SOCIAL AND EMOTIONAL LEARNING IN ACTION

Social and Emotional Learning in Action

Creating Systemic Change in Schools

edited by

Sara E. Rimm-Kaufman
Michael J. Strambler
Kimberly A. Schonert-Reichl

Foreword by Aaliyah A. Samuel

THE GUILFORD PRESS
New York London

A Division of Guilford Publications, Inc.
370 Seventh Avenue, Suite 1200, New York, NY 10001
www.guilford.com

Printed in the United States of America

This book is printed on acid-free paper.

Last digit is print number: 9 8 7 6 5 4 3 2 1

Library of Congress Cataloging-in-Publication data is available from the publisher.

ISBN 978-1-4625-5204-7 (paperback)
ISBN 978-1-4625-5205-4 (hardcover)

To my parents, Sylvia and Alfred Rimm
—SERK

To my mom, Betty Ann Strambler
—MJS

To my husband, Arleigh,
and to my sons, Griffin and Gray
—KASR

About the Editors

Sara E. Rimm-Kaufman, PhD, is the Commonwealth Professor at the School of Education and Human Development at the University of Virginia. Since 2000, she and her team have conducted research on schools with the goal of using evidence to improve the quality and equity of learning experiences. Dr. Rimm-Kaufman has studied a range of programs, including Connect Science, EL Education, Leading Together, Responsive Classroom, RULER, and Valor Collegiate and Compass, among others. She has authored more than 100 chapters, articles, and blog posts, yet she wrestles with the reality that researchers' extensive knowledge about social and emotional learning is rarely made accessible to educators. This book is one example of her efforts to bring SEL knowledge to a broad audience.

Michael J. Strambler, PhD, is Associate Professor of Psychiatry at the Yale University School of Medicine and Director of Child Wellbeing and Education Research at The Consultation Center at Yale, where he is also Senior Evaluation Consultant for YaleEval. Dr. Strambler's work focuses on the role of social environments in the academic, psychological, social, and behavioral well-being of children and youth. Much of his work occurs in the context of partnerships between researchers and practitioners, such as the Partnership for Early Education Research, which he directs among three Connecticut communities. Dr. Strambler is a recipient of the Kenneth B. and Mamie P. Clark Early Career Grant from the American Psychological Foundation and the Postdoctoral Award from the Ford Foundation.

Kimberly A. Schonert-Reichl, PhD, is the NoVo Foundation Endowed Chair in Social and Emotional Learning and Professor in the Department of Psychology at the University of Illinois Chicago. Prior to her graduate work, she worked as a middle school teacher and as a teacher at an alternative high school for adolescents at risk. Dr. Schonert-Reichl is a recipient of the Janusz Korczak Medal for Children's Rights Advocacy; the EdTech Postsecondary Leader of the Year Award from MindShare Learning Technology; the Joseph E. Zins Distinguished Scholar Award from the Collaborative for Academic, Social, and Emotional Learning; and the Paz Buttedahl Career Achievement Award from the Confederation of University Faculty Associations of British Columbia.

Contributors

Pilar Alamos, PhD, is a postdoctoral researcher at the University of Virginia's Center for Advanced Study of Teaching and Learning (UVA-CASTL) within the School of Education and Human Development. She is part of the Collaborative for Academic, Social, and Emotional Learning (CASEL) Weissberg Scholars program, and her research focuses on teacher–child interactions and relationships.

Stacey Alicea, PhD, is the Director of Early Learning Strategy at the Newark Trust for Education, where she leads efforts to strengthen Newark's early childhood ecosystem to support children's equitable healthy development and learning. In addition to her doctorate in Psychology and Social Intervention, she holds an MPH in Population and Family Health.

Jocelyn V. Artinger, MAT, is the Principal at Markham Elementary School (Mt. Lebanon, Pennsylvania) and has been a school leader in urban and suburban settings. She has served in traditional public and charter schools, across a variety of student demographics, and is also a doctoral student with K–12 Principal Certification.

Joyce Barnes, EdS, has nearly three decades of experience as a PreK–12 teacher, special education administrator, and program/resource developer. Now a freelance writer and editor based in Louisville, Kentucky, she has provided editing support to the Aspen Institute National Commission on Social, Emotional and Academic Development and the American Association of School Administrators (AASA) SEL Impact Project and currently serves as a writer/editor for the Global Youth and Education division of Special Olympics International.

Tia Navalene Barnes, PhD, is Assistant Professor in Human Development and Family Sciences at the University of Delaware. Her research examines the social and emotional well-being of minoritized populations. Dr. Barnes is the 2021 recipient of the Joseph E. Zins Award for SEL Research from CASEL.

Bloodine Barthelus, EdD, serves as the Director of Practice Innovations at CASEL. She specializes in program development and professional learning that leverages adult SEL to shift practice and construct equitable learning spaces for young people.

Aaron Benavot, PhD, is Professor of Global Education Policy at the University at Albany, with interests in comparative education. Previously he served as Director of the United Nations Educational, Scientific and Cultural Organization (UNESCO) Global Education Monitoring Report, which analyzes progress toward international education targets. Dr. Benavot works with both Networking to Integrate SDG Target 4.7 and Social and Emotional Learning into Educational Materials (NISSEM) and the Monitoring and Evaluation of Climate Change Education (MECCE) Project, a 6-year study of climate change education.

Sheldon Berman, EdD, served as superintendent of four districts in three states spanning 28 school years and is currently AASA's Lead Superintendent for Social–Emotional Learning. He was the 2003 Massachusetts Superintendent of the Year and has received lifetime achievement awards from the AASA, CASEL, and Character.org for his national leadership and the implementation of SEL in his districts.

Jean Bernard, EdD, is a senior partner at Spectacle Learning Media, a network of writers, illustrators, and designers of print and digital media. At UNESCO (2004–2009), she coordinated the development of global policies and strategies for integrating peace and human rights education into textbooks and other learning materials.

Jennifer O. Briggs, PhD, is a developmental researcher in the Literacy and Learning Division at The Office of Child Development, University of Pittsburgh. Her research and practice interests focus on early childhood learning and development around the topics of social justice and equity, particularly related to teacher training and practice.

Jocelyn E. Brown, EdD, is a Supervisor of Instruction in the Capital School District (Dover, Delaware), where she works with instructional and mental health staff to support the implementation of multi-tiered systems of support. As an educator and licensed mental health clinician, Dr. Brown is committed to ensuring access, equity, and progress through systems change and advocacy.

Alexcia Bryant is an undergraduate student in the Department of Health Sciences at the University of Delaware, studying to obtain a bachelor's degree in nursing.

Elise Cappella, PhD, is Vice Dean for Research and Professor of Applied Psychology at New York University's Steinhardt School. Dr. Cappella engages in research–practice partnerships to understand and support school and afterschool contexts of social–emotional and academic learning in PreK to eighth grade. She is a former fourth-grade teacher.

Christina Cipriano, PhD, EdM, is Assistant Professor at the Yale Child Study Center and Director of Research at the Yale Center for Emotional Intelligence at the Yale University School of Medicine. Dr. Cipriano's research focuses on the systematic examination of SEL assessment and intervention for marginalized student and teacher populations.

Jenna Conway, MBA, is Deputy Superintendent of Early Childhood Care and Education for the Virginia Department of Education, where she leads efforts to ensure that all Virginia children have the opportunity to enter kindergarten ready. For more than a decade, she has worked in different states to change how we see, fund, and manage our birth-to-5, public–private early childhood care and education systems.

Abigail Eveleigh, MRes, is Lab Manager and Assistant Research Scientist at New York University's LEARN (Language Experience and Acquisition Research at NYU) Lab. Previously she was a postgraduate research associate at the Yale Center for Emotional Intelligence, where she worked with the RULER for All team. Her prominent research interests are developmental disorders, autism spectrum disorder, special education, and SEL.

Tyralynn Frazier, PhD, MPH, is Chief Scientist at the Center for Contemplative Science and Compassion-Based Ethics at Emory University. She leads the development of a research program on the global implementation of SEE Learning, the implementation of Cognitively Based Compassion Training for educators, and the science of compassion, ethics, and prosociality throughout development.

Dionne Grayman, MEd, is a staff developer for the Morningside Center for Teaching Social Responsibility, where she provides support around the implementation of restorative practices to reimagine schools as centers of belonging and joy.

Anne Gregory, PhD, is Professor in School Psychology at Rutgers, the State University of New Jersey. Dr. Gregory is driven by an urgency to eradicate racial and gender disparities in school discipline. She examines restorative practices and equity-oriented SEL and recently received the Joseph E. Zins Early Career Contributions Award from CASEL.

Deirdre Hon, PhD, is Assistant Professor and Director of the Specialty in SEL program in the School of Education at the University of Portland. Her research focuses on exploring how preservice teachers acquire the skills and dispositions to implement high-quality SEL once they enter the field.

Jurni Jackson is a junior Honors Human Services major and Psychology minor at the University of Delaware. She has been working in Dr. Tia Barnes's research lab since her sophomore year and thanks Dr. Barnes and the rest of the team for giving her the opportunity to contribute to this work.

Robert J. Jagers, PhD, is Vice President of Research at CASEL. Among his various CASEL duties, Dr. Jagers is leading work with partner districts to explore how SEL can be leveraged to promote equitable learning environments and local developmental imperatives, especially for youth and adults in underserved school communities.

Jacqueline Jodl, PhD, is Chief of Global Youth & Education at Special Olympics. Previously, Dr. Jodl was Associate Professor at the University of Virginia's School of Education and Executive Director at the Aspen Institute, leading the National Commission on Social, Emotional, and Academic Development.

Olivia A. Johnson, PhD, is a Postdoctoral Research Fellow at CASEL. Her research explores how theories of care inform policy interpretation in underserved districts and schools.

Julia Mahfouz, PhD, is Assistant Professor in the School of Education and Human Development at the University of Colorado Denver and a CASEL Weissberg scholar. Her research explores the social, emotional, and cultural dynamics of educational settings, with an emphasis on adult SEL, specifically the integration of systemic SEL into principal preparation programs.

Natalie May, MA, is a doctoral student in the Applied Psychology Department at New York University's Steinhardt School. Her research, which seeks to increase the accessibility and cultural relevance of SEL interventions by leveraging community knowledge and resources, takes a practitioner-focused approach informed by her time teaching and evaluating classroom interventions.

Lauren H. Naples, EdD, is a postdoctoral associate at the Yale Child Study Center in the Yale Center for Emotional Intelligence, Yale University School of Medicine.

Dr. Naples is a National Board-Certified mental health counselor, and her research focuses on the development and evaluation of strengths-based programming to promote student well-being among diverse learners.

Ednah Nwafor, MA, is a Research Associate at CASEL. A native of the Greater Newark area, her childhood experiences anchor a deep commitment to optimal developmental outcomes for marginalized youth through the centering of equity, cultural sensitivity, and antiracism.

Brendan Ozawa-de Silva, PhD, is a Senior Lecturer at the Center for Contemplative Science and Compassion-Based Ethics at Emory University. His work has focused on developing and researching programs that bring contemplative and compassion-based practices into schools and prisons, as well as the promotion of higher education in prisons.

Gabrielle Rappolt-Schlichtmann, EdD, is Executive Director and Chief Scientist at EdTogether, a not-for-profit research and development organization focused on empowering youth with disabilities to imagine and realize a meaningful education by harnessing the power of emotion in learning.

Tamilah Richardson, EdD, is Director of Early Childhood Learning for the Virginia Department of Education. Broadly focused on birth-to-5 classroom supports that promote learning and development, she works closely with UVA-CASTL on several projects, including the Virginia Kindergarten Readiness Program and an Early Childhood Mental Health Consultation Program.

Julie Riley, EdD, is Director of Curriculum and Instructional Technology for the Manchester Essex Regional School District in Massachusetts.

Sara E. Rimm-Kaufman, PhD (see "About the Editors").

Julie Sauve, MA, MAT, is a doctoral candidate in the Human Development, Learning, and Culture Program at the University of British Columbia, and Adjunct Professor in the School of Education at the University of Portland. As a former teacher and instructional coach, she is passionate about research that advances knowledge about teaching practices, SEL, and teacher well-being.

Kimberly A. Schonert-Reichl, PhD (see "About the Editors").

Margaret Sinclair, DPhil, DUniv, has worked with United Nations High Commissioner for Refugees (UNHCR), UNESCO, Education Above All, and NISSEM (as co-convenor) in the fields of education planning, education in emergencies and for refugees, protection of education from attack, and planning curriculum for learning to live together, social cohesion, and conflict resolution.

Alexandra Skoog-Hoffman, PhD, is Director of Research–Practice Partnerships at CASEL, where she directs key practice-focused research initiatives designed to support and scale the continuous improvement processes and impacts of high-quality SEL implementation in partner states, districts, schools, and communities.

Andy Smart, BA, is an education and publishing consultant and a co-convenor of NISSEM, with a background in teaching and educational and children's publishing. He specializes in textbook policy, planning, and development; English- and Arabic-medium primary curriculum; and children's reading.

Caitlin F. Spear, PhD, is Director of Literacy and Learning at the Office of Child Development at the University of Pittsburgh. Her work focuses on topics of social justice and equity, particularly as they relate to early childhood racial and disability identity, language and literacy development, and teacher education.

Melissa Stoffers, MS, worked as a special educator before returning to academia to pursue a doctoral degree in Human Development and Family Sciences at the University of Delaware. She is interested in research about social relationships for individuals with disabilities.

Michael J. Strambler, PhD (see "About the Editors").

Shannon B. Wanless, PhD, is Associate Professor in Health and Human Development and Director of the Office of Child Development at the University of Pittsburgh School of Education. She develops adult learning communities that focus on social justice and early childhood.

Allison Rae Ward-Seidel, EdM, is a doctoral student in Educational Psychology at the University of Virginia, studying social–emotional development and equity in schools. She is a former teacher, which brought her to study school climate and discipline disparities to improve racial equity and social justice.

Amanda G. Wells, MA, is a Nationally Certified School Psychologist who primarily serves students with complex special education needs and leads efforts to promote positive outcomes for all students in Capital School District (Delaware).

James H. Williams, EdD, is Professor and Chairholder, UNESCO Chair in International Education for Development, at the Graduate School of Education and Human Development and the Elliott School of International Affairs, The George

Washington University. Recently he coedited a special issue of the *Journal on Education in Emergencies* on Psychosocial Support and Social and Emotional Learning.

Amanda P. Williford, PhD, is the Batten Bicentennial Professor of Early Childhood Education at the Center for Advanced Study of Teaching and Learning in the School of Education and Human Development at the University of Virginia. Her applied research focuses on young children's mental well-being, social–emotional development, and school readiness.

Yu Xia, MS, is a graduate student and research assistant in the Department of Human Development and Family Sciences at the University of Delaware. Her research focuses on SEL in children. She is also interested in seeking ways to promote better learning experiences from studying the teacher–student relationship.

Acknowledgments

It goes without saying that books do not write themselves. We are beyond grateful to the contributors to this book. From them, we learned that raw pearls of ideas develop in beautiful ways with input and time. We especially appreciate the contributions of authors and coauthors who work for districts, state governments, schools, and nonprofit organizations, who bring their own unique and tremendously valuable perspective to systemic social and emotional learning (SEL). We thank our contributors for their dedication and patience, and especially Craig Thomas, our editor at The Guilford Press, for his enduring enthusiasm for this book from start to finish. Of course, we are grateful to our families for supporting this endeavor and our careers.

We—Sara, Mike, and Kim—spent hours on the phone talking about the promise and challenges in our field and the many facets of putting SEL into action in schools, families, and communities. We agree that social, emotional, and behavioral skills are a natural part of development and that schools stand at center stage. We constantly came back to this reality in our efforts to avoid the politicization of SEL. As we worked, we imagined the full range of possible readers and edited, revised, and constantly strived to reach the broadest audience possible for this book.

How can schools contribute to student flourishing? How can schools promote adult well-being? Can schools offer opportunities that meet the needs of each and every student who dwells there? Can schools amplify strengths in the families and communities they serve? Are there better ways to create policies and direct resources to improve adult and student experiences in schools? How do we engage students and educators in meaningful ways that honor their voices and perspectives? These are just a few questions that guided our conversations, editing, and direction for this book.

The pandemic conditions meant that we were each other's hallway buddies and for that, we're grateful. We had family losses, an international move, our kids' development, and even a new marriage. Together, we wrestled with the pandemic, political changes, racial strife, and international war conditions. At each and every historical moment, we discussed how these sociopolitical realities played out in schools. How are kids learning normal social skills if they need to stay 6 feet away from each other? What is it like for a Black boy in high school to see a video of a police killing on his phone between third and fourth period and then sit down to learn math? Can we create equitable access to opportunities in schools, given that youth experience so much inequity outside of school? What are communities doing to make sure kids can attend school remotely while their parents work two or three jobs? What new environmental challenges will today's children face 20 and 30 years in the future, and what social skills will they need to identify and act on solutions to those problems?

As we wrap up this project, we will be turning our attention to a new journal, *Social and Emotional Learning: Research, Practice, and Policy.* We hope questions that linger at the completion of this book will take shape in exciting ways in this new journal—the passion project of our dear colleague and mentor, Roger P. Weissberg, in the last months of his life. Roger consistently told us that it is through collaboration that the field of SEL will grow and flourish. We hope that this book inspires collaboration as we all strive to put SEL into action and create a world where all children can thrive.

Foreword

The field of social and emotional learning (SEL) is surrounded by more excitement than ever before. Nearly three decades since the Collaborative for Academic, Social, and Emotional Learning (CASEL) first introduced the term, interest in SEL has ballooned a once-niche field into a global education movement.

Demand has surged among parents, educators, policymakers, researchers, employers, and students themselves. For example, 83% of school principals believe it's "very important" to promote SEL (Atwell & Bridgeland, 2019). Three-quarters of high school students say that they would benefit from schools that focus strongly on SEL (DePaoli, Atwell, Bridgeland, & Shriver, 2018), and 92% of executives surveyed by the *Wall Street Journal* said social and emotional skills such as problem solving and communicating clearly are equal to or more important than technical skills—yet 89% said they have a difficult time finding employees with those skills (Davidson, 2016).

Additionally, the substantial evidence base on SEL continues to expand. Already, meta-analyses across multiple countries have demonstrated that SEL programs are as effective at improving academic achievement as programs that are focused specifically on academics (Mahoney, Durlak, & Weissberg, 2018). Across the world, researchers are continuing to study what makes SEL effective in different contexts (e.g., in international communities and out-of-school time); how it can be leveraged toward a range of goals (e.g., academic achievement, mental wellness, school safety, civic engagement, and workforce readiness); what is required to ensure SEL practices are culturally responsive and benefit all groups of students (including students of color, those with disabilities, and students from rural and low-income communities); and what conditions are necessary for sustaining and improving SEL implementation.

What we know about schooling has expanded over the past few decades. But as researchers, educators, and policymakers have dug deeper into the critical pieces of learning and development, consistent ingredients persist across all ideals of quality education: safe in-person environments, caring relationships, attention to students' holistic well-being, and engaging instruction. SEL creates a foundation for all these key components.

We will continue deepening our insights for decades to come, but the scientific consensus is already clear. As the National Commission on Social, Emotional, and Academic Development's Council of Distinguished Scientists states:

> Compelling research demonstrates what parents have always known—the success of young people in school and beyond is inextricably linked to healthy social and emotional development. Students who have a sense of belonging and purpose, who can work well with classmates and peers to solve problems, who can plan and set goals, and who can persevere through challenges—in addition to being literate, numerate, and versed in scientific concepts and ideas—are more likely to maximize their opportunities and reach their full potential. (Jones & Kahn, 2017)

I have personally come to this work as a parent, a former teacher and principal, and a policy influencer. All these experiences have solidified a belief in me that there is nothing more vital to our young people's future than an education anchored in social, emotional, and academic learning. In schools I have visited across the country, I have heard the same urgency from educators, custodians, school leaders, counselors, students, family members, and more. In rural, tribal, urban, and suburban communities across red and blue states, educators and parents from all backgrounds share a few fundamental principles. They want their children to achieve their goals, have healthy relationships, and develop skills that will help them succeed in their careers and lives. This has always been important, but the case for SEL has never been more compelling.

Our education system faces significant challenges that have accelerated over the past few years: the long-term unraveling of the impacts from a global pandemic that disrupted all our lives, increasing attention to a crisis around youth mental health, persistent inequities in educational opportunities and outcomes, and divisive politics that have seeped into school board meetings and classrooms. Meanwhile, preparing students for their lives beyond school has become increasingly complex. Not only are the jobs of the future rapidly shifting—an estimated 85% of jobs that will exist in 2030 don't yet exist today (Dell Technologies, 2018)—but youth who will enter the workforce in the coming years are also more entrepreneurially minded than previous generations (Sawyer, 2021).

All of these challenges have underscored a new charge for our education systems: to prepare a generation for a world that is more complex, globally connected, and technologically advanced than we have ever experienced. The students of today will need deep self-awareness, an ability to adapt to and navigate diverse contexts, dynamic relationship-building skills, and strategies for collaborative problem solving. In other words, SEL is integral to every child's education across every stage of development, from early childhood to workforce preparation.

But how to bring this charge to fruition? This is the urgent question for our field. Growing attention has expanded, shifted, and complicated the very notion of SEL, giving rise to many layers that encompass all that is wrapped into the term. Depending on who is asked, SEL is described as an individual developmental progression, a discrete program or curriculum, a set of pedagogical practices for academic learning, a broad focus on relationship building, or an entire approach to education systems. There are also similar and competing terms for SEL: *whole-child education, life skills, character education, 21st-century skills, workforce skills, essential skills,* and others. Not surprisingly, educators and education leaders intrinsically understand the value and importance of SEL but often grapple with the concrete steps required to fully support students' social, emotional, and academic learning and development. Indeed, among schools and districts that do *not* use SEL, the top reason cited is a lack of clarity on where to start with implementation (Bryant, Crowley, & Davidsen, 2020).

Similarly, parents and caregivers show broad agreement around what social and emotional skills are essential for their children's education and success, but they are often perplexed by, and at times skeptical of, what SEL in schools entails. Large majorities of parents (80–90%) agree when asked whether schools should teach specific skills such as setting and achieving goals, navigating social situations, or empathizing with others (Tyner, 2021). But the murky picture of SEL implementation leaves them worried that it will shift attention away from academics, call on teachers to become therapists, or result in students being labeled for their behaviors (Learning Heroes, 2018). Of course, those who implement high-quality, evidence-based SEL know that many of these fears are based on misconceptions. But they reflect a consistent thread of confusion around education jargon and acronyms.

In my travels across the country, the resounding demand for SEL also gave rise to repeated questions from parents, business leaders, policymakers, community members, and others: *What actually is SEL? What does it look like and sound like in schools? What's the role of parents and caregivers? What's the role of districts and states?* Frequently, the responses to these questions are narrow—a daily community-building activity, an anti-bullying policy, a grant for mindfulness programs. These types of programmatic responses often dot the canvas around an image of SEL but fail to capture the full vision.

The contributors to this book open the aperture to answer these questions through the lens of *systemic SEL.* Far beyond a weekly lesson on empathy or emotion regulation, systemic SEL is a vision of education that centers the full and healthy development of all children. More specifically, SEL is:

> an approach to create equitable learning conditions that actively involve all PreK to Grade 12 students in learning and practicing social, emotional, and academic competencies that are important for success at school and in life. These conditions require aligned policies, resources, and actions at state and district levels that encourage local schools and communities to enhance the personal and professional capacities of adults to: implement and continuously improve evidence-based programs and practices (EBPs); create an inclusive culture that fosters caring relationships and youth voice, agency, and character; and support coordinated school–family–community partnerships to enhance student development. (Mahoney et al., 2021, p. 2)

This conceptual shift in SEL requires attention to both the teaching and practice of social and emotional competencies, as well as the environments, policies, relationships, and interactions that surround young people in all the places where they live and learn. The challenge is that a systems-level focus often feels so big that practitioners and policymakers don't know where to begin. Here we can lean on the advice of tennis great and civil rights advocate Arthur Ashe: "Start where you are. Use what you have. Do what you can."

In the previous decade, educators and education leaders have already applied solutions that embed SEL into district systems and structures, such as staff meeting structures and hiring practices that emphasize social and emotional competencies. Researchers have demonstrated the effectiveness of strategies for aligning SEL across in-school and out-of-school time (e.g., Schwartz et al., 2020), with academic content areas (e.g., Rimm-Kaufman & Merritt, 2019), and across school climate and culture (e.g., Osher & Berg, 2017). Policymakers have standardized developmental benchmarks that help guide local implementation decisions, connect SEL to workforce readiness skills, and help braid funding streams to support the infrastructure for SEL (Dusenbury & Weissberg, 2018).

At CASEL, we have also spent the last decade learning alongside school, district, and state partners as they implement systemic SEL (CASEL, 2021). We have documented these learnings in a theory of action focused on four key areas:

1. Building foundational support for SEL through engaging stakeholders in a shared vision and plan, and aligning resources to support and sustain SEL.
2. Strengthening adult SEL competencies and capacity through high-quality professional learning and cultivating a trusting staff culture.
3. Promoting SEL for students through EBPs, integration of SEL with academics, and family and community partnerships.
4. Reflecting on data for continuous improvement through ongoing processes for measuring and reflecting on implementation and outcomes.

By bringing together these insights, examples, and evidence, *Social and Emotional Learning in Action: Creating Systemic Change in Schools* unearths practices that make systemic SEL come alive and work well in schools. There is no quick-fix solution found within these pages. Instead, the deep work of systemic SEL rests on a long-term commitment to continuously iterating our school systems to promote the academic, social, and emotional learning and development of every single child more fully.

Despite challenges, the field of SEL is getting stronger and will continue to grow. In the coming years, we will see more diverse perspectives and voices joining the movement—parents and business leaders; rural, suburban, and urban communities; leaders of early childhood and educator preparation; and the global community. When we bring all these people to the table, it will require deep listening and collaboration to come up with solutions together—and that is exactly why our social and emotional skills are so crucial in this moment and beyond.

We have already lit the bright path forward. You can read about it in the chapters that follow. You can see it in the classrooms where teachers are engaging students in reflection and perspective taking. You can feel it in the partnerships between schools, families, and communities. You can hear it in the collaborative solutions that young people are bringing forward.

This is the promise of SEL. Together, we continue to envision and champion a bright future for our nation's young people.

AALIYAH A. SAMUEL, PhD,
President and CEO, Collaborative for Academic, Social, and Emotional Learning;
Deputy Assistant Secretary, Local, State and National Engagement, U.S. Department of Education;
Senior Fellow, Center on the Developing Child, Harvard University

REFERENCES

Atwell, M., & Bridgeland, J. (2019). Ready to lead: A 2019 update of principals' perspectives on how social and emotional learning can prepare children and transform schools. Retrieved from *https://casel.s3.us-east-2.amazonaws.com/casel-resources-ready-to-lead-2019.pdf.*

Bryant, G., Crowley, S., & Davidsen, C. (2020). Finding your place: The current state of K–12 social emotional learning. Retrieved from *https://d1hzkn4d3dn6lg.cloudfront.net/production/uploads/2020/07/finding-your-place_the-current-state-of-k-12-social-emotional-learning.pdf.*

CASEL. (2021). 2011 to 2021: 10 years of social and emotional learning in U.S. school districts. Retrieved from *https://casel.s3.us-east-2.amazonaws.com/casel-resources-emerging-insights.pdf.*

Davidson, K. (2016). Employers find "soft skills" like critical thinking in short supply. Retrieved from *www.wsj.com/articles/employers-find-soft-skills-like-critical-thinking-in-short-supply-1472549400.*

Dell Technologies. (2018). Realizing 2030: A divided vision of the future. Retrieved from *www.delltechnologies.com/content/dam/delltechnologies/assets/perspectives/2030/pdf/realizing-2030-a-divided-vision-of-the-future-summary.pdf.*

DePaoli, J., Atwell, M., Bridgeland, J., & Shriver, T. (2018). Respected perspectives of youth on high school & social and emotional learning. Retrieved from *https://casel.s3.us-east-2.amazonaws.com/casel-resources-respected.pdf.*

Dusenbury, L., & Weissberg, R. (2018). Emerging insights from states' efforts to strengthen social and emotional learning. Retrieved from *https://casel.s3.us-east-2.amazonaws.com/casel-resources-emerging-insights.pdf.*

Jones, S., & Kahn, J. (2017). The evidence base for how we learn: Supporting students' social emotional, and academic development. Retrieved from *www.aspeninstitute.org/wp-content/uploads/2017/09/sead-research-brief-9.12_updated-web.pdf.*

Learning Heroes. (2018). Developing life skills in children: A road map for communicating with parents. Retrieved from *https://r50gh2ss1ic2mww8s3uvjvq1-wpengine.netdna-ssl.com/wp-content/uploads/2018/05/dls-report-2018-for-distribution-single-pages.pdf.*

Mahoney, J., Durlak, J., & Weissberg, R. (2018). An update on social and emotional learning outcome research. *Phi Delta Kappan, 100*(4), 18–23.

Mahoney, J., Weissberg, R., Greenberg, M., Dusenbury, L., Jagers, R., Niemi, K., . . . Yoder, N. (2021). Systemic social and emotional learning: Promoting educational success for all preschool to high school students. *American Psychologist, 76,* 1128–1142.

Osher, D., & Berg, J. (2017). School climate and social and emotional learning: The integration of two approaches. Retrieved from *www.prevention.psu.edu/uploads/files/rwjf443059-schoolclimate.pdf.*

Rimm-Kaufman, S. E., & Merritt, E. G. (2019). Let's power our future: Integrating science and social and emotional learning to improve collaborative discourse and science understanding. *Science and Children, 57*(1), 52–60.

Sawyer, A. (2021). How business and education can help Gen Z reframe the future. Retrieved from *www.ey.com/en_gl/corporate-responsibility/how-business-and-education-can-help-gen-z-reframe-the-future.*

Schwartz, H., Hamilton, L., Faxon-Mills, S., Gomez, C., Huguet, A., Jaycox, L., . . . Wrabel, S. (2020). Early lessons from schools and out-of-school time programs implementing social and emotional learning. Retrieved from *www.rand.org/pubs/research_reports/rra379-1.html.*

Tyner, A. (2021). *How to sell SEL: Parents and the politics of social–emotional learning.* Thomas B. Fordham Institute.

Contents

Chapter 1

Introduction

Meeting the Moment with Systemic SEL

Sara E. Rimm-Kaufman, Michael J. Strambler,
and Kimberly A. Schonert-Reichl

In 2015, I (Sara) received a phone call from Dianne Garcia, a soon-to-be colleague from rural, western Virginia asking, "Our schools are trying to move from good to great. Do you think social and emotional learning can help?" The question surprised me. I immediately sized up the situation and asked, "What's not working?" Little did I know that we were about to embark on a long-standing partnered process to cultivate systemic social and emotional learning (SEL) in two small rural school districts. Together, these two districts served 3,000 students—roughly 90% White, 10% Black, with just one or two students from other ethnic groups. About half of the students were eligible for free/reduced lunch. Geographically, one district served the small city and the other served the county that wrapped around it. There was considerable rivalry between these two districts, yet they shared common challenges. Both districts faced student population declines common in rural Appalachia. Both had difficulty accessing teacher professional development. And, most importantly, both districts experienced mistrust and/or disengagement from many of the families that they served.

Low kindergarten readiness and student behavioral problems were two big issues that the districts were confronting and SEL seemed like a natural place to start. Fortunately, this community has a unique asset in that it has a small foundation, The Alleghany Foundation, that was formed when the community sold its nonprofit hospital. Many foundations like this invest in community health or business infrastructure, but this foundation also focused on partnering with the schools and channeling its efforts to support children and youth from birth into postsecondary education. My colleagues at the foundation, Dianne Garcia and Mary Fant Donnan, began work with the superintendents, school board, teachers, and other educators in the community to invite engagement in conversations about improving education in their districts.

In 2014, Dianne Garcia assembled a group of teachers, principals, and other school staff to look at SEL programs and identify pros and cons of different programs and approaches, find time to visit schools using these programs, and understand what school conditions needed to be in place to use them. Next, our research team conducted a needs assessment involving surveys and interviews of educators, families, and students. We used data gathered to guide next steps and worked with the school superintendents and foundation leaders to identify six main targets of growth (e.g., social and emotional learning, kindergarten readiness). For each, we created workgroups that included school leaders and community members. Each group was tasked to identify new ways to improve various aspects of children's experience from birth into postsecondary education. Once the workgroup developed proposals, these were shared with school leaders and the foundation, and if the stakeholders agreed, the work was funded and would move forward. The hope was that by engaging community members, a broader range of people would generate new ideas, and more people would be invested in launching these ideas and seeing them implemented well (Rimm-Kaufman et al., 2018).

One workgroup focused on SEL. The group began to explore a full range of programs, identified a source of funds for professional development, and began to implement evidence-based SEL in their schools, starting with preschool and elementary years and working up. They began to think through how to evaluate the programs and discussed short-term and long-term goals for students. When these SEL ideas were brought forward to school leaders and foundation members, the early conversations covered reactive approaches to discipline to proactive approaches to cultivating social and emotional skills in students. Over a few months, I noticed that the conversation migrated to new and broader topics. Were teachers meeting the developmental needs of students? Did teachers feel prepared, valued, and energized to do their best work? Did teachers and administrators trust one another and did these trusting relationships lead to collaboration and elevate the quality of teaching in the schools? Was district leadership (central office) focused on SEL and did they "walk the walk" not just "talk the talk"?

Within the first 2 years of partnered work, we saw a shift in conversation. When people talked about SEL, they didn't just talk about students' skills. People were asking whether classrooms, schools, and organizations in the community were creating opportunities for students to develop, use, and practice their social and emotional skills. SEL was no longer viewed as a single program or a few programs tethered together, but rather as a culture that the districts were trying to cultivate with the goal of supporting students' development. At around this time, I recall a question from the foundation director: "Is there such a thing as a community growth mindset?" My thoughts at the time were "Yes, there is a community growth mindset, and it is present here."

What I observed was *SEL in action*. I watched this community work together to create systemic change in their schools.

Here are a few examples of the transformation. In 2016, the Virginia Department of Education released "The Profile of a Virginia Graduate," designed to shift Virginia schools to focus on skills needed to help students be "life ready"—defined as "prepared for college and/or work and to be successful in life" (Virginia Department of Education, 2016). In this policy document, the Board of Education called attention to the "five C's"—critical thinking, creative thinking, collaboration, communication, and citizenship. In essence, the expectation was that schools would trade out course expectations and replace them with opportunities for authentic workplace experiences, so that students would be "eligible and competitive" for job opportunities. The response in the Alleghany Highlands was exciting. The high school principals, community college, and district leaders gathered with people from local businesses to talk about some of the life skills that students need to develop. Then they worked with local businesses to design internship experiences that would help students develop adaptability, communication, and organization skills and identified ways that these skills could be integrated into high school life.

The schools leaned into SEL to respond to pressures present in their schools. For instance, one middle school principal realized the pressures of testing and accountability on teachers, not just students. He identified ways to tune-in on the needs of the teachers and to figure out how to improve the sense of connection and collaboration among the adults at the school. The teachers, administrators, and other school personnel met weekly for conversation and community building to improve teacher well-being, so that teachers had more capacity to meet the needs of their students.

Realizing that not everyone felt like they belonged at schools—especially given that many parents did not have a positive experience in school themselves—the schools found new inroads to connect with parents. Instead of expecting families to come to school for curriculum night, the teachers went to various church events, with the goal of connecting with local families. The community adopted the Dolly Parton Reading Program from birth to 5 that sent books to homes for free in an effort to support families in preparing children for school. The local librarians identified new ways to connect with families. At first glance, a skeptic might ask how these efforts relate to SEL. The answer is that connecting to families signaled community commitment to a *whole-child approach*—school is not just about academic learning, but about developing good human beings.

These districts are located in the southern United States and have inherited a history of slavery, then segregation, and now entrenched patterns of racial inequality. Key stakeholders in this process understood the barriers and the ways in which schools may not have created a sense of belonging for the Black students in their community. The workgroups included Black families, and school leaders aspired toward not only producing achievement-oriented students but also creating a positive culture—one designed to give students a feeling of belonging and connection at school. How they navigate racial inequities in opportunities is still a work in progress.

Reflecting back, I realize that I witnessed a 7-year transformation of these districts as they aligned priorities. Initially, the schools viewed social and emotional skills as something students either had or didn't have. Now, there is a common shared understanding about the importance of developing a culture that supports student *and* adult development of SEL. In time, these districts underwent a transformation, and now *systemic SEL* is in the foreground of how the two districts function.

In 2022, these districts decided to merge. My colleagues reached out to me, because the community knew that the merger was much more than a business decision. The districts needed to consider the psychological experiences of administrators, teachers, and other school personnel who faced changes in their day-to-day life due to the merger. The leadership was keenly aware that the merger would only succeed if they planned carefully to address the well-being of the adults involved.

This example from two small rural districts in western Virginia shows SEL *in action*. Educators now speak a new language in which academic learning and SEL are viewed as complementary skills that come together to promote the healthy development of children and youth. Their conversations are forward-thinking and systemic in nature. At its core, the focus of these efforts has been to elevate students' social and emotional skills by creating opportunities for whole-child development in the spaces where students spend their time. Perhaps most importantly, the districts spent time and resources supporting the adults in schools, knowing that educators can only do their job well if they are supported, treated well, and given opportunities for professional growth, so they can bring their "best self" to their work and show up in school (and nonschool settings) with a positive attitude toward kids.

Goals of This Book

All three of us have engaged in research–practice partnerships involving close work with schools and districts as they cultivate SEL at a *systemic* level. Over the last three decades, we have seen the proliferation of SEL programs—including those to which we have contributed—and become aware of how SEL takes hold in school settings. High-quality SEL connects in meaningful ways with teachers and students, and improves attitudes, knowledge, and skills in the adults and youth in schools. Decades of research supports this finding (Durlak et al., 2011; Taylor et al., 2017), and economic analyses show that the benefits of SEL outweigh the costs; $1 invested in SEL leads to $11 in gains to youth and society (Belfield et al., 2015). However, just because a school has adopted an SEL program does not mean it will work. Many well-meaning SEL efforts fail because of poor implementation. Schools, communities, districts, and states need to create certain *conditions* to make SEL work. High-quality SEL—to reemphasize our point—only takes hold if the teachers, school leaders, and district and state goals are aligned and organized around improving students social, emotional, and academic learning in schools and creating equitable opportunities that engage all youth at their schools.

Systemic SEL involves creating conditions that are conducive to SEL implementation. The term *systemic SEL* has been defined as

> aligned policies, resources, and actions at state and district levels that encourage local schools and communities to enhance the personal and professional capacities of adults to: implement and continuously improve evidence-based programs and practices (EBPs); create an inclusive culture that fosters caring relationships and youth voice, agency, and character; and support coordinated school–family–community partnerships to enhance student development. (Mahoney et al., 2020, p. 1129)

In the last decade, we have seen exciting examples of systemic SEL developing across the United States (e.g., Schwartz et al., 2022). Districts in Washoe County, Anchorage, Louisville, and Nashville offer just a few examples. Unfortunately, we often lack access to some of the most important insights from the stakeholders immersed in these activities. Educators are too busy to write these stories, and researchers (accidentally) bury some of the most exciting ideas in the methods sections of their research articles. We have come together to write this book with the hope that we can advance the field by unearthing ideas and practices that make systemic SEL come alive and work well in schools. In this book, we hear the stories of Capital School District in Dover, Delaware; Manchester–Essex Regional School District in Massachusetts; statewide efforts in Virginia; international examples from India, Bangladesh, and Ethiopia, and many others to gain a rich understanding of how systemic SEL takes hold.

Together with our contributing authors, we envision this book supporting and inspiring those who work to enable districts, schools, and classrooms to cultivate positive social skills, teach self-management, and instill an approach to ethical decision making. The chapter authors drew from practical experiences, as well as theory and research in developmental and educational psychology, to describe contemporary issues in systemic SEL. Issues of promoting equity and cultural competence are integrated throughout the book. When we talk about school and societal systems, we know that structural racism is a fixed feature that needs to be noticed and addressed so the systems can be rebuilt without perpetuating a harmful historic legacy. In each chapter, researchers worked closely with practitioner partners to develop the ideas in this book because we wanted each chapter to be relevant, authentic, and high quality. We know that the path toward systemic SEL is complex and packed with successes and challenges. We applaud the effort and courage of all the authors in this book for their willingness to describe complex partnerships and share victories—as well as ideas that fell flat.

In this book, we address two broad questions: "What conditions need to be in place in systems (including states, local areas, districts, schools, classrooms, etc.) to support the development of SEL?" and "What actionable steps can we take to create those conditions?" In the rest of this chapter, we define SEL and systemic SEL, describe the contents of this book, and call attention to four common themes present throughout this book: equitable opportunities, intergroup understanding, adult development of social and emotional skills, and effective leadership.

What Is SEL?

Each generation faces its own challenges. In the 21st century, we need to come to terms with the reality that children and youth face an increasingly uncertain future. Global population growth, environmental issues, intergroup conflict, an intense racial reckoning, gun violence, trauma, and learning loss and mental health issues due to COVID present a tremendous range of challenges. Children and youth need opportunities to become fully equipped with all the skills, drive, and attitudes to meet these challenges now and in the future. The ability to listen to and communicate with people who are different than oneself, anticipate the consequences of individual and collective actions, show caring toward others even if it means giving up something one is privileged to have, take other people's perspectives, and show courage to stand up in the face of injustice are all crucial skills needed for our society to advance.

The skills and attitudes we have mentioned all fit beneath the umbrella of *social and emotional learning,* defined as "the process through which all young people and adults acquire and apply the knowledge, skills, and attitudes to develop healthy identities, manage emotions and achieve personal and collective goals, feel and show empathy for others, establish and maintain supportive relationships, and make responsible and caring decisions" (CASEL, 2022). Healthy SEL leads to a positive sense of one's own identity, the ability to be aware of one's own and others' emotions, the ability to manage strong emotions, the capacity to establish and work toward goals individually and collectively, and skills to cooperate with others, show empathy and caring for people similar and different than oneself, and create and maintain healthy supportive relationships (CASEL, 2022). See Appendix 1.1 at the end of this chapter (pp. 28–32) for a description of social and emotional competencies, and the conditions that cultivate them. Like many competencies that people develop—whether it's learning to sing or becoming a competent driver—these skills do not just appear magically. Children and youth learn new skills and knowledge from the opportunities and people around them. If the settings in which youth spend their time create the conditions conducive to skill development, then youth are more likely to develop skills. In the absence of settings filled with opportunities, development will be slow and stunted at an enormous cost to society. We cannot afford to let this happen.

There is a reason why SEL is so important for people during the first two decades of life. Children and youth are constantly experiencing physical, social, emotional, relational, ethical, and identity development. Their back-and-forth interactions with activities and people are the engines of that development (Bronfenbrenner & Morris, 2006). If the people around them create spaces and relationship opportunities that support their healthy development, children and youth thrive by latching onto some of the best opportunities available to them. If not, children and youth will find places where they fit in, where they feel like they matter, where they have a sense of agency—think of toxic middle school peer groups or neighborhood gangs—and those spaces are not necessarily productive and healthy. This means that it is our jobs as adults in youth lives to think carefully and creatively to create the best possible environments for youth.

One inherent challenge (and opportunity) of SEL is that children and youth are changing rapidly between the preschool years through high school. Efforts to teach SEL need to be finely attuned to youth's developmental needs, identities, and interests. Otherwise, the efforts will flop, because there will be no uptake from the students themselves. (This is akin to joining a gym but never going and then saying that the gym does not work.) Picture a fourth-grade teacher teaching a lesson about empathy and then showing a lack of empathy to students in their classroom. Fourth graders do not miss a trick! They will imitate their teachers' actions, thereby negating any skills taught. Imagine middle school students from racially/ethnically diverse classrooms rolling their eyes at SEL lessons that are designed for young kids, or lessons that are centered on stereotypical, all-White, middle-class characters. Those lessons will not work, and if anything, the efforts will backfire. Imagine high school students assigned to do community service without any choice about what service that will be. Those types of experiences feel irrelevant to them and will do nothing to produce engaged citizens.

As we strive to create engaging and meaningful SEL experiences, we need to remind ourselves that development of knowledge, skills, behaviors, and attitudes occurs (or does not occur) in the places in which youth spend their time. Classroom and school environments are important contexts for the development of these skills, as are families, communities, places of worship, peers, and afterschool environments, as well as the sociopolitical environments to which youth are exposed. Unfortunately, social and emotional development has become a political flashpoint in recent years, with politicians and families striving to ban SEL in schools and suggesting that SEL is a form of indoctrination (Meckler, 2022). Recognizing a few points related to the realities of SEL may help us understand a path forward.

First, students learn behaviors at school. Educators can either be intentional and choose the behaviors they want students to learn or leave that up to chance. Let us imagine educators trying to do their jobs *without* SEL practices—whether or not they are formally identified as such. To start, it would be impossible for educators to create learning spaces that are physically and psychologically safe and therefore conducive to academic learning. Without SEL, teachers would have no way of teaching life and career skills that are highly desired by future employers (Solberg et al., 2022). Furthermore, it would be extremely difficult for teachers to confer discipline in ways that are healthy and keep students engaged in school.

Consider disciplinary action as an example. School suspensions are common, with roughly 5–6% of students having one suspension per year (U.S. Department of Education Office for Civil Rights, 2018), yet they have been shown to have negative effects on youth, including absenteeism, lower grades, and decreased likelihood of graduating (LiCalsi et al., 2021). Also, disciplinary practices such as suspensions are disproportionately issued to students of color and students with disabilities. One recent study on suspension showed five times more lost days of school among Black than among White students and double the loss of school days among students with disabilities compared to nondisabled peers (Losen & Whitaker, 2018). Alternative approaches to discipline that incorporate SEL principles offer promise; for instance, Gregory, Ward-Seidel, and Grayman (Chapter 3, this volume) describe the role of restorative practices that balance empathy and accountability. Using these practices focuses on relationship-building prevention efforts, as well as disciplinary interventions that help youth understand the impact of their behavior on others and support them to make things right again (Gregory et al., 2016). Research on the responsive discipline strategies involving this approach shows promise for reducing misbehavior and discipline problems and enhancing school climate (Darling-Hammond et al., 2020). Work by Okonofua, Paunesku, and Walton (2016) examined the impact of empathic instead of punitive attitudes toward students. In their study, middle school math teachers were recruited into a randomized controlled trial of an empathic mindset intervention. Those in the intervention condition received two 45-minute sessions that led to understanding why students were showing behavior problems and gave suggestions for handling behavior problems in ways that conveyed respect and empathy. Results showed that students in the empathic-mindset classrooms were half as likely to be suspended during the school year compared to those who did not receive the intervention (Okonofua et al., 2016).

Recently we have heard a very loud, vocal minority protesting against SEL, but an even stronger, more prevailing call from educators acknowledges that SEL is critical to rebound from the damages of COVID. SEL practices are prevalent in schools. Recent survey work shows that 76% of principals said their school used a SEL program or curriculum in 2021–2022 (Schwartz et al., 2022). A national survey shows that 93% of principals believe that their schools should place fair or a great deal of emphasis on developing students' social and emotional competencies (Atwell & Bridgeland, 2019). Further, stress has been stated as the most common reason that people are leaving public school teaching (Dilberti et al., 2021), and many SEL strategies have been linked to improved teacher well-being, resulting in increased use of SEL.

Federal school reopening guidelines called attention to the importance of social and emotional learning after COVID, particularly for students who have been affected disproportionately by the pandemic, for instance, students of color, students with disabilities, and students from families with low incomes (U.S. Department of Education, 2021). The American Rescue Act of 2021 disbursed $122 billion to schools for safe reopening, with the specification that at least 5% of each state's allocation must go toward evidence-based interventions that respond to students' academic, social, and emotional needs (Office of Elementary & Secondary Education, 2021). Between November 2019 and April 2021, the spending on SEL in schools and districts increased from $530 million to $765 million (Tyton Partners, 2021). Taking these developments together, we see that SEL is a force in today's schools. Whether the intended outcome is long-term career skills, student well-being, or issues of equity, it is hard to ignore the growing use of SEL to support students' skills for life and learning.

What Is Systemic SEL?

To understand systemic SEL, we need to talk about the definition of a *system*. The Merriam-Webster dictionary defines it as "a regularly interacting or interdependent group of items forming a unified whole." Children, youth, their families, teachers, school leaders, adults in the community, and all levels of policy (e.g., municipal, regional, state, federal) are indeed "items" of a system that interact with one another to form the "unified whole." Items in a system are interdependent, so a change in one item impacts the others.

Here's an example. We know that when children make the transition into adolescence, their needs change. Picture a district that implements a new major policy that shifts schools from a K–5 to a K–8 structure. School leaders and teachers will need to reorganize their structures and routines, and think through how changes to the student body will impact other students, families, teachers, and so forth. (In other words, the decision to change school composition represents one "item" that will produce changes for students, families, and teachers that are also "items" in the same system.) New questions will arise. What does it mean that kindergarteners will be mixing with eighth graders? Are there ways to do this intentionally and well, so that positive, mentor-like relationships can form? With adolescents, it seems critical that relevant sociopolitical events outside of school are integrated into conversations, advisories, and the curriculum. Are there practices, such as whole-school meetings, that will need to be adjusted? Will shifting to a K–8 school mean that peer interactions on the morning bus ride will be affected? How can educators work with families and youth to create bus guidelines with intention?

Systemic SEL involves aligned policies, resources, and actions across administrative levels (states, districts, schools) and developmental levels (PreK to adulthood) to produce equitable learning conditions focused on the growth of social, emotional, and academic competence (Mahoney et al., 2020). When done well, all children and youth living in these systems will experience relationships, activities, and experiences that meet their developmental needs from the preschool years until after graduation. As such, we can think of systemic SEL as a universal intervention that can operate at the population level and improve public health for all people (Greenberg & Abenavoli, 2017). Just as we put fluoride in the water and conduct vision tests for all children in the early elementary school years, efforts to boost all students' social and emotional learning are intended to enhance their mental health and SEL skills so they can operate effectively in society (Greenberg et al., 2017).

When we establish SEL as a universal intervention, we need to think carefully about what that means. Universal interventions are about boosting skills for all children and youth, but the ways that these skills take form will vary. One of our greatest assets in schools is the diversity of our students (race, ethnicity, language, gender, sexual orientation and identity, religion). This diversity means that SEL as a universal intervention needs to be adjusted to meet people's individual needs in ways that match their desired outcomes of development, which may be rooted in religious, cultural, or even political stances. One sixth-grade teacher demonstrated this idea when I (Sara) asked him how he taught his students to be respectful. He explained:

> "Especially working in a culturally diverse school where there are lots of different norms around respect, it's [about] really being explicit and clear and generative with the kids [and asking] 'What is respect going to look like in this situation?' "

The teacher explained how he introduced a game called Tank, a communication game in which one student is blindfolded and moves around trying to pick things up and toss them at different objects with the help of their nonblindfolded peers.[1] Before introducing the game, he led a conversation about respect, eliciting responses from students about their families' ways of showing respect to one another, so the students and the teacher could notice and point out similarities and differences between home and school. Then he talked about the game and asked the kids to generate ways of showing respect while playing the game, so that they could have a common definition. By having this conversation, he showed that he valued students' home definitions while creating a shared common definition of respect in their classroom. In this scenario, the cultivation of respect was a part of a universal approach, yet the organic process to develop shared norms of behavior engendered curiosity about diversity and reflected the unique cultural experiences of the students in their classroom.

[1] The nongendered pronouns *they* and *their* are used throughout this book when describing nonspecific or hypothetical individuals, or when preferred by a specific individual.

How Systemic SEL Can Lead to Equity

How do we make sure that all youth have opportunities to spend time with people in settings that support their healthy development of social and emotional competencies? The answer is complex—it includes teachers, families, schools, out-of-school activities, communities, neighborhoods, and religious organizations. The answer involves policies—standards and laws at the federal, state, and local levels that direct funds toward some settings rather than others. Unfortunately, we live in a society plagued by existing systemic inequities, where Black and Brown students and students from families with limited economic means have less access to opportunities that contribute to healthy growth and development, an issue that has been amplified by pandemic conditions (American Academy of Pediatrics, 2021; Institute of Education Sciences, 2022).

Many stakeholders need to come together effectively to make sure that SEL is promoting equity, not perpetuating existing systemic inequality. Our definition of equitable SEL draws from work by Ramirez et al. (2021); equitable SEL involves safe, inclusive learning environments that affirm diverse identities; the recognition and inclusion of family strengths, cultural values and practices; efforts to cultivate a positive sense of identity; promotion of students' voice and sense of agency; and explicit discussion of issues of inequality, bias, and power, accompanied by efforts to disrupt the status quo. Given this definition, equity at the systemic level means transforming the existing systems so that students can spend their time in spaces conducive to equity.

It is important to clarify what we mean by *equity*, because this term is used in so many different ways. For instance, a commonly uttered phrase at (coeditor) Mike's son's preschool was "Fair is not always equal." Equity is a way of providing individuals with the resources they need to achieve the outcomes they deserve. This may mean providing some individuals different levels of resources to work toward the same goal. For example, a student with a reading disability may need more resources to reach the same grade-level expectation as a student who does not have a disability. We call this "equity in opportunity." This approach stands in contrast to the idea of "equality," which infers that everyone gets the same resources regardless of their needs.

But equity is also sometimes referred to as an outcome, as in "achieving equity" or "equitable outcomes." What does an outcomes-focused equity mean? Some view equitable outcomes as students achieving the same outcomes regardless of their condition or background. Certainly, there is great value in this conceptualization. For example, we do not want one's income or race to be a determining factor in their educational outcomes. However, in the SEL world, if we focus on SEL outcomes only, we expect all youth to conform to dominant cultural behaviors that conflict with norms learned at home and may invalidate youth's cultural identity (Ramirez et al., 2021). Even worse, we run the risk of using SEL with youth of color as a way of garnering compliance and control (Simmons, 2021).

A different perspective—the one offered in this book—focuses on *equity of opportunity*. This perspective argues for creating high-quality learning opportunities that are available to everyone—again, regardless of one's background or condition. Critically, this view also acknowledges that providing the same opportunities to students may still result in *unequal outcomes* because of the different starting points coming in to school, different opportunities outside of school, or different priorities among students and their families. Equity of opportunities requires educators to be carefully attuned to their students to know who needs what and when. This requires cultural competence and psychologically healthy teachers who feel well supported by leadership and the systems around them.

We live in a country with systemic inequities. As a result, youth spend a lot of their time in spaces that lack equity in opportunities. For example, imagine two students who want to participate in a sports program after school that involves a small fee. For one student, the fee is not a concern. For the other, the fee means the student needs to go through the extra paperwork and possible humiliation to acquire a fee waiver, which means the student may not even try to engage. Our goal for schools is to make sure that the main places in which youth spend their time offer equitable access to the resources they need to buffer them against harmful realities and develop their strengths and skills. If schools are successful in creating equitable opportunities, youth will learn and be empowered not only to face but also to transform and improve the equity of those broader societal systems that limit progress.

Contents of This Book

Our book is organized in four parts. We begin with chapters that describe systemic SEL in action. The chapters in Part I, *Supporting Systemic SEL*, do the equivalent of opening the door to the kitchen so we can watch the chef make a glorious dinner and learn from our observations. In Chapter 2, Tia Navalene Barnes, Jocelyn E. Brown, Melissa Stoffers, Jurni Jackson, Yu Xia, Amanda G. Wells, and Alexcia Bryant describe partnered work in a diverse urban district to create systemic SEL that counteracts dominant White, middle-class-oriented approaches to SEL. Through those efforts, the district makes sure that all students (including those living in poverty and/or experiencing high mobility, students of color, English learners, and students with disabilities) have equivalent access to high-quality SEL. To mention just one of many gems in the chapter, the project team identified all of the current district and school initiatives, programs, practices, and processes (PreK–12)—140 in all—and examined whether they exacerbated inequities, were applied equitably, and were actually needed or could be consolidated to streamline the process.

Next, in Chapter 3, Anne Gregory, Allison Rae Ward-Seidel, and Dionne Grayman describe the integration of racial equity initiatives, restorative practices, and SEL. They focus on the role of school leaders in systemic SEL and show the importance of alignment between ideas and actions. The chapter also describes the remarkable value of adult learning, reflection, and coach support to expand leaders' capacity to produce equitable opportunities. The inspiring real-world examples from a 6th- to 12th-grade school show the vulnerability that comes with leaders' efforts to break old habits to adopt equitable practices. We see bold efforts to engage students and improve upon existing practices.

Chapter 4 broadens the lens internationally. Andy Smart, Jean Bernard, James H. Williams, Aaron Benavot, and Margaret Sinclair show the role of textbooks in systemic SEL. Many countries around the world strive to meet the United Nations Sustainable Development Goals focused on human rights, peace, and appreciation of cultural diversity, and these ideas require students' development of social and emotional skills (NISSEM, 2022). The chapter draws from international contexts, particularly low- and middle-income countries, where pedagogical ideas printed in a textbook help teachers steer away from rote instruction and toward student-centered approaches that incorporate SEL. Examples from India, Ethiopia, and Bangladesh show efforts to create alignment between governmental policies and school practices.

In Part II, *Fostering Adult SEL: Insights for Preservice Education and Professional Development*, the chapters focus on the adults in schools, showing how adult skills, growth, and engagement are crucial for systemic SEL. Chapter 5, by Olivia A. Johnson, Bloodine Barthelus, Alexandra Skoog-Hoffman, Ednah Nwafor, and Robert J. Jagers, examines the skills and actions of adult leaders and describes *transformative social and emotional learning* (tSEL)—a form of SEL that brings an explicit, justice-oriented frame and creates opportunities for adults and youth to discuss inequities and construct solutions that are available to everyone. In doing so, tSEL is designed to engage people in civic and school life. In this chapter, the authors follow guidelines emanating from the Building Equitable Learning Environments (BELE) network and focus on how adults can engage in tSEL for their own growth and development so they can better meet the needs of youth. After the murder of George Floyd in 2020, the principal at one school launched into new conversations with her staff about racial inequities. These conversations led to a fresh vision for replacing a centrally placed mural at their school that depicted students in stereotypical ways. Instead, the new mural will affirm the racial and ethnic identities of the adults and students at school, offering an insight into adult tSEL.

Next, Chapter 6, by Deirdre Hon, Julie Sauve, Julia Mahfouz, and Kimberly A. Schonert-Reichl, describes what preservice teacher preparation programs can do to cultivate *SEL-ready teachers*. In their chapter, the authors identify foundational skills and knowledge needed by SEL-ready teachers and provide a framework that teacher education programs can use to improve practice. This chapter describes a range of teacher education programs; some offer SEL courses, others provide SEL specialties or certifications, and still others fully integrate SEL at the programmatic level. The chapter offers rich examples throughout, engenders an understanding of what teachers know (or do not know) when they enter the workforce, and generates ideas for new approaches.

Shannon B. Wanless, Caitlin F. Spear, Jocelyn V. Artinger, and Jennifer O. Briggs wrote Chapter 7 to call attention to a crucial issue that tends to be sidelined in conversations about SEL. Districts all over the country rely on expert facilitators for SEL professional development in their schools. Yet we seldom consider whether these facilitators have developed the skills they need to lead challenging conversation about race. If facilitators have developed these skills, they can speak boldly and frankly, create safe spaces for conversation about racial equity, and craft conditions for educators to unlearn problematic habits that come (inadvertently) from living in a society that privileges some but oppresses others. If facilitators do not have these skills, these conversations get shoved under the rug, which perpetuates the status quo and leads educators of color and students of color to feel greater mistrust toward their schools and districts as they wonder: "Am I being seen for who I am? Am I being heard? Are my ideas valued here?" In their chapter, the authors describe the role of SEL in racial equity facilitation and draw from contemporary research and experiences.

Part III, *Cultivating Student SEL: Creating School Conditions Conducive to Skill Development,* focuses on the question: What are the skills that we want youth to develop? As we explore this question, we recognize that schools are a place where children and youth learn from the people around them. If educators are intentional about that learning, youth are more likely to develop the positive skills and attitudes that we envision for them. This section begins with Chapter 8, by Elise Capella, Stacey Alicea, and Natalie May, who focus on interpersonal skill development—cooperation, perspective taking, and empathy. These skills emerge in children and youth when they have daily opportunities for positive engagement with adults and peers around them. To foster the development of these skills, schools need to make sure that their school activities and routines are guided by values of equity so that all students, including those from groups who are often marginalized because of their race, ethnicity, language, income, (dis)ability, or gender, benefit from skill development opportunities. The authors remind us that the outward appearance of these skills vary by culture, disability, and age. The chapter describes how schools can shift their routines and activities so that the conditions are present for the healthy development of these skills.

In Chapter 9, Tyralynn Frazier and Brendan Ozawa-de Silva turn the focus inward by talking about the emotional life of children and the adults around them. They bring together SEL and contemplative frameworks, and give an example of how compassion-based meditation practices can change children's inner dialogue, appraisal of themselves, self-control, and management of their strong emotions. For intrapersonal development to occur, students need to feel safe and secure, and experience settings that are culturally and developmentally aligned. In this chapter, the authors provide a checklist of systems-level conditions that need to be met to create equitable opportunities for intrapersonal development.

Part IV, *Identifying Roadmaps for SEL in Action*, rounds out our book. We close with examples of SEL in action, with the goal of providing roadmaps for others making policy and practice decisions. In Chapter 10, Sheldon Berman, Jacqueline Jodl, and Joyce Barnes provide guidelines for action. This chapter explains that each district needs to make choices about SEL, and that integration and implementation needs to be customized for it to be effective. Berman and colleagues describe the need to align instructional practices, discipline systems, and professional capacity with SEL values, and they give examples of typical roadblocks. One common rut is organizing SEL around the dominant cultural norms and values without tapping into the racial, ethnic, and cultural heritages of the students in the classroom. Meaningful connections between classroom and community life need to be established. The authors close with two recommendations for success—make sure the first step is successful, and build from that by thinking through how the elements of a plan connect with each other. These closing points remind us that with systemic SEL, action in one component of the system creates reaction in other components.

Chris Cipriano, Gabrielle Rappolt-Schlichtmann, Julie Riley, Lauren H. Naples, and Abigail Eveleigh describe a new framework, the Collaboratory for Inclusion, to bring SEL practice to adults and students in school communities. Chapter 11 reminds us that during periods of school change, the same voices tend to get heard. There is seldom enough energy and effort expended to amplify the voices of those who tend to be most marginalized from decision making—students with disabilities, student of color, English learners, and/or students from families with low income. The focus on SEL for children with disabilities takes on new and exciting forms as the authors bring together ideas from culturally responsive pedagogy and universal design for learning, integrate perspective taking and youth voice, and apply these ideas in a school district striving to implement SEL.

In Chapter 12, Pilar Alamos, Jenna Conway, Tamilah Richardson, and Amanda P. Williford describe systemic SEL writ large by describing a statewide measurement effort. This chapter describes a 7-year process that led to the measurement of self-regulation and social skills for all kindergarten children in Virginia. These teacher-reported data can be analyzed at classroom, school, district, or state levels to assess growth, establish benchmarks, and identify patterns of inequity. Having access to these data is one important milestone, but interpreting these data effectively and using these data to improve practice is an equivalently important challenge. In this chapter, Tamilah Richardson, a former preschool teacher, reflects on how the teacher-reported data measure actual student behavior and teachers' perception of those students. These insights shed light on how measurement of social and emotional skills can be used to enhance equity and family engagement.

Finally, we close with Chapter 13, our Conclusion, led by Michael J. Strambler with Kimberly A. Schonert-Reichl and Sara E. Rimm-Kaufman. This chapter pulls together several important themes on the current trends, ongoing challenges, and future directions of SEL and includes reflections from children and youth about their SEL experiences in schools.

Common Themes

Four common themes emanate from this book, as we describe here. Each of these speak to the way that this book meets the moment in our society.

SEL Can Be Leveraged toward Equity

Issues of equity are prominent in every chapter in this book. Considerable disagreement remains about the relation between equity and SEL. One ongoing question is whether we can work within our existing school systems to create equity or whether we need to transform them completely to produce educational improvement. The chapters in this book grapple with this question. They describe lessons learned in efforts to create equitable spaces and show a variety of approaches in pursuit of this goal.

Many schools implement SEL by adopting programs. The examples in this book show ways to use systemic SEL to create an overarching umbrella of aligned priorities and policies, then adopt programs to achieve goals within schools. Often, to be successful, the implementation of programs means retaining the critical aspects of the programs but making adaptations of those programs to match the student body with which schools or teachers are working. The chapters in this book also demonstrate the need for new programs that are designed to be culturally responsive by matching the culturally specific knowledge and providing instruction to facilitators on how to use culturally responsive strategies (Barnes, 2019). Furthermore, given the composition and training of the teacher workforce, adult capacity building is essential so that teachers can grow to better meet the needs of diverse youth (Ramirez et al., 2021). See Johnson et al., Chapter 5, Hon et al., Chapter 6, and Wanless et al., Chapter 7, this volume.

Each chapter raises crucial issues related to equity, leaving us perhaps with more questions than answers. For example, one action for addressing equity is to center practices around the students in the classroom. However, centering practices around some students means educators are decentering practices from others. We are drawn to the idea of systemic SEL because we see it as our best hope for achieving enduring change in the inequitable systems in which students spend their time. This begs the question—how do we strive toward systemic SEL that will be *better* than past approaches? We know that the existing systems are biased against groups of people who have been historically marginalized. If we have the same people sitting around the table examining the same problems, we are likely to get the same answers we generated one or two decades ago. We need to expand the circle of people who are creating change (e.g., see Cipriano et al., Chapter 11, this volume). That means more than "checking the box" to make sure that decision-makers are from different racial groups. It means thinking broadly about the definition of diversity—making sure that age, racial/ethnic, disability, gender identity, and political diversity are fully present. It is not enough to just invite diverse people around the table. The increasingly diverse groups must be given the power to transform the existing processes and structures. Without such efforts, new systems will simply rebuild the old and inequitable systems once again.

SEL Can Support Intergroup Understanding

Unfortunately, in the United States, most people spend most of their time in segregated spaces—segregated by income, race/ethnicity, politics, or religion. However, there are many schools in the United States where considerable diversity is present. We hold out hope for schools as a place where students can learn to understand and respect people who are different from themselves. Using race as an example, between one-half and two-thirds of U.S. students attend schools with a diverse racial composition (defined as fewer than 75% of students from a single race; Nowicki, 2022). (Worth noting: This figure is far less than what is possible given that almost 8,000 highly segregated schools in the United States are within 5 miles of each other and thus could be integrated [Lehrer-Small, 2022] and that segregation within schools can be as stark as between schools because of tracking [Siegel-Hawley, 2020].) Our take-home message is that more than half of U.S. students are in schools where educators can leverage the existing racial diversity to create opportunities for cross-racial conversations and friendships.

Such diversity can elevate students' awareness about people who are different from them and help students notice inequality and injustice. These experiences are a healthy step toward develop *critical consciousness*, that is, "the ability to recognize and analyze systems of inequality and the commitment to take action against these systems" (El-Amin et al., 2017, p. 18). For example, if teachers are sufficiently prepared for race-based conversations (Wanless et al., Chapter 7, this volume), these conditions lend themselves to opportunities to teach the language of inequality, create space to discuss issues of racism, and teach students how to take action against inequality (El-Amin et al., 2017). Even if some schools lack diversity, we need to prepare *all* youth to be curious and interested in people who are different from them, a topic raised by Capella et al. (Chapter 8, this volume). We need to give all students a chance to collaborate with people from different backgrounds so that students learn to take others' perspectives and understand that there is more than one way to be in this world. There is a lot of room for innovative ideas to support intergroup understanding. Technology can be used creatively in classrooms to create intergroup experiences that otherwise would not be available. Smart and colleagues

(Chapter 4, this volume) describe exciting ways to embed SEL into textbooks and other educational materials that can be widely distributed. This approach can be scaled-up to be used in millions of classrooms.

Adult SEL Is Foundational to Successful SEL

Every chapter in this volume calls attention to the need to support adult SEL, not just growth in children and youth. These chapters were written during the pandemic period during which schools have witnessed a dramatic increase in mental health issues, overwork, burnout, and staffing shortages (Pressley, 2021; Steiner & Woo, 2021). A national survey conducted in January 2022 showed that teachers and principals were twice as likely to experience frequent job-related stress compared to typical workers. Burnout, symptoms of depression, and inability to cope well with job-related stress were all higher among teachers and principals than others in the workforce. Further complicating issues, many educational environments appear to be hostile toward people of color, with 48% of principals of color and 36% of teachers of color indicating that they had experienced at least one occurrence of racial discrimination since the beginning of the school year (Steiner et al., 2022). If we want to improve settings for students, we need to upgrade the adult experiences in school.

The importance of teacher–student relationships is just one of many reasons why adult SEL matters. One of the clearest and most consistent findings in education research is that high-quality relationships between teachers and students leads to improved student outcomes. When teachers are attuned to students' interests, sensitive and responsive to students' needs, and show caring and respect, students have fewer behavior problems, better social skills, improved emotion regulation, higher engagement in learning, and better academic outcomes (Merritt et al., 2012; Hamre & Pianta, 2005; Rimm-Kaufman et al., 2015; Roorda, Koomen, Spilt, & Oort, 2011; Wentzel, 1997). These positive teacher–student relationships have even greater consequence for students of color (Gregory et al., 2016; Vega et al., 2015) and students from families with low income (Roorda et al., 2011). Yet teachers can only develop positive relationships with students if they have capacity to do so, which means teachers need to be psychologically and physically healthy themselves, which is a challenge given the stressful nature of teaching (Steiner & Woo, 2021). SEL interventions have been shown to improve teacher well-being (Jennings et al., 2019) and the quality of teacher–student relationships (Baroody et al., 2014).

Adult SEL is also critical for student SEL, because U.S. teachers teach students who are different from them. In U.S. public schools, 80% of the teachers are White, but 51% of the students are students of color (National Center for Education Statistics [NCES], 2016). Almost all teachers have college degrees, but 8% of students live in households in which no parent completed high school (NCES, 2022). The majority of teachers are middle class (NCES, 2018), but roughly one in seven children live in poverty (Children's Defense Fund, 2022). For many reasons, teachers do not automatically develop the skills needed to work with students who are different from them—an issue that plays out in unfortunate ways, such as low expectations and disproportionate disciplining of students of color or students with disabilities. Chapter 12 by Alamos et al., this volume, offers the example that teachers' past experiences and backgrounds affect their perception of the social and emotional skills of their students.

Just as teachers acquire skills to teach reading or math effectively, the skills to teach across difference can be learned, too. Teachers need to become increasingly self-aware and socially-aware. That means teachers need opportunities to unlearn prejudicial habits, learn about their students and their families, and listen carefully to the needs of their students (Rimm-Kaufman & Thomas, 2021). Professional development is necessary to develop key adult competencies including critical self-awareness that comes from reflecting on one's own practices, emotions, interactions and behaviors; the ability to build warm, reciprocal relationships that convey high expectations for youth; and the ability to shift power to students to create student-centered experiences in schools (Ramirez et al., 2021).

Teachers are the people who actually implement SEL programs and practices in school settings (Schonert-Reichl, 2017), and teachers' own SEL competence and well-being play a critical role in influencing the learning context and the degree to which they are successful at infusing new practices into classrooms and schools (Aarons et al., 2009; Larson et al., 2018).

School Leaders Matters for SEL

We see the crucial role of school leaders in successful systemic SEL. In Barnes et al. (Chapter 2, this volume), we see principals needing to "manage up" while also adjusting the district initiatives to meet the needs of students within their schools. In Gregory et al. (Chapter 3, this volume), we see the vulnerability of principals as they take challenging risks. In Johnson et al. (Chapter 5, this volume), we see a principal identifying a visible symbol of inequity in their school and creating unity among adults and students in the schools as they work to change that symbol.

Research evidence points to the important role of school principals. A large-scale meta-analysis (a study that summarizes results from many other, smaller empirical studies) shows that an effective elementary school principal has the equivalent impact of an extra 2.7 and 2.9 months of extra instruction in reading and math, respectively (Grissom et al., 2021). For a principal to be effective, teachers need to trust them. Each social interaction or communication between a principal and teacher offers an opportunity for teachers to discern whether their leader is trustworthy or not. Research tells us that teacher–principal trust hinges on genuine caring for teachers; honesty, integrity, and fairness; openness toward ideas of the staff; competence as a school leader; and consistency over time (Tschannen-Moran & Gareis, 2015). What makes a principal's role especially difficult is the balance between effective social relationships and task orientation, so that the work of the school gets accomplished well in the presence of supportive relationships. This feat unto itself requires adult social and emotional skills.

Most U.S. principals endorse SEL. For instance, a recent survey of nationally representative surveys of 884 public school principals in PreK–12 schools showed that almost all principals (98%), regardless of their location or type of school, believed that students from all backgrounds benefit from SEL in schools (DePaoli et al., 2017). We know that effective principals have profound impact on schools. Yet principals are more likely to be successful at implementing SEL extensively if their central office, superintendents, and district leaders showed buy-in to SEL (DePaoli et al., 2017).

For readers, we hope the theme of leadership calls attention to crucial questions that need to be addressed in every district. For example, who are the decision-makers in your district (or school)? Are there people around the decision-making table who think every day about the caring culture of the school and whether students feel like they belong? For instance, are there school psychologists or school counselors present? Are disciplinary approaches proactive, justice-oriented, and focused on child growth and development, or reactive and punitive?

Our Aspiration for This Book

We hope that this book will be read by school board members, administrators, and other educators from all over the country—rural, urban, and suburban districts—who have interests in SEL. As faculty ourselves, we were excited by the idea of including this book in undergraduate and graduate school classes. We envision this book being used by professional learning communities, grade-level meeting groups, school boards, educational organizations, innovators, and all-school book clubs in the United States and beyond.

As you read this book, we hope that you will naturally make connections to your work. We offer a few questions for reflection here:

- What are the connections of this chapter to your own practice?
- What challenges and roadblocks does this chapter raise about SEL? How have you addressed these challenges and roadblocks in your practice? Who have been your partners in this work? What have you learned from these experiences?
- Are there aspects of SEL that are available to some students but not others because of systemic inequities in your school and communities, or society at large? If so, what children and youth dwell on the margins and are not exposed to opportunities for social and emotional growth? What steps can you take to address these inequities? Who can partner with you in this work?
- Given what you have just read about SEL, what are two or three actionable steps that you can take tomorrow?

Every setting or organization has an opportunity to create a more equitable space in what, unfortunately, is an inequitable world. We have seen equity audits in which a group of community members or educators look at the policies and examine how they may advantage some students more than others. One take-home message from this book is that schools can reach out to students and families and look for their strengths—whether it is their ability to navigate complex systems as they immigrated to the United States, their tight family relationships that enable a teacher to connect to an uncle or brother to support a struggling student, or their linguistic skills in another language.

Yet another goal in writing this book is to address the big gap between what we know works and what actually gets implemented in schools. The most effective SEL educators can take programs or curricula and make them come alive in their classroom or school. That magic only happens when educators have a deep understanding of *why* a classroom practice matters. In these cases, they are not just implementing SEL practices superficially because someone told them to do so.

Knowing the "why" behind SEL deepens educators' practices. For example, effective teachers know that children thrive when they feel safe, feel liked and respected by their teachers, and feel like they belong. If this is an organizing principle that a teacher has in mind as they enact SEL, the SEL efforts will flourish. For example, I (Sara) had the privilege of Zooming with a brilliant group of elementary school teachers who were preparing for their students to come back to school in person in February 2021, during COVID times. These teachers knew *why* they needed to implement SEL—they understood the magnitude of the transition ahead, they knew that children thrive when they feel safe and feel liked and respected by their teachers and peers, and they knew they could apply SEL principles and practices to their classroom to ease the students' transitions back to school. The teachers met (virtually) and engaged in conversation. First, they took their students' perspectives to understand the full range of experiences (and emotions) they had over the past 6 months. Then they discussed children's needs to be social, yet safe, and brainstormed how to accommodate these needs in pandemic conditions. They also anticipated that their students would feel anxious about being near so many people after being told to avoid others. The results were exciting. The teachers planned conversations with students to adjust classroom norms to include physical safety, decided to offer opportunities for children to draw pictures about how school was different at home than in the school building, and created opportunities for young children to practice reminding others to wear their masks properly in ways that were kind and reflective of their shared safety goals. These teachers knew why they were implementing these practices. They knew students would have a lot of "big emotions" as they returned to school, and they thought through how to support students in their awareness and management of those emotions before focusing in on academic learning.

To cultivate an understanding of *why* we use SEL practices, each chapter concludes with questions for discussion and reflection. We know every reader will bring their own point of view, and we hope these questions spark ideas for teachers, principals, school psychologists, occupational therapists, speech–language pathologists, school nurses, parents, and others who work with children and youth. We encourage readers to choose from these questions and discuss those that are most relevant.

Concluding Points

The field of psychology reminds us that we, as humans, go through tremendous mental exercises to protect our delicate sense of self-worth. It is human nature. We like being right. We like feeling wise. We all want affirmation for our hard work. As you dig into this book, we hope you will find affirmations of your best practices. When that happens, pause, and allow yourself to appreciate your accomplishments, the victories at your school, organization, or community. Take time to notice the progress that you have made since you've set out to improve the school and community conditions in ways that will contribute to SEL. But affirmation is not the only experience we want you to take from this book. We urge you to identify new ideas that you haven't tried and consider partnerships that may seem overwhelming at first glance but within reach upon further consideration. We anticipate that you will read ideas that are surprising, provocative, and question your assumptions. Sit with those moments of discomfort and learn from them. Our hope is that these moments will energize you to say, "I can think about SEL challenges in a new way" or "Our community can do more." Please use this book to first notice and then face new challenges that lie ahead. We—the readers, editors, chapter authors—are a community of people who care deeply about youth. Please view us as your partners in the challenging and important work that you do.

REFERENCES

Aarons, G. A., Fettes, D. L., Flores, L. E., Jr., & Sommerfeld, D. H. (2009). Evidence-based practice implementation and staff emotional exhaustion in children's services. *Behaviour Research and Therapy, 47*(11), 954–960.

American Academy of Pediatrics. (2021, October 19). AAP-AACAP-CHA Declaration of a National Emergency in Child and Adolescent Mental Health. Retrieved from *www.aap.org/en/advocacy/child-and-adolescent-healthy-mental-development/aap-aacap-cha-declaration-of-a-national-emergency-in-child-and-adolescent-mental-health.*

Astor, R. A., Benbenishty, R., & Estrada, J. (2009). School violence and theoretically atypical schools: The principal's centrality in orchestrating safe schools. *American Educational Research Journal, 46*(2), 423–461.

Atwell, M. N., & Bridgeland, J. M. (2019). Ready to Lead: A 2019 update of principals' perspectives on how social and emotional learning can prepare children and transform schools. Retrieved from *https://casel.org/casel-resources-ready-to-lead-2019/?view=true.*

Barnes, T. N. (2019). Changing the landscape of social emotional learning in urban schools: What are we currently focusing on and where do we go from here? *The Urban Review, 51*(4), 599–637.

Baroody, A. E., Rimm-Kaufman, S. E, Larsen, R. A., & Curby, T. W. (2014). The link between Responsive Classroom training and student–teacher relationship quality in the fifth grade: A study of fidelity of implementation. *School Psychology Review, 43*(1), 69–85.

Battistich, V., Solomon, D., Watson, M., & Schaps, E. (1997). Caring school communities. *Educational Psychologist, 32*(3), 137–151.

Belfield, C., Bowden, A. B., Klapp, A., Levin, H., Shand, R., & Zander, S. (2015). The economic value of social and emotional learning. *Journal of Benefit-Cost Analysis, 6*(3), 508–544.

Benard, B., & Slade, S. (2009). Listening to students: Moving from resilience research to youth development practice and school connectedness. In M. J. Furlong, R. Gilman, & E. S. Huebner (Eds.), *Handbook of positive psychology in schools* (2nd ed., pp. 353–368). Routledge/Taylor & Francis Group.

Braun, S. S., Schonert-Reichl, K. A., & Roeser, R. W. (2020). Effects of teachers' emotion regulation, burnout, and life satisfaction on student well-being. *Journal of Applied Developmental Psychology, 69*, 101–151.

Bronfenbrenner, U., & Morris, P. A. (2006). The bioecological model of human development. In R. M. Lerner (Ed.), *Handbook of child development: Vol. 1. Theoretical models of human development* (6th ed., pp. 793–828). Wiley.

Bryk, A., & Schneider, B. (2002). *Trust in schools: A core resource for improvement.* Russell Sage Foundation.

Charney, R. (2002). *Teaching children to care: Classroom management for ethical and academic growth, K–8.* Center for Responsive Schools.

Children's Defense Fund. (2022). The state of America's children in 2021. Retrieved from *www.childrensdefense.org/state-of-americas-children/soac-2021-child-poverty.*

Collaborative for Academic, Social and Emotional Learning. (2020). CASEL'S SEL framework: What are the core competence areas and where are they promoted? Retrieved from *https://casel.org/fundamentals-of-sel/what-is-the-casel-framework.*

Collaborative for Academic, Social and Emotional Learning. (2022). Fundamentals of SEL. Retrieved from *https://casel.org/fundamentals-of-sel.*

Collie, R. J., & Perry, N. E. (2019). Cultivating teacher thriving through social–emotional competence and its development. *Australian Educational Researcher, 46*(4), 699–714.

Collie, R. J., Shapka, J. D., & Perry, N. E. (2012). School climate and social–emotional learning: Predicting teacher stress, job satisfaction, and teaching efficacy. *Journal of Educational Psychology, 104*(4), 1189–1204.

Cook, C. R., Fiat, A., Larson, M., Daikos, C., Slemrod, T., Holland, E. A., . . . Renshaw, T. (2018). Positive greetings at the door: Evaluation of a low-cost, high-yield proactive classroom management strategy. *Journal of Positive Behavior Interventions, 20*(3), 149–159.

Darling-Hammond, S., Fronius, T. A., Sutherland, H., Guckenburg, S., Petrosino, A., & Hurley, N. (2020). Effectiveness of restorative justice in U.S. K–12 schools: A review of quantitative research. *Contemporary School Psychology, 24*, 295–308.

DePaoli, J. L., Atwell, M. N., & Bridgeland, J. (2017). Ready to lead: A national principal survey on how social and emotional learning can prepare children and transform schools (A report for CASEL). Retrieved from *https://files.eric.ed.gov/fulltext/ED579088.pdf.*

Diliberti, M., Schwartz, H. L., & Grant, D. M. (2021). *Stress topped the reasons why public school teachers quit, even before COVID-19*. RAND.

Durlak, J. A., Weissberg, R. P., Dymnicki, A. B., Taylor, R. D., & Schellinger, K. B. (2011). The impact of enhancing students' social and emotional learning: A meta-analysis of school-based universal interventions. *Child Development, 82*(1), 405–432.

El-Amin, A., Seider, S., Graves, D., Tamerat, J., Clark, S., Soutter, M., . . . Malhotra, S. (2017). Critical consciousness: A key to student achievement. *Phi Delta Kappan, 98*(5), 18–23.

Greenberg, M. T., & Abenavoli, R. (2017). Universal interventions: Fully exploring their impacts and potential to produce population-level impacts. *Journal of Research on Educational Effectiveness, 10*(1), 40–67.

Greenberg, M. T., Domitrovich, C. E., Weissberg, R. P., & Durlak, J. A. (2017). Social and emotional learning as a public health approach. *Future of Children, 27*(1), 13–32.

Gregory, A., Clawson, K., Davis, A., & Gerewitz, J. (2016). The promise of restorative practices to transform teacher–student relationships and achieve equity in school discipline. *Journal of Educational and Psychological Consultation, 26*(4), 325–353.

Gregory, A., & Fergus, E. (2017). Social–emotional learning and equity in school discipline. *Future of Children, 27*, 117–136.

Gregory, A., Skiba, R. J., & Mediratta, K. (2017). Eliminating disparities in school discipline: A framework for intervention (Special issue on equity in school). *Review of Research in Education, 47*, 253–278.

Gregory, A., Ward-Seidel, A. R., & Carter, K. (2020). Twelve indicators of restorative practices implementation: A framework for educational leaders. *Journal of Educational and Psychological Consultation, 31*(2), 147–179.

Grissom, J. A., Egalite, A. J., & Lindsay, C. A. (2021). How principals affect students and schools: A systematic synthesis of two decades of research. Retrieved from *www.wallacefoundation.org/principalsynthesis*.

Hamre, B. K., & Pianta, R. C. (2005). Can instructional and emotional support in the first-grade classroom make a difference for children at risk of school failure? *Child Development, 76*(5), 949–967.

Heifetz, R. A., & Linsky, M. (2002). Leading with an open heart. *Leader to Leader, 26*, 28–33.

Institute of Education Sciences. (2022). 2022 School Pulse Panel: Student behavior. Retrieved from *https://ies.ed.gov/schoolsurvey/spp*.

Jagers, R., Rivas-Drake, D., & Borowski, T. (2018). *Equity and social and emotional learning: A cultural analysis*. CASEL.

Jennings, P. A., Doyle, S., Oh, Y., Rasheed, D., Frank, J. L., & Brown, J. L. (2019). Long-term impacts of the CARE program on teachers' self-reported social and emotional competence and well-being. *Journal of School Psychology, 76*, 186–202.

Jennings, P. A., & Greenberg, M. T. (2009). The prosocial classroom: Teacher social and emotional competence in relation to student and classroom outcomes. *Review of Educational Research, 79*, 491–525.

Jones, S., Bailey, R., Brush, K., & Kahn, K. (2017). Kernels of practice for SEL: Low-cost, low-burden strategies. EASEL Lab, Harvard Graduate School of Education. Retrieved from *www.wallacefoundation.org/knowledge-center/pages/kernels-of-practice-for-sel-low-cost-low-burden-strategies.aspx*.

Jones, S. M., Bailey, R., & Jacob, R. (2014). Social–emotional learning is essential to classroom management. *Phi Delta Kappan, 96*(2), 19–24.

Larson, M., Cook, C. R., Fiat, A., & Lyon, A. R. (2018). Stressed teachers don't make good implementers: Examining the interplay between stress reduction and intervention fidelity. *School Mental Health, 10*, 61–76.

Legette, K. B., Rogers, L. O., & Warren, C. A. (2022). Humanizing student–teacher relationships for black children: Implications for teachers' social–emotional training. *Urban Education, 57*(2), 278–288.

Lehrer-Small, A. (2022). "Low-hanging fruit": Thousands of same-race schools within miles of each other. Retrieved from *www.the74million.org/article/low-hanging-fruit-thousands-of-same-race-schools-within-miles-of-each-other.*

LiCalsi, C., Osher, D., & Bailey, P. (2021). An empirical examination of the effects of suspension and suspension severity on behavioral and academic outcomes. Retrieved from *www.air.org/sites/default/files/2021–08/nyc-suspension-effects-behavioral-academic-outcomes-august-2021.pdf.*

Losen, D., & Whitaker, A. (2018). 11 million days lost: Race, discipline, and safety at U.S. public schools. Retrieved from *www.aclu.org/report/11-million-days-lost-race-discipline-and-safety-us-public-schools-part-1.*

Mahfouz, J. (2018). Mindfulness training for school administrators: Effects on well-being and leadership. *Journal of Educational Administration, 56*(6), 602–619.

Mahfouz, J., Greenberg, M. T., & Rodriguez, A. (2019). *Principals' social and emotional competence: A key factor for creating caring schools.* Edna Bennett Pierce Prevention Research Center, Pennsylvania State University (Robert Wood Johnson Foundation Brief).

Mahoney, J., Weissberg, R., Greenberg, M., Dusenbury, L., Jagers, R., Niemi, K., . . . Yoder, N. (2020). Systemic social and emotional learning: Promoting educational success for all preschool to high school students. *American Psychologist, 76*, 1128–1142.

Meckler, L. (2022, March 28). In "social–emotional learning," right sees more critical race theory. Retrieved from *www.washingtonpost.com/education/2022/03/28/social-emotional-learning-critical-race-theory.*

Merritt, E. G., Wanless, S. B., Rimm-Kaufman, S. E., Cameron, C., & Peugh, J. (2012). The contribution of teachers' emotional support to children's social behaviors and self-regulatory skills in first grade. *School Psychology Review, 41*(2), 141–159.

Moreno, A. J., Baker, S., Varey, K., & Hinze-Pifer, R. (2018). Bringing attention restoration theory to the classroom: A tablet app using nature videos to replenish effortful cognition. *Trends in Neuroscience and Education, 12*, 7–21.

National Center for Education Statistics. (2016). Status and trends in the education of racial and ethnic groups 2016. Retrieved from *https://nces.ed.gov/pubs2016/2016007.pdf.*

National Center for Education Statistics. (2018). A closer look at teacher income. Retrieved from *https://nces.ed.gov/blogs/nces/post/a-closer-look-at-teacher-income.*

National Center for Education Statistics. (2022). Characteristics of children's families. Retrieved from *https://nces.ed.gov/programs/coe/indicator/cce/family-characteristics.*

NISSEM. (2022). United Nations Target 4.7 and SEL. Retrieved from *https://nissem.org/sel.*

Noddings, N. (1992). *The challenge to care in schools: An alternative approach to education.* Teachers College Press.

Nowicki, J. M. (2022). K–12 Education: Student population has significantly diversified, but many schools remain divided along racial, ethnic, and economic lines. Retrieved from *www.gao.gov/products/gao-22–104737.*

Office of Elementary and Secondary Education. (2021). American rescue plan elementary and secondary school emergency relief. Retrieved from *https://oese.ed.gov/offices/american-rescue-plan/americanrescue-plan-elementary-and-secondary-school-emergencyrelief.*

Okonofua, J. A., Paunesku, D., & Walton, G. M. (2016). Brief intervention to encourage empathic discipline cuts suspension rates in half among adolescents. *Proceedings of the National Academy of Sciences USA, 113*(19), 5221–5226.

Osher, D., & Berg, J. (2017). *School climate and social and emotional learning: The integration of two approaches.* Edna Bennet Pierce Prevention Research Center, Pennsylvania State University.

Pressley, T. (2021). Factors contributing to teacher burnout during COVID-19. *Educational Researcher, 50*(5), 325–327.

Ramirez, T., Brush, K., Raisch, N., Bailey, R., & Jones, S. M. (2021). Equity in social emotional learning (SEL) programs: A content analysis of equitable practices in PreK–5 SEL programs. *Frontiers in Education, 6,* Article 679467.

Rimm-Kaufman, S. E. (2021). *SEL from the Start.* Norton.

Rimm-Kaufman, S. E., Baroody, A., Larsen, R., Curby, T. W., & Abry, T. (2015). To what extent do teacher–student interaction quality and student gender contribute to fifth graders' engagement in mathematics learning? *Journal of Educational Psychology, 107*(1), 170–185.

Rimm-Kaufman, S. E., Donnan, M. F., Garcia, D., Snead-Johnson, M., Kotulka, E., & Sandilos, L. (2018). A partnered approach to school change in a rural community: Reflections and recommendations. *Foundation Review, 10*(4), 103–118.

Rimm-Kaufman, S. E., & Thomas, K. (2021). How white middle class teachers can apply psychology to teach students who are different from them (Education Practice Brief and Podcast). Retrieved from *https://apadiv15.org/education-practice-briefs.*

Rivers, S. E., Brackett, M. A., Reyes, M. R., Elbertson, N. A., & Salovey, P. (2013). Improving the social and emotional climate of classrooms: A clustered randomized controlled trial testing the RULER approach. *Prevention Science, 14,* 77–87.

Roorda, D. L., Koomen, H. M. Y., Spilt, J. L., & Oort, F. J. (2011). The influence of affective teacher–student relationships on students' school engagement and achievement: A meta-analytic approach. *Review of Educational Research, 81,* 493–529.

Sauve, J. A., & Schonert-Reichl, K. A. (2019). Creating caring classroom and school communities: Lessons learned from social and emotional learning programs and practices. In J. Fredricks, A. L. Reschly, & S. L. Christenson (Eds.), *The handbook of student interventions: Working with disengaged youth* (pp. 279–295). Elsevier.

Schonert-Reichl, K. A. (2017). Social and emotional learning and teachers. *Future of Children, 27*(1), 137–155.

Schwartz, H. L., Bongard, M., Bogan, E. D., Boyle, A. E., Meyers, D. C., & Jagers, R. J. (2022). Social and emotional learning in schools nationally and in the Collaborating Districts Initiative: Selected findings from the American teacher panel and American school leader panel surveys (RR-A1822–1, 2022). Retrieved from *www.rand.org/pubs/research_reports/RRA1822-1.html.*

Shirley, D., Hargreaves, A., & Washington-Wangia, S. (2020). The sustainability and unsustainability of teachers' and leaders' wellbeing. *Teaching and Teacher Education,* 92(2), 1–12.

Siegel-Hawley, G. (2020). A single garment: Creating intentionally diverse schools that benefit all children. Retrieved from *www.hepg.org/hep-home/books/a-single-garment.*

Simmons, D. N. (2021). Why SEL alone isn't enough. *Education Leadership, 78*(6), 30–34.

Simmons, D. N., Brackett, M. A., & Adler, N. (2018). *Applying an equity lens to social, emotional, and academic development.* Edna Bennett Pierce Prevention Research Center, Pennsylvania State University.

Solberg, V. S. H., Donnelly, H. K., Kroyer-Kubicek, R., Basha, R., Curtis, G., Jaques, E., Schreiber, K. (2022). *Condition of career readiness in the United States.* Coalition for Career Development Center and the BU Center for Future Readiness.

Steiner, E. D., Doan, S., Woo, A., Gittens, A. D., Lawrence, R. A., Berdie, L., . . . Schwartz, H. L. (2022). Restoring teacher and principal well-being is an essential step for rebuilding schools. Retrieved from *www.rand.org/pubs/research_reports/rra1108-4.html.*

Steiner, E. D., & Woo, A. (2021). Job-related stress threatens the teacher supply. Retrieved from *www.rand.org/pubs/research_reports/RRA1108-4.html.*

Taylor, R. D., Oberle, E., Durlak, J. A., & Weissberg, R. P. (2017). Promoting positive youth development through school-based social and emotional learning interventions: A meta-analysis of follow-up effects. *Child Development, 88*(4), 1156–1171.

Tschannen-Moran, M., & Gareis, C. R. (2015). Faculty trust in the principal: An essential ingredient in high-performing schools. *Journal of Educational Administration, 53*(1), 66–92.

Tyton Partners. (2021). Finding your place 2021: Social Emotional Learning Supplier Index. Retrieved from *https://tytonpartners.com/post-pandemic-schooling-emphasizing-social-emotional-learning.*

U.S. Department of Education Office for Civil Rights. (2018). 2015–2016 Civil Rights Data Collection: School climate and safety. Retrieved from *www2.ed.gov/about/offices/list/ocr/docs/school-climate-and-safety.pdf.*

U.S. Department of Education, Office of Planning, Evaluation and Policy Development. (2021). ED COVID-19 Handbook, Volume 2: Roadmap to reopening safely and meeting all students' needs. Retrieved from *www2.ed.gov/documents/coronavirus/reopening-2.pdf.*

Vega, D., Moore, J. L., III, & Miranda, A. H. (2015). In their own words: Perceived barriers to achievement by African American and Latino high school students. *American Secondary Education, 43,* 36–59.

Virginia Department of Education. (2016). Progress Report for Profile of a Graduate. Retrieved from *www.doe.virginia.gov/boe/committees_standing/accountability/2016/06-jun/progress-report-for-profile-of-a-graduate.pdf.*

Wentzel, K. (1997). Student motivation in middle school: The role of perceived pedagogical caring. *Journal of Educational Psychology, 89,* 411–419.

APPENDIX 1.1. Definitions and Examples of Social and Emotional Competencies and Conditions That Support Them

Note. We define SEL using the CASEL (2022) framework that describes social, emotional, behavioral, and attitudinal competencies that develop throughout childhood, into adolescence, and throughout adulthood. The definitions below bring an equity orientation informed by Gregory and Fergus (2017), Jagers et al. (2018), and Johnson et al. (Chapter 5, this volume). Each competency below includes a few illustrative examples of competencies for students, teachers, and school leaders to develop, along with examples of the conditions conducive to the development of these skills.

Relationship skills		
Definition and description	Examples of relationship skills	Examples of conditions conducive to these skills
Relationship skills are the ability to develop and sustain healthy, positive relationships with people. These skills include communication, listening to one another, cooperation, resisting peer pressure, managing and addressing conflict well, standing up for others, and seeking and offering help as needed (CASEL, 2022). One challenge is that different settings have different rules for what social engagement and cooperation look like. For this reason, adults can mistakenly interpret that students with strong relationship skills will have social activity with other students who are quiet, peaceful, and indicate compliance with an adult request. When students are truly socially engaged, it may be loud. Conflict is a normal part of peer work, because students are practicing their relationship skills. Growth in children's ability to navigate challenging situations, especially with people who are different from them and hold values that contrast with their own, show highly competent relationship skills.	• Students talk and listen to each other during a think–pair–share in math class. • Students discuss a conflict instead of avoiding it. • Students know ways of approaching the teacher to ask for help and assistance. • Teachers collaborate on curriculum development efforts in their grade-level teams. • Teachers have early-in-the-year conversation with children's families and listen for strengths evident in those families. • Teachers greet their students at the door or move around the classroom to connect with each student before class begins. • School leaders convey trustworthiness by explaining an unpopular decision to their staff, parents, and/or students. • School leaders listen carefully to the concerns of others and approach decisions with an open and accepting attitude instead of making arbitrary decisions.	• There are classroom- and/or school-level norms that convey an ethic of care on how a setting should look, sound, and feel (Noddings, 1992). • There are regular small-group student gatherings (e.g., daily meetings, advisory) of that allow student–student and teacher–student relationships to thrive (Battistich, Solomon, Watson, & Schaps, 1997; Charney, 2002). • Teachers gather information from students on what teachers can do to show they care. • There are regular structures for educators to connect with one another professionally, reflect on their collective practices, and know each other personally (Shirley et al., 2020). • Educators develop and implement plans for positive approaches to student discipline that are culturally responsive and take a restorative approach (Gregory et al., 2017; Gregory & Fergus, 2017). • School leaders develop positive relationships with parents and families by providing regular opportunities to meet and hear their perspectives and suggestions to build relational trust (Bryk & Schneider, 2002).

Social awareness		
Definition and description	Examples of social awareness	Examples of conditions conducive to these skills
Social awareness is the ability to take the perspective of other people from different backgrounds and cultures. It means showing empathy toward people—not only toward our closest friends and family but also to people who differ from us and hold views with which we may not agree. It involves understanding norms for behavior, how social norms differ depending on context, and how what is considered a desired norm to one person may not be a desired norm to another. Social awareness also means recognizing teachers, family members, and people in the community as resources who can offer support. Becoming socially aware also means understanding others in terms of the ways their experiences may have been influenced by systematic inequality in the United States and how others may have experienced a different level of privilege than one's own. Social awareness can help students size up the power dynamics in a situation and consider the ways that they may be disadvantaging others (Jagers et al., 2018).	• Students have skills to think about other people's ideas that may be different than their own. • Students show empathy to a newcomer in their school by inviting them into conversations and activities. • Students notice who has or hasn't stated their opinion in a conversation and create space for the people who are shy or more soft-spoken. • Students are aware of the adults who can help them and offer support, if needed. • Teachers focus on the strengths of their students and offer personalized lessons that build on these strengths. • Teachers recognize how larger systemic and social inequalities can impact their interactions with students. They take action to create an inclusive environment, so that each student feels seen, heard, and respected for who they are. • School leaders regularly express gratitude to their staff, teachers, and students. • School leaders notice which teachers or families have decision-making power at their school and work to amplify the voices of people who otherwise would go unheard. • School leaders lead with compassion and do not rush to judge a person's behaviors. • School leaders work collaboratively to create a community that addresses injustices.	• There are formal structures in the school (e.g., all school meetings) to bring together the larger school community to share their opinions and perspectives about school policies and procedures (Bryk & Schneider, 2002). • There is a positive approach to school discipline that takes a restorative approach that allows varied perspectives to be heard and respected (Gregory et al., 2020). • Teachers hold high and realistic expectations for students and create positive, caring relationships with them (Rimm-Kaufman, 2021). • Teachers and school leaders have opportunities to become culturally competent and equity literate educators by having regular professional development and discussions that build their awareness of their privilege, implicit bias, and microaggressions. The educators receive support (e.g., coaching) to environments where students, teachers and families experience a sense of belonging, support, respect, and safety (Simmons et al., 2018). • Both in the classroom and in the school, there are regular opportunities for student engagement and voice. For example, students' input is sought on issues relating to school culture and climate (Benard & Slade, 2009).

Self-management		
Definition and description	Examples of self-management	Examples of conditions conducive to these skills
Self-management refers to the competence at regulating one's emotions, thoughts, and behaviors in ways that match situations. We see self-management as stress management, self-motivation, setting and working toward goals, impulse control, and code-switching between home and school. One challenge with self-management is that educators can prize and praise self-management so much that it suppresses students' joy and agency and results in compliance. This is particularly an acute issue in classrooms serving students who are Black, Indigenous, and people of color (BIPOC; Simmons, 2021). Other skills include setting goals and using organizational skills to organize work toward those goals, taking initiative even in challenging situations, and demonstrating individual and collective agency. English learners use self-management each time they determine which language to use depending on the context. Listening carefully to others also involves self-management.	• Students can use a "toolkit" of strategies when they feel frustrated or angry; the toolkit may include seeking social support from an adult or peer, mindful breathing, walking away from a situation or other. • Students demonstrate agency by speaking up when they see an injustice in how one classmate treats another. • Students can identify the steps they need to achieve a goal, such as listing the steps needed to accomplish or complete a science project. • Teachers can use healthy stress-reduction strategies when they feel overwhelmed. • Teachers' plan, organize, and implement evidence-based SEL programs and practices. • School leaders demonstrate courage and leadership by identifying injustices in their schools and encouraging difficult conversations. • School leaders support or acknowledge their own emotions and model productive ways of dealing with strong emotions. • School leaders identify and implement their own healthy stress reduction strategies.	• Teachers and leaders foster the creation of supportive, participatory, school and classroom routines. For instance, the classroom/school may have a charter (Cook et al., 2018). • Teachers and leaders spend time to get to know each student, and foster student autonomy in ways that allows each student to stretch their self-management skills (Battistich et al., 1997; Sauve & Schonert-Reichl, 2019). • Teachers provide students with specific strategies and places (e.g., a calm down corner) that support students' strategies to calm down (Jones et al., 2014; Moreno et al., 2018). • Teachers and school leaders can learn to notice and manage the racially motivated aspects of their emotional reactions and perceptions of Black students, thus reducing their deficit perspective and improving their relationships with Black youth (Legette et al., 2022). • School leaders are open to new experiences and are sensitive to school and community concerns (Astor et al., 2009; Heifetz & Linsky, 2002).

Self-awareness		
Definition and description	Examples of self-awareness	Examples of conditions conducive to these skills
Self-awareness refers to a person's ability to notice and understand their own emotional states and internal thoughts and know how their emotions and thoughts influence their behavior. Self-awareness involves the ability to size up one's strengths and limitations. Self-awareness can lead to optimism and self-confidence, in ideal situations. Self-awareness also includes an understanding of one's own identity (reflecting ethnicity, race, religion, gender, etc.). This can include beliefs about how that identity is important to their sense of self and also, how that identity automatically connects them to some groups more than others (Jagers et al., 2018). Self-awareness can involve understanding some of the advantages or disadvantages that have been conferred automatically by society because of aspects of that identity.	• Students show self-awareness when they let others in their classroom share their ideas, instead of talking nonstop. • Students realize when they are stuck on a hard problem and need to figure out a different way to solve it or get help from a friend or teacher. • In a conflict with a peer, students are able to name their emotions and demonstrate an understanding of how the situation evoked their emotions in the moment. • When struggling with a difficult assignment, students can identify the strategies they need to implement and learn in order to find success—demonstrating a growth mindset. • Teachers acknowledge their own mistakes to their students and apologize—serving as a role model for honesty and integrity. • Teachers are aware of their own implicit biases and prejudices, recognize how these can influence their interactions and discipline approaches with their students, then work to address these in proactive ways. • School leaders acknowledge their strengths and limitations and work to create a collaborative leadership team that can help address their limitations. • School leaders reflect and explicitly identify their sense of purpose for the type of leader they aspire to become.	• Teachers implement evidence-based SEL programs and practices that help to promote students' abilities identify and understand their emotions (e.g., Rivers et al., 2013: Jones et al., 2017). • Teachers recognize that their own social and emotional competencies and well-being (cultural competency skills, self-efficacy) affects their abilities to implement SEL programs and practices and impacts their students' well-being (Braun et al., 2020; Collie et al., 2020; Collie & Perry, 2019; Jennings & Greenberg, 2009; Schonert-Reichl, 2017). • School leaders recognize the importance of counteracting systemic racism and create a safe place for teachers to explore and counteract their implicit biases and prejudices that can interfere with their effective teaching. • School leaders encourage teachers to engage in programs and practices that support their own well-being (Greenberg et al., 2017; Jennings et al., 2019). • School leaders engage in their own professional development to support their well-being and cultural competence through evidence-based programs to promote adults SEL (Mahfouz, 2018; Mahfouz et al., 2019).

Responsible decision making		
Definition and description	Examples of responsible decision making	Examples of conditions conducive to these skills
Responsible decision making is the ability to make productive choices about social interactions and personal behaviors in ways that consider what is safe, ethical, socially realistic and attuned to the well-being of self and others. One aspect of effective decision making involves understanding the consequences of one's actions. What makes responsible decision making so difficult to describe is that what some people describe as responsible, others would not describe this way. Decision making involves being open-minded and curious. Becoming an effective decision-maker involves analyzing what is fact versus fiction and synthesizing the information available to inform a decision.	• Students engage in responsible decision making when they find a $5 bill on the floor and bring it to their teacher, make the effort to use a reusable water bottle because they know it's better for the planet, or decide that it's better to hand in an assignment late instead of copying answers from a friend. • Teachers demonstrate responsible decision making when they do not rush to judgment and remain open-minded and curious. • Teachers demonstrate responsible decision making when they recognize how their disciplinary actions toward one student may impact the well-being of all of their students. • Teachers recognize how their racialized perspective on the world impacts their decision making related to academic decisions and discipline and behaves in ways that counteract those internalized stereotypes (Legette et al., 2022). • School leaders demonstrate responsible decision making when they come to a reasoned judgment for a student's disruptive behavior after analyzing information, data, and all of the facts that may have influenced the behavior. School leaders who reflect and acknowledge how their actions and/or decisions for one teacher or staff member may impact their overall school community are demonstrating responsible decision making.	• Teachers create time and space to discuss ethical dilemmas, that is, scenarios involving moral issues where there is not necessarily one right answer to a problem. Youth literature, recent news controversies, or environmental issues can provide raw material for these conversations. • Teachers and school leaders (with their students) can develop schoolwide commitments (e.g., integrity, accountability, respect). When situations arise that test those commitments, they discuss the dilemmas and use those challenges to strengthen their resolve toward those commitments. • School leaders and teachers make decisions in ways that show that their values are aligned with their actions. • School leaders and educators need to scrutinize their school environments and ask, "If students are making problematic decisions, why? What is that they might be avoiding? Do they feel marginalized at schools? What can we do to reengage this student in school and learning?" • Educators can develop restorative justice approaches to bring compassion and humanity to their approach to discipline. • School leaders and teachers can include trauma-informed practices in ways that are accessible, sustainable, evidence-based, and culturally responsive to provide a context in which ethical decisions can implemented (Osher & Berg, 2017).

Part I Supporting Systemic SEL

Chapter 2

Increasing Equity in SEL for Students from Marginalized Populations

Tia Navelene Barnes, Jocelyn E. Brown, Melissa Stoffers, Jurni Jackson, Yu Xia, Amanda G. Wells, and Alexcia Bryant

Capital School district is a midsize district in Dover, Delaware. Located in Kent County, Dover is the capital of Delaware and is the second largest city in the state. The school district encompasses a diverse geographic area that includes urban, suburban, and rural areas. As a city in the first state, Dover boasts a long and rich history. It is home to Delaware State University, which is a public historically Black university, and it houses an Underground Railroad route, which helped more than 3,000 slaves reach freedom in the 19th century. Additionally, Dover is home to a thriving Amish community, the Dover International Speedway that hosts multiple NASCAR events each year, and the Dover Air Force Base, which is home to the Department of Defense's largest aerial port and nearly 9,000 service members, civilians, and families.

Capital School District serves over 6,000 students in grades PreK–12 in 12 school buildings, including seven elementary schools, two middle schools, and one comprehensive high school. In addition, the district has two special education programs that serve students with significant educational needs throughout the county. Within the school community, about 50% of students identify as Black, 29% as White, and 13% as Hispanic. 7.8% of students are eligible for English language services, with Spanish (69%) and Haitian Creole (20%) being the primary spoken languages. Approximately 51% of students within the district meet the state's low-income criteria, qualifying the district as a Title I district. Currently, 3% of students experience homelessness, and almost 1% of students reside in a foster care setting.

The community and geographic makeup of Dover lends itself to a wide range of benefits and challenges for the school community to explore. In spring 2016, as part of its strategic planning, Capital School District embarked on a new approach to meet the needs of its diverse school community. This robust systems-change effort, which included an in-depth needs assessment and implementation plan, resulted in a paradigm shift in how students are prepared with the skills, attitudes, and behaviors necessary to reach their full potential and to live a fulfilling life. The district's approach applies the principles of implementation science and policy coherence to ensure that all students, including those from traditionally underserved populations, can enjoy the benefits of social and emotional learning (SEL).

As discussed in Chapter 1, the ongoing changes in the demographic makeup of the nation have impacted the diversity of students enrolling in public schools and has challenged schools with finding the best ways to support children with a diverse range of needs, such as English language learners (ELLs), children with disabilities, and children living in poverty—all of whom are often underserved in schools and are more likely to face increased rates of adverse outcomes in social–emotional development and educational achievement (Council on Community Pediatrics, 2016). Considering the growing focus on student SEL, school districts like the Capital School District now face the challenge—and the opportunity—to ensure that this programming is accessible to their entire student population.

Many schools have adopted SEL practices to teach emotion management and interpersonal skills (Jagers et al., 2019). While SEL is intended to improve children's academic, emotional, and social success, many of the prevalent SEL school practices fail to address the inequities that face today's schools (Gregory & Fergus, 2017). The challenge of SEL and inequity is twofold: Traditional approaches to SEL prioritize the prevailing White, middle-class, American culture and thus disability, poverty, and language are often absent from this work, and there is inequitable access to SEL across various populations within the school environment. Inequity has been a fixture in schools, but we can uproot it with SEL practices that acknowledge and work to reform the inequitable history of this country and its schools. Two possible solutions to reach this ideal include introducing SEL that is adaptable to the student populations within each school district and increasing access to SEL. We discuss and describe both of these challenges.

Here, we focus on students who experience poverty and residential mobility, students of color, ELLs, and students with disabilities (SWDs). Using findings from implementation science, the field of science that studies how to translate evidence-based research into applied policies, programs, and practices (Peters et al., 2014), the district developed policy coherence in SEL programming to serve students with varying needs. *Policy coherence* refers to the process in which schools and school district central offices work together to continually negotiate the fit between external demands on schools and schools' own goals and strategies (Honig & Hatch, 2004). We begin with an overview of the literature on our populations of interest; discuss the importance of implementation science for the purpose of ensuring need, fit, sustainability, and policy coherence when engaging in systemic integration; and provide a case study of one district's use of these concepts to provide equitable access to SEL programming for all students.

Populations of Interest

In this chapter, we focus on students who experience poverty and residential mobility, students of color, ELLs, and students with disabilities (SWDs). For these populations that are often underserved in schools, equitable access to education programs is particularly important as these students face increased rates of adverse outcomes in social–emotional development and educational achievement (Council on Community Pediatrics, 2016). SEL with a systematic approach can allow for accommodations and adjustments to the program to ensure alignment with the needs of diverse student populations.

Poverty and Residential Mobility

Poverty and residential mobility are two issues that can be detrimental to student educational success. Students living in poverty experience challenges such as limited access to academic and social resources, exposure to conditions that may negatively affect their health, and a lack of access to social capital (Williams et al., 2017). Poverty is also associated with residential mobility. For instance, district administrators in New York suggest that students living in poverty are the most likely to experience frequent moves (Schafft, 2006). Residential mobility contributes to disengagement, as students may miss instructional time, experience an inconsistent academic foundation, and feel isolated from school (Shankar-Brown, 2017).

Fortunately, educators can ameliorate these challenges by building respectful relationships with students and families, providing additional resources to students, and creating a collaborative environment (Mullen & Kealy, 2013). These actions support student engagement, which is positively related to academic achievement (Lee, 2012). Additionally, protective factors such as belonging to positive peer networks that provide social and emotional support and facilitate academic achievement, caring teachers, family and community assets, and intrinsic and extrinsic motivators increase the likelihood that students living in poverty and those with high mobility will achieve academic success (Williams et al., 2017).

Students of Color

Research consistently shows that school environments do not adequately support students of color. These students often experience psychological distress, peer victimization, and academic difficulty in schools. For example, students of color, including African Americans, Asian Americans, and Latines, report higher levels of stress and psychological distress, including depression, low self-esteem, suicidal ideation, and higher instances of bullying than their White peers (Wang et al., 2016). Moreover, children with these stressors and negative experiences are more likely to face challenges associated with academic performance, school adjustment, and engagement (Buhs et al., 2010).

Well-established SEL intervention programs can be effective with diverse student populations if racial, ethnic, and cultural diversity are considered (Brown et al., 2018). For instance, the Imani Rites of Passage program is an SEL intervention created for African American student populations (Whaley & McQueen, 2004). As part of this intervention, children receive tutoring support and cultural activities to strengthen their racial/ethnic identities. Additionally, African American guest speakers serve as models for career aspiration and successful coping in adulthood. Finally, a family component provides support and fosters community and common goal setting among families. Findings from exploratory studies of this intervention suggested that participants had an enhanced cultural identity and had higher expectations for their future selves.

English Language Learners

ELLs are a rapidly growing student population whose social and emotional well-being must be considered in schools. Although bilingual or multilingual children demonstrate greater ability in perspective taking (Greenberg et al., 2013) and executive functioning (Yang et al., 2011), they concurrently experience a variety of environmental challenges such as language barriers and low familial socioeconomic status (SES; Niehaus & Adelson, 2014). ELLs must interact in two or more linguistic environments, and this discontinuity in the use of language can pose acculturative stress in reconciling between the native and host culture (Castro-Olivo et al., 2014). This can lead to academic, social, and behavioral challenges (Niehaus & Adelson, 2014).

Much as with students of color, cultural adaptations to SEL interventions can support ELLs. Moreover, these interventions should also consider linguistic diversity in their adaptations. For instance, Castro-Olivo (2014) found that the Jóvenes Fuertes program, a culturally adapted version of the Strong Teens SEL program, which has the appropriate language and examples to support Latine immigrant adolescents in coping with the acculturation process, was effective in strengthening teens' resilience and SEL knowledge.

Students with Disabilities

SWDs are less likely to feel a sense of belonging in school settings (Espelage, Rose, & Polanin, 2016). Multiple studies indicate that SWDs are at greater risk of experiencing peer rejection, social isolation, and weaker prosocial behaviors (Koller et al., 2018; Stiefel et al., 2018). Consequently, SWDs have an increased likelihood of victimization that may contribute to a decreased sense of school safety and lead to an increase in internalizing symptoms such as depression and anxiety (Espelage et al., 2016).

Though research on SEL programming for SWDs is limited, available studies suggest that it may be an effective solution for supporting SWDs (Espelage et al., 2016). For instance, Espelage and colleagues found that SWDs reported that they were more likely to intervene in a bullying situation after receiving the Second Step: Student Success through Prevention intervention, which could help reduce the bully victimization rate among this population.

Systemic SEL and Coherence

SEL holds great promise in its ability to meet the needs of diverse student populations. Its focus on developing a universal skill set among students, attention to creating connection and community in schools, and focus on enhancing one's own identity and appreciating differences can support flourishing for all students. A systemic approach to SEL implementation, or systemic SEL, is needed to ensure equity in access to SEL (Mahoney et al., 2021). The key to successful systemic SEL implementation in schools is policy coherence at the state, district, and local school levels. To ensure coherence, stakeholders must work together toward a common agenda, identify what works, and make meaning of their findings over time (Fullan & Quinn, 2016). Mahoney and colleagues (2021) suggest four key areas to address at the state, district, and school level to support systemic SEL that include (1) building a shared plan and supports for implementation, (2) strengthening adult SEL competencies and capacity, (3) promoting SEL for students, and (4) engaging in continuous improvement. The Capital School District team focused on these key areas, as well as others, as they moved toward incorporating systemic SEL at the district level. See Figure 2.1 for a summary of the district's process.

Case Study: Capital School District

As part of its systemic implementation of SEL, and in accordance with evidence-based practices, Capital School District leaders engaged multidisciplinary teams of stakeholders that included board members, administrators, instructional coaches, teachers, and related service providers in a comprehensive strategic planning process, with the goal of furthering educational excellence within the district. The district leaders engaged stakeholders with the understanding that their involvement would increase the likelihood that future initiatives would be implemented with fidelity, which in turn would lead to improved outcomes (Bohanon & Wu, 2014).

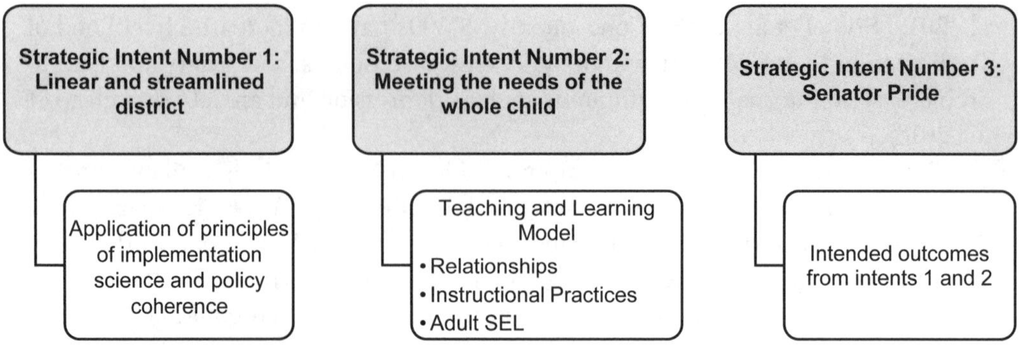

FIGURE 2.1. Summary of Capital School District's process for incorporating systemic SEL.

The stakeholder activities aligned with Mahoney and colleagues' (2021) first area of systemic SEL implementation—building a shared plan and providing supports for implementation.

Building a Shared Plan and Supports for Implementation

The Capital School District Board of Education and Superintendent initiated a systems-change initiative to build a shared plan that included the identification of school and district needs through an in-depth review of data and culminated in the development of three strategic intents that were used to guide decision making around policy and practice development within the district. The development of the strategic intents helped ensure that stakeholders' work was guided by a shared vision that aligned with the allocation of resources, selection of practice, and instructional approaches within the district. The key focus areas of the strategic intents included (1) creating a linear and streamlined district characterized by clear communication, cohesive initiatives aligned with district goals, and consistency in educational experiences for students; (2) meeting the needs of the whole child; and (3) creating "Senator Pride," which is defined as a highly visible culture of pride that is demonstrated through the behaviors, beliefs, values and symbols within and across the school community. We discuss the strategic intents in more detail below.

Strategic Intent 1, *Creating a Linear and Streamlined District,* refers to clear, consistent communication with stakeholders and streamlining initiatives so they are cohesive and aligned with district goals. This includes the tasks of (1) improving the consistency of the educational expectations and experiences of students, parents, and the community at all grade levels; (2) improving communication with stakeholders; (3) reducing the number of transitions students must make between schools to facilitate the alignment of course material across grade levels; and (4) leveraging resources that align with district goals. To achieve this intent, which focuses on cohesiveness, district stakeholders engaged in a variety of activities, including a review of policies and practices and an evaluation of district coherence to those policies and practices. Teams worked together to identify over 140 district and school initiatives, programs, practices, and processes (PreK–12) centered around instructional practices, academic and SEL curricula, student support services, and community engagement. Examples of initiatives included the adoption and implementation of a consistent SEL curricula across schools, developing plans for building staff capacity for blended learning and digital convergence, auditing and mapping curricula, and building capacity of stakeholders around multi-tiered systems of support (MTSS). The team determined that to ensure every student had equitable access to necessary resources, initiatives would need to be systematically integrated, coordinated, and collaborated across the district and schools. When redundancy or inconsistency was identified, implementation science was utilized to select the most appropriate resource.

Strategic Intent 2, *Meeting the Needs of the Whole Child,* included a focus on children's behavior, mental health, social and emotional health, academic rigor and supports, and entrepreneurship. Targeted activities entailed (1) increasing social–emotional professional learning; (2) systemic change related to scheduling at the student, classroom, and building level; (3) developing a district response to the intervention team to create framework; and (4) advocacy. This strategy ensured a coherent framework, as well as faithful implementation of a common language, and set of expectations that support the needs of students and families within the district was in place. Strategic Intent 3, *Senator Pride,* described the ideal characteristics that a Capital School District student (referred to as a "Senator," which is the district's mascot) possessed upon graduation. This included behaviors, beliefs, and values believed to result in benefits such as student development into productive citizens, improved school safety, retention of premier educators, and positive relationships with community partners. Efforts focused on (1) recruiting/retaining quality staff, (2) engaging Capital families and the community (collaboration), and (3) marketing/branding the district.

In addition to creating strategic intents, the stakeholder groups created an instructional model to support implementation. The instructional model provided a vehicle through which the district streamlined its instructional practices and prioritized meeting the needs of the whole child. District stakeholders ensured the alignment and allocation of resources to support the academic, social, emotional, and behavioral needs of students through this model. The implementation of the instructional model also ensured equity and access to every student by prioritizing standards-based, personalized, rigorous instruction in a safe and supportive environment, as well as the measurement of outcomes through dynamic assessment. Though the instructional model provided the Capital School District's educators with a clear intent for their work, there was a need to provide a roadmap that outlined clear and actionable steps toward actualizing the strategic intents. To meet this need, stakeholder groups identified the evidence-based strategies that aligned with district needs as determined by district data sources. Over a period of about 4 years, these strategies were translated into actionable practices and instructional approaches that could be incorporated into lesson planning and instruction. The model gave way to instructional, environmental, and SEL strategies that are proven to impact positive outcomes for students (i.e., high yield). These strategies fell into three categories that aligned with Mahoney and colleagues' (2021) strategic implementation areas: (1) strengthening adult SEL competencies and capacity, (2) promoting SEL for students through relationships, and (3) engaging in continuous improvement of instructional practices. The district stakeholders then prepared to implement these strategies.

Preparing for High-Yield Strategy Implementation

Using the instructional model to guide the process, district personnel identified funding opportunities that supported a sustainable investment in student mental health. District administrators allocated resources to ensure that every student and family had access to multiple qualified, school-based mental health team members, including school counselors, licensed clinical social workers (LCSWs), school psychologists, and additional contracted providers to support their social, emotional, and mental health needs.

School-based mental health team members actively participated on established tiered problem-solving teams, which provided a continuum of evidence-based supports. MTSS is a framework that typically includes a continuum of prevention and intervention supports including universal screening to identify students who need additional support, the delivery of evidence-based interventions that match identified student needs, and ongoing progress monitoring that is informed by assessments (August et al., 2018). To ensure sustainability, SEL was not only integrated with academic instruction but was also intentionally embedded into existing tools and structures. For instance, aspects of SEL were reflected in items such as lesson planning and professional learning community (PLC) resources, teacher evaluation tools, and school building goal-setting templates. Once this groundwork was laid, district teams moved to integrate the high-yield SEL strategies systematically and effectively into the education system. Below are some examples from each of the three strategies within the district.

Strengthening Adult SEL Competencies and Capacity

Capital School District administrators offered professional development (PD) opportunities around the high-yield SEL strategies to build adult capacity and competence in ways to support and implement SEL initiatives, ensuring that adults serve as models of SEL throughout the school community. PD opportunities focused on the implementation of high-yield SEL strategies and included teachers, administrators, district- and building-based instructional coaches, school-based mental health providers, nurses, disciplinarians, paraprofessionals, support staff, and related service providers. The PD plan outlined a cohesive strategy of ongoing professional learning opportunities that were provided to all throughout the school year, rather than to only to a small group of adults during designated PD days or events.

The process of introducing SEL and the high-yield SEL strategies was planned strategically by district administrators to encourage support and buy-in from adults in schools and the community. Often, when new SEL programs are introduced, educators ask, "Why are we doing this?" To address this frequently asked question, the adults engaged in a series of PD opportunities that introduced SEL and its documented benefits for students, staff, and the greater community. Sharing this information increased support of SEL instruction among adults, who were then able to set meaningful goals, utilize relevant data points to review and measure progress, and measure and understand the impact of SEL initiatives on the school community. Once the "why" was clear, adults were introduced to the "how." Educators were provided with practical strategies for making connections between social, emotional, or moral lessons with content that they were already teaching and were provided with a "toolbox" supplied with descriptions of each practice, as well as resources and actionable strategies to facilitate their integration into their daily instruction (toolbox available through second author). For instance, teachers who wished to explore culturally responsive teaching practices to establish an equitable learning environment were provided with resources such as videos, lessons, and graphic organizers around engaging students in project-based learning, providing experiential learning opportunities such as service-learning activities, and youth participatory action research to increase social, civic, and academic skills across diverse groups of students.

Promoting SEL for Students through Relationships

Building positive relationships is a key component in creating engagement and reducing detrimental outcomes for diverse student populations (Mullen & Kealy, 2013). Over time, the Capital School District Student Support team developed a system that promoted and fostered an inclusive culture that helped students and their families to feel valued, supported, and ultimately empowered. To accomplish this, school teams worked collaboratively within the district, as well as with community partners, to develop and establish trusting relationships between school staff, students, and families, and to provide access to services to mitigate the impact of conditions such as residential mobility.

Relationships played an important role in the team's efforts to support families faced with residential mobility. Authentic partnerships with families characterized by warmth and support served as the foundation for meeting family and student needs. One common challenge encountered was the gaps that existed between schools and community support agencies. As a result of such gaps, families encountered obstacles that prevented them from easily accessing needed resources. This led to frustration and unmet basic needs. District staff addressed this in a variety of ways. For example, District Homeless Liaisons (also known as Visiting Teachers) worked to develop and enhance relationships and partnerships between the district and community agencies. By establishing relationships with community partners and agencies to coordinate services, and by accessing available grant funding, resources that were once only accessible outside of the school building, were brought into the schools. For example, the district staff partnered with a local hospital, resulting in a Wellness Center in Dover High School staffed by a nurse practitioner and LCSW. Similarly, individual schools created and managed pantries stocked with food, personal hygiene items, and cleaning supplies within the school building for families to access. The district also used an app to communicate specific tangible student needs (anonymously) that were fulfilled by the donations of community members. Because of these efforts, families no longer needed to interact with multiple outside agencies, but instead with their school support person, who linked them with readily available resources. This elimination of "red tape" facilitated the development of trusting relationships between students, families, and their school liaisons, and increased the likelihood of an equitable learning environment for students experiencing poverty and residential mobility.

One barrier to building relationships with families of ELLs was the lack of communication options. District administration and English Language team members began to research ways to share information more effectively with linguistically diverse families as a means of increasing their engagement in the learning process. The district staff discovered and adopted new practices, including a drop-down menu on the school website that allowed information to be translated into multiple languages, and established a partnership with a contracted agency that translated written documents. In addition, school teams had access to professional translators who could be invited to attend scheduled meetings and also be utilized to translate telephone conferences. Teachers and families also had access to an app that enabled them to communicate through a human translator rather than through an automated computer translation system. Furthermore, English Language teachers visited the homes of families to provide individualized information and assistance with accessing educational content or technology, and schools created opportunities for students and families to meet with instructional staff during scheduled evening sessions to receive support with academic content or to navigate technology, regardless of the language spoken.

Another challenge identified in the Capital School District was around diversity of staff. Administrators found after reviewing staff demographic data that the staff member demographics did not sufficiently match the ethnic and racial composition of the schools. Research indicated that employing diverse staff can lead to immediate and long-term benefits for students of color including increases in academic engagement, high school graduation, and college enrollment and decreases in racial disproportionality in exclusionary discipline (Gershenson et al., 2017). With this understanding, the Capital School District administration worked to attract, recruit, and retain diverse staff members. Members of the Human Resources team sought out and participated in professional learning opportunities to learn strategies for recruiting candidates from diverse backgrounds, and to identify recruitment opportunities at specialized events and locations within Delaware and throughout the region. Plans for developing culturally responsive hiring and retention include reviewing job postings for cultural bias, creating a position for a human resources specialist with expertise in reaching diverse candidates, and creating support networks for newly hired staff to facilitate the establishment of professional and personal connections within the community in an effort for retention.

Special education services are provided for Capital SWDs in their least restrictive environment, with the goal of taking a "whole-child" approach to student success. Due to the district's increased effort to provide equity, emphasis was placed on ensuring that SWDs have access to and interaction with typically developing peers. When student needs warranted the provision of services outside of the general education environment, district team members made efforts to provide supported opportunities for peer socialization to foster connectedness and social–emotional well-being (Eisenman et al., 2017). One way these goals were realized was through extracurricular opportunities that promoted SEL for SWDs. For example, active high school students with and without disabilities participated together on Special Education Unified Sports teams and established a Best Buddies International chapter that allowed them to develop genuine friendships with one another. Participation in these opportunities provided many social–emotional benefits for all students, such as the ability to connect with individuals from diverse populations and enhanced community relationships through an atmosphere of shared inclusive pride.

Engaging in Continuous Improvement of Instructional Practices

When educators place an emphasis on providing appropriately challenging and meaningful work, and maintain that all students can and will succeed, students are more likely to achieve academic success (Yoder, 2014). Ensuring that high-quality instructional practices are available to all students begins with a focus on policy and extends through all levels to the school building. Each year, policies relative to

ELLs, SWDs, students experiencing residential mobility, and other marginalized populations were reviewed and adjusted to align with the most current state and federal statutes and regulations, and language within the policy was reviewed to ensure cultural responsiveness and relevance to the needs of students. In addition to policy review, the district evaluated its organizational structure to determine how well it allowed students and staff to access necessary supports. For example, an administrative reorganization allowed English language staff to access additional support from district administration and instructional coaches. This change empowered English language teachers by providing them with an increased voice and opportunities to advocate for programs, practices, and resources that benefit students. For instance, the advocacy of this group led to increased access of translation services to all stakeholders, a restructuring of the common planning and professional learning community process, and increased opportunities for collaboration and professional learning. As a result of this organizational shift, teachers were provided with the resources necessary to design and implement rigorous instructional practices that align with the specific and unique needs of the students they support.

To ascertain the level of rigor of assignments, as well as their alignment to standards, a group of elementary and secondary teachers, coaches, and administrators engaged in a comprehensive analysis of literacy assignments. This initiative provided valuable information about the tasks and assignments developed for students in general education and inclusive English Language Arts classes. The group members engaged in a variety of reflections and discussions about the tasks they assigned and the assignment's alignment with grade level standards, level of cognitive challenge and writing output, relevancy (cultural responsiveness), and opportunities for student independence. This professional discourse led to additional PD activities, a shared and consistent understanding of the critical role classroom assignments play in preparing students for rigorous college and career ready standards, a review of culturally responsive teaching practices, and a shared language around rigor. The goals of the audit were to ensure that educators developed an understanding of the critical role that classroom assignments play in preparing every student for the rigors of college and career. While the initial analysis has been completed, the work around academic rigor and high expectations for all students is ongoing.

Next Steps

Capital School District created a strong foundation for sustainable and equitable districtwide SEL by employing the principles of implementation science and coherence to create district-level initiatives in collaboration with school stakeholders. To plan for continuous growth and improvement, SEL teams continue to meet regularly to review and reflect on outcome data, assess progress toward goals, and make necessary changes to enhance student outcomes.

While district initiatives are streamlined and aligned with the district vision, there is a need to ensure that district initiatives continue to align with state initiatives. On October 7, 2018, Delaware Governor, John C. Carney, signed Executive Order #24, making Delaware a trauma-informed state. This order provides direction for the Family Services Cabinet Council to help mitigate the impact of adverse childhood experiences (ACEs) and to build resilience in children, adults, and communities. This designation also ensures that dedicated funding opportunities around trauma are available to schools and community agencies. Recently, Delaware was one of five states that was awarded a $7 million Trauma Recovery Demonstration Project grant entitled Project THRIVE, which is a 5-year grant project funded by the U.S. Department of Education for state education agencies to develop trauma-specific therapeutic service delivery models for the most vulnerable students within MTSS. The prioritization of mental health on a state level further legitimizes the work done in the Capital School District and facilitates the acquisition of resources, training, and support.

To ensure that students and families in need can access necessary services, district stakeholders must be informed of the resources that are available both locally and throughout the state. As a means of strengthening the MTSS process, academic and mental health teams facilitate an in-depth resource mapping process to identify and understand the resources that are available within the state, district, and building teams. Team members increase their awareness of available services by collaborating with colleagues across the state through various coordinated activities and events.

Capacity building around the Capital School District's SEL high-yield strategies will continue. Targeted PD will occur specifically around the strategy of student voice and choice. This concept will become a common SEL thread that will run through school and district initiatives over the next school year. Student voice is a critical component of systemic SEL implementation. When students are provided with agency and develop the skills to effect positive change, the entire system benefits. Students feel more connected to their school, educators can make informed decisions that will benefit all learners, and the organization functions more effectively (Shafer, 2016). In addition, when educators are attuned to the needs of students, they can appropriately address these needs by providing relevant opportunities.

The work of providing equity through SEL will continue with an increased focus on ensuring access to SEL for all students, including those with disabilities. Capital School District stakeholders strive to propel the success of SWDs in the least restrictive environment, with the goal of continually increasing the number of students regularly accessing the general education environment, which includes SEL. In this effort, consideration of equitable access for SWDs to both human and material resources must continue as these resources grow throughout the district. Furthermore, enhancing the knowledge of all staff in meeting the needs of the whole student with a disability is critical. Incorporating more opportunities for typically developing students to learn about disabilities and to participate in discussions about their learning will also further enhance relationships, improve social–emotional skills, and contribute to overall positive outcomes.

Key Messages and Recommendations for Action

Based on the experiences within the Capital School District, the following are recommendations for districts undertaking a similar process of improving equitable access to SEL within their district using systemic SEL implementation:

- *Incorporate the voices of school and community stakeholders.* Previous research suggests that stakeholder participation is critical to successful adoption of a program (Collaborative for Academic, Social, and Emotional Learning [CASEL], 2012; Redding & Viano, 2018). Incorporating the voices of various members and partners of the school community allows the district to engage in strategic planning and development of a shared vision. Giving voice to members of the school community can help increase buy-in, which is also important to fidelity of implementation and sustainability of a program (Meyers et al., 2019).

- *Increase coherence in district SEL initiatives.* Recognizing that schools and districts must act as coordinated units to effectively enact change (Chrispeels et al., 2008), the district developed a more cohesive, evidence-based system that would meet the needs of all students. The goal was to create a common language and understanding of SEL, which helped to ensure equitable learning opportunities for students across the district. The shared vision focuses on the unique needs of the district and considers the resources, practices, and instructional approaches valued by the community. Additionally, a shared vision can ensure uniformity in understanding the intended goals of a program, which can help schools within a district to implement programs in a uniform manner (Chrispeels et al., 2008).

- *Examine ways to embed SEL.* The district embedded SEL strategies into daily instruction and existing practices to reduce the potential of teachers feeling overburdened by delivering SEL. Naturally integrating SEL into the school day guides systemic change (CASEL, 2012). The district also redesigned the lesson planning process to include consideration of SEL, created opportunities for discussion about SEL in professional learning communities, required principals to incorporate SEL within their annual school success plans, and encouraged teachers to include SEL as a student improvement goal in their teacher evaluations as ways to further entrench students and teachers in SEL.

- *Ensure a focus on SEL PD.* Research about successful implementation of school programming suggests that schools and districts should provide PD to teachers to ensure success (Chrispeels et al., 2008; Meyers et al., 2019). The Capital School District is focusing on building capacity of stakeholders through various PD opportunities. All stakeholders are included in the PD plans for the district, which also helps to build a sense of cohesion across the district. The adoption of a coaching model allowed for mentorship and assistance for instructional support personnel. Additionally, in alignment with CASEL's (2012) guidelines for selecting evidence-based SEL programs, the district sought to embed PD in SEL by establishing a committee that supports the development of SEL competence and by encouraging engagement in activities that improve overall well-being for school personnel.

- *Recognize and address issues of inequity.* The district established community partnerships that have led to greater student access to mental health and medical services, and access to food for families facing food insecurity to help meet the needs of diverse learners. The district has also addressed various inequities through intentional recruitment of diverse staff members, access to translation services for ELL families, and an increased commitment to placing SWDs in the least restrictive environment. These initiatives demonstrate a commitment to inclusiveness and an intent to support all members of the school community in their social and emotional development.

Through a robust systems-change effort, this systemic SEL implementation in Capital School District resulted in a paradigm shift around the way students are educationally prepared with the skills, attitudes, and behaviors necessary to reach their full potential and to live fulfilling lives. This approach ensures that SEL initiatives are sustainable and accessible to every student, regardless of their background or circumstances.

DISCUSSION QUESTIONS

1. In Capital School District, teams identified 140 different district and school initiatives (e.g., programs related to instruction, SEL interventions, support services, and community engagement). Think about the schools/districts that you've worked with in the past. Does this seem like a typical number of initiatives or too many to be successful? What are some factors that help determine the manageable number of initiatives for a school/district? What challenges affect sustainment when a school or district has many initiatives? What challenges should a school or district consider when making the decision about whether to drop some of their initiatives? How would you prioritize initiatives?

2. In strengthening adult SEL competencies and capacity, the district leaders first established *why* the PD was important before explaining *what* the PD entailed. The goal here was to create buy-in and engagement for new learning.
   a. Reflect on learning experiences you have experienced where the *why* came before the *what*. How did this affect your motivation to learn?
   b. Think about an upcoming PD that you are planning, leading, or bringing to a school. How can you establish the *why* before introducing the *what*? In what ways can you use this principle to increase interest and motivation for the people experiencing the PD?
3. The Capital School District built "a highly visible culture of 'Senator Pride'" as a way of envisioning student aspirations and creating a culture in which schools are safe, students become productive citizens, excellent educators are retained, and the schools have positive relationships with community partners. Choose one of the following categories: students of color, students with high mobility who are living in poverty, ELLs, or students with special needs. What practices can be put into place to ensure that those students fully experience Senator Pride? How would you evaluate progress with the "Senator Pride" initiative?

ACKNOWLEDGMENTS

Our thanks to the Capital School District Board of Education and Interim Superintendent, Dr. Sylvia Henderson, for supporting this project. We also acknowledge and appreciate the support of district and partner SEL champions; the K–12 Director of Instruction, Paul Dunford; the School-Based Mental Health Team; the Departments of Student Support and Special Services; District Administrators, Staff, Students, Families and Community Partners; the District SEL Committee; the Johns Hopkins University Development and Learning Systems IDEALS Institute; and Rowan University Partnerships for Educational Equity and Research (PEER) Lab.

REFERENCES

August, G. J., Piehler, T. F., & Miller, F. G. (2018). Getting "SMART" about implementing multi-tiered systems of support to promote school mental health. *Journal of School Psychology, 66*, 85–96.

Bohanon, H., & Wu, M.-J. (2014). Developing buy-in for positive behavior support in secondary settings. *Preventing School Failure, 58*(4), 223–229.

Brown, C., Maggin, D. M., & Buren, M. (2018). Systematic review of cultural adaptations of school-based social, emotional, and behavioral interventions for students of color. *Education and Treatment of Children, 41*(4), 431–456.

Buhs, E. S., Ladd, G. W., & Herald-Brown, S. L. (2010). Victimization and exclusion: Links to peer rejection, classroom engagement, and achievement. In S. R. Jimerson, S. M. Swearer,

& D. L. Espelage (Eds.), *Handbook of bullying in schools: An international perspective* (pp. 163–172). Routledge.

Castro-Olivo, S. M. (2014). Promoting social–emotional learning in adolescent Latino ELLs: A study of the culturally adapted strong teens program. *School Psychology Quarterly, 29*(4), 567–577.

Castro-Olivo, S. M., Palardy, G. J., Albeg, L., & Williamson, A. A. (2014). Development and validation of the Coping with Acculturative Stress in American Schools (CASAS-A) scale on a Latino adolescent sample. *Assessment for Effective Intervention, 40*(1), 3–15.

Chrispeels, J. H., Burke, P. H., Johnson, P., & Daly, A. J. (2008). Aligning mental models of district and school leadership teams for reform coherence. *Education and Urban Society, 40*(6), 730–750.

Collaborative for Academic, Social, and Emotional Learning. (2012). Effective social and emotional learning programs: Preschool and elementary school edition [CASEL Guide]. Retrieved from *https://casel.org/resources-support.*

Council on Community Pediatrics. (2016). Poverty and child health in the United States. *Pediatrics, 137*(4), Article e20160339.

Eisenman, L. T., Freedman, B., & Kofke, M. (2017). Focus on friendship: Relationships, inclusion, and social well-being. In K. Shogren, M. Wehmeyer, & N. Singh (Eds.), *Handbook of positive psychology in intellectual and developmental disabilities* (pp. 127–144). Springer.

Espelage, D. L., Rose, C. A., & Polanin, J. R. (2016). Social–emotional learning program to promote prosocial and academic skills among middle school students with disabilities. *Remedial and Special Education, 37*(6), 323–332.

Fullan, M., & Quinn, J. (2016). *Coherence: The right drivers in action for schools, districts, and systems.* Corwin.

Gershenson, S., Hart, C. M. D., Lindsay, C. A., & Papageorge, N. W. (2017). The long-run impacts of same-race teachers. Retrieved from *http://ftp.iza.org/dp10630.pdf.*

Greenberg, A., Bellana, B., & Bialystok, E. (2013). Perspective-taking ability in bilingual children: Extending advantages in executive control to spatial reasoning. *Cognitive Development, 28*(1), 41–50.

Gregory, A., & Fergus, E. (2017). Social and emotional learning and equity in school discipline. *Future of Children, 27*(1), 117–136.

Honig, M. I., & Hatch, T. C. (2004). Crafting coherence: How schools strategically manage multiple, external demands. *Educational Researcher, 33*(8), 16–30.

Jagers, R. J., Rivas-Drake, D., & Williams, B. (2019). Transformative social and emotional learning (SEL): Toward SEL in service of educational equity and excellence. *Educational Psychologist, 54*(3), 162–184.

Koller, D., Le Pouesard, M., & Rummens, J. A. (2018). Defining social inclusion for children with disabilities: A critical literature review. *Children and Society, 32*, 1–13.

Lee, J. S. (2012). The effects of the teacher–student relationship and academic press on student engagement and academic performance. *International Journal of Educational Research, 53*, 330–340.

Mahoney, J. L., Weissberg, R. P., Greenberg, M. T., Dusenbury, L., Jagers, R. J., Niemi, K., . . . Yoder, N. (2021). Systemic social and emotional learning: Promoting educational success for all preschool to high school students. *American Psychologist, 76*, 1128–1142.

Meyers, D. C., Domitrovich, C. E., Dissi, R., Trejo, J., & Greenberg, M. T. (2019). Supporting systemic social and emotional learning with a schoolwide implementation model. *Evaluation and Program Planning, 73*, 53–61.

Mullen, C. A., & Kealy, W. A. (2013). Poverty in school communities. *Kappa Delta Pi Record, 49*(2), 70–77.

Niehaus, K., & Adelson, J. L. (2014). School support, parental involvement, and academic and social–emotional outcomes for English language learners. *American Educational Research Journal, 51*(4), 810–844.

Peters, D. H., Adam, T., Alonge, O., Agyepong, A., & Tran, N. (2014). Implementation research: What it is and how to do it. *British Journal of Sports Medicine, 48*(8), 731–736.

Redding, C., & Viano, S. L. (2018). Co-creating school innovations: Should self-determination be a component of school improvement? *Teachers College Record, 120*(11), 1–32.

Schafft, K. A. (2006). Poverty, residential mobility, and student transiency within a rural New York school district. *Rural Sociology, 71*(2), 212–231.

Shafer, L. (2016, August 18). Giving students a voice: Five ways to welcome student input and bolster your school's success. Retrieved from *www.gse.harvard.edu/news/uk/16/08/giving-students-voice*.

Shankar-Brown, R. (2017). Layers of estrangement: Social–emotional and educational implications of homelessness on K–12 students. *National Youth-At-Risk Journal, 2*(2), 81–91.

Stiefel, L., Shiferaw, M., Schwartz, A. E., & Gottfried, M. (2018). Who feels included in school?: Examining feelings of inclusion among students with disabilities. *Educational Researcher, 47*(2), 105–120.

Wang, F., Leary, K. A., Taylor, L. C., & Derosier, M. E. (2016). Peer and teacher preference, student–teacher relationships, student ethnicity, and peer victimization in elementary school. *Psychology in the Schools, 53*(5), 488–501.

Whaley, A. L., & McQueen, J. P. (2004). An Afrocentric program as primary prevention for African American youth: Qualitative and quantitative exploratory data. *Journal of Primary Prevention, 25*, 253–269.

Williams, J. M., Bryan, J., Morrison, S., & Scott, T. R. (2017). Protective factors and processes contributing to the academic success of students living in poverty: Implications for counselors. *Multicultural Counseling and Development, 45*(3), 183–200.

Yang, S., Yang, H., & Lust, B. (2011). Early childhood bilingualism leads to advances in executive attention: Dissociating culture and language. *Bilingualism: Language and Cognition, 14*(3), 412–422.

Yoder, N. (2014). *Teaching the whole child: Instructional practices that support social and emotional learning in three teacher evaluation frameworks*. American Institutes for Research Center on Great Teachers and Leaders.

Chapter 3

Striving for Racial Equity through Restorative Practices and SEL

Anne Gregory, Allison Rae Ward-Seidel, and Dionne Grayman

Principal Miles leads a 6th- to 12th-grade school in which the majority of students are Black and Brown. The school is located in a neighborhood, long plagued by governmental neglect, of working-class families and a large, multinational immigrant population. The majority of the staff are also Black, including the principal. Four of the teachers and the assistant principal are White. Quite a few of the current staff are former students. Turnover is rare; many of the teachers, including the principal, have been at the school for at least two decades.

Principal Miles was asked if he was interested in working with a nonprofit whose staff coach and support schools in a rethinking discipline process. Principal Miles jumped at the chance to partner with them. Thus began a 3-year restorative practice (RP) initiative that aimed to weave together a restorative approach to discipline, an explicit focus on racial equity, and opportunities for social and emotional learning (SEL; Manassah et al., 2018).

Similar to other education leaders across the United States, Principal Miles recognized the negative effects of rigid zero-tolerance discipline policies and exclusionary discipline. For him, protocols need to be easily malleable to best meet the moment. He has a firm belief in the power of established relationships as the driving force fueling decision making and action. He leads with his heart and, as the leader, models what that looks like. He also invites others to lead from the same space, with the recognition that the tiniest crease of heart space in adults may yield something hopeful and transformative.

> Dionne Grayman (known as "Ms. G.") from Morningside Center for Teaching Social Responsibility partnered with Principal Miles in 2018. With 26 years supporting schools and as a former teacher herself, Ms. G. was no stranger to the complexity of school change. For 3 years, they worked together to shift the school toward a more relational approach to student behavior and social-emotional well-being. In doing so, they faced complexities and challenging day-to-day decisions.

Here, we describe examples of Principal Miles and Ms. G. grappling with the challenges of individual-level and systems-level change in a single secondary school. We offer commentary about the case examples to elucidate how, despite the challenges, two conditions in the school facilitated the implementation of equity-oriented RP and SEL. Before doing so, we describe the research driving school discipline reform across the nation. We offer detail about an equity-oriented, restorative, and SEL approach to student and staff behavior as an example of one community-based organization's work with schools to support schoolwide change. We also describe two research- and field-based conditions that support implementation of their whole-school initiative (Gregory, Ward-Seidel, & Carter, 2020). Condition 1 is that effective school leaders need to embody an equity, RP, and SEL approach through words and deeds and bold leadership for change; Condition 2 is that adults need opportunities for learning and reflection—opportunities that are supported by coaching and training. Adult learning and reflection advances the challenging work of excavating personal beliefs about race and equity, and breaking habitual behavior in order to adopt new equitable practices with minoritized students.

The Context for Change

Over the last two decades in the United States, school discipline reform has been shifting away from harsh zero-tolerance discipline policies toward a relational, support-oriented approach to the development of social skills and community in schools (Gregory et al., 2021). Shifts are in reaction to practices and policies that have been documented as harmful. Beginning in the 1990s and associated with the war on crime, zero-tolerance discipline policies led to increased out-of-school suspension rates (Ritter, 2018). Since then, studies have documented the detrimental effects of exclusionary school discipline (e.g., Noltemeyer, Ward, & Mcloughlin, 2015). Students who are suspended have lower academic achievement (Noltemeyer et al., 2015), higher dropout rates (Anderson et al., 2019), and a greater likelihood of juvenile justice system involvement (Fabelo et al., 2011; Mittleman, 2018).

Disparities in school discipline sanctions have been documented for decades (Children's Defense Fund, 1975), with persistent gaps between Black and White students and those with and without disabilities. For example, in 2015–2016, Black students were suspended at twice the rate (8%) of White students (3.8%) and Latine students (3.5%). Students with disabilities were also suspended (8.6%) at rates twice as high as students without disabilities (4.1%; Harper et al., 2019). Moreover, that same year, American Indian and Alaska Native students were 10 times more likely than White students to receive suspension (Whitford et al., 2019).

Driven by a racial and social justice perspective, educators, families, students, policymakers, and researchers have advocated for school discipline reform (Fiester, 2015). Study after study has shown that when accounting for a range of student-, family-, and school-level contributors (e.g., student achievement; student socioeconomic status; teacher-, parent-, and self-reported behavior), Black and White disparities in student receipt of exclusionary discipline remain significant (e.g., Bradshaw et al., 2010; Gopalan & Nelson, 2019; Huang & Cornell, 2017; Huang, 2020; Owens & McLanahan, 2020). In other words, the prevailing research indicates harsh, unjust treatment of Black students relative to treatment of their White peers with similar behavior and socioeconomic backgrounds.

Recognizing persistent disparities in exclusionary discipline, we conceptualize equity-oriented reform in a robust manner (Gregory et al., 2021; Osher, Pittman, et al., 2020). A robust approach to equity means educators think critically about how their own school practices reflect cultural, structural, and historical factors related to institutional racism, implicit racial bias, and punitive approaches to students of color. Along these lines, discipline reforms aim to increase cultural responsiveness and bias awareness (Gregory et al., 2017). This includes both adults and students developing social awareness about diverse racial and cultural groups, increasing perspective taking about how structural inequalities and racism affect well-being, and fostering skills in building trusting relationships across identity lines (e.g., ability status, sexual/gender identity; Gregory et al., 2021).

A robust approach to equity also means recognizing that school discipline and student–staff behavior are embedded in relational and instructional contexts (Osher, Cantor, et al., 2020). This means discipline reforms need to interconnect with efforts to reduce opportunity gaps. Discipline policies/practices can aim to build an inclusive school community that place high value on academic engagement and achievement. Regardless of background, circumstances, or ability status, all students need access to academic rigor and challenge, along with access to academic, social–emotional, behavioral supports, and restorative interventions.

Weaving Efforts for Racial Equity, Restorative Practice, and SEL

Educators know that adding a disjointed new reform initiative to teachers' and administrators' already full plates is not sustainable. Thus, community-based organizations are aiming to *integrate* racial equity initiatives, restorative practices, and equity-conscious SEL into existing infrastructure. In this chapter, we profile just one of those efforts through the work of Morningside Center. Their RP initiative aims to draw on schools' existing strengths and explicitly address racial (in)equity, increase SEL, and transform approaches to building community and repairing harm when conflict/discipline incidents occur. They strive to build the capacity of school leaders, staff, students, and families in the ways detailed below.

Principals receive coaching to foster a restorative mindset and utilize brave leadership skills for implementing racial equity reform (Roderick, 2018). Alongside coaching, principals work with an RP staff developer to assemble a restorative leadership team that is intentionally diverse. The diverse leadership team allows a simultaneous top-down and bottom-up process for garnering buy-in and supporting the initiative. The team engages in a series of racial equity conversations. Leveraging their learning, team members then lead monthly, schoolwide staff racial equity conversations. Staff developers also help facilitate discipline policy reform that aligns with restorative and equitable values (Manassah et al., 2018).

Staff developers also train adults to lead RP community-building circles with students and implement an SEL and equity-focused curriculum during those circles. Community-building circles are based in Indigenous traditions in which participants sit in a circle and pass a talking piece to strengthen relationships or resolve conflict with agreed-upon values (Boyes-Watson & Pranis, 2015; Valandra Waŋbli Wapȟáha Hokšíla, 2020). The circle prompts elicit reflection/discussion and follows a sequenced SEL curriculum addressing social–emotional competencies and building connections across difference. More specifically, modules include specific SEL skills (e.g., empathy, assertiveness, anger triggers) and equity topics (e.g., institutionalized oppression, the challenge of being an ally). Teachers and staff participate in student circles and adult circles, where they can develop self-awareness about their racial identity and emotion management, especially in challenging conversations about race and equity.

Based on principles of RP that disrupt traditional power hierarchies, family members and students take on leadership roles in the whole-school initiative. Students are trained as circle facilitators and peer mentors. Student leadership roles are purposefully inclusive of students who are typically marginalized or disciplined. The notion is that developing leadership capacity with students who have been repeatedly disciplined can foster a sense of connection to the school and increase empathetic perspective taking for adults. Family members participate in community-building circles that engage in SEL activities (e.g., self-care, acknowledging the diversity of racial and cultural identities) and address racial trauma and healing.

Conditions for Change

School districts and community-based organizations are drawing the link between RP and equity efforts (Davis, 2019; Winn, 2018) or SEL and equity efforts (Jagers et al., 2019). Yet the field is in early stages of explicating how to strategically integrate these areas. Despite this need for additional implementation studies, research and practice indicate two conditions that support equity-oriented and integrated RP and SEL initiatives. The conditions relate to (1) equity-oriented school leadership and (2) adult opportunities for self-reflection and guided learning with coaching and workshop supports.

Condition 1. Equity-Oriented School Leadership

Committed principals lay the groundwork for integrative and transformative work on school discipline and student behavior. In fact, research has shown that principals are influential gatekeepers in the discipline decision-making process. Skiba and colleagues (2014) found that principal perspectives on discipline (e.g., prevention vs. suspension) were more predictive of suspension rates than individual student characteristics, including type of student behavior. Yet principals need to go beyond a focus on prevention. They also need to "walk the talk" and "live the walk" in terms of their commitment to equity-oriented and integrated RP/SEL initiatives. Said differently, they need to embody the work in mindset and bold leadership decisions.

The study of principal leadership has offered compelling ideas about what it means to be a culturally responsive school leader (e.g., Khalifa et al., 2016). Culturally responsive leaders are open to self-reflection and continuous learning as they strive for equity and eradication of marginalizing practices. For instance, they interrogate their own assumptions, low expectations, or deficit beliefs about minoritized groups in their schools (e.g., false beliefs that low income parents are less supportive of their children's educational success than high-income parents). Culturally responsive leaders critically appraise the sorting and tracking of students in their schools, which often occurs along racial and socioeconomic lines and can lead to differential access to educational opportunities, behavioral supports, and rigorous high-quality instruction. Culturally responsive leaders reflect on how they have been raised, taught, and trained in educational settings bound by *structural and systemic racism,* which is defined as an interlocking constellation of individual and institutional beliefs, behaviors and policies, developed over at least 400 years, that propel and maintain socioeconomic power of those with lighter skin color over those with darker skin color (Skiba et al., 2022). According to Khalifa and colleagues (2016), culturally responsive leaders also "identify, protect, institutionalize, and celebrate" the assets and cultural practices of students of color (p. 1278).

Culturally responsive leaders challenge educators to reject a color-evasive approach and disrupt practices that criminalize youth of color (Bonilla-Silva, 2018; Gooden, 2012; Kennedy, 2019). Holding color-evasive beliefs, a teacher might say, "I don't see color" and assert that this means they are reducing discrimination. Yet, as Fergus (2017) states, "Refusing to recognize race means that persons of color, in particular, cannot be fully understood because a significant part of their experience is being ignored" (p. 35). Moreover, when not seeing race, an educator denies the everyday impacts of institutional racism and discrimination. Ultimately, a color-evasive approach is harmful because it perpetuates the status quo. Here, note that we use the term *color-evasive* instead of *color-blind.* As Annamma et al. (2017, p. 153) write, "Color-evasiveness . . . resists positioning people with disabilities as problematic as it does not partake in dis/ability as a metaphor for undesired."

Ethnographic research has documented that principals leading RP initiatives face pressures from internal and external stakeholders (Lustick et al., 2020). Pressure against change can come from teachers who exclusively attribute the problem of student misconduct to student and family factors, without considering the contribution of educational policies and practices (Gregory & Mosely, 2004). Parents, district leaders, and school board members can also create pressure to resist change. Given pressures to maintain the status quo, educational leaders may need to confront "knee-jerk" punitive responses to student behavior. Effective leaders courageously push teachers and staff to challenge racialized outcomes and not let concerns about White fragility (DiAngelo, 2018) or the politics of politeness (King, 1963) squelch adult learning and growth. Educational leaders are called upon to remain firm in their conviction to center equity in RP/SEL initiatives, even in the face of push-back from diverse stakeholders.

Condition 2. Opportunities for Adult Reflection and Learning

Staff can vary in their beliefs about discipline and whether teachers should take an authoritative or an authoritarian stance with students (Hoy & Weinstein, 2006). They can also hold a range of beliefs about the utility of praising students (Shernoff et al., 2020) and the degree to which relationship-building should be prioritized relative to a singular focus on delivering academic content (Gregory & Hitchman, 2019). Social–emotional competencies including relationship-building skills with students can also vary among educators. Moreover, they can range in their openness to critical self-reflection about how schools contribute to racially disparate school outcomes (Pollock et al., 2016). Along these lines, time for self-reflection may support growth for many educators who have had the privilege of not seeing themselves as racialized beings socialized through the systems of structural racism (Valandra Waŋbli Wapȟáha Hokšíla, 2020). In fact, given the tremendous range of beliefs and skills, adults need opportunities to examine implicit or explicit beliefs and develop skills before they can successfully implement equity-oriented RP and SEL initiatives. Thus, adults need opportunities to build their capacity to implement equity-oriented RP and SEL initiatives (Aspen Institute, 2018; Delpit, 2012).

Research has demonstrated that teachers can learn to shift away from a tendency to reprimand and toward a habit of praising positive behavior (Gion et al., 2022). Findings from a recent study suggest that teachers taking the time to reflect on student perspectives of discipline incidents and the power of positive student–teacher relationships has promise to shift biased beliefs about Black students as "troublemakers" (Okonofua et al., 2020). Beyond time for reflection, school staff also need support as they try out implementing new practices.

A concern is that districts invest in "one-off" equity, RP, and SEL workshops for their faculty. This follows a "train and hope" strategy (Stokes & Baer, 1977) whereby administrators hope that practice shifts will arise out of workshop-induced knowledge gains. Yet there is a profound need for one-on-one coaching and consultation to support teachers' facility in using RP (Acosta et al., 2019; Mayworm et al., 2016; Thorsborne & Blood, 2013) and in developing a racial equity lens (Gregory et al., 2020; Wadhwa, 2020).

Now, we provide practice-based case examples to highlight the two aforementioned conditions for implementation. Reading the examples below, note how the school leader, Principal Miles, "walks the talk" and "lives the walk" in terms of his commitment to equity-oriented and integrated RP/SEL initiatives. Also note the opportunity for adult learning through crisis, and the role of coaching and consultation led by Ms. G., the RP/SEL staff developer. Importantly, the examples also demonstrate the real-world complexity of school change as Principal Miles and Ms. G. navigate two profound student events. To protect confidentiality, names and details are altered.

Equity-Oriented School Leadership: Empathy Rather Than Efficiency

Offering perspectives from the field, Ms. G. shares:

"Even before the COVID-19 pandemic, Principal Miles's school was very familiar with the process of loss and grief. More than a few of his young people were victims of deadly intercommunal violence. One former student was killed in Afghanistan while serving his country. A few students died as a result of preexisting medical conditions, such as cancer and asthma. In one instance, a student, Shayla, who was severely asthmatic, died in the fall following her graduation. Immediately upon hearing the tragic news, Principal Miles went into action.

"Principal Miles gathered all of Shayla's friends and teammates from the girls' swim team in the auditorium, along with the swim coach, guidance staff, teachers on prep time, and the Assistant Principal (AP). He had lunch delivered to the auditorium, and he instructed his secretary to postpone or outright cancel all of the meetings on his schedule. He had Shayla's graduation photo blown up and hung several copies at various points along the school corridors. Principal Miles led the entire school community through a moment of silent reflection. He used that time to also talk about his own relationship with Shayla, including what he cherished and would miss the most about her. He had all of the afternoon classes shift to advisory so faculty members, who had received a list of resources available to the school, could lead students in talking about pain and sadness, and what they could do to honor how they felt. Principal Miles designated his office as the meeting space so that Shayla's closest friends could plan a memorial service and appointed one of the guidance counselors to serve as liaison to the family. In the days leading up to the memorial service, he checked in with the students he knew would be most impacted, including those identified by the guidance staff as needing extra support because of their own mental health struggles.

"Two of Principal Miles's greatest strengths are his ability to be flexible and to pivot on a moment's notice. Whenever a crisis arises, he seems to respond intuitively. His default is empathy rather than efficiency, being purposeful rather than productive. His approach comes from thinking that is anchored deeply in building and sustaining genuine relationships. The young people in his school learn that they are his priority, and they rely on his compassion with a certainty and security found lacking, sadly, in the experience of many of their peers. When a few teachers complained that crucial instructional time was being lost, he offered them per-session pay to hold extra enrichment classes for students in need."

Opportunities for Learning and Reflection: Shifting from Condemnation to Compassion

Again, from Ms. G.:

"Principal Miles is unwavering in his stance on giving young people unlimited chances to get it 'right.' Kyle and David, two friends, had been accused of stealing an envelope containing approximately $300 collected for a student trip from an unlocked desk drawer after school. When the staff member realized the envelope was gone, the pair could be seen entering and leaving the room on the security video. The next morning, Principal Miles confronted them both and gave them multiple opportunities to 'come clean.' When they continued to deny their involvement, Principal Miles threatened to call the police, thinking that fear would provide motivation to tell the truth. When that failed, he was forced to make good on his own threat.

"Rather than deal with unknown entities, Principal Miles called the Community Affairs officers from the local precinct directly, because they were frequent visitors to the school and known by many. He then instructed all of the teachers to remain in their rooms with their students and had available staff members stand in front of staircases and along the hallway leading to the elevators to prevent students from seeing their classmates being arrested. When the officers came, he asked them if they would pray with him and his two students, who were visibly afraid, as the handcuffs were being placed onto their wrists. Miles received assurances from the two officers that Kyle and David would be placed in an office away from the holding cell until their parents arrived. The elevator doors hadn't closed completely before he was dialing.

"Administratively, Miles was compelled to begin initiating a long-term suspension, which, at minimum, is 30 days. The following day, he asked me to facilitate a restorative circle for staff to process the anger, betrayal, hurt, and disappointment many were expressing and to garner feedback for next steps. The majority of the staff agreed that a full suspension was warranted, but a smaller number, including the AP, advocated for expulsion to give them a fresh start at a new school, believing that was the more restorative process for them. Giving the staff space and time to express their feelings, inquire as to the well-being of the families, and offer opinions on what should happen with their students was difficult but necessary.

"There were some who believed that Principal Miles, because of his unwavering belief in RP, had created conditions that gave students permission to run wild and do whatever they wanted, like stealing. Both Kyle and David were star athletes on the school's baseball team and when they made the 'worst mistake of their lives,' they should have been at practice with their teammates fighting for a spot in the citywide playoffs. The day after the arrest, Jordan, Kyle's brother, who was also on the team, got into a very loud argument with a friend for 'spreading lies' about his brother and placing the blame solely on him for tanking their shot at playoff glory.

"Paul Wilson, an educational associate whose role is to support students with learning needs, had been aware of the 'facts' students were sharing and believed it to be a matter of time before Jordan, who was fiercely protective of his younger brother, would feel the need to physically defend Kyle's reputation. He asked if I would co-lead a restorative circle with him and wanted the boys' baseball coach, who was also the school's dean, to be included.

"Mr. Wilson went to Principal Miles to request permission for the team to miss a class and to secure space for their meeting. When we were all assembled, Jordan glared at teammates who nervously laughed and shifted in their seats, wiping imaginary specks of dust off of already pristine sneakers. I began by introducing myself and why I was there to work with the staff. I shared more about restorative circles, why we had convened, and how they might play a role in surfacing and repairing harm anyone may have experienced as a result of the arrest incident. I told them this was also an invitation to discuss the impact on the team and to provide input as to the consequences their teammates should face. I wasn't surprised that no one spoke up. They didn't know me, even though some may have seen me in passing. We didn't have a relationship.

"But they knew Mr. Wilson. I asked him if there had been a time, when he was a young person, that he had made a bad decision. He began by telling a story of his own arrest at the age of 16 when he had been a student at the same school and how he felt being in the same police station where Kyle and David had been. He talked about how frightened he was, how hard he tried not to cry, and his worry over his mother's reaction. The group of juniors and seniors were silent and still as he recounted the details.

"When Mr. Wilson finished, Coach/Dean Owens talked about the time he cut school back in his home country and how that set off a chain of events that began with his father leaving work to look for him because he 'wasn't that type of kid.' The whole team laughed when he said that after four terrified hours of hiding under his bed and listening to his father call family and friends to find him, he went to his father to confess.

"As the laughter faded, Jordan began to talk about how fearful and embarrassed Kyle was when his parents brought him home from the precinct. He opened up about his own feelings of disappointment and anger with his brother, and agreed that it sucked that the team may pay a price for their action. He asked his teammates what they would have done if faced with access to an envelope of cash. Only about a third said they would not have given into the temptation. With that question, he changed the energy of the room from condemnation to compassion.

"Some talked about their own encounters with hostile police and admitted to the terror they experienced and how they had never talked about that before. Others, who had been spared from overaggressive policing, listened attentively. When Coach/Dean Owens reminded them of his previous talks about integrity, the young men in the room talked about wanting their peers back in school, the necessary steps they would need to take to be welcomed back, including apologies to everyone and the kinds of community service they should be made to complete. They also agreed that suspension from the team was warranted even if that meant they would be knocked out of playoff contention. They were willing to sacrifice their chance if it was for the good of their friends. With very little prompting from me or the other adults in the room, the young people went through a restorative process that allowed them to surface feelings, process emotions, be vulnerable, and provide supportive solutions.

"In a completely characteristic move, Principal Miles shortened the suspension to 2 weeks. He requested that I lead a reentry circle for Kyle and David to welcome them back. While most of the staff were not surprised, some vocalized their frustration at Miles for being too soft on students, believing that the arrest and 2 weeks out of school was not nearly punishment enough to have them appreciate the consequences of their actions. From a place of faith and as a premium feature of his leadership, Principal Miles holds strong convictions about the importance of restorative justice grounded in the attributes of redemption, forgiveness, and grace. What he lacked was familiarity with the protocols necessary for such a process. He had never participated in a formal reentry process and had his secretary clear his schedule so he could participate.

"I arranged for the reentry circle to be held in a guidance counselor's office and asked that the counselor, along with Coach/Dean Owens, be present. Kyle was there with Jordan and their mother; David, with his mother and sister. Including Principal Miles, we were a total of eight assembled to better understand Kyle and David's thinking at the time of the incident and to co-craft a way forward. After explaining the steps to everyone and asking the young men what happened, the *why* became clearer: David's heartbreak over his father's decision to return to his country of origin had been manifesting as an escalation of poorly made choices. When David began to cry, head in his lap sobbing, Principal Miles went over to him and wrapped his arm around his shoulders and told David that he understood, that he forgave him, and that while he wasn't David's father, he was his family. The other adults all talked about watching David's backward slide in failing grades, unexcused absences, and bursts of anger in classes and on the field, and no one knew why. They all talked about feeling guilty for never asking why David was behaving differently than usual. His mother admitted to knowing why but feeling powerless to help her son and trusted that the school would see that David had been struggling and would know precisely the kind of support her son needed. The school personnel, however, had allowed their assumptions to guide their thinking in generating success strategies for David without knowing *the why*. That would be like a doctor offering a course of treatment based on observing symptoms without benefit of an actual diagnosis.

"Care was present; the adults in the room deeply cared about the pair, but it is not enough that adults care. Care should be a given—a baseline from which to operate. Without the appropriate structures, procedures and protocols, RP will fail to make the necessary inroads in developing and strengthening a community of care, positive relationships, deep belonging, and joy in schools. Actions and decisions that arise from a place of care are at the core of RP. The expression of care will vary from school to school, yet some elements are common and necessary to facilitate RP. Schools need to have programming that supports consistent and intentional blocks of time for community building, protocols for repairing harm when harm happens, and dedicated staff members to establish, track, and provide follow-up for all of the above. Clearly, Principal Miles's 'bluff' backfired in a way he hadn't imagined, which he later admitted regretting, because he knew full well to what they might have been subjected. He allowed that his anger and frustration got the better of him. He owned that had he been thinking clearer, his decision making would have reflected that clarity: He never would have called the police. I believe his guilt was the primary factor in shortening the suspension.

"One of the constant adult refrains at Principal Miles's school is that because he makes the students think they are special, he is setting them up for harsh lessons and disappointment 'in the real world.' Principal Miles's counter is that because the real world can be harsh and disappointing, school is the perfect setting to provide students with tools to transform joy into a renewable source of strength and belonging."

Commentary on the Principal Miles Case Examples

Ms. G.'s powerful case examples illustrate two challenging scenarios that were met well because key conditions were in place in the school: (1) equity-oriented school leadership and (2) adult opportunities for reflection and learning. Here, we briefly highlight the key conditions found in the first example, then do the same with greater depth in the second example.

Principal Miles's school leadership highlights the interconnection of restorative values, racial equity efforts, and SEL opportunities. In his response to the death of a student, he acknowledged the trauma and loss for the school community by immediately making space for processing grief in schoolwide advisory circles. Often schools in Black and Brown communities are subject to strict academic oversight and rigid, less engaging instructional routines than schools in White affluent neighborhoods (Delpit, 2012). Recognizing the whole humanity of his students, Principal Miles did not hesitate to flex the schedule and provide extra time and resources to meet students' social–emotional needs in the moment. When teachers were concerned about lost academic instructional time, he remained committed to the social–emotional processing and healing time, and he provided funding for teachers to supplement academic support. In addition, Principal Miles honors Shayla's close friends' leadership and voices to support their planning a memorial, and he allocates guidance resources to support Shayla's family. Principal Miles prioritized empathy, relationships, and social and emotional connection.

In the second case example, Principal Miles brings to life Condition 1 in his embodiment of equity-oriented restorative leadership through his mindset and bold decisions. For example, his awareness of the profound negative consequences for involving the police with two young men of color was clear. Rather than unquestioningly following a law enforcement protocol for Kyle and David, Principal Miles did everything he could to disrupt the practices that criminalize youth of color by calling familiar Community Affairs officers and taking steps to mitigate shame and fear. He ensured that other students and staff did not observe the officers escort the young men off campus, advocated for Kyle and David's humane treatment throughout the process, and immediately communicated with families. His commitment to minimizing exclusionary practices with students of color is further illustrated when he confronts the "knee-jerk" reaction from some staff, including the AP, for longer, harsher punishment or expulsion. It was a bold leadership move to prioritize repairing harm and community, including Kyle and David's reentry, over the fear-based accusation that his response was too "soft." With bold leadership, the principal not only confronted the typical school power structure but he also challenged educators to jointly reflect and understand their own emotional reactivity to the incident through a circle process.

As seen in the case example, Principal Miles and Ms. G. made opportunities for adult learning and reflection, Condition 2, to increase adults' critical self-awareness and strengthen relationships. In the baseball team's restorative circle, adults as well as students, reflected on their own experiences making mistakes. Through the format of a circle, teachers were given the opportunity to consider the student perspectives of the discipline incident that may have helped disrupt deficit thinking about Kyle and David. The principal himself engaged in critical reflection about his action of calling the officers, and he leaned into genuine listening and learning from Kyle's perspective during the reentry circle.

Ms. G.'s role is another illustration of Condition 2 as a consistent implementation support, including her provision of ongoing coaching, consultation, and cofacilitation. As a staff developer in Principal Miles's school, her role was primarily to support staff learning and reflection. Over 3 years, she guided an RP leadership team in systems-level policy change (e.g., integrating consistent community-building time in the schedule for students and for staff circles, revising discipline policy with protocols for repairing harm) and trained and coached staff for individual-level change in classrooms (e.g., developing self-awareness about racial identity, confronting bias, supporting adults' and students' facility in using RP). For example, Ms. G. and Principal Miles worked in concert to resolve harm with Kyle and David, including a restorative circle with the baseball team, a circle with staff to address feelings about fairness and accountability, and a reentry circle for Kyle and David. Each circle was a learning and reflection opportunity for all those involved.

Ms. G. modeled her own priority for empathy and relationships during the baseball team circle. She cofacilitated the circle to foster adult RP skills development, and importantly, she invited Mr. Wilson to share and reflect on his feelings about the situation rather than pressing the students to speak up first. Furthermore, Principal Miles called on Ms. G.'s expertise to facilitate the reentry circle, allowing for accountability and adult learning in the process. This included the principal deepening his own understanding of Kyle's contributing stressors.

Key Takeaways and Recommendations for Next Steps

In this chapter, we have provided case examples and offered two conditions that support equity and integrated RP and SEL initiatives: (1) equity-oriented school leadership, (2) supported adult opportunities for learning and reflection. The conditions that foster implementation, along with the case examples drawn from a 6th–12th grade school, point to the imperative that school leaders need to be bold in prioritizing the social–emotional needs of diverse students and staff members. Decisiveness and wholehearted conviction take courage and steadfastness given the pull toward maintaining the status quo of punitive and color-evasive approaches to student behavior and adult–student interactions. Educators are called on to confront racist policies and practices entrenched in our institutions and deep-seated biased assumptions and structures.

It is recommended that school staff and leaders bolster their commitment to "rethinking" the schools' approach to discipline, behavior, and equity through regular reflection and clear communication with colleagues, students, and families. Staff opinion leaders and administrators might use a set of screening questions that prompt self-reflection when developing new policies or practices, such as the following:

- How does this policy/decision align or contrast with our equity-oriented core values?
- How might this policy/practice affect the social–emotional wellness and development of diverse students and staff?
- How might this policy/practice inadvertently perpetuate or purposefully disrupt the marginalization of students?

It is also recommended that schools schedule monthly time for staff members to honestly reflect on implementation challenges. Adults need regular opportunities for growth and learning, especially in the midst of implementing complex new initiatives. Joint problem solving is a chance to course correct and increase the sense that "we are in this together." Honest reflection includes considering the social and emotional impacts of those challenges and surfacing unspoken beliefs about discipline, racism, and what constitutes "appropriate" behavior in school.

As a staff developer, Ms. G. urges us to consider joy and belonging in her concluding thought: "When students feel seen and heard, they are more likely to positively respond with trust and respect—the lifeblood of any community or organization. But because of built-in power dynamics and color-evasiveness, many teachers too often fail to miss the opportunity to tap into the power of relationships rooted in joy and belonging."

DISCUSSION QUESTIONS

1. Consider the situation raised by Ms. G., Principal Miles's response to the death of a student. Take the perspective of Shayla's friends and discuss how they experienced Principal Miles's reactions to this challenging situation. Then, take the perspective of classroom teachers at the school and/or Shayla's family—how did they experience Principal Miles's reactions? Principal Miles shifted the daily routine (e.g., afternoon classes became advisory). How might teachers see the trade-offs in the change in routine?
2. Consider the challenging situation Principal Miles had with Kyle and David. What trusting adult relationships were present at the school that made the restorative practices useful and successful? In the restorative circle, why did the adult sharing of their own experiences increase the authentic emotional exchange among the students?

3. This chapter emphasizes the importance of school leadership for schools to use SEL and restorative practices toward equity goals.
   a. What does the research reviewed in this chapter say about school leadership and equity?
   b. School leaders need to act boldly and align their values and actions. Think about your school or a school you've worked with closely. What stakeholders place pressures on school leaders, especially when they advance equity-focused initiatives? As the school (or district) works toward systemic equity-focused SEL, what changes outside of the school could be made to support school leaders?
4. One of the recommendations in this chapter was to identify adult opportunities for self-reflection and guided learning with coaching and workshop supports.
   a. Picture your own school or a school with which you've worked closely. What kinds of workshops and coaching would you recommend to address equity issues? What kinds of workshops and coaching experiences would not be successful?
   b. If you were introducing new workshops and coaching, how would you evaluate if and how it's working? What information (data) would you want to collect?

REFERENCES

Acosta, J., Chinman, M., Ebener, P., Malone, P. S., Phillips, A., & Wilks, A. (2019). Evaluation of a whole-school change intervention: Findings from a two-year cluster-randomized trial of the restorative practices intervention. *Journal of Youth and Adolescence, 48*(5), 876–890.

Anderson, K. P., Ritter, G. W., & Zamarro, G. (2019). Understanding a vicious cycle: The relationship between student discipline and student academic outcomes. *Educational Researcher, 48*(5), 251–262.

Annamma, S. A., Jackson, D. D., & Morrison, D. (2017). Conceptualizing color-evasiveness: Using dis/ability critical race theory to expand a color-blind racial ideology in education and society, *Race Ethnicity and Education, 20*(2), 147–162.

Aspen Institute. (2018). Executive summary of the social, emotional, and academic development landscape Analysis. Retrieved from *www.aspeninstitute.org/events/introducing-the-social-emotional-and-academic-development-field-landscape-analysis.*

Bonilla-Silva, E. (2018). *Racism without racists* (5th ed.). Rowman & Littlefield.

Boyes-Watson, C., & Pranis, K. (2015). *Circle forward.* Living Justice Press.

Bradshaw, C. P., Mitchell, M. M., O'Brennan, L. M., & Leaf, P. J. (2010). Multilevel exploration of factors contributing to the overrepresentation of Black students in office disciplinary referrals. *Journal of Educational Psychology, 102*(2), 508–520.

Children's Defense Fund. (1975). *School suspensions: Are they helping children?* Washington Research Project.

Davis, F. (2019). *The little book of race and restorative justice.* Good Books.

Delpit, L. D. (2012). *Multiplication is for White People: Raising expectations for other people's children.* New Press.

DiAngelo, R. (2018). *White fragility: Why it's so hard for white people to talk about racism.* Beacon Press.

Fabelo, T., Thompson, M. D., Plotkin, M., Carmichael, D., Marchbanks, M. P. I., & Booth, E. A. (2011). Breaking schools' rules: A statewide study of how school discipline relates to students' success and juvenile justice involvement. Retrieved from *https://knowledgecenter.csg.org/kc/system/files/breaking_school_rules.pdf.*

Fergus, E. (2017). Confronting colorblindness. *Phi Delta Kappan, 98*(5), 30–35.

Fiester, L. (2015). Tilling the field: Lessons about philanthropy's role in school discipline reform. Retrieved from *www.atlanticphilanthropies.org/research-reports/tilling-the-field.*

Gion, C., McIntosh, K., & Falcon, S. (2022). Effects of a multifaceted classroom intervention on racial disproportionality. *School Psychology Review, 51*, 67–83.

Gooden, M. A. (2012). What does racism have to do with leadership? Countering the idea of color-blind leadership: A reflection on race and the growing pressures of the urban principalship. *Educational Foundations, 26*, 67–84.

Gopalan, M., & Nelson, A. A. (2019). Understanding the racial discipline gap in schools. *AERA Open, 5*(2), 1–26.

Gregory, A., & Hitchman, S. (2019). Shifting adult systems towards restorative practices in a U.S. middle school. Retrieved from *https://journals.openedition.org/ries.*

Gregory, A., & Mosley, P. M. (2004). The discipline gap: Teachers' views on the overrepresentation of African American students in the discipline system. *Equity and Excellence in Education, 37*(1), 18–30.

Gregory, A., Osher, D., Jager, R. J., & Sprague, J. (2021). Good intentions are not enough: Centering equity in school discipline reform [Special issue]. *School Psychology Review, 50*(5–6), 206–220.

Gregory, A., Skiba, R. J., & Mediratta, K. (2017). Eliminating disparities in school discipline: A framework for intervention [Special issue]. *Review of Research in Education, 47*, 253–278.

Gregory, A., Ward-Seidel, A. R., & Carter, K. (2020). Twelve indicators of restorative practices implementation: A framework for educational leaders. *Journal of Educational and Psychological Consultation, 31*(2), 147–179.

Harper, K., Ryberg, R., & Temkin, D. (2019). Black students and students with disabilities remain more likely to receive out-of-school suspensions, despite overall declines. Retrieved from *www.childtrends.org/publications/black-students-disabilities-out-of-school-suspensions.*

Hoy, A. W., & Weinstein, C. S. (2006). Student and teacher perspectives on classroom management. In C. M. Evertson & C. S. Weinstein (Eds.), *Handbook of classroom management: Research, practice, and contemporary issues* (pp. 181–219). Erlbaum.

Huang, F. L. (2020). Prior problem behaviors do not account for the racial suspension gap. *Educational Researcher, 49*(7), 493–502.

Huang, F. L., & Cornell, D. (2017). Student attitudes and behaviors as explanations for the Black–White suspension gap. *Children and Youth Services Review, 73*, 298–308.

Jagers, R. J., Rivas-Drake, D., & Williams, B. (2019). Transformative social and emotional learning (SEL): Toward SEL in service of educational equity and excellence. *Educational Psychologist, 54*(3), 162–184.

Kennedy, K. (2019). Centering equity and caring in leadership for social-emotional learning: Toward a conceptual framework for diverse learners. *Journal of School Leadership, 29*(6), 473–492.

Khalifa, M. A., Gooden, M. A., & Davis, J. E. (2016). Culturally responsive school leadership: A synthesis of the literature. *Review of Educational Research, 86*, 1272–1311.

King, M. L., Jr. (1963, April). Letter from Birmingham Jail. In M. L. King, Jr. (Ed.), *Why we can't wait.* Harper & Row.

Lustick, H., Norton, C., Rey Lopez, S., & Greene-Rooks, J. H. (2020). Restorative practices for empowerment: A social work lens. *Children and Schools, 42*(2), 89–97.

Manassah, T., Roderick, T., & Gregory, A. (2018). A promising path toward equity: Restorative circles develop relationships, build communities, and bridge differences. *Learning Forward, 39*(4), 36–40.

Mayworm, A. M., Sharkey, J. D., Hunnicutt, K. L., & Schiedel, K. C. (2016). Teacher consultation to enhance implementation of school-based restorative justice. *Journal of Educational and Psychological Consultation, 26*(4), 385–412.

Mittleman, J. (2018). A downward spiral?: Childhood suspension and the path to juvenile arrest. *Sociology of Education, 91*, 183–2014.

Noltemeyer, A. L., Ward, R. M., & Mcloughlin, C. (2015). Relationship between school suspension and student outcomes: A meta-analysis. *School Psychology Review, 44*(2), 224–240.

Okonofua, J. A., Perez, A. D., & Darling-Hammond, D. (2020). When policy and psychology meet: Mitigating the consequences of bias in schools. *Science Advances, 6*(42), eaba9479.

Osher, D., Cantor, P., Berg, J., Steyer, L., & Rose, T. (2020). Drivers of human development: How relationships and context shape learning and development. *Applied Developmental Science, 24*(1), 6–31.

Osher, D., Pittman, K., Young, J., Smith, H., Moroney, D., & Irby, M. (2020). Thriving, robust equity, and transformative learning and development: A more powerful conceptualization of the contributors to youth success. The Readiness Projects. Retrieved from *https://forum-fyi.org/wp-content/uploads/2020/07/Thriving.Equity.Learning.Report.pdf.*

Owens, J., & McLanahan, S. S. (2020). Unpacking the drivers of racial disparities in school suspension and expulsion. *Social Forces, 98*(4), 1548–1577.

Pollock, M., Bocala, C., Deckman, S. L., & Dickstein-Staub, S. (2016). Caricature and hyperbole in preservice teacher professional development for diversity. *Urban Education, 51*(6), 629–658.

Ritter, G. W. (2018). Reviewing the progress of school discipline reform, *Peabody Journal of Education, 93*(2), 133–138.

Roderick, T. (2018). *Whole school racial equity (RE) program personal and professional leadership coaching for principals: A manual for coaches.* Unpublished Morningside Center for Teaching Social Responsibility internal report.

Shernoff, E. S., Lekwa, A. L., Reddy, L., & Davis, W. (2020). Teachers' use and beliefs about praise: A mixed-method study. *School Psychology Review, 49*(3), 256–274.

Skiba, R. J., Chung, C. G., Trachok, M., Baker, T. L., Sheya, A., & Hughes, R. L. (2014). Parsing disciplinary disproportionality contributions of infraction, student, and school characteristics to out-of-school suspension and expulsion. *American Educational Research Journal, 51*, 640–670.

Skiba, R. S., Fergus, E., & Gregory, A. (2022). The new Jim Crow at school: Exclusionary discipline and structural racism. In E. Sabornie & D. Espelage (Eds.), *The handbook of classroom management* (3rd ed., pp. 211–230). Routledge.

Stokes, T. F., & Baer, D. M. (1977). An implicit technology of generalization. *Journal of Applied Behavioral Analysis, 10*(2), 349–367.

Thorsborne, M., & Blood, P. (2013). *Implementing restorative practices in schools: A practical guide to transforming school communities.* Jessica Kingsley.

Valandra Waŋbli Wapȟáha Hokšíla, E. C. (Ed.). (2020). *Colorizing restorative justice: Voicing our realities.* Living Justice Press.

Wadhwa, A. (2020). "What do you want, reparations?": Racial microaggressions and restorative justice. In E. C. Valandra (Ed.), *Colorizing restorative justice: Voicing our realities* (pp. 159–170). Living Justice Press.

Whitford, D. K., Gage, N. A., Katsiyannis, A., Counts, J., Rapa, L. J., & McWhorter, A. (2019). The exclusionary discipline of American Indian and Alaska Native (AI/AN) students with and without disabilities: A Civil Rights Data Collection (CRDC) national analysis. *Journal of Child and Family Studies, 28*(12), 3327–3337.

Winn, M. T. (2018). *Justice on both sides: Transforming education through restorative justice.* Harvard Education Press.

Chapter 4

Integrating SEL into Textbooks and Instruction in Low- and Middle-Income Countries

Andy Smart, Jean Bernard, James H. Williams, Aaron Benavot, and Margaret Sinclair

THE HAPPINESS CURRICULUM IN INDIA

What makes a good life? This is the question that Delhi's education system has prioritized in addressing the urgent needs of children growing up in extremely adverse conditions. By the early 2010s, childhood depression had become a serious issue in India, along with an alarming increase in teen suicides. Education in public schools had been oriented toward making a living but was failing to provide vulnerable students with the skills needed to make a good life. With the support of the Delhi Government, and building on a curriculum pilot initiated in 2015, a team of change makers—teachers, mentor teachers, and nongovernmental organizations (NGOs)—set out to create an innovative program rooted in the cultural context of India and dedicated to the goal of developing emotionally sound students capable of sustaining healthy social relationships. In 2018, the Happiness Curriculum was launched in 1,030 schools with continued advocacy from Deputy Chief Minister Shri Manish Sisodia. As of the start of the 2020 school year, 800,000 students in grades K–8 have engaged every day in a variety of games, storytelling, and other activities designed to build essential life skills alongside academic competencies. Implementation of the Happiness Curriculum in Delhi schools can be seen as a landmark first step in expanding a public education system to focus on the holistic development of all learners to invest in their well-being, and improve the overall quality of education (V. Talreja, personal communication, July 17, 2021).

REFORMED PEDAGOGY IN BANGLADESH'S PRIMARY SCHOOL TEXTBOOKS

In 2015, the government of Bangladesh undertook a major refinement (review) of primary school textbooks in an effort to support a new competency-based curriculum and improve the quality of education. The new approach for social studies reduced the amount of content and shifted to an innovative pedagogical approach that was designed not only to be easy to teach, by providing scaffolding to teachers and students alike, but that also conveyed key messages. Social and emotional learning (SEL) topics already in the curriculum—such as helping others, communicating effectively, and respecting others' opinions—are now presented in simpler language in the textbook. This allows for deeper understanding of key ideas rather than rote memorization of facts, with space for students to offer their own thoughts and engage in interactive discussion. The textbooks' content and pedagogy also reflect the diversity of the people of Bangladesh, thereby contributing to students' understanding of people different than themselves and creating opportunities in the classroom to rehearse specific social awareness and relationship skills. Formative assessments are frequent. Distributed to each pupil each year and regarded as the core element of instruction, Bangladesh's refined primary school textbooks have been instrumental in leading a reform of classroom teaching and learning. Although teachers reported struggling with the new format at first, they have come to appreciate the refinements, as well as the classroom practices they embody. (Badrul Alam, personal communication, July 21, 2021).

In recent years, a number of low- and middle-income countries (LMICs)—from Afghanistan to Kenya, Morocco, Colombia, Thailand, and others—have been exploring curricular or pedagogical reforms to support SEL. Initiatives such as those described above illustrate contemporary efforts to overcome a widespread and entrenched reliance on rote teaching and to introduce new curriculum priorities. However, implementing such reforms in very low-resource settings typically means facing numerous constraints. Dilapidated buildings, overcrowded classes, and limited material resources are often the norm. Abysmally low salaries force many teachers to take second and third jobs, leaving little time for reflection, professional development, or innovation. Curricular policy emanating from ministerial authorities allows schools very little autonomy to experiment with new approaches, and overburdened teachers may understandably resist departures from well-entrenched practices. Overly dense, information-packed textbooks effectively embody the national curriculum, even in classrooms where the only copy is the one in the teacher's hands. The often-centralized nature of education systems in developing countries means that textbooks both communicate policy and shape practice. In these types of settings, the design, organization and content of textbooks can have a disproportionately large influence on classroom teaching. As such, they can also act as essential levers for systemic improvement.

Textbooks as Levers of Change

In rich and poor countries alike, textbooks often provide the core structure for teaching and learning. Even in government schools in Finland, for example, it is not uncommon for teachers to rely on textbooks as a vital element of the official curriculum even though multiple resources are readily available (Pudas, 2013; Smart & Jagannathan, 2018). In LMICs, nationally authorized textbooks tend to play an even more prominent role by determining not only *what* is taught but also *how* it is intended to be learned.

> It's so important to the life of a child and a teacher in Africa, for example. This is where the whole socialization of schooling and everything comes from. The textbook is central to this, so if you can get a textbook—which teachers and students are so familiar with—to be used differently, you have a big chance to really transform a school and education. (K. Akyeampong, personal communication, December, 2020)

To bring SEL to life in poorly resourced classrooms worldwide, coordinated efforts are needed to introduce its foundational concepts into national education policies and core subject curricula. However, this is not enough. To achieve systemic SEL and help ensure that it is implemented in a systematic and meaningful way in such contexts, and not simply as an "add-on" to the curriculum, the thematic and pedagogical dimensions of SEL must also be integrated into textbooks, teachers' guides, and assessment practices.

Despite their centrality in shaping what actually goes on in classrooms, textbooks used in resource-constrained settings tend to lack genuine pedagogy—in other words, they are virtually devoid of a teaching methodology that maps onto how children actually learn. The term *pedagogy* as used here does not simply refer to instructional method or teaching practice, but to the act of teaching in relation to the ideas that inform and explain it: "Pedagogy . . . encompasses both the act of teaching and its contingent theories and debates" (Alexander, 2009, p. 927). Textbooks that lack a pedagogical rationale for how students learn particular subjects at particular levels in particular contexts often lead to a default, rote-teaching methodology that pays little attention to students' developmental, social, and emotional needs. This puts up a barrier, hindering both students and teachers from engaging in activities that can help them nurture and build social and emotional competencies alongside academic skills.

Without such a rationale, especially in elementary grades, textbooks foster intensively teacher-directed instruction that offers few opportunities for student autonomy, social interactions among peers, independent goal setting, or reflection on open-ended questions that do not have a single correct answer (which teaches perspective taking) and so forth. While textbooks and learning media typically used in high-resource systems have evolved beyond the single-perspective model, textbooks in many low-resource systems (and some well-resourced systems, too) are designed primarily to help teachers prepare their students for high-stakes, content-driven examinations.

Researchers in LMICs in Africa, Asia, and Latin America will testify to generations of textbooks based on passages of densely written text—which may not be written in the students' home language—followed by narrow comprehension questions that do not attempt to stimulate deeper thought or draw out students' opinions. Such textbooks may be thought of as *barriers to*—rather than *carriers of*—learning. Not only do they fail to guide classroom instruction in engaging but practical ways but also their overloaded content cannot communicate effectively with most learners.

Instead, textbooks can become levers of change by embedding sound, SEL-based pedagogy, and by building teachers' capacities to move away from rote teaching and learning methods. They can provide examples of content that engages students' interests and introduces (or exemplifies) socially and emotionally competent behaviors and attitudes with a pedagogy that is *both teacher-centered and student-centered rather than textbook-centered*, thereby providing opportunities for students to practice social and emotional competencies such as goal setting, planning, good listening, and communicating about ideas with their peers.

Figure 4.1 shows how SEL-based pedagogy can be integrated into a science textbook, based on discussions with educators in India. The lesson is on microorganisms, vaccines, and misinformation.[1] Since it is relevant to students' lives, it is likely to be engaging. In addition, it embeds opportunities for students to learn responsible decision making as they make reasoned judgments after analyzing information and facts. Furthermore, the lesson offers opportunities to learn relationship skills through Pair Talk, in which students turn and talk to one another, exchange views, listen, and collaborate within a framework of prosocietal application of knowledge and critical thinking activities that are appropriate for the context in India. It also includes role play activities that allow students to exercise relationship-building skills and engage in critical thinking.

In countries committed to putting SEL into practice in a meaningful, systematic way, complete revision of a country's textbooks with embedded SEL content and pedagogies is the ideal. However, given the expense and time involved in curriculum and textbook reform, less costly interventions may take more practical first steps, even if student assessment methods remain unchanged and determine much of the teaching approach, especially in senior grades. Such interventions may take the form of teacher activity guides, supplementary reading materials, or extracurricular activities such

[1]The overall objectives of the unit from which this lesson is taken are (1) to deepen knowledge and understanding about microorganisms and about their impact on health; (2) to know what vaccines are and understand how they work; (3) to understand that vaccination campaigns require large numbers of people to be vaccinated; (4) to appreciate that misinformation can prevent some people from agreeing to be vaccinated; (5) to form the intention to protect one's own health and that of the family and society through appropriate actions (sharing information about vaccination, avoiding crowds, isolating if infected, etc.).

CASE STUDY

Keeping COVID-19 out of Dharavi

Different students should read each bullet point aloud:

- COVID-19 is caused by a virus that spreads easily through the air and when people talk, cough or sneeze. This happens especially when they live and work in a crowded place.
- Some people with COVID-19 get a high fever and find it hard to breathe. Sadly, some will die. Most people have mild symptoms or none at all.
- COVID-19 caused a pandemic. It infected hundreds of millions of people across the world, and several million of them died.
- Because COVID-19 is viral, there are no medicines to cure it. We must try to stop it spreading.

The crowded streets of Dharavi during the COVID-19 pandemic - about 1,000,000 people live in an area of 2.2km²

Dharavi, on the edge of Mumbai, is one of the most crowded places on Earth.

When a 56-year-old garment seller from Dharavi died of COVID-19, public health officials knew they must act fast. If COVID-19 was allowed to spread in overcrowded Dharavi, thousands would die.

A team of public health workers visited the man's family. They made a list of all the people he had been in contact with and the places he had visited. The team tracked everyone, tested them for the virus, and quarantined them

4 **6 MICROORGANISMS**

They disinfected the buildings that the man had visited.

They also created an app to track what was happening.

There was a strict lockdown. Basic supplies were provided for everyone so they would stay at home and would not spread the virus.

As a result of these public health efforts to track, trace and quarantine people in contact with COVID-19, the number of infections in Dharavi stayed low, in spite of the crowded conditions.

Dharavi is an example of what can be done by good public health work.

PAIR TALK

How do lockdowns help prevent the spread of COVID-19? Describe to your partner how the idea of an epidemic and a lockdown makes you feel. What changes would you make in your own behaviour if there was a new epidemic?

CLASS TALK AND ROLE PLAY

Discuss: How might different people react to a public health lockdown if schools, temples, mosques and public places are closed and people are told to wear a mask in public?

Carry out a role play: Choose a role from the left-hand box and one option from the middle box. In your chosen role, tell others your opinion about having a lockdown and wearing a mask. Say which sources of information you are using to support your opinion. There are some examples of sources in the right-hand box. You can also use your Pair Talk and notes from the Activity Table you made to get ideas.

Role		Source
• The mother or father of six children. • A shop keeper. • A local politician. • A public health officer. • A teenager who likes to meet up with friends. • A local doctor.	**Information** **Misinformation**	• neighbours • books • parents • the internet • teachers • public health officials

6 MICROORGANISMS 5

FIGURE 4.1. Sample pages from a grade 8 textbook (unpublished) for science education in India. Reprinted by permission of NISSEM. Photo copyright © 2020 Manoej Paateel, courtesy of Dreamstime.com.

as clubs, games, or performances. Citing the high cost and complexity of creating new editions of textbooks, Mexican curriculum planners charged with implementing *Goals for 21st Century Education* decided to start by creating *fichas didacticas*, or books of lessons as a resource for teachers. In the words of Elisa Bonilla-Rius, who was involved with the Mexican SEL initiative, "We gave every teacher a handbook per grade, with *fichas didacticas*, specific activities to do in classrooms . . . in case there was not going to be enough money for the textbook" (Bonilla-Rius, personal communication, January 22, 2021). With the *fichas didacticas*, Mexico's SEL-focused strategy reflected the textbook policy and the economic climate, as well as policymakers' views of the degree of autonomy allocated to the teaching cadre.

Emerging SEL Practices in Low-Resource Settings

Even when SEL initiatives have strong government support, curricular and pedagogical reforms often face numerous constraints, including objections from parents and communities. Attempts to bolt on new "child-centered" pedagogy, imported from other contexts and lacking a basis in a social–emotional adjustment by teachers themselves, have frequently failed to take root (Tabulawa, 2003; Schweisfurth et al., 2020). Governments may embrace ambitious policy reforms and even provide a rationale for their implementation, but deeply ingrained implicit and explicit cultural values and social attitudes are naturally resistant to change, and innovations may be viewed as an imposition of external (or top-down) values and agendas. Education reforms need to be consensually developed and implemented through an adaptive, widespread, and sustainable process. Policymakers, however, find it difficult to allocate sufficient time and resources for such processes with long-term goals.

In systems where new SEL initiatives have been introduced alongside the academic curriculum, as in Delhi's Happiness Curriculum (HC), resources for training, mentoring, and supporting teachers have proven essential to success. As Ankit Pogula, a classroom teacher and filmmaker who contributed to the HC design, observed, "Despite a skepticism whether things could be better in the education system, the curriculum created the ground where people felt that teacher entrants are getting better, teachers are getting more motivated, there's a lot of teacher training happening" (Pogula, personal communication, March, 2021). Initial training on conducting HC lessons is followed up by regular visits from experienced mentors. Each teacher is provided with a level-appropriate, step-by-step activity guide that explains not only what to teach but how.

Vishal Talreja, cofounder of the organization Dream a Dream,[2] which worked with the Delhi government, was instrumental in developing and implementing the

[2]Dream a Dream, one of the four major NGOs participating in the HC development process, is dedicated to "empowering children and young people from vulnerable backgrounds to overcome adversity and thrive in a fast-changing world." For additional information, see *www.dreamadream.org*.

HC. He explains that mentor teachers were trained to work with children using contextualized, empathy-based pedagogies and a focus on life skills, approaches based on a philosophical concept called *madhyasth darshan* (coexistential thought). "According to this philosophy, happiness can be achieved by being aware of the self, body, family, society, nature and universe in order to live in harmony" (Talreja, personal communication, July 17, 2021). Fostering attitudes and values grounded in this overarching concept addresses the students' emotional and mental needs by creating a stimulating environment through mindfulness, critical thinking, storytelling, and experiential, play-based activities. In the Happiness classes, learning is not about being right or wrong; it is about students being allowed to express themselves, without judgment. Teachers are not required to finish the HC syllabus, but rather, to ensure that all children internalize and understand the concepts taught and have the opportunity to participate (Talreja, personal communication, July 17, 2021). Many of these desired outcomes resemble familiar SEL frameworks in North America, such as the one established by the Collaborative for Academic, Social, and Emotional Learning (CASEL; 2020) competencies (self-regulation, self-awareness, social awareness, relationship skills, responsible decision making). The design of the HC by Talreja, Pogula, and others represents a collaboration of civil society actors in support of government and shared goals. As with all curricular reforms, the initial positive anecdotal evidence for its impact now needs to be followed by rigorous research.

It is noteworthy that several promising SEL-based programs have originated in countries with alarmingly high numbers of out-of-school children. For example, a Speed School program that has run for nearly a decade in rural, southern Ethiopia[3] condenses the formal government curriculum for lower primary schooling but teaches it with a different pedagogy, seeking "not only faster but also deeper and more effective learning" (Akyeampong et al., 2018). This SEL-based program helps marginalized, out-of-school children between ages 9 and 14 to reintegrate into grade 3 or 4 of government schools after just 10 months of "accelerated" learning instruction.

The Speed School approach to inclusive classroom pedagogy fosters more symmetrical and less authoritarian social relations between students and teachers, drawing on familiar child–adult relations from the home setting. In Speed School classrooms, the social and emotional dimensions of learning—building on values and beliefs about learning that are contextual to the setting—are recognized as critical to academic attainment. Kwame Akyeampong, a professor at the Open University (United Kingdom) who led the program evaluation, describes a threefold emphasis on (1) learning that is culturally responsive, social, creative and emotional; (2) identification and reflection on the ways children learn at home and in the community; and (3) encouraging students to think for themselves and to work with peers

---

[3]The Speed School program was first created by the Strømme Foundation, a Norwegian development organization, as a community-driven initiative to address the needs of out-of-school children in Mali, Niger, and Burkina Faso. Speed School programs in Ethiopia and Liberia began operation in 2011.

to find solutions to practical problems (Akyeampong, personal communication, December, 2020).

According to a post-Speed School survey, those who finished the program have tended to remain more "reflexive, autonomous and resilient." Their academic achievements have been greater than those of their formally educated peers, with gains sustained into secondary school. The program's impact on the children's families' socioeconomic circumstances was also noticeable.[4]

Bangladesh's Institute of Educational Development (IED), part of BRAC—one of the largest NGOs in the world—embraces SEL as the centerpiece of its approach to teaching and learning. BRAC's Education Programme serves out-of-school children and youth in Bangladesh and other countries, as well as in refugee contexts in Asia and Sub-Saharan Africa. To date, over 12 million children have completed BRAC schooling. Working with marginalized children, the BRAC Education Programme has consistently prepared students who perform as well as more advantaged children in the public school system (Nath, 2006; Chabbott & Chowdhury, 2015; Ahmed et al., 1993).[5]

IED's executive director, Erum Mariam, is a champion of SEL. In her words,

> Traditional education focuses only on academics, but education is much more important than that for children. It takes a child through a process of socialization, of learning, and of socio-emotional development. While socio-emotional learning builds a child's confidence, self-esteem, empathy, kindness, compassion, and more, a student's environment also contributes to motor development, cognitive development, and language development. Skills related to problem-solving or conflict resolution also begin to get honed. (E. Mariam, personal communication, December 27, 2020)

During the period of school and work closures due to COVID-19, beginning in March 2020, BRAC rushed to develop or reboot several innovative initiatives for promoting millions of children's physical, cognitive, language, and social–emotional development that could be facilitated at a distance using accessible technologies. For example, the *Pashe Achhi* or "Play Labs" model, which had been in use in certain government primary schools around Bangladesh and in Rohingya refugee camps, was adapted for interactive, remote learning using basic mobile phones operating over widely available, inexpensive 3G network services. Play Leaders were trained to engage with children and caregivers over the phone through activities such as reciting Bangla rhymes, offering psychosocial support and providing tips on how to stay safe from the virus.

---

[4] From 2011 to 2017, household assets of Speed School students improved by about 45%, and the average livestock increased by about 88%—in real terms an increase of about two times the livestock of a household. For Government and Link School households, assets and average livestock stayed almost the same for the same period (Akyeampong et al., 2018).

[5] Key to the Programme's success is a thorough ongoing research and evaluation process, carried out since 1972 by BRAC's Research and Evaluation Division.

The Speed School program and BRAC's nonformal schools, as well as BRAC's work with Rohingya refugee children, all seek to address salient social issues through improved teacher–student relationships and pedagogy in low-resource settings. Speed Schools aim to reengage children with schooling, while BRAC's programs target rural and displaced children's mental health, as well as academic learning. Both are developmentally based, while reflecting culturally informed, home-based, adult–child relationships rather than typical, formal school environments. Both are also aimed at preprimary- and primary school-age children, where policy reforms may be less constrained by pressures to prepare students for competitive examinations. On the other hand, both of the programs are run by NGOs and are therefore not part of official government policy and do not receive government funding.

Expansion of NGO-initiated innovations requires that more resources and support be made available to a much larger number of schools. For systemic SEL to gain traction in the postpandemic era, the principles articulated by Akyeampong and Mariam need to be embedded more broadly in newly energized and well supported processes of curriculum and textbook innovation, coupled with thoughtful implementation and processes of scale.[6]

Integrating SEL, Textbooks, and Pedagogy

Textbooks, we argue, can provide structure and direction to classroom instruction everywhere but have an especially elevated role in most LMICs, where they are often the most visible manifestation of the curriculum. In contexts where instructional resources are limited, the textbook—whether there is one per student or just a single copy—has an enormous influence. Where teachers have few opportunities for inservice training or peer mentoring, and where testing drives instruction, even more authority is likely given to the content of the textbook.

To foster systemic SEL into classrooms around the world in ways that are firmly grounded in local cultural and physical contexts, we recommend that textbooks, teachers' guides, and all instructional materials can be developed around the principle of strong content and strong pedagogy. *Strong content* focuses on enriching the priority elements of academic content through connecting with the challenges of personal development and societal issues. It emphasizes deeper understanding of a select number of concepts rather than broad but often superficial understanding of many concepts. It serves to help learners make connections internally within the academic curriculum, as well as externally to responsible decision making in personal life and society. The textbooks—contingent on the aims of the national curriculum framework—can promote values and dispositions that reinforce connections

---

[6]BRAC has learned a great deal about scaling of programs and extension to international contexts (Chabbott, with Chowdhury, 2015).

through inclusion, collaboration, negotiation, and volunteerism, and apply those values to societal and environmental concerns.

Strong pedagogy is based on sociocultural theories of learning. As Vygotsky (1978) put it, "Human learning presupposes a specific social nature and a process by which children grow into the intellectual life of those around them" (p. 88). Therefore, an SEL-based pedagogy—which is multirelational within the classroom—should include learning experiences that are designed, for example, to welcome differences in response rather than identical responses. This reflects the contrast between factual learning, which may be learned by rote, and conceptual, meaning-based learning that benefits from diversity of thinking and from discussion, even where diversity and discussion are new to teachers' practice. Such pedagogy can build on what is already present in the school system, taking into account the teaching–learning culture of teachers, students, and community.

A third-grade social studies textbook from Bangladesh, showing a lesson for teaching the curricular topic of empathy, can serve as an example.[7] This textbook exemplifies efforts to offer strong content and strong pedagogy in what we describe as a *strong–strong framework*. For instance, Chapter 2, "Living Together," shows strong content by addressing an issue of societal importance in the Bangladesh context—the importance of respecting others even if they are different than oneself. It shows strong pedagogy by including opportunities for students to speak and write about their ideas and then to identify someone in their community who needs their help. These instructional stages provide a scaffold for students to role-play "being helpful." The topic closes with a small assessment to help check for understanding. To create this revised topic, the length of text in the previous textbook chapter—for the same national curriculum—was reduced significantly, allowing teachers more time to focus on comprehension, higher-order skills, and student commitment. The chapters of the textbook were divided into a series of double-page spreads per topic, with the right-hand page comprising four parts that move from a semistructured, whole-class, oral activity to a guided writing activity, and concluding with an activity intended to allow students to apply their learning (Smart et al., 2019). The SEL is part of the content and the textbook offers scaffolding to help the teachers enact it.

Integrating SEL into textbooks and pedagogy demands attention not only to the local meanings and manifestations of social and emotional life but also to existing school and instructional cultures.[8] Efforts to move from weak to strong pedagogy and weak to strong curricula can be evaluated based on three separate continua described by Schweisfurth et al. (2020).

---

[7]The full text is available at *https://infoworld247.files.wordpress.com/2018/08/primary-2018-class-3-bgs-pdf-web.pdf.*

[8]One such initiative, the Smithsonian Science for Global Goals program, illustrates the role of local social–scientific issues in encouraging students to build an identity committed to positive local and global futures (Blanchard et al., 2019).

1. *From knowledge as a fixed entity to knowledge as fluid:* Moving from a conception of knowledge as known, unchanging, and external to the teacher and student to an understanding of knowledge as a process of developing understanding, in which students and teachers are contributors.
2. *From learner as recipient of learning toward a notion of learner as active creator:* This continuum moves from a view of students as blank slates or a "bank" in which knowledge is inscribed or deposited (Freire, 2020) to a view of students who actively construct knowledge, building on past knowledge and educational stimuli inside and beyond the classroom.
3. *From teacher–learner relationships based on hierarchy, authoritarianism and accountability to more symmetrical relationships based on trust, mutual agreement, and support.* This continuum involves developing learning environments where students and teachers feel secure to explore knowledge together based on mutual trust. The teacher is seen as a respected authority rather than a feared source wielding power granted by the education system.

Innovations based on the teaching of positive SEL will benefit from thinking in terms of these continua, with particular regard to culture and context. Well-designed textbooks can help facilitate these processes for teachers themselves, and also for students. Incorporating SEL into textbooks in a systematic way, in terms of both strong content and strong pedagogy, should be grounded in appropriate cultural, as well as organizational and instructional, contexts.

Context and Culture Matter When Introducing SEL

One question might have occurred to our readers: Just why is it so important to contextualize SEL in non-Western settings and school systems? Are relationship skills, for example, not universal?

At an abstract level, the need for relationship skills is certainly universal. But the answer to what makes a "good relationship" varies from community to community and from one context to another. As a simple example, in some cultural contexts, eye contact is expected as a sign of engagement with the speaker, whereas in others, respect is shown by averting one's eyes. Misunderstandings arise if teachers and students come from different cultural backgrounds and are unaware of the assumptions they bring to the classroom, or if evaluation instruments use eye contact as a measure of engagement or the quality of the relationship. Similarly, some instructional cultures place a high value on active class participation: Students who raise their hands, pose questions, and express opinions, even if different than those of their teachers, are considered to be bright and engaged. In other contexts, posing questions or articulating views in class may be considered disrespectful or a challenge to the teacher's status and expertise. SEL materials or instruction created on the assumption of a Western, middle-class model of active student participation might confuse students, undermine classroom culture, or teach them behavior that would get them into trouble in other classrooms or in the community. The new materials might be met with resistance by teachers, students, and parents.

Critical thinking is another skill viewed by many educators as important in academic, social, and emotional life, yet critical thinking is bounded by cultural constraints that are often invisible. For example, only *some* schools in the capitalist West are ready to have children question systemic inequalities and the unequal distribution of wealth in their countries. In other contexts, some years back, Singapore and Hong Kong revised their curricula to promote entrepreneurship, creativity, and critical thinking in different but bounded ways. Singapore sought to foster entrepreneurialism among its students, coupled with respect and loyalty to the state as governed. Hong Kong placed more emphasis on individual rights, at the same time emphasizing its historical cultural rather than current political ties to Mainland China. The word for "critical thinking" in Japanese has negative connotations; thus, Japanese educators may prefer to use the English term. Indeed, most societies encourage students to be critical in certain areas but not others—for example, critical of corrupt practices in the marketplace but not of existing regimes. Despite similar language, the words *critical thinking* can mean very different things in different cultural settings.

Context and culture certainly matter in the realm of values and nonacademic skills. NISSEM's third volume of Global Briefs (Smart & Sinclair, 2022), with the title *SEL in Context*, explored diverse SEL approaches and frameworks in non-anglophone, non-Western contexts. Torrente et al. (2015), having surveyed citizenship education (also referred to as "civic, ethics, or moral education"), found that "whereas Europe and Latin America commonly emphasized links with human rights, Asia and Sub-Saharan Africa highlighted connections with a return to indigenous cultural and religious values." Nishimura and Williams (in press) find that creativity in the context of Japanese schools refers less to novelty (coming up with "new" ideas) than with improvement (coming up with "better" ideas). Critical thinking, noted earlier, relies less on *questioning* and *challenging* existing ideas than on *understanding the assumptions* of existing ideas, *verifying* and *improving* them. These subtle differences lead to quite different kinds of lessons. *Empathy* is taught directly and indirectly in Japanese classrooms, especially in early education, often obscuring, we might argue, more abstract universal principles such as human rights.

Thus, it is reasonable to conclude that the major features of SEL—including, for example, notions of self-awareness, self-management, relationship skills, social awareness, decision making, critical thinking, and so on—can be identified and discussed in a wide array of cultural and educational contexts. However, the particular behaviors or skills that fit under these headings, or that are meant to be embodied in learners as a consequence of educational interventions, are likely to depend on the specific cultures in which children live.

Erum Mariam, talking about BRAC's approach to designing curriculum and teacher development for Rohingya refugees or for government primary schools in Bangladesh, also observed:

> Culture plays a very important part here. In the designing of the pedagogy, also in the designing of the capacity building modules [for teachers], there's very important cultural alignment, and it needs to be relevant for the culture. So, we always say a bottom-up approach. What we have done is very much Bangladeshi, and very much Rohingya. This is not based on something that we have found from the USA. This kind of home-grown contextualization is very important, because the home-grown part of it is really about us (Mariam, personal communication, December 27, 2020).

Therein, in Mariam's words, lies the "social" of SEL.

Propositions for Integrating SEL into Textbooks and Pedagogy in Low-Resource Settings

- ***Proposition 1:*** *Textbooks and curricular materials can, in terms of both their content and their pedagogy, provide a fulcrum to support systemic SEL reforms.* Textbooks, through the content they include *and* exclude, and through the general and subject-specific pedagogy they promote, provide a reference and anchor for all school stakeholders. They can clarify and illustrate the intentions of policymakers, which are often expressed in broad aspirational terms, and can provide a powerful lever for system improvements, especially in LMICs. They also guide classroom instruction in powerful ways.

- ***Proposition 2:*** *Textbooks can and should support students' emotional and social learning.* Official curricular policy needs to prioritize textbook frameworks that recognize and integrate the interlinking of the affective and the cognitive. Classroom content should engage students' interests (emotionally) before building and consolidating their knowledge. Textbook writers should be guided to prepare textbooks that engage both the cognitive and affective learning dimensions.

Similarly, the social dimension of learning can be enhanced by linking cognitive content and affective learning to broader societal goals, as well as national commitments to the UN Sustainable Development Goals, through a curriculum framework that is supportive of prosocietal purposes (e.g., sustainability, social inclusion, mutual respect, democratic voice). Within this framework, subject content and pedagogy may provide opportunities to explore the implications of academic content for future citizenship. Authentic examples and carefully constructed exercises can guide teachers and students in practicing prosocial behaviors such as perspective taking, empathic understanding of others, and conflict resolution.

- ***Proposition 3:*** *Textbooks can and should support instruction that is both student-centered and teacher-centered rather than textbook-centered.* When textbooks are dense with content (often expressed in difficult language) and designed with little or no pedagogy or affect, both teachers and students lose agency and revert to rote-learning approaches. Just as student-centered implies agency for the student, teacher-centered implies agency for the teacher. Both are vital. Without such agency, SEL, higher-order thinking skills, and student (and teacher) engagement are difficult to achieve. On the other hand, where there is political and stakeholder support, including adequate time and resources, textbooks can be transformed to help teachers incorporate social and emotional competencies, drawing and building on the positive aspects of their own teaching–learning culture and the many social and emotional resources that students and teachers bring to class. Textbooks can include learning experiences written in collaboration with local teachers, who can moderate what is possible and desirable in typical low-resource classrooms.

- ***Proposition 4:*** *Systemic SEL—throughout the classroom, school, and system—can be planned by means of a "strong–strong model."* Moving beyond textbook-centered rote learning requires textbooks and curricular materials that are strong in both content *and* pedagogy. To support the development of such materials and anchor a systemic approach to integrating SEL with academic learning, NISSEM has developed a model that can be applied in many contexts, including resource-constrained systems. In these systems, the goal for curriculum and textbook developers will be the top right-hand quadrant of the diagram in Figure 4.2.

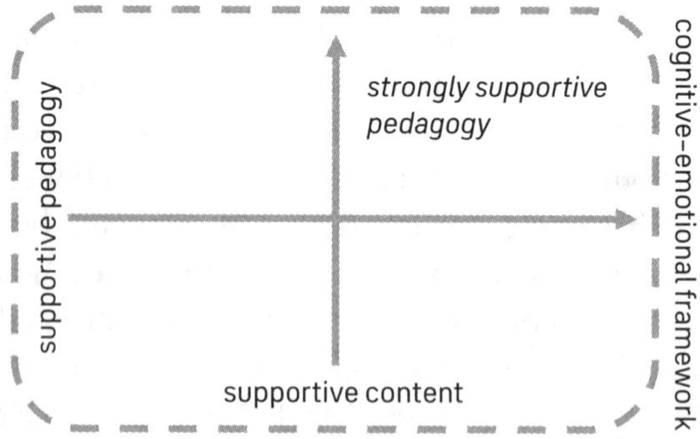

FIGURE 4.2. The strong–strong textbook model, in which both content and pedagogy can be strongly supportive of prosocial themes and SEL within a cognitive–emotional framework (Smart et al., 2019).

- ***Proposition 5:*** *"Culture eats strategy for breakfast."* This famous quote, attributed to the organization theorist Peter Drucker, conveys the idea that no matter how strong your strategic or reform plan, success is assured only by means of those implementing it. This is not only cautionary to international organizations but also to policymakers. If teachers and educators from diverse cultural backgrounds are not involved in the reform process, and if they perceive the content of the reform to be at variance with their own context and everyday instructional or cultural practices, the reform is unlikely to be implemented as intended. Education reform plans, in particular for SEL elements, cannot simply be lifted off the shelf.

Where Do We Go from Here? Implications and Future Directions

This chapter has focused on the challenges of integrating SEL into instruction and textbooks in LMICs. These include issues such as the difficulties of managing instruction through top-down policies alone and a scarcity of supplementary teaching–learning materials. We note operational challenges such as lack of resources, overcrowded classrooms, underprepared and underpaid teachers, poorly designed and written textbooks, and the pressure to focus on high-stakes examinations as conditions that complicate the systemic integration of SEL. The largest barrier is one of systems-level implementation rather than lack of awareness. Well-functioning SEL reforms at a somewhat smaller scale, such as the Happiness Curriculum in India (with just over 1,000 schools) and the Speed Schools program in Ethiopia (with under 500 schools), typically recognize and draw on local sources of knowledge, including national NGOs, projects, universities, and local champions. Successful efforts often follow an adaptive decision-making process and use a well-designed implementation loop that includes good communications with implementers, thereby allowing teachers and local education managers to respond to problems as they emerge. "Before the Happiness Curriculum came in in 2018, almost three years were spent in workshops . . . talking to a lot of teachers, a lot of principals" (Pogula, personal communication, March, 2021). This information was used to make recommendations on what materials to focus on and how to use those materials in the future.

Having accumulated extensive and varied experience working in LMIC education systems, we believe that the presence of certain factors can increase the successful integration of systemic SEL into settings constrained by low resources and weak infrastructures. These may serve as ideas for further investigation and refinement in this emergent area of practice and research. In our view, the implications of what we have observed are that SEL initiatives in such settings are most likely to succeed when they meet the following criteria:

Conditions Needed in the Classroom

- Build on what teachers value, know, and can do.
- Enhance the skills and agency of both teachers and students.
- Guide teaching and learning interactions rather than focusing on content alone.
- Provide opportunities for higher-order thinking, practice, deep understanding, and multiple opportunities to connect cognitive and affective dimensions of learning.
- Target specific, relevant SEL competencies to be acquired and assessed in tandem with academic learning outcomes that are embedded throughout the curriculum and integrated into textbooks as a permanent rather than optional or add-on feature.

Conditions Needed in the System

- Draw on contextual knowledge, including that of NGOs, community-based organizations, and appropriate research and ideas from other contexts that fit into, build on, and are sensitive to:
  - Cultural norms and values of the community.
  - Teaching–learning cultures of the learning space.
- Draw on collaboration and consultation, engaging curriculum specialists, teachers and learners, and textbook authors and illustrators.
- Permeate the entire system of education—that is, in policy, curriculum, teaching and learning materials, teacher training, evaluation and assessment of learning outcomes—with textbooks acting as a foundation, fulcrum, and point of reference.

Future Directions

The pandemic has highlighted the critical role of SEL in enhancing the well-being and academic achievement of learners. In Erum Mariam's words, "Perhaps COVID has shown us why the social–emotional is so important, but *we always knew it was important*. We now really need to mobilize our resources" (Personal communication, December 27, 2020; emphasis added). The reality for LMICs is that there are fewer resources to mobilize than in other country contexts. The enduring centrality of textbooks, whether in print or electronic form, makes them an excellent medium for shaping what happens in classrooms, particularly where resources for teachers are scant.

We have argued that our strong–strong model for textbooks and learning resources represents an explicit process that can help to develop the existing capacities of teachers in low-resource contexts worldwide to scaffold students' social and emotional competencies. Ultimately, the policy and practice of SEL need to become culturally "at home" in places distant from the classrooms, schools, and research centers of the United States and Europe. At present, virtually all research on SEL implicitly assumes well-resourced settings, individualistic cultures, and democratic/human rights discourses associated with Western cultures.

For this reason, NISSEM is embarking on a new venture aimed at developing an online resource base that will provide examples of newly developed textbook units that bring SEL to life, with the goal of creating levers for systemic change. These sample units will be based on the strong–strong model of contextualized content and pedagogy. Starting with customized materials developed by teams of experienced textbook writers, curriculum specialists, and teachers in specific countries, NISSEM will develop illustrative textbook and teachers' resource samples that respond to the call, "If you can't illustrate your advice, don't give it!" Figure 4.1, developed with colleagues in India, is an example of this. Using the open-access principle behind the Global Digital Library (*https://digitallibrary.io*), which has made hundreds of reading books freely available in dozens of languages, we intend that this new resource base will begin to make available to LMICs a new generation of teaching and learning materials that fully integrate SEL and link academic content to prosocietal and pro-environmental themes and values. In doing so, such materials can become powerful tools for generating systemic change.

DISCUSSION QUESTIONS

1. This chapter describes that at an abstract level, social and emotional competencies are universal across cultures. However, some of the behavioral markers of those social and emotional competencies differ between cultures. (We used eye contact for showing respect as one example.)
   a. Generate examples of behavioral markers of social and emotional skills that appear to vary by cultural background. Then, discuss how those examples can cause confusion and misinterpretations of behaviors.
   b. At times, we see as much variation within cultures as between cultures in how individuals express or show their social and emotional skills. Can you generate an example of this phenomenon based on your school or a school with which you've worked closely?
2. Smart and colleagues (2020) make the argument for using textbooks as a lever for change in low- and middle-income countries. Specifically, they describe that textbook materials can have strong content *and* strong pedagogy, so that learning social and emotional skills is integrated smoothly into students' learning experience. Choose a few pages from a textbook or a science or social studies unit that describes instructional activities. In what ways can students' engagement in

these instructional activities contribute to students' development of social and emotional skills?

3. Discuss the "strong–strong" framework. Generate examples from your school or a school in which you've worked where this strong–strong framework was present (or absent). Support the argument with actual examples from the school.

REFERENCES

Ahmad, J., Mariam, E., Sadaf, B. H., Sarwar, S. S., Siddique, S. N., & Zaman, S. S. (2020). Mental Health and learning: BRAC's response in Bangladesh during Covid-19. Retrieved from *https://earlychildhoodmatters.online/issues/early-childhood-matters-2020.*

Ahmed, M., Chabbott, C., Joshi, A., Pandi, R., & Prather, C. J. (1993). *Primary education for all: Learning from the BRAC experience: A case study.* Project ABEL, Academy for Educational Development.

Akyeampong, K., Delprato, M., Sabates, R., James, Z., Pryor, J., Westbrook, J., . . . Tsegay A. H. (2018). Speed School Programme in Ethiopia: Tracking the progress of Speed School Students: 2011–17 (Research report). Retrieved from *http://sro.sussex.ac.uk/id/eprint/79134.*

Alexander, R. (2009). Towards a comparative pedagogy. In R. Cowen & A. M. Kazamias (Eds.), *International handbook of comparative education* (pp. 923–942). Springer.

Blanchard, K. P., Gibson, H., & O'Donnell, C. (2019). *Understanding yourself as a foundation for exploring the world.* NISSEM Global Briefs.

Chabbott, C., with Chowdhury, M. (2015). *Institutionalizing health and education for all: Global goals, innovations, and scaling up.* Teachers College Press.

Collaborative for Academic, Social, and Emotional Learning (CASEL). (2020). What is the CASEL framework?: A framework creates a foundation for applying evidence-based SEL strategies to your community. Retrieved from *https://casel.org/fundamentals-of-sel/what-is-the-casel-framework.*

Freire, P. (2020). *Pedagogy of the oppressed* (30th anniversary ed.). Bloomsbury.

Nath, S. R. (2006). *Quality of BRAC Education Programme: A review of existing studies* (Research Monograph Series No. 29). BRAC: Research and Evaluation Division (RED).

Nishimura, M., & Williams, J. H. (in press). Socio-cultural differences in creativity and critical thinking: Epistemological diversity or fragmentation in the education system? In A. Smart & M. Sinclair (Eds.), *Teaching and learning transversal competencies in ASEAN countries and their neighbours.*

Pudas, A.-K. (2013). Investigating possibilities to develop textbooks to implement global education in basic education instruction. *IARTEM e-Journal, 5*(2), 1–22.

Rogoff, B. (2003). *The cultural nature of human development.* Oxford University Press.

Schweisfurth, M., Thomas, A. M., & Smail, A. (2020). Revisiting comparative pedagogy: Methodologies, themes and research communities since 2000. *Compare: A Journal of Comparative and International Education, 52,* 560–580.

Smart, A., & Jagannathan, S. (2018). *Textbook policies in Asia: Developing, publishing, printing, distribution, and future implications.* Asian Development Bank.

Smart, A., & Sinclair, M. (Eds.). (2022). *Educating for the social, the emotional, and the sustainable. Volume III: SEL in context.* Retrieved from *www.nissem.org/NGB3.*

Smart, A., Sinclair, M., Benavot, A., Bernard, J., Chabbott, C., Russell, S. G., & Williams, J. (Eds.). (2019). Educating for the social, the emotional and the sustainable. Retrieved from *www.nissem.org/ngb1.*

Smart, A., Sinclair, M., Benavot, A., Bernard, J., Chabbott, C., Russell, S. G., & Williams, J. (2020). *Learning for uncertain futures: The role of textbooks, curriculum, and pedagogy.* UNESCO.

Tabulawa, R. (2003). International aid agencies, learner-centred pedagogy and political democratisation: A critique. *Comparative Education, 39*(1), 7–26.

Torrente, C., Alimchandani, A., & Aber, J. L. (2015). International perspectives on SEL. In J. A. Durlak, C. E. Domitrovich, R. P. Weissberg, & T. P. Gullotta (Eds.), *Handbook of social and emotional learning: Research and practice* (pp. 566–587). Guilford Press.

Vygotsky, L. (1978). *Mind in society: Development of higher psychological processes.* Harvard University Press.

Part II Fostering Adult SEL

Insights for Preservice Education and Professional Development

Chapter 5

"What We Saw on the Wall"

Adult Transformative SEL as a Lever for Equity and Excellence in Schools

Olivia A. Johnson, Bloodine Barthelus, Alexandra Skoog-Hoffman, Ednah Nwafor, and Robert J. Jagers

Words like "freedom," "justice," "democracy" are not common concepts; on the contrary, they are rare. People are not born knowing what these are. It takes enormous and, above all, individual effort to arrive at the respect for other people that these words imply.

—JAMES BALDWIN

For nearly a decade, from 2012 to 2021, many in the King Elementary School community walked past the mural in their front hallway without giving the artwork much thought. The mural showcased portraits of real King students grouped over symbolic landscapes: an African savanna, a beach where a sombrero leans casually upon a cactus, and the Statue of Liberty. When Dr. Lena Matthews became King's principal in 2017, she noted that the image reduced students to stereotypes, and their segregation—the Black student portraits over the savanna, the Asian student portraits over a Chinese-style dragon—troubled her.

The school, located in one of the most impoverished areas of the United States, has served a majority minority student population. In 2021, just 3% of King's student population identified as White—a contrast to the surrounding community's 50% White population. King's students largely identify as either Black (40%) or Latine (34%), and nearly 50% of its teaching staff identify as Black. According to community data from the National Center for Education Statistics (NCES), 34% of the community's residents identify as Black, 50% as White, and 8% as Latine. King Elementary, then, is less White than the community that surrounds it. The town itself, located in the southeastern United States, has a history of frontline involvement in the Civil Rights movement. The mural and its segregated, overly simplified—if not wholly incorrect—depictions of race and ethnicity, sharply contrasted with the school, its community, and its history.

Dr. Matthews had a number of casual conversations over the years with teachers and school staff about their perceptions of the often-ignored mural. By her fourth year as principal, she had become increasingly vocal about the mural's troubling representations with her staff. Not only had she become more comfortable with asserting her own opinion—that the mural should be removed—the increasing civil unrest across the United States provided a greater sense of urgency. After the 2020 murder of George Floyd, and throughout the COVID-19 pandemic, Dr. Matthews and the King staff engaged in many frank conversations about racial equity and justice—conversations critical to the lives of their predominantly Black and Brown student and staff populations. Through these conversations, they realized that current issues "in the world did not match what we saw on the wall." Dr. Matthews noted that in 2012, the mural was likely meant to honor King's diverse students, but "the question now is who does it really honor?" This question of honor, a sense of curiosity, and the local community's history of civic engagement intertwined to become the impetus for a new mural—a project that began in Spring of 2021.

The King Mural project is an important example of how adults can practice and model the core competencies of social and emotional learning (SEL), serving not only as a foundational support for building student SEL competencies, but to initiate and potentially sustain communitywide equity and civic engagement—a beautiful demonstration of adult transformative SEL (tSEL). The main aim of the mural project was to paint a new mural that reflected and affirmed the identities of the King community. The work to address this aim called for deep engagement—among staff, caregivers, community stakeholders first, and then to students—in service of creating systems of authentic partnership. This drive for a systemic shift toward greater equity that is rooted in historical understandings of context, as well as the strong foundation of SEL in the school and district, has allowed for an interesting case study of adult transformative SEL in action. As adults in the King community engaged with the work and each other, they modeled actions that they hoped to see among King students. These actions among adults then shifted the nature of their interactions with youth. We argue in this chapter that adult opportunities for personal transformative development are critical to the facilitation of similar developmental opportunities among youth.

The CASEL Updated Definition of SEL

The field of SEL grew out of a desire to make sure all students received an education that allowed them to be happy, healthy, and well prepared for adulthood. As a pioneer in the field, the Collaborative for Academic, Social, and Emotional Learning (CASEL) has helped grow SEL from a promising theory to an essential part of education. Through a dedication to working alongside researchers, policymakers, and practitioners to ensure high-quality, evidence-based SEL for all, CASEL has built the shared knowledge base of SEL, driven quality implementation of SEL by translating research into action, helped guide supportive legislation by informing policy at the state and federal levels, and informed and convened SEL champions of the field. The accumulated research points to the positive contributions of well-implemented SEL programs to an array of desired short- and long-term academic, social, and emotional outcomes for children and adolescents (Sklad et al., 2012; Taylor et al., 2017; Wiglesworth et al., 2016).

Despite the growth and impact of SEL, it has not been free from criticism (Pondicio, 2021; Zhao, 2020). Many practitioners, researchers, policymakers, and funders have expressed concern about the tendency for SEL to be dismissive of contextual factors, misconstrued, and used as a behavioral management tool for students of color (e.g., use of the construct "grit" by educators and researchers illustrates the tendency to drill down into the idea of self-management, focusing on emotion regulation in a controlled learning environment rather than seeing students holistically, allowing for a varied range of appropriate emotion) (Credé et al., 2017). Furthermore, there has been an expressed need for more explicit articulation and demonstration of the ways that SEL addresses the developmental imperatives of families and youth residing in underserved communities. Leaders of the Science of Learning and Development (SoLD) Alliance suggest that schools should be attuned to diverse students in ways that support optimal learning outcomes, including using SEL practices that foster a caring, supportive learning environment that includes relational trust and respect among students and adults (school staff, caregivers, and community members) (Immordino-Yang & Gotleib, 2017; Darling-Hammond et al., 2018).

Through CASEL's exploration of SEL as potentially transformative in the development of youth and adults—and our efforts to articulate forms of SEL—we offer an updated definition of SEL that incorporates issues of equity and excellence, placing greater emphasis on affirming the strengths, experiences, and identities of young people and adults from diverse backgrounds and settings, especially those who have been underserved in the current educational system. Key considerations include attention to (1) social identity and goals and (2) making explicit the features of the learning contexts that support such competence development. The updated definition advanced in 2020 states:

> Social and emotional learning (SEL) is an integral part of education and human development. SEL is the process through which all young people and adults acquire and apply the knowledge, skills, and attitudes to develop healthy identities, manage emotions and achieve personal and collective goals, feel and show empathy for others,

> establish and maintain supportive relationships, and make responsible and caring decisions.
>
> SEL advances educational equity and excellence through authentic school–family–community partnerships to establish learning environments and experiences that feature trusting and collaborative relationships, rigorous and meaningful curriculum and instruction, and ongoing evaluation. SEL can help address various forms of inequity and empower young people and adults to co-create thriving schools and contribute to safe, healthy, and just communities. (CASEL, 2020)

This updated definition sets a vision for what high-quality, systemic SEL is and how it might be achieved. As part of this work, CASEL advances the role of transformative SEL as a means to promote engagement in school and civic life. It is a form of SEL that intentionally points to competencies and highlights relational and contextual factors that help promote equitable learning environments and foster desirable personal and collective outcomes. Where the updated definition of SEL raises the impetus for both personal responsibility and a participatory form of SEL, transformative SEL adds a more explicit, justice-oriented frame that encourages adults and youth collaboration to unpack inequities and co-construct solutions that benefit all (Jagers, Rivas-Drake, & Williams, 2019).

Conceptualizing tSEL

Critics of SEL also point out that much of the larger conversation about SEL focuses on youth and places too much responsibility on children themselves. We argue that youth SEL can only occur within the context of adult SEL processes. The same, then, is true for tSEL processes. The initial work on tSEL identifies skills-building in various areas: *identity*, *agency*, *belonging*, *collaborative problem solving*, and *curiosity*. These areas have emerged as the five focal constructs, or ideas, of tSEL. However, the emergence of these skills in youth is contingent on adult tSEL and adults creating a school community that values and encourages youth tSEL skills. Transformative SEL amplifies many of the important ideas in systemic SEL—it is about the systems that cultivate youth development. For example, the superintendent of King Elementary's home district envisioned an SEL approach that did not force students to shoulder the responsibility of bringing about change to their classrooms through adjustments of their personhood (e.g., show more self-control), but instead by supporting adults to become abundantly clear on their role to cultivate and model the very competencies we say are necessary for student thriving.

We offer, then, that tSEL is a process whereby "young people and adults build strong and respectful relationships that facilitate co-learning to critically examine root causes of inequities and to develop collaborative solutions" (Jagers et al., 2021, para. 7) across differences that lead to improved academic, social, and emotional outcomes for children, adolescents, and adults in the school community. This form of SEL can help meet the growing political, economic, and health challenges faced in local communities across the United States and around the world. Transformative SEL suggests that proximal and distal contextual factors help define and shape the rights and responsibilities associated with being a good person and how to best engage extant social and institutional relations. Developmental relationships and experiences foster guided self-reflection on who one is and illuminate the pathways and resources needed to become who one aspires to be.

Anchoring on the existing CASEL schoolwide SEL framework and the long-term outcome of engaged citizenship is therefore generative (see Figure 5.1). The framework explicitly points to the importance of strengthening adult SEL, in addition to building foundational support, as part of an intergenerational learning process intended to support young people in developing knowledge, skills, and attitudes needed for meaningful engagement in schools and other social institutions as they grow from childhood into adulthood.

We resonated positively with this, as the literature reveals that an informed and engaged populace is vital to individual well-being (Hart & Sulik, 2014) and to the health of democratic societies (Flanagan & Levine, 2010). As such, civically engaged adults—and youth—are critical to maintaining and improving local, national, and global communities (Lerner et al., 2014; Weissberg et al., 2015).

The ongoing public health crisis (e.g., COVID pandemic) and civil discord makes it tempting to limit tSEL to issues of race and/or ethnicity. However, this would be overly simplistic. For example, people in the same "racial group category" can and do vary in terms of race-related beliefs, attitudes, and behaviors. Additionally, other personal characteristics or social dimensions such as social class, career/job category, political party, gender, ability status, and age can be equally salient to understanding the complex, layered nature of person–environment fit and what it means to thrive in U.S. society.

Focal Constructs for tSEL

The focal constructs of tSEL—identity, agency, belonging, collaborative problem solving, and curiosity—serve as equity-based expressions of the five CASEL competencies (self-awareness, self-management, social awareness, relationship skills, and responsible decision making). Each construct is grounded in practice and research, and all are interrelated with the potential to be synergistic and mutually reinforcing. See Figure 5.2, the CASEL Profile of a Graduate, for a visualization of these constructs and their connections to the core competencies.

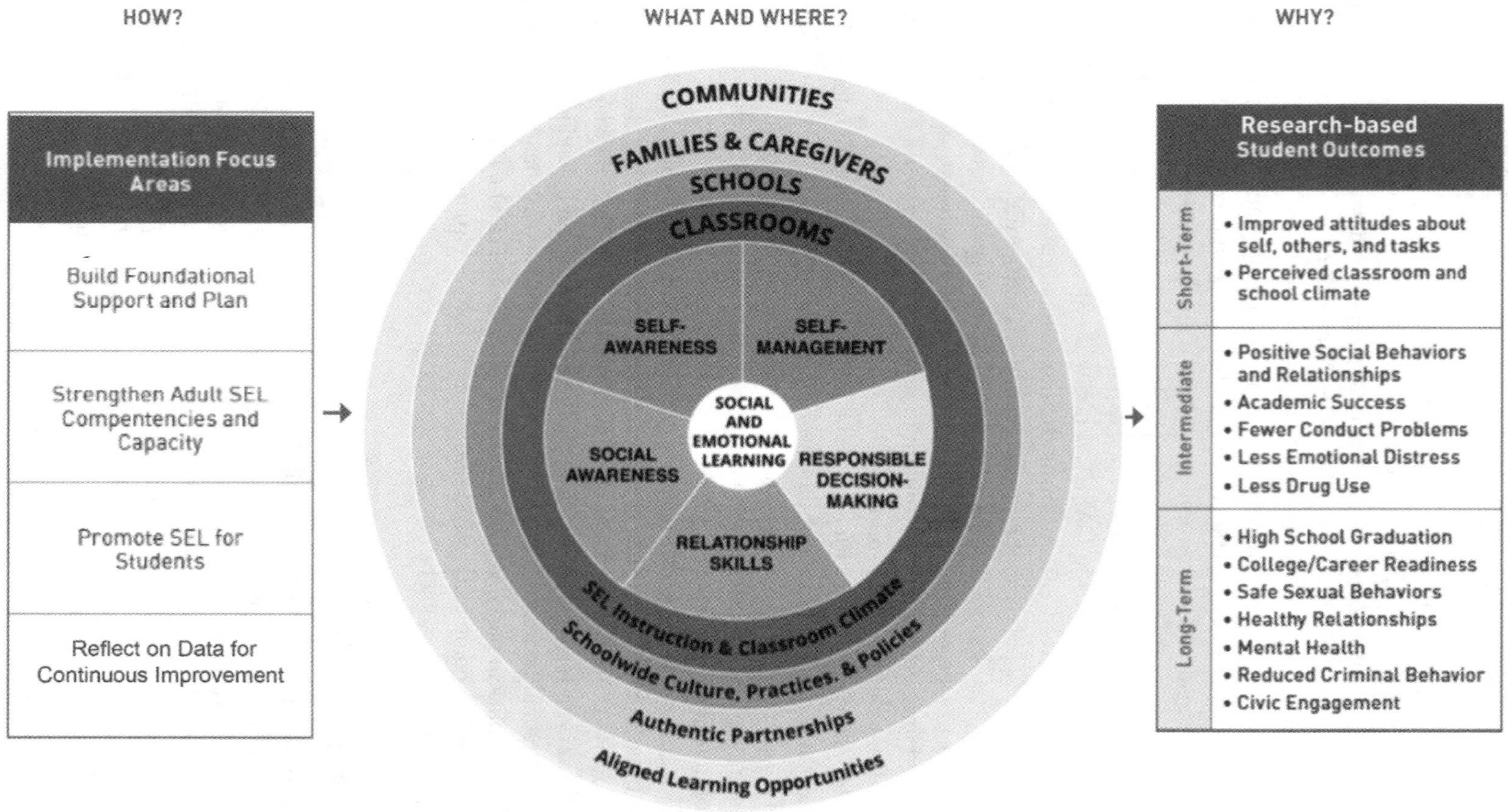

FIGURE 5.1. CASEL's Schoolwide SEL Framework. Copyright © 2020 CASEL (*casel.org*). Reprinted by permission.

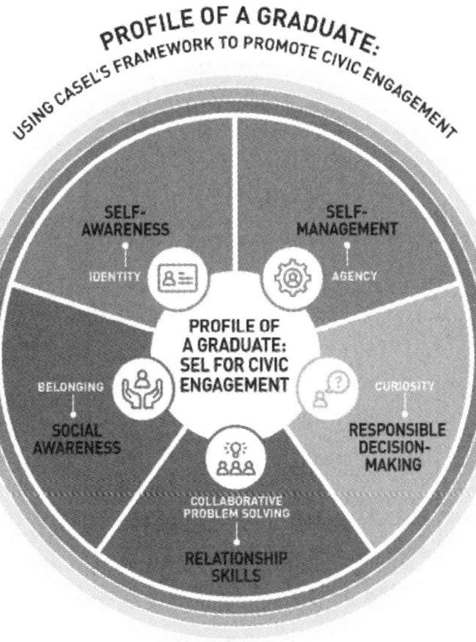

FIGURE 5.2. The CASEL Profile of a Graduate. Copyright © 2021 CASEL (*casel.org*). Reprinted by permission.

Research–Practice Partnerships as an Approach to tSEL

There are many CASEL partner districts working to connect their equity work to SEL, and that work to their broader communities. However, our exploration of systemic tSEL implementation has only just begun. This exploration has been facilitated by the role of CASEL within the Building Equitable Learning Environments (BELE) network. In 2019, we entered into the BELE network, a diverse collaborative of organizations—from academic institutions to fellow nonprofits—that are working to advance equity in education. BELE network partners share a bold vision of thriving youth, families, caregivers, and communities—and of education systems that are co-created with those they are intended to serve, to foster academic, social, emotional, and cognitive growth and well-being. CASEL is part of the BELE Network research and learning arm, and as such is responsible for documenting the network learnings surrounding its collective learning agenda, aims, and essential actions (see Figure 5.3).

Opportunities such as the King Mural project serve to develop the knowledge base of practices, strategies, and eventual resources that can support implementation of tSEL in classrooms, schools, and other youth serving organizations.

For us, BELE district work is focused specifically on tSEL implementation in service of equity and civic engagement. When launching our BELE district partnerships, we refined ongoing work with our Collaborating District Initiative (CDI)

THE BELE ESSENTIAL ACTIONS

1. TRANSFORM CLASSROOM EXPERIENCE
2. MAKE SYSTEMS HUMAN-CENTERED
3. SHARE POWER WITH YOUTH
4. PARTNER WITH CAREGIVERS
5. INVEST IN STAFF
6. MEASURE WHAT MATTERS
7. ALLOCATE RESOURCES EQUITABLY

FIGURE 5.3. The seven BELE essential actions (*belenetwork.org*).

partner districts, with the goal of creating new pathways to develop proof points for practices, policies, and programming for tSEL. The focus of these districts' work is on addressing an identified district challenge, specifically around SEL implementation in service of equity and excellence, and applying intensive resources to unpack, address, and construct sustainable solutions. For example, one BELE district chose to focus on how districtwide tSEL implementation could address exclusionary practices that disproportionately impacted their Black, Indigenous, and people of color (BIPOC) students. These partnerships require a 2-year commitment with an initial 4- to 5-month planning period between a group of cross-office district team members and CASEL coaches.

Through a research–practice partnership (RPP) model using a design-based implementation (DBIR) approach, we aim to investigate the best processes for combining rigorous research methodology with a recognition of practical, actionable findings generated by and for practitioners (Coburn & Penuel, 2016). This paradigm offers a unique collaborative experience with a dual benefit: Practitioners get the chance to collaborate and participate in research that has meaningful applications for their work, while researchers have access to a rich, "real-time" opportunity to test and assess their hypotheses.

Interested districts engage in discussion with CASEL to determine their readiness to co-learn as partners, and to codesign a process that addresses identified problems of practice (PoPs) impacting students who have been historically underserved. Some of the readiness indicators include the collaboration of a cross-office district team including SEL, equity, and research and evaluation leads; a commitment to dismantling inequitable policies, programming, and practices that perpetuate harm; protected time to convene, plan, implement, and evaluate; and a cohort of schools with engaged leadership focused on addressing the identified PoP. The implementation work in these districts has allowed for further development of tSEL and its constructs. Ideally, the partnership is represented by team members with expertise in research, SEL implementation, and diversity, equity and inclusion practices, so that the "research" and "practice" components framed with the priority of equity are present from each department. It fosters a dynamic bidirectional process of communication and learning between research and practice. In addition, planning for and setting aside the time to adequately identify and review data, determine what these data reveal, and work collaboratively to determine research and practice priorities is critical.

Through BELE work, we have focused on four "essential actions" that are integral to effectively integrating tSEL into systemic implementation models. In our work, these four essential actions have proven useful and can serve as priorities for other organizations striving to use tSEL to create more equitable schooling experiences. Additionally, the following provide organizational clarity and direction for our emerging findings on the form and function of tSEL in schools and communities:

1. Invest in staff.
2. Share power with youth.
3. Partner with caregivers.
4. Measure what matters.

tSEL for Adults: Investing in Staff

The CASEL updated definition of SEL highlights family–school–community partnerships. This speaks to the need for adult SEL with an emphasis on learning about one's own social, emotional, and cultural competencies, seizing opportunities for collaboration, and serving as models for young people of how the competencies appear in practice. The focus of educational equity and excellence is one that requires a collaborative approach through active partnerships with students rather than their positioning as passive recipients of decisions made by adults. For tSEL to become systemic, there must be a recognition that SEL is the work of all stakeholders with several entry points for this work: adults in schools, families, and communities.

Historically, our work has focused primarily on supporting and tracking the efforts of key state and district administrators to enact organizational improvements, with less attention given to the school communities—a top-down approach, if you will. To realize the principles and goals of tSEL, we now also pursue opportunities for collaborative inquiry with local practitioners (e.g., teachers, youth workers), families, and youth, representing a bottom-up approach.

Engaging in Productive Partnerships in Service of Adult tSEL

As researchers and practice specialists, we recognize that to implement adult tSEL in a way that is systemic and sustainable, the approach must be different. Our partnerships with districts necessitate both a willingness to interrogate the inequities evidenced as we codevelop plans and modeling processes that draw on the expertise of stakeholders who best understand their needs, and contexts. As we seek to strengthen adult tSEL competencies, we create space for bidirectional sharing, a redistribution of power often represented through shared voice and decision making, and assume the role of a co-learner, recognizing that our current knowledge is limited. Broadening our perspective for a more complete narrative requires listening to the often-silenced stories of those we serve. Finally, employing a stance of collaborative reflection, curiosity, and analysis supports us in applying a robust continuous improvement lens that is fitted to see beyond a limited scope of data review and decision making.

Collaborative partnerships can serve as a vehicle for developing adult tSEL. We have seen this through the ongoing development process of an Adult Learning Series that CASEL is engaged in with a Midwest high school, focused on infusing tSEL into the culture of their school community. For several years, the school leadership team has strived to create a learning environment that focuses on the developmental, cognitive, and social–emotional needs of their students and foster opportunities for well-being. A collaboration with the high school seemed optimal as we sought to develop a six-part adult learning series dedicated to the five focal constructs of tSEL and a final session focused on integrated implementation.

Before the work began, the school leader expressed concern regarding staff morale, educator identity, and well-being. He wanted to address these concerns in a way that modeled the tenets of tSEL prior to developing additional content. Although the school community's student-centered approach had yielded significant gains (i.e., increased engagement of students, more supportive educator–student relationships, and a responsive approach to discipline), the school had to navigate the global pandemic, school closures, the ongoing unresolved racial discourse, and the resulting repercussions and trauma response of each issue. As a result, their positive approach to student learning began to wane as school staff managed their own trauma and that of their students, along with mounting work demands. The result of this request led to CASEL's facilitation of a session focused on the following participant objectives:

- Engage in and create spaces of empathy that support healing and connection [Belonging].
- Leverage self-awareness and self-management to elevate an educator identity that acknowledges and embraces the current assets and opportunities [Identity, Agency, Curiosity].
- Identify and leverage agentic practices that affirm one's identity and supports well-being [Agency, Curiosity].
- Employ practices and strategies that can buffer personal triggers and reinforce self-care, compassion, and aligned action [Agency, Collaborative Problem Solving, Curiosity].

Each objective connected to one or more of the focal constructs, and the full session acknowledged the humanity of educators, centered their experiences, and created space for deep reflection and curiosity regarding their own personal positioning and that of the community. In addition, collaborative problem solving was leveraged as staff members engaged together to construct next steps and strategies to practice necessary self-compassion and increased connectedness across teams. The session, which served as an initial journey into adult tSEL, was met by positive reviews, with over 80% of school staff stating that they would welcome an opportunity to engage in another session.

As of the writing of this chapter, the high school Instructional Support Team (IST), comprising members of the school leadership team, instructional coaches, and several teachers, have begun meeting regularly with CASEL to develop content for the full Adult Learning Series focused on tSEL. The following paragraphs highlight how tSEL is addressed in the series for the adult educator through each of the focal tSEL constructs:

In Session 1, *identity* remains nested among the self-awareness competencies and refers to how educators view themselves. Healthy identity can serve as a buffer against negative and traumatic experiences, and contribute to positive developmental outcomes (Rivas-Drake et al., 2014). Educators' understanding of their professional identity allows for reflection of the impacts other aspects of their identities have on those they are tasked to serve and positions them to develop supportive relationships with all youth and creates an openness to identities, cultures, and assets of others.

In Session 2, *agency* relates to the competency of self-management, speaking to the perceived and actual ability to make desired change through one's coordinated actions. It involves a redistribution of power that creates opportunities for shared voice, choice, and ownership. It also recognizes that educators are individuals who are experts on how they operate best. If educators are trusted, they have the capacity for self-direction, self-management, and goal setting that will result in achievement of personal and collective goals.

In Session 3, *belonging* relates to social awareness and implies the felt experience of respect, acceptance, and connection. A sense of belonging is both a fundamental human need and a foundational element to career, school, and life success. Building belonging requires a rich focus on identity, encouragement of empowered action, and a commitment to fostering a school community that is co-created, where all members are fully recognized and experience an increased sense of self-worth (Stroman, 2021).

In Session 4, *collaborative problem solving* relates to relationship skills and refers to an individual's capacity to engage in a process of solving a problem with others. It is based on a collectivist orientation that honors the strengths, skills, and intelligence of the community rather than the individual, and creates the necessary space to work together to solve challenges. Collaboration can resolve issues and result in shared power across many, rather than the centralization of power among a select few. Schools and classrooms are sites where adults and young people with various competencies and from various backgrounds learn to interact, argue, work together (and, we hope, derive new knowledge and solutions to local and broader social challenges), ultimately modeling the opportunities and challenges of democracy (Flanagan et al., 2007; see also Torney-Purta et al., 2007). In this regard, we see collaborative problem solving as a central consideration that often serves to activate the remaining competencies.

In Session 5, *curiosity* relates to responsible decision-making competencies and can inspire critical analysis of the self and the world. The sense of curiosity helps a person envision a better possible world, which in turn, motivates them toward change. Just as responsible decision making comes as a result of the interrelated nature of the other four SEL competencies (self-awareness, self-management, social awareness, and relationship skills), the same is so for curiosity set in responsible decision making. One who is curious possesses a sense of agency and has the ability to connect with others to create communities of belonging. These traits contribute to well-informed, responsible decisions that support aligned outcomes. Curiosity acknowledges that there is always more to learn, more to understand, and accepts that "no one knows everything, about anything." Compassionate curiosity with reflection supplants judgmental questioning and enhances self-development and social analysis that supports responsible decision making, yielding authentic partnerships with students, caregivers, and colleagues.

Regardless of their own backgrounds, essential actions for adults in schools include replacing deficit-oriented perceptions with more affirming views of students. As such, educators have a responsibility to conduct (and administrators have a responsibility to support) a critical analysis of their curriculum, textbooks, and other materials to ensure they are engaging, rigorous, relevant to, and respectful of their students (Rivas-Drake et al., 2014). Additionally, educators should respect and strive to learn about families' and communities' funds of knowledge, which requires them to understand their own culture and approach learning about others' cultures and communities with curiosity and humility (Gonzalez et al.).

Partnering with Caregivers

In order for adult tSEL to act as a lever for systemic educational equity, each of the five focal tSEL constructs must be present at multiple levels of the system—from the home to the superintendent's office. When the tSEL constructs are organized, embedded, and cultivated into the culture of a system, then systemic change is possible. For example, *collaborative problem solving* must be a norm in SEL team meetings, as well as in parent–teacher conferences. Teachers and staff should engage in regular and intentional explorations of *identity*, from self to community, and examinations of how identity impacts decisions and actions. This is the groundwork adults must do in service of modeling tSEL for youth, and to create environments where tSEL flourishes and is sustained. Without the interaction of the five constructs, systemic change will be hindered.

King Elementary's Mural Project has been supported with BELE resources and personnel networks toward engaging the community, particularly young people and caregivers, as decision-makers related to the goals of the project. One of the primary interests of the King and district teams has been to learn how schools could create authentic partnerships with the community and caregivers, and what that partnership looked like in practice. The team invested in leveraging that partnership to co-create learning environments that supported the thriving of all students. The elevation of King students' voices was central to their long-term goals—mural and beyond.

The centrality of *collaborative problem solving* to tSEL was evident in the adult work on the King Mural Project. Though it was Dr. Matthews who originally pushed her staff to see the previous mural as she saw it, when the SEL Specialist at King heard about Dr. Matthews's plans, she and the rest of the SEL department immediately wondered, "How can we take this moment and this energy and idea that Dr. Matthews had and really engage students in a way that represents their identity and accesses their agency?" Together, they began to envision the new mural as an opportunity to pull the King community together around an exploration of identity. The old mural, which reinforced racial stereotypes of students, did not represent the true nature of the King community—a civically minded, justice-oriented, racially diverse school. In collaboration with CASEL, the SEL team and Dr. Matthews brainstormed ways to not only recreate the mural but also to involve students, teachers, district departments, families, and community stakeholders in the effort. All told, 13 partners—from the district's grants department to parents—were involved in the project. The King SEL Specialist, who was promoted to district SEL Director, frequently touched on the importance of collaborative problem solving among adult stakeholders to move the project forward and gain traction (see Figure 5.4).

Two teams planned the work locally: the district planning team and the school-level team. The planning team focused on aligning the scope and aims of the project to the district's vision and policies, and the school-level team was in charge of delivering tSEL-aligned instruction. Members of CASEL's practice and research teams participated in the planning meetings and worked to connect the team to an experienced local community artist. Though we acted as primary collaborators, all planning meetings were led by the district.

In the spring of 2022, all King staff participated in two professional learning sessions—codesigned by CASEL's practice team and the district planning team—the first on adult SEL, and the second on tSEL and its centrality to the mural project. Staff responded positively to both sessions, indicating a growing excitement for the new mural and fostering the tSEL competencies among the King community. Additionally, two focus groups with parents and caregivers were held, organized by the school's parent liaison and co-led by the district's SEL Director and the community artist. These sessions were designed to gain insight into their hopes for the mural project, the future of the district as an equitable space where they feel a sense of belonging, their identities are validated, and they feel empowered to advocate for themselves and their children. The ideas from these sessions were incorporated into the final mural design.

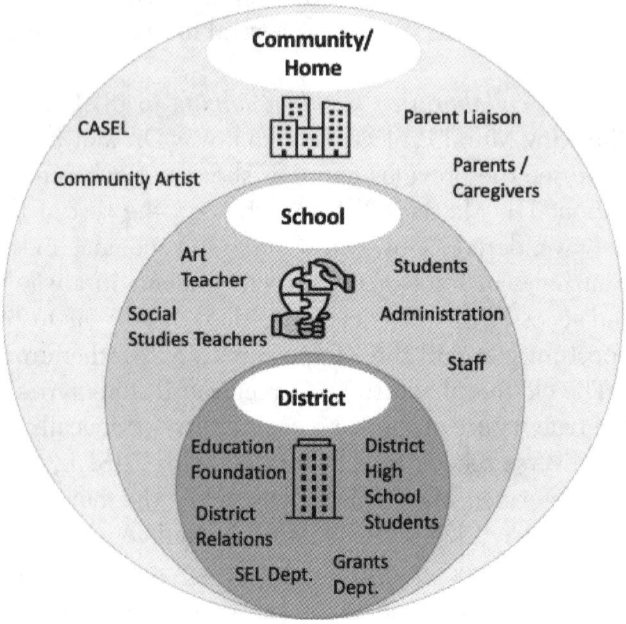

FIGURE 5.4. Mural project partners.

The constructs of *identity* and *agency* were also evident in the district and school's intentional work on equity and an informed sense of community identity. As mentioned in the introduction to this chapter, King is located in a highly impoverished area of the United States, and the town was also an important site in the Civil Rights Movement of the 1950s and 1960s. Given this history, Dr. Matthews noted, "You would think that in a community like ours, the issue of equity and inclusion and diversity would come naturally, but it doesn't always." About 5 years ago, the district commissioned an equity audit by the consulting group the Groundwater Institute. The results of the analysis on racial inequity were troubling, indicating the need for a systems-level reckoning. The district displayed de facto racial segregation—White students tended to be in schools with majority White peers, and Black students tended to be in schools with majority Black peers. The King Elementary student body was majority non-White, just one example of the cross-district segregation that the report unearthed (see Figure 5.5). These pieces of context provided some of the background and preconditions for the mural project, and contributed to Dr. Matthews's drive to paint over the previous mural. "It doesn't represent what we've learned and where we need to go from here," she noted.

Over the course of the past year, CASEL has also engaged in a process of updating its SEL Dialogue Series for Caregiver–School Partnerships. While the first series was focused on creating a shared understanding of SEL between educators and caregivers, the updated version leans into tSEL and aims to help caregivers and school staff grow together as partners while supporting all children as they practice social and emotional skills. In addition, it elevates existing opportunities for authentic partnerships between caregivers and schools through increased agency.

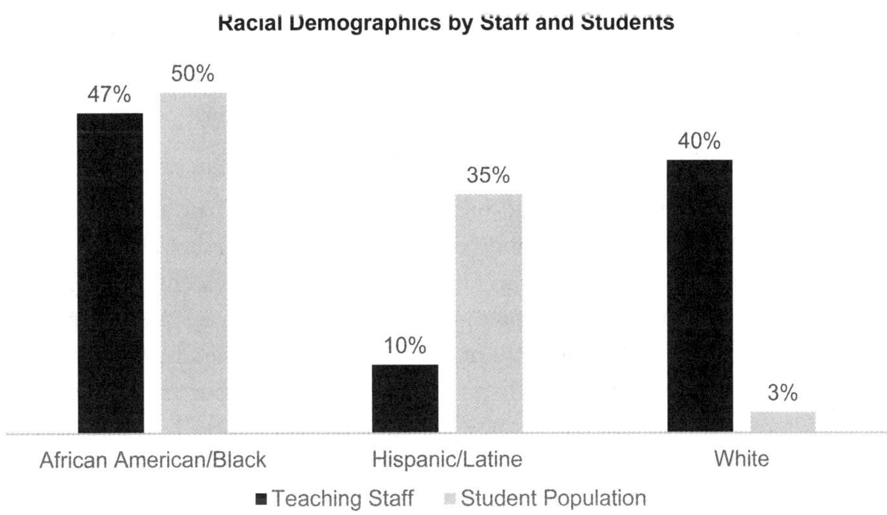

FIGURE 5.5. King racial demographics by staff and students.

Sharing Power with Youth

Curiosity was evidenced throughout the project in its driving implicit and explicit questions: How can we build authentic partnerships? What does equity mean for our school community? How can we do better in service of our students? How can this project forward structural change? When Dr. Matthews spoke to King's teachers about the previous mural, she talked through its visual representations. "What would I say to you," she asked them, "if I walked into your classroom and saw your students like this? That you have the White students front and center and you have everybody grouped by some preconceived notion about their race or their ethnicity?" This line of questioning opened the door for new ideas about art and representation, and the curiosity of all the parties involved in the King Mural Project acted as the gas that kept the metaphorical car running.

Over the summer of 2021, Dr. Matthews, in collaboration with the SEL and Service–Learning Departments, hosted summer school for some of King's students. Local high school students, some former King students, were recruited to participate in the project to earn credit. All the lessons centered around exploring King students' *identity*, *agency*, and sense of *belonging*. Lesson plans were codesigned by the participating high school students and King's SEL Specialist.

In a continuation of this summer work, tSEL constructs were interwoven into the district and school team's plans for instruction in the spring of 2022. This tSEL-centered instruction took place during students' Social Studies and Art classes. All tSEL-oriented instruction was bolstered by the groundwork of adults, and their own explorations of the focal constructs in relation to the mural redesign. In their art classes, students were able to offer insights into their vision for the mural—and King Elementary's future. These instructional plans were the result of another focal construct, *collaborative problem solving*, again illustrating the centrality of this tSEL construct to both adult and youth tSEL.

Measuring What Matters to Drive Adult Change

The King Mural Project is just one example of adult tSEL in action. There are a number of other recent applications of tSEL that are worth touching upon, as they highlight adult-level change as a critical component to Systemic tSEL. District stakeholders have recognized the potential for SEL data strategies to drive adult conversations and focus more sharply on equity. Many districts have analyzed disaggregated data to highlight racial disproportionality in teacher assessments of students' social and emotional competencies, school climate, and discipline practices. They have used these analyses to address the root causes of those disparities and inform SEL-related policies and practices that promote greater equity. Exploring these root causes has exposed the need for adult tSEL, not just student tSEL, to produce desired changes.

A few districts have examined climate, academic, and discipline data for inequities and used these data to drive root cause analysis and decision making. For example, the Chicago Public School reviewed discipline data and revealed that subjective infractions such as "persistent defiance," were applied to higher percentages of Black students than to their classmates. This led to partnering with student, parent, and community groups to revise their discipline policies to better align with the district's commitment to a more consistent, equitable policy that keeps students in class. Palm Beach County Schools developed a Master Schedule Analysis Protocol to examine racial disparities in access to advanced coursework. This analysis was used as a coaching tool to help staff members reflect on their perceptions of race and achievement and to critically examine how these perceptions might contribute to limiting some students' access to advanced coursework.

District level leaders are, of course, implicated in whether and in what ways districts address issues of educational equity. A core assumption is the need to bring together a diverse group of educational stakeholders to envision, plan, and animate the local equity-focused educational innovations. In addition to education leaders, the stakeholder group should include some combination of department leads, classroom teachers, caregivers, community members and young people.

We are also learning what happens in classrooms and schools when teachers systematically collect student experience data. In one BELE school, teachers recently met to discuss their learnings from the first administration of a survey given to assess classroom learning conditions. At first, the group members expressed surprise at the results, but upon further discussion, admitted that while the results were unexpected, the survey helped them pinpoint what needed support. One teacher noted that he was making efforts to change the culture of his classroom and giving students the power to make decisions about how the class was set up. Throughout the discussion, teachers relied on their own tSEL competencies—*curiosity* and *collaborative problem solving* in particular—to examine their own teacher identities in service of student experience and SEL.

In contrast, teachers in another BELE district reviewed data from the same survey and had a largely negative response, with many teachers claiming that the data were "wrong." This choice to distrust and even ignore student voices—in this case expressing the desire for greater teacher caring and classroom community—is one example of where existing adult tSEL competencies should actively work against these reactions. When adults come to discussions of student data from a space of *curiosity*, grounded in awareness of their identities as persons and teachers, systemic change in service of schoolwide tSEL is cultivated.

King Elementary, as with all BELE district schools, has engaged in data-informed SEL implementation efforts, administering an SEL implementation survey to all staff to gauge their perceptions and attitudes toward SEL, and implementing SEL work aligned with the CASEL indicators of schoolwide SEL. Their winter 2021–2022 SEL implementation survey found that King educators had demonstrated a strong commitment to cultivating positive adult SEL practices over the past year, demonstrating relative stability (with a slight increase) in staff members who strongly endorsed frequent participation in professional learning on how their interactions with students could promote students' social and emotional competence. Perhaps due to the administration period falling during the pandemic, there was a 17% decrease in staff members who agreed that they felt supported and connected to colleagues over this period. However, there was a 6% increase in staff who strongly agreed that staff members at their school interacted in a way that modeled social and emotional competence.

When narrowing in on the historical data that highlights issues of equity, King promoted positive student interactions and outcomes. However, there was an 8% decrease—from 100% in March 2020 to 92% in winter 2021—in staff members who agreed that students of all races are treated fairly. Additionally, there was a 5% decrease in staff who strongly agreed that they can help students feel safe while they are at this school.

The staff implementation survey data also allowed Dr. Matthews to gather information on staff perceptions of caregivers and community involvement. For example, one question asked about agreement with the statement, "Parent/guardians are influential decision-makers in this school." Another prompted, "The community we serve is supportive of this school." These data were used for informed decision making and strategic partnerships. Furthermore, this information allowed for a periodic snapshot of the staff relationships with King families and caregivers. Her desire to honor the history of the local community through the mural project—to acknowledge past, present, and future—was viewed as a productive way to build, maintain, or repair community relationships, now and into the future.

Recommendations for Action

For those wondering where to start when it comes to enacting and implementing the five focal constructs of adult tSEL, it is critical to begin with one's approach to the work. We recommend employing an investigative approach, one that allows for all who are engaged to remain open to new discoveries. Whether the work begins at the district or school level, creating a space for honest dialogue and feedback from educators, caregivers, community organizations, and students opens avenues that lead to systemic change. Grounding the work in a shared understanding that transformative work, by nature, takes time, is an important foundational step. While a continuous improvement model may feel burdensome initially, allowing the necessary space to adjust and implement again based on observations and lessons learned is a crucial aspect of implementation work.

The implementation of tSEL in the CASEL BELE partner districts has illuminated key learnings and recommendations for action:

1. Invest in the time necessary to authentically partner with and collaborate with educators, students, and caregivers in service of SEL and equity.
2. Expand the decision-making—and tSEL implementation—table to include those who are most impacted by the work itself. This work cannot be completed in silos, without input from all stakeholders.
3. A model of a cohort of schools can offer extensive professional learning opportunities for staff to engage in deep, critical self-reflection and examine the status of their own tSEL competencies.
   a. School cohorts launching SEL implementation should begin by engaging in conversations around the context and communities they serve, and exploring data related to community health, well-being, and economic indicators.
   b. In multiyear cohort models, staff members could have the opportunity to engage in an action research project after their first year of work.
   c. Models could offer opportunities for peer mentoring and collaborations in pursuit of districtwide solutions for equity. In this case, more experienced schools adopting SEL and equity practices could mentor newer cohorts for a multiyear period.
4. Adult tSEL should be a central consideration in all professional development.
   a. Generally, professional development should be tailored to accommodate the expressed needs of adults.
   b. Professional learning should be data-driven and well matched to the needs of the school.
   c. Principals can provide resources for educator professional development that support beliefs and practices that allow all young people to thrive. This includes attention to implicit and explicit biases, the implementation of culturally responsive education, and managing student discipline in a supportive manner, especially with students of color and those from underresourced communities.
5. The hiring of experienced, highly competent teachers is also relevant to the pursuit of adult tSEL (Burroughs et al., 2019).
   a. The hiring of teachers of color may make an especially important contribution to a school climate since, compared with their White colleagues, teachers of color are preferred and linked to better performance by students from all backgrounds and can be especially relevant to educational outcomes of Black boys (Cherng & Halpin, 2016; Gershenson et al., 2021).
   b. If hiring teachers of color is not possible, bring into the school community members who match the racial/ethnic composition of the school as partners, presenters, and instructional resources to improve students' experience.

Conclusion

It is sobering to write about and engage in SEL implementation work during this moment in time. As we collectively look toward a future in which SEL and tSEL, and their mutually reinforcing competencies and focal constructs, are increasingly threatened, we must also realize and trust that they are increasingly necessary. The ideas discussed in this chapter are by no means prescriptive, though we posed many necessary prerequisites. Transformative SEL in service of equity, excellence, and civic engagement requires patience, persistence, attention to detail, and continual reflection on oneself as part of a greater collective.

DISCUSSION QUESTIONS

1. Choose one or two practices or approaches that you have seen used to develop any of the five CASEL competencies in adults in schools (e.g., self-awareness, self-management social awareness, relationship skills, and responsible decision making). Reflect on those common practices and competencies. What aspects of those practices/approaches would need to be changed in order to cultivate identity (in addition to self-awareness), agency (as part of self-management), belonging (in addition to social awareness), collaborative problem solving (not just relationship skills), and curiosity (in addition to responsible decision making)?
2. This chapter emphasizes the importance of research–practice partnerships for improving practice in schools. Based on the examples given here, what do these partnerships offer that can improve tSEL implementation? What are some concrete ways that stakeholders (e.g., teachers, families, administrators) can show collaborative problem solving (or identity or agency) in their work together?
3. We live in a society where many educators hold deficit views toward students from traditionally marginalized groups (e.g., students of color, students with disabilities) and do not realize the ways that bias impacts their behavior. Consider your school or a school with which you have worked closely. What steps would you want to take to prepare the adults at school for tSEL?
4. Many people are familiar with tSEL for youth but have not considered how tSEL takes shape for the adults at their school. Discuss a problem that often occurs at a school with which you're familiar. How can tSEL be used to address that problem? How will those solutions have positive consequences for adults and students?

REFERENCES

Burroughs N., Gardner, J., Lee, Y., Guo, S., Touitou, I., Jansen, K., & Schmidt, W. (2019). *Teaching for excellence and equity: Analyzing teacher characteristics, behaviors and student outcomes with TIMSS*. International Association for the Evaluation of Educational Achievement.

CASEL. (2020). Fundamentals of SEL. Retrieved from *www.casel.org/what-is-sel*.

Cherng, H., & Halpin, P. (2016). The importance of minority teachers: Student perceptions of minority versus White teachers. *Educational Researcher, 45*(7), 407–420.

Coburn, C. E., & Penuel, W. R. (2016). Research–practice partnerships in education: Outcomes, dynamics, and open questions. *Educational Researcher, 45*(1), 48–54.

Credé, M., Tynan, M. C., & Harms, P. D. (2017). Much ado about grit: A meta-analytic synthesis of the grit literature. *Journal of Personality and Social Psychology, 113*(3), 492–511.

Darling-Hammond, L., Cook-Harvey, C., Flook, L., Gardner, M., & Melnick, H. (2018). *With the whole child in mind: Insights from the Comer School Development Program*. Association for Supervision and Curriculum Development.

Flanagan, C., & Levine, P. (2010). Civic engagement and the transition to adulthood. *The Future of Children, 20*(1), 159–179.

Flanagan, C. A., Cumsille, P., Gill, S., & Gallay, L. S. (2007). School and community climates and civic commitments: Patterns for ethnic minority and majority students. *Journal of Educational Psychology, 99*(2), 421–431.

Gershenson, S., Hart, C. M. D., Hyman, J., Lindsay, C., & Papageorge, N. W. (2021, February). *The long-run impacts of same-race teachers*. National Bureau of Economic Research.

Gonzalez, N., Moll, L. C., & Amanti, C. (2005). *Funds of knowledge: Theorizing practices in households, communities, and classrooms*. Erlbaum.

Hart, D., & Sulik, M. J. (2014). The social construction of volunteering. In L. M. Padilla-Walker & G. Carlo (Eds.), *Prosocial development: A multidimensional approach*. Oxford University Press.

Immordino-Yang, M. H., & Gotlieb, R. (2017). Embodied brains, social minds, cultural meaning: Integrating neuroscientific and educational research on social-affective development. *American Educational Research Journal, 54*(1, Suppl.), 344S–367S.

Jagers, R. J., Rivas-Drake, D., & Williams, B. (2019). Transformative social and emotional learning (SEL): Toward SEL in service of educational equity and excellence. *Educational Psychologist, 54*(3), 162–184.

Jagers, R. J., Skoog-Hoffman, A., Barthelus, B., & Schlund, J. (2021, Summer). Transformative social and emotional learning. Retrieved from *www.aft.org/ae/summer2021/jagers_skoog-hoffman_barthelus_schlund*.

Lerner, R. M., Wang, J., Champine, R. B., Warren, D. J. A., & Erickson, K. (2014). Development of civic engagement: Theoretical and methodological issues. *International Journal of Developmental Science, 8*(3–4), 69–79.

Pondicio, R. (2021, October). The unexamined rise of therapeutic education: How social–emotional learning extends K–12 education's reach into students' lives and expands teachers' roles. Retrieved from *www.aei.org/research-products/report/*

the-unexamined-rise-of-therapeutic-education-how-social-emotional-learning-extends-k-12-educations-reach-into-students-lives-and-expands-teachers-roles.

Rivas-Drake, D., Seaton, E. K., Markstrom, C., Quintana, S., Syed, M., Lee, R. M., . . . Ethnic and Racial Identity in the 21st Century Study Group. (2014). Ethnic and racial identity in adolescence: Implications for psychosocial, academic, and health outcomes. *Child Development, 85*(1), 40–57.

Sklad, M., Diekstra, R., De Ritter, M., Ben, J., & Gravesteijn, C. (2012). Effectiveness of school-based universal social, emotional, and behavioral programs: Do they enhance students' development in the area of skill, behavior, and adjustment? *Psychology and Schools, 49*, 892–909.

Stroman, C. (2021). Structures for belonging: A synthesis of research on belonging–supportive learning environments. Retrieved from *https://studentexperiencenetwork.org/structures-for-belonging-a-synthesis-of-research-on-belonging-supportive-learning-environments.*

Taylor, R., Oberle, E., Durlak, J. A., & Weissberg, R. P. (2017). Promoting positive youth development through school-based social and emotional learning interventions: A meta-analysis of follow-up effects. *Child Development, 88*, 1156–1171.

Torney-Purta, J., Barber, C. H., & Wilkenfeld, B. (2007). Latino adolescents' civic development in the United States: Research results from the IEA Civic Education Study. *Journal of Youth and Adolescence, 36*(2), 111–125.

Weissberg, R. P., Durlak, J. A., Domitrovich, C. E., & Gullotta, T. P. (Eds.). (2015). Social and emotional learning: Past, present, and future. In J. A. Durlak, C. E. Domitrovich, R. P. Weissberg, & T. P. Gullotta (Eds.), *Handbook of social and emotional learning: Research and practice* (pp. 3–19). Guilford Press.

Wiglesworth, M., Lendrum, A., Oldfield, J., Scott, A., ten Bokkel, I., Tate, K., & Emery, C. (2016). The impact of trial stage, developer involvement and international transferability on universal social and emotional learning programme outcomes: A meta-analysis. *Cambridge Journal of Education, 46*, 347–376.

Zhao, Y. (2020). Another education war?: The coming debates over social and emotional learning. *Phi Delta Kappan, 101*, 42–48.

Chapter 6

Cultivating SEL-Ready Teachers

SEL in Teacher Preparation

Deirdre Hon, Julie Sauve, Julia Mahfouz,
and Kimberly A. Schonert-Reichl

Since 2009, social and emotional learning (SEL) has been explicitly integrated into a postbaccalaureate, 11-month, elementary teacher preparation program in the Faculty of Education at the University of British Columbia (UBC) in British Columbia, Canada. Specifically, each year, the teacher education program at UBC welcomes approximately 400 elementary preservice teacher candidates (TCs). TCs have the opportunity to select from nine specialty areas, and SEL is one option. Two cohorts of 36 students each, per year, choose to focus on SEL.

TCs in the SEL cohorts at UBC take the regular course requirements for teacher certification, and embedded within these are courses specifically designed to include materials and experiences on educational research and contemporary issues in SEL. Throughout the 11-month program, TCs learn to embed SEL in all areas of students' development and learn strategies to connect youth's academic learning with the development of social and emotional competencies, including social awareness, self-awareness, self-management, relationship skills, and social responsibility. In the program, students also are provided with opportunities to attend 1-day workshops on topics including SEL games, cooperative learning, building resiliency, restorative practices, educator SEL, and neuroscience and SEL, to name a few. Moreover, all of the TCs in the SEL cohorts are placed into classrooms with sponsor teachers with expertise and experience in integrating SEL programs and practices into classroom instruction, who serve as mentors and role models for TCs on the integration of SEL programs and practices during their field experience. Finally, integrated throughout the program are opportunities for the TCs to engage in inquiry and action research on SEL to advance their understanding of teaching practices that advance SEL. At the end of their program, students engage in a capstone project in which TCs demonstrate their learning and integration of SEL through an action research project that is then shared with all TCs in the program via a poster session.

The SEL preservice teacher education program was initiated by Shelley Hymel and Kimberly Schonert-Reichl, two professors in the UBC Faculty of Education who received support from the Edith Lando Charitable Foundation to develop the program, SEL courses, and create an SEL resource library. This program was initially inspired, in part, via a graduate course on SEL with a yearlong practicum that began in 2006. The SEL graduate course created excitement, interest, and visibility in SEL among faculty and students in the UBC Faculty of Education. The SEL resource library includes many popular SEL programs (e.g., Second Step, PATHS, RULER, MindUP, Tribes), books, and other SEL resources. The library has grown and has become a popular and invaluable resource for TCs in the SEL cohort and students in the larger teacher education to use when creating their lesson plans for their student teaching.

To our knowledge, UBC was the first teacher education program in North American with an SEL focus. The larger educational policy context in British Columbia played a critical role for the buy-in and implementation for the program at UBC. Indeed, the effort was catalyzed, in part, by the designation of "human and social development" as a core goal of the British Columbia education system in its Vision for Student Success (British Columbia Ministry of Education, n.d.), as well as the identification of the promotion of students' personal and social competencies as a central component of the K–12 curriculum in British Columbia.

Why Preservice SEL Education?

A common theme has emerged across educational contexts: Supporting the social and emotional competencies of our students is imperative for their development and learning (e.g., Durlak et al., 2011; Humphrey, 2013; Jones & Kahn, 2017; Mahoney et al., 2021; Sklad et al., 2012; Taylor et al., 2017; Wiglesworth et al., 2016). One strategy to achieve this goal is to integrate SEL into preservice education, as illustrated by the program at UBC. Because teachers are the engines that drive SEL programs and practices in schools (Schonert-Reichl, 2017), there is a growing expectation that new teachers will know how to implement SEL effectively. In turn, there is growing attention to the importance of teachers' own social and emotional skills as foundational for them to be able to support their students effectively, bridge cultural gaps to promote equity, and buffer the impacts of chronic stress brought on by teaching.

One major problem in teacher education is that programs vary widely in the extent to which they teach SEL (Shriver & Weissberg, 2020; Stevenson & Markowitz,

2019). In turn, we need programs to increase their focus on SEL and prepare SEL-Ready teachers. We address this thorny problem in this chapter in several ways. First, we outline the foundational skills and knowledge that preservice teachers need to become SEL-Ready teachers who implement SEL effectively. In doing so, we call attention to the reality that effective SEL needs to be culturally responsive. Next, we provide a framework for teacher education programs to support preservice teachers' acquisition of the skills and knowledge to promote high-quality SEL. We close with recommendations for action by programs eager to integrate SEL into teacher preparation. Teacher preparation programs have the potential to help TCs develop their own SEL skills and provide formalized training in SEL implementation, creating a ripple effect that leads to widespread high-quality SEL implementation.

Teacher SEL Needs to Come First

Extensive research indicates that teaching is one of the most stressful professions, and the proportion of teachers reporting chronic job stress is on the rise (Diliberti et al., 2021; Kyriacou, 2011). Chronic job stress is often cited as a reason why teachers choose to leave the field prematurely and has been linked to negative health outcomes (Montgomery & Rupp, 2005; Ingersoll, 2001; Katz et al., 2016). Prior to the COVID-19 pandemic, it was estimated that 30–50% of teachers leave the profession within the first 5 years of beginning their careers—a phenomenon known as *early career attrition* (Gray & Taei, 2015; Ingersoll & Strong, 2011). Unfortunately, the COVID-19 pandemic has exacerbated levels of teacher stress and burnout, while also depleting teacher morale (Diliberti et al., 2021). Results from studies have shown that regardless of years of teaching experience, a growing number of teachers are more likely to leave the profession now than prior to the onset of the pandemic (Fullard, 2021; Gadermann et al., 2021). This is alarming given that attrition costs the United States up to $7 billion a year, with teacher turnover disproportionately occurring more frequently in high-poverty schools with a high percentage of minority students (Greenberg, Brown, & Abenavoli, 2016; Carver-Thomas & Darling-Hammond, 2019).

Fortunately, a growing body of research has shown that teachers' own social and emotional skills can support their well-being, buffer the impact of the stress of teaching (Jennings & Greenberg, 2009; Katz et al., 2018), and enable them to better support their students. For example, studies indicate that using SEL practices can strengthen the quality of student–teacher interactions (Abry et al., 2013), the closeness of student–teacher relationships (Baroody et al., 2013), and is positively related to teacher efficacy (Rimm-Kaufman & Sawyer, 2004).

As we look toward the future of education, scaling up SEL in schools and districts depends on the skills of educators to drive this work. Teachers who have developed strong social and emotional skills and have a deep knowledge of SEL are likely to recognize the importance of SEL and be better prepared to lead the implementation of SEL programs, policies, and practices in their schools (Jones et al., 2013). We acknowledge that there are many different pathways into the teaching profession. As of 2015–2016, while 82% of teachers came in through university programs, about 18% of public school teachers entered teaching through an alternative route to certification program (National Council on Teacher Quality, 2015). There are other approaches to preservice training as well (e.g., Teach for America, New York City Teaching Fellows; Devier, 2019). In this chapter, we focus attention on university-based preservice teacher education programs, but many of the key ideas apply to other programs designed to support teachers before they enter the teaching workforce. Any teacher preparation program—within or outside of a university program—can cultivate these skills in teachers before they enter the classroom, helping them to "hit the ground running," and make SEL the foundation of their teaching.

Current Trends in Preservice Teacher Education and SEL

Until recently, the field had little information about the prevalence of SEL in preservice education. We do know that there is neither consistent nor thorough coverage of SEL and students' mental health and behavior problems in schools in preservice teacher education. We also know that students leaving teacher education programs vary in the degree to which they feel prepared to become teachers. There are a few areas where these needs appear to be the greatest. For instance, both first-year teachers and experienced teachers report inadequate training in their teacher education programs to identify and management mental health concerns of their students (Koller et al., 2004). A national study of educators showed that teachers (especially first-year teachers) feel inadequately prepared for classroom management and identify professional development in classroom management as a high priority (Coalition for Psychology in Schools and Education, 2006). Both of these areas—student mental health and classroom management—can be enhanced with more preparation in SEL.

In order to provide more comprehensive data regarding the degree to which SEL is included in teacher preservice education, Schonert-Reichl et al. (2017) scanned SEL courses in teacher preparation programs across the United States. This scan was the first, and only (as of the date of this publication), comprehensive scan of SEL content in preservice teacher education programs that has been conducted. The scan involved a detailed content analysis of 3,916 required courses in teacher preparation programs in 304 colleges of education in the United States (representing 30% of all U.S. colleges). Schonert-Reichl et al. found that few teacher education programs included content that explicitly addressed five core SEL competencies identified by the Collaborative for Academic, Social, and Emotional Learning (CASEL). These competencies include self-awareness, self-management, social awareness, relationship skills, and responsible decision making (CASEL, 2013, 2015). Specifically, 13% of the programs evaluated had at least one course that included information on relationship skills, 7% for responsible decision making, 6% for self-management, 2% for social awareness, and approximately 1% for self-awareness. Overall, 63% of the course descriptions analyzed did not address any of the five social and emotional competencies identified by CASEL. Courses most likely to have SEL content included Curriculum, Instruction, and Methods; Foundations; Psychology; and Special Education. The findings of this study reveal that despite the demands for teachers to develop social and emotional skills, colleges and universities are not providing the comprehensive coursework needed for teachers to fully develop these competencies.

The review by Schonert-Reichl et al. (2017) also included the current status of the degree to which states had SEL standards integrated into the teacher certification requirements. They found that only six states had comprehensive standards including all areas of SEL. The most frequently addressed area in the state standards for teacher SEL was responsible decision making, followed by social awareness and relationship skills. The least found areas were self-awareness and self-management. Many teacher preparation programs currently have no established curricula, guidelines, or "best practices" for their instructors to disseminate knowledge of SEL to preservice teachers, either to implement SEL at schools or to develop their skills in promoting SEL for their own well-being. While it is positive that most states have at least some coverage of SEL areas in their teacher certification standards, how colleges and universities are interpreting and/or meeting these standards in their preparation programs is not clear.

In summary, while many teacher preparation programs include elements related to cultivating SEL in their courses, such as building meaningful relationships with students and creating warm and welcoming classrooms, the prevalence of such content was surprisingly low. Plus, more than three out of five courses reviewed contained no content about SEL at all, suggesting that efforts to bring whole-child development approaches into schools are likely thwarted from the start.

Further complicating issues, enhancing teacher's knowledge of SEL alone is not enough to promote high-quality SEL in schools. Researchers suggest that it is a combination of teachers' beliefs and values, personal social and emotional competence, and pedagogical skills that influence SEL implementation (Jones & Bouffard, 2012), as well as school conditions, which of course, are beyond the scope of what teacher preparation programs can control. There has yet to be a thorough study to examine whether the type of skills being taught are adequately preparing TCs to promote SEL in schools. Thus, the question remains: *What exactly are the essential social and emotional skills and knowledge that teachers need as they begin their careers?* Within the following section we have drawn on the literature related to SEL prominent theories from the fields of educational and developmental psychology, as well our collective experiences as educators to explore this question.

Cultivating SEL-Ready Teachers

It has been argued that TCs who are exposed to SEL during their training programs may be better equipped to teach social and emotional skills to students, as well as have a greater capacity to establish and maintain the types of caring and supportive learning environments in which students' social, emotional, and academic development can thrive (Katz et al., 2020; Schonert-Reichl, 2017). We posit that the SEL-Ready teacher needs the following skills and knowledge to support student SEL and development: (1) a deep understanding of social and emotional development; (2) their own social and emotional skills; (3) ability to promote positive classroom and school climates; (4) wide knowledge of SEL frameworks, programs, and pedagogy; and (5) strategies for assessment and continuous improvement to monitor SEL development. Each of these areas is described below.

A Deep Understanding of Social and Emotional Development

Human development is both social and emotional in nature (Immordino-Yang & Damasio, 2007) and is shaped by the environments and contexts that an individual experiences throughout a lifetime (Pianta, 1997; Wertsch, 1985). Classroom and school environments play a critical role in shaping their developmental trajectories (Hamre & Pianta, 2010), and research has for decades shown that children can thrive when their school environments provide them with experiences that help them feel connected, safe, and secure (Jones & Kahn, 2017). Educators who understand the development of children and youth are better equipped to provide learning experiences for students that support student outcomes (Hamre & Pianta, 2006; Rimm-Kaufman & Hamre, 2010).

Understanding of Cultural Diversity

Cultural identity plays a critically important role in the social and emotional well-being of students, especially marginalized and historically underserved students (e.g., Alim & Paris, 2017; Brittian-Loyd & Williams, 2017; Gee et al., 2019; Jagers et al., 2019). The development and expression of social and emotional skills (for both teachers and students) are affected by cultural identities such as race, religion, ethnicity, sexual orientation, socioeconomic status, or location (Mahfouz & Anthony-Stevens, 2020) and other factors such as social-historic context, including epistemic beliefs (i.e., about the nature of knowledge) and power dynamics (i.e., groups or individuals that, whether consciously or not, exhibit greater influence or power than others; Apple, 2011; Bang & Medin, 2010).

Thus, an SEL-Ready teacher effectively incorporates culture, adopts a strengths-based lens, and engages in integrating the cultural assumptions that underpin educational practices as a way to recognize and serve all young people.

An SEL-Ready teacher is also involved in critical discussions and reflections of the complex cognitive, political, and social ecologies that result in bias toward students. For example, students from traditionally marginalized groups learn how to navigate social spaces that were not necessarily designed with them in mind. As a result, students who are emerging English learners need to create bridges to understand what is occurring in school—they need to bridge the gap between their home culture and school culture, understand a new idea in a language that is unfamiliar to them, plus understand the new concept that is being taught. An SEL-Ready teacher is aware of these needs and able to address these obstacles. For instance, using texts that match the culture of students in the classroom, can mean less stretching for this student. In that sense, the SEL-Ready teacher supports the academic, social, and emotional development of children and creates a space where all students feel they are valued and belong.

The SEL-Ready teacher brings a strengths-based perspective to supporting students by focusing on the cultural and personal assets of students and their families, then leveraging those strengths toward new roles and skills in the schools. For instance, a teacher could be working with a child who has endured poverty and identify ways that the child shows persistence and resilience. The teacher may point that persistence out to the child and identify ways to support the growth of that persistence in classroom life. In another instance, a teacher working with a recent refugee may notice the way that a middle school student is stepping up and translating for their family, which can translate into strong leadership skills. An SEL-Ready teacher has the knowledge and skills to identify strengths in the families and youth with whom they work and harnesses these to support the students' development and community involvement.

Teachers' Social and Emotional Skills

The demands of teaching require that teachers not only have the ability to support their students' social and emotional development, but also the strategies to manage their own emotions and model these skills with their students. Social and emotional skills serve as a foundation from which a teacher draws in order to foster a safe, caring, and equitable learning environment for all students (Jagers et al., 2019; Markowitz et al., 2018). This process of developing social and emotional skills requires deep self-awareness about their strengths and weaknesses in these areas, as well as a deep understanding of their sociopolitical identity and positionality to help them explore how their implicit biases and stereotypes might impact their teaching. This work enables them to model social and emotional skills more fluidly and regularly. Research has demonstrated that supporting teachers' social and emotional development results in improvements in teachers' own well-being and coping strategies, as well as the quality of their classroom interactions and student engagement (Brown et al., 2010; Jennings et al., 2017).

Ability to Promote a Positive Classroom and School Climate

Establishing and nurturing SEL-supportive learning environments requires promoting a positive climate in schools and classrooms. The quality and characteristics of the learning environments provided to students influence their social, emotional, and academic development (Darling-Hammond et al., 2020; Hamre & Pianta, 2010); thus, it is critical that students are embedded within learning environments in which they feel safe, cared for, and supported as they practice developing social and emotional skills (Sauve & Schonert-Reichl, 2019).

An SEL-Ready teacher uses SEL as a foundation from which to create a sense of community and build equitable and inclusive learning environments that support a diversity of students (Katz et al., 2020; Mahfouz & Anthony-Stevens, 2020) by actively exploring their own beliefs and biases and modeling SEL-promoting behaviors while interacting with students, colleagues, parents, and community members (Mahoney et al., 2021). These behaviors are imperative for reinforcing a diverse, equitable, and inclusive learning environment in which all students experience a sense of belonging, feel valued, and experience caring.

Wide Knowledge of SEL Frameworks, Programs, and Pedagogy

There is a large, ever-expanding body of SEL frameworks, programs, and pedagogy (Schonert-Reichl, 2019), and various online tools are available so that teachers can easily explore these resources. Some examples include the CASEL Program Guide (*https://pg.casel.org*), the "Explore SEL" Project by the EASEL Lab (*http://exploresel.gse.harvard.edu*), and the SEL Resource finder (*www.selresources.com/sel-resources*). An SEL-Ready teacher has a broad and deep understanding of multiple SEL definitions, frameworks, approaches, and programs, as well as knowledge about how to help an educational community identify how SEL promotion might work most effectively in their community. They also understand that SEL is not a stand-alone program but a way of designing classroom and school life such that children and youth are exposed to a culture and a constant flow of experiences that promote their social and emotional development (Katz et al., 2020; Mahoney et al., 2021; Markowitz & Bouffard, 2020).

Strategies for Assessment and Continuous Improvement

To determine if their efforts are having positive impacts on all students, SEL-Ready teachers need skills to effectively and efficiently monitor student participation and growth in SEL. An SEL-Ready teacher knows that the purpose of using assessment is not to label students or develop behavioral compliance plans. Instead, an SEL-Ready teacher views assessment as a tool to measure students' strengths, needs, and areas of growth to inform their teaching practices. Furthermore, an SEL-Ready teacher knows that meaningful assessment invites students to participate in evaluating their own development. This requires teachers and students to define the goals and objectives they have related to the social and emotional development. An SEL-Ready teacher can then utilize formative and summative assessment strategies that can help them monitor the impact of the SEL programming and practices used within their classrooms and schools. This includes using both quantitative and qualitative measures to develop robust continuous improvement plans that involve creating implementation strategies, tracking progress, examining outcome data, and making appropriate adjustments to implementation based on the specific needs of the educational community. These assessment strategies are already taught in many teacher-preparation programs and applied to other content-area learning. Working with students so they see how assessment practices in reading or math apply to SEL implementation and SEL skills will not only help preservice teachers deepen their understanding through inquiry, but it may also push further research and innovation in an area of education that is rapidly developing.

A Framework for Teacher Education Programs

Empowering teachers with skill sets to implement SEL requires weaving knowledge and practice of SEL throughout their preparation programs (see Figure 6.1). Since preparation programs serve a variety of students, who all have very different needs—undergraduates majoring in education, graduate students seeking licensure, or nonmatriculated students seeking professional development—a one-size-fits-all program will not be sufficient. In turn, we suggest that teacher preparation programs wanting to promote deep knowledge of SEL and a wide breadth of pedagogical skills focus on three areas in their program: (1) coursework in SEL with opportunities to practice implementing SEL, (2) personal social and emotional skills development, and (3) programmatic elements that support SEL Promotion. In many programs, these three areas and the content in them overlap across the different contexts (e.g., coursework, practicum experiences) of a teacher preparation program.

Coursework in SEL

Courses that address the components of SEL and give novice teachers the opportunity to learn and practice implementing their new knowledge are critical. We recommend that teacher preparation programs include multiple courses in which preservice teachers learn foundational knowledge in social and emotional development and practice teaching SEL in order to deliver high-quality SEL to students. The suggested content of such courses follows.

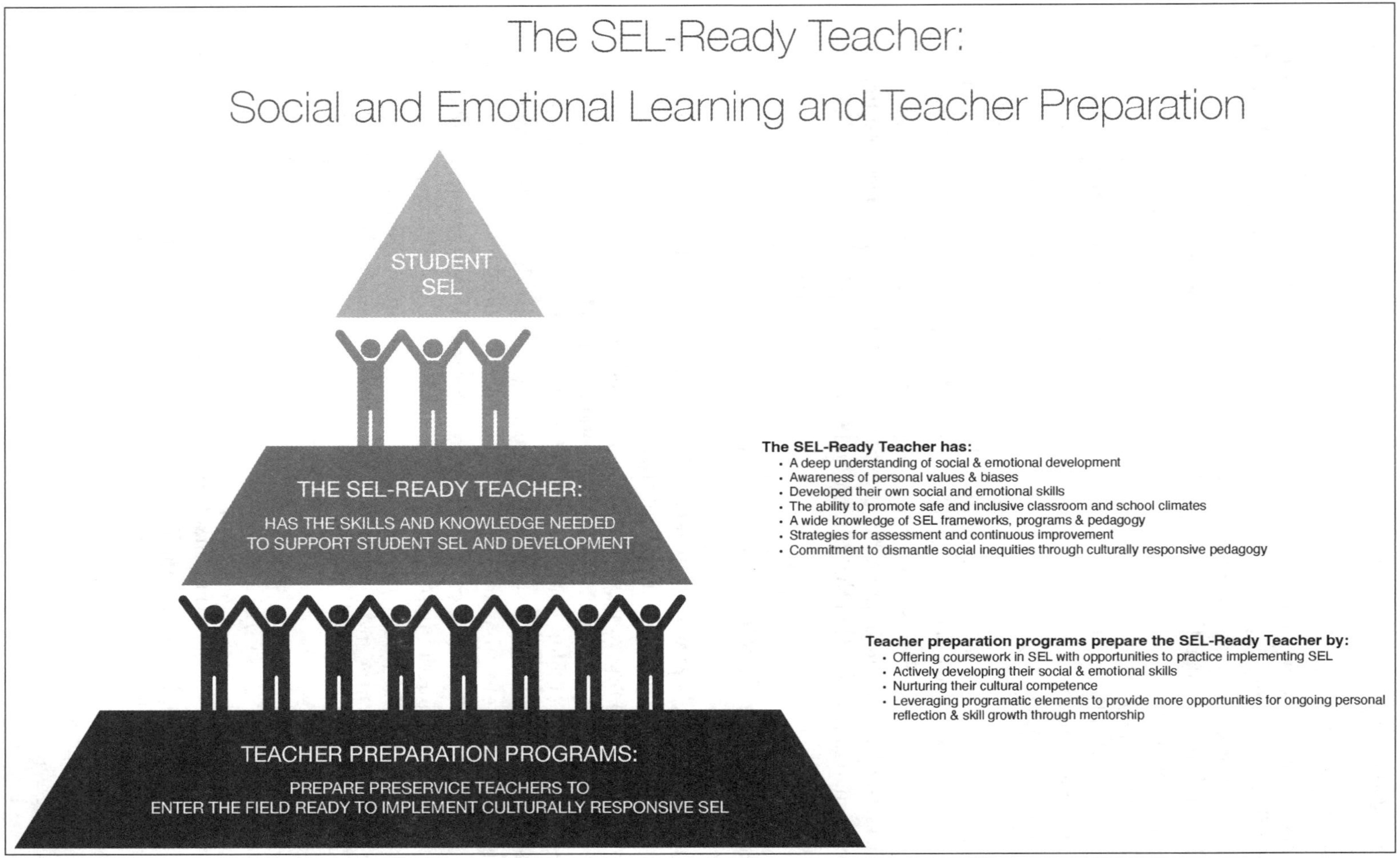

FIGURE 6.1. The SEL-Ready Teacher.

Deep Knowledge of Social and Emotional Development

As outlined earlier, teachers must have a solid understanding of the core of SEL: the intrapersonal experience of emotion, and the interpersonal experience of social relations in society that deeply considers culture as the central framework through which learning occurs. In order to be culturally relevant, SEL curricula in teacher education programs need to call attention to the ways that complex social-historical landscapes influence learning, create spaces for teachers to engage in discussions of deep cultural analysis, and include the development of social political consciousness (Anthony-Stevens et al., 2020; Jagers et al., 2019; Ladson-Billings, 1995, 2014; Mahfouz & Anthony-Stevens, 2020). It is important to note that students' needs are largely based on their developmental stage, and the student–teacher relationship looks different within each of these stages (Eccles & Roeser, 2003). As such, teacher education programs need to highlight the various developmental needs of students based on the grade levels students plan to teach.

Opportunity to Observe and Practice SEL

Students need practice, so they can hone their skills at implementing high-quality SEL. This requires that preservice teachers have opportunities to (1) observe others teaching SEL, (2) implement SEL practices and procedures themselves, (3) learn how to weave SEL-based practices and procedures into the fabric of a classroom or school's culture even if there isn't a universally adopted program, and (4) practice utilizing formative assessment strategies.

Teacher preparation programs need to provide preservice teachers with the time and opportunity to explore the content of multiple evidence-based SEL programs. Within the field, the UBC in Vancouver, British Columbia, serves as an excellent example of how this may be done. Here, all education students have access to an SEL-exclusive library, where they can check out entire SEL curricula and accompanying program materials.

Teacher preparation programs with access to such a library, for example, can provide TCs with the opportunity to practice developing and implementing SEL lessons and units that are SAFE. SAFE lessons include (1) the use of a **S**equenced, step-by-step training approach; (2) an emphasis on **A**ctive forms of learning that require students to practice new skills; (3) specific attention and time given to **F**ocus on skill development; and (4) **E**xplicit definition of the social and emotional skills being promoted. The CASEL Program Guide is also an excellent resource that highlights multiple SAFE programs (*https://pg.casel.org*). Providing preservice teachers with the opportunity to use this guide helps teacher candidates not only develop familiarity with the various SEL programs and practices available but also decipher which of the programs and practices fit the specific subjects or classes they intend to teach.

Practice with Action Research

Teacher preparation programs can integrate SEL-focused action research into their courses so that preservice teachers have the opportunity to understand the needs of their classrooms and schools, and how they can implement SEL. Action research also helps students understand how SEL skills are measured and monitored through formative and summative assessment for the purpose of evaluating teachers' efficacy implementing SEL or showing the influence on students' social and emotional development or understanding the process of the school's SEL implementation. Practice with action research helps teachers develop new skills and knowledge directly related to their classrooms, enables teachers to have agency in how they integrate SEL, and reinforces the connection between the theories and frameworks learned and the actual teaching practice. Engaging students in this process, for example, through the use of reflective journaling, the creation of portfolios, or conducting student-led conferences, can also help the SEL-Ready teacher empower students to take ownership of their own social and emotional development.

Personal Social and Emotional Skills Development

Teachers need ample opportunities to continually develop their own social and emotional skills in order to teach, model, and foster student development (Jennings & Greenberg, 2009; Katz et al., 2020). Helping preservice teachers cultivate their own social and emotional skills and resilience requires (1) providing of safe spaces to identify, reflect, and unpack their own stereotypes, biases, and privilege, so they can become aware of their positionality; (2) guiding them through exploration and strengthening of their own social and emotional skills; and (3) creating a toolkit of strategies to manage their emotions, promote their own well-being, and cultivate culturally responsive practices into their teaching. This requires that preparation programs not only provide preservice teachers with foundational knowledge about the cultivation of adult SEL but also offer opportunities for them to reflect on their cultural competency, practice self-care, and utilize their developing regulatory strategies, so that their personal social and emotional development becomes intertwined with their professional identity. This self-awareness journey can take place in courses, as well as in the context of mentorships with cooperating teachers and university personnel, so that the practice of preventive ways of being starts early on in their careers, creating the potential to increase teacher resilience and reduce burnout and attrition among teachers.

Some university programs are creating these opportunities for self-exploration and growth in creative ways. For example, the University of Colorado Boulder has developed a teacher and SEL specialization that focuses on helping teachers explore their own emotional well-being. They provide courses such as "The Teacher's Social and Emotional Learning" and "Teacher SEL: Programs, Possibilities, and Contexts." Other programs, such as the one at the University of Portland, ask students enrolled in SEL courses to make a "personal resilience plan" after reading Elena Aguilar's (2018) book *Onward: Cultivating Emotional Resilience in Educators.* San Jose State grounds all their preservice education coursework and mentoring in Markowitz and Bouffard's (2020) seven anchor competencies for the development of social, emotional, and cultural competencies. Developing this plan uses myriad formative assessments, such as personal reflection and frequent skill monitoring—activities that enable the students to evaluate their growth over the course of their teaching program.

Programmatic Elements

Teacher preparation programs need to consider broader aspects of their program that could help cultivate SEL-Ready teachers through mentoring relationships, teacher educators well versed in SEL, as well as offering majors, certificates, and area of focus in SEL.

Mentoring Relationships

Teacher education programs can support preservice teachers' SEL skill development by integrating personal and supervisor reflection on SEL skills throughout the program. Faculty and teaching supervisors, as well as the students themselves, have the opportunity to track the acquisition and development of these skills as they progress in their program. For example, university personnel could work with them to develop an individualized growth plan for their own social and emotional development from the start of the program to finishing their teacher preparation. Simulations, role-play activities based on adult transformative learning theories, could also be useful tools to allow students to apply their skills, strategies, and knowledge practically. These activities can be the focus of one or multiple courses and may include the practicum phase of the preservice program.

One example of the integration of social and emotional skill development into the teacher preservice programs to support collaborative assessment between mentors and preservice teachers is the use of the Social–Emotional Dispositions Inventory and the *social and emotional dimensions of teaching and learning* (SEDTL) model developed by Markowitz and colleagues (2018) from San Jose State University. The model has three foci: (1) SEL competencies of teachers; (2) teachers' skills in managing the social–emotional context of the classroom; and (3) teachers' skills in fostering social–emotional competencies of students. Using this model, preservice teachers are assessed on their social and emotional dispositions and skills at the beginning of the school year, midyear, and end of the year. This inventory can then be used to guide the development of SEL practices and effective teaching.

Teacher Educators' Knowledge and Skills in SEL

Having a cadre of teacher educators and classroom supervisors with the necessary SEL knowledge and skills is a necessary prerequisite for incorporating domains of SEL into preservice education. Thus, colleges and faculties of education need to provide professional development for their current faculty in this area and, possibly, hire new personnel with the required expertise in SEL.

An example of this can be found in the UBC teacher education program. First, some of the teacher educators in the UBC program are teachers with knowledge in both the research and practice of SEL, who are invited in from local school districts to teach the SEL courses and to supervise teacher candidates in the SEL preservice cohort. Second, because the UBC Faculty of Education also has an SEL concentration in its MEd and MA in the Human Development, Learning, and Culture Program, teacher candidates are taught coursework by graduates from the SEL concentration.

Majors, Certificates, Specialties, and Areas of Focus

Education departments may want to work with their university and state Departments of Education to create areas of concentration, a certificate in SEL, or a credential that appears on teachers' licenses. Requirements vary by state and university, but acquisition of these types of certificates or credentials offers new teachers the opportunity to share their expertise when entering the field. Providing opportunities for credentials associated with SEL knowledge and skills has the potential to make new teachers more marketable to schools that are making SEL a priority.

Examples of SEL in Teacher Preparation Education Programs

We emphasize that the integration of SEL into any given preservice teacher education program must fit the unique needs of that program. Indeed, it is not a "one-size-fits-all" approach. Rather, it is important that efforts to incorporate SEL into the existing coursework, practices, and procedures be scaled-up according to the unique context of each program. In this section, we highlight some of the ways by which schools of education have integrated SEL to teacher preparation. These include providing (1) SEL-explicit course offerings, (2) SEL specialties or certifications, and (3) SEL integrated at the programmatic level. Each of these approaches is described below, and examples are offered in Tables 6.1 through 6.3.

SEL-Explicit Course Offerings

Many schools are beginning to offer courses to preservice teacher candidates that are explicitly founded upon SEL principles. Various topics are often included in these types of courses, including (but not limited to) SEL and development for children and adults, the neuroscience of teaching and learning, developing a supportive learning environment, SEL for inclusion and equity, and positive classroom management. Frequently offered by a School of Education or School of Psychology, SEL-based courses can be included as part of a teacher candidate's required coursework or offered as an elective option (see Table 6.1 for examples).

SEL Specialties or Certifications

Several schools now offer preservice educators the option to obtain an "add-on" specialty or certification in SEL while concurrently earning their initial teaching licensures. In such cases, students typically complete the regular requirements for the desired degree and teaching licensure, as well as courses or requirements specific to SEL. These types of "add-on" specialties or certifications often result in the newly certified teacher having a specific SEL designation listed on their teaching licensure, in addition to any other acquired endorsements, specialties, or certifications (see Table 6.2 for examples).

TABLE 6.1. Examples of SEL Course Offerings

University and program	Course name(s) and foci
University of Pittsburgh (Pittsburgh, PA) School of Education *Yearlong psychology course offered as part of a dual-degree program for Master of Arts in Teaching (MAT) students*	**Course:** *Attentional Teaching Practices* **Preservice teachers learn to:** • Develop own social and emotional skills to strengthen teaching practices, navigate the psychological dynamics of the classroom, and improve personal psychological competence.
University of Virginia (Charlottesville, VA) School of Education and Human Development *Multiple courses offered to those seeking initial teaching licensure at the undergraduate or graduate level*	**Courses:** *Mindfulness in Health and Human Development; Mindfulness for Teachers; The Trauma-Sensitive Classroom; Teaching Mindfulness in Schools; Social and Emotional Learning* **Preservice teachers learn to:** • Apply mindfulness within schools to support the social, emotional, and academic development of students.
Fort Lewis College (Durango, CO) Teacher Education Department *Course offered to undergraduate and graduate preservice teachers*	**Course:** *Instructional Equality* **Preservice teachers learn to:** • Develop cultural and social competency to support egalitarian and collaborative learning environments.

TABLE 6.2. Examples of SEL Specialties or Certifications

University and program	Specialty or certification
University of Portland (Portland, OR) School of Education *Specialty in SEL that spans three semesters offered to undergraduate preservice teachers or graduate students*	*Specialty in SEL* notated on educators' Oregon Teaching License **Requirements for completion:** • Coursework includes three courses: *Foundations of Social and Emotional Learning in Schools*; *Social–Emotional Learning Programs and Practices*; *Continuous Improvement in SEL Implementation* • Fieldwork integrated into all courses
University of Iowa (Iowa City, IA) College of Education *SEL Track offered to undergraduate and Master of Arts in Teaching (MAT) preservice teachers as part of completion of a Teacher Leader Certificate*	*SEL Teacher Leader Certificate* indicated on Level 1 Educator Certification **Requirements for completion:** • Coursework includes a series of six SEL-intensive workshops • Fieldwork of 10 hours of volunteer work in schools • Requires completion of Level 1 Google Educator Certification
Lehigh University (Bethlehem, PA) College of Education *Certificate focused on the social, emotional, and mental health of PreK–12 students offered to preservice (postbaccalaureate) or inservice teachers (MEd or MA)*	*Certificate in Social, Emotional, and Behavioral Wellness* leading to endorsement on teaching licensure **Requirements for completion:** • Coursework includes four courses (total of 12 credits); students choose from a variety of courses • Fieldwork integrated into several courses

SEL Integrated at the Programmatic Level

A few schools have established SEL as an integral part of their preservice teacher education programs. This means that rather than view SEL as an "add-on" to the traditional coursework and experiences offered by a teacher education program, SEL is weaved into the very fabric of all the program has to offer. As mentioned previously, integrating SEL at the programmatic level into the existing structures, practices, and procedures of any preservice teacher preparation is not a "one-size-fits-all" approach. What works for one preservice teacher preparation program may not work for another; thus, the unique needs specific to each program must be considered. Examples of integrating SEL at a programmatic level may include partnering with local school districts to ensure that teacher candidates are placed in SEL-promoting schools while completing their student teaching, collaboration with local school districts and policy leaders to align teaching standards with current K–12 SEL standards established for their state, providing ongoing instruction in SEL-based topics to the faculty and staff within the preservice teaching program, or explicitly weaving SEL into the content of all courses offered throughout a program (see Table 6.3 for examples).

TABLE 6.3. Examples of SEL Integrated at the Programmatic Level

University and program	Key features of program
University of British Columbia (Vancouver, BC, Canada) Faculty of Education *Postbaccalaureate, preservice teachers have the option to join the "SEL cohort" as they complete courses and seek initial licensure in elementary education*	• "Personal and social competence" is one of the core standards for all K–12 curricula across British Columbia; all teacher candidates across the province receive basic instruction in SEL as part of teacher preparation. • At UBC, preservice elementary teachers can complete their program as part of an "SEL cohort." • Members of the SEL cohort complete the traditional teacher preparation program while considering all topics, instruction, or experiences through an SEL lens. • UBC partners with champion districts and educational organizations to ensure that students in the SEL cohort are offered fieldwork, professional experiences, and student-teaching placements that emphasize SEL **Preservice teachers learn to:** ○ Critically discuss established theories and current educational issues through a social and emotional lens. ○ Integrate SEL-promoting practices and procedures into all aspects of their pedagogy. ○ Develop a deep understanding of SEL programs and practices and how to utilize them in the classroom. • Continuing education in SEL is offered to inservice teachers, counselors, and other school professionals through MA and MEd programs.
San Jose State University (San Jose, CA) College of Education *A 1-year program where prospective K–8 elementary teachers can obtain Multiple Subject Credentials (MSC) combined with a Master of Arts in Education; emphasis is placed on the development of cultural, social, and emotional competence*	• The development of preservice teachers' cultural competence and social and emotional skills underscores all course offerings, fieldwork, and experiences provided through this program. • SJSU partners with selected districts to ensure that teacher candidates experience a student teaching placement that allows them to intentionally practice developing cultural competence and social and emotional skills. **Preservice teachers learn to:** ○ Develop a deep understanding of their own cultural, social, and emotional biases, competence, and capacity. ○ Utilize culturally responsive and SEL-promoting teaching strategies that nurture equitable, culturally responsive, safe, and caring learning environments. ○ Integrate culturally responsive and SEL-promotive practices into all pedagogy/curricula. • SJSU partners with the Center for Teaching and Reaching the Whole Child (CTRWC; *http://crtwc.org*) to provide ongoing, in-depth training in cultural, social, and emotional competence to inservice teachers and graduates, co-operating teachers, and educators associated with the program.

Conclusion

Teachers' own social and emotional competence (SEC) and their role in promoting SEL is receiving increased attention in education. This recognition highlights the need for teachers to be well versed in SEL implementation. SEL used well can begin to address the needs of students and promote the safe, welcoming, inclusive schools we strive to create. This requires extensive training, practice, and forethought by educators. Preservice teachers who have substantial training in SEL in their teacher education programs and have been guided through the cultivation of their own SECs will be better equipped to implement meaningful SEL in schools. Teacher education programs are well positioned to offer preservice teachers valuable knowledge of how to implement meaningful, culturally responsive SEL at the classroom and school level.

How do we turn this into action? We provide the following recommendations for practitioners and policymakers with the goal of advancing SEL in teacher preparation programs, with the long-term goal of creating welcoming equitable SEL focused schools:

1. Include SEL coursework in teacher preparation programs.
2. Prepare instructors in preparation programs to implement SEL by having them practice teaching lessons and designing units that build SEL skills over time.
3. Create program policies and guidelines that ensure teachers in preparation programs have the necessary support and time needed through mentorship and guidance to cultivate, reflect on, and practice their social and emotional skills.
4. Identifying the available faculty strengths and community resources that can be leveraged to enhance preservice teachers' experience. Then, engage in a strategic integration that can result in features such as an SEL library, SEL-enriched practicum experiences, or other strategies mentioned earlier.
5. Create state-level standards for teacher preparation programs that ensure the programs include specific education and practice in SEL during training programs.

With these recommendations in mind, teacher preparation programs can approach the work of instilling these skills in a variety of ways, as outlined by the myriad exemplary approaches discussed in this chapter. The ripple effect of teaching teachers about SEL and supporting them as they cultivate their own social and emotional skills in their preservice programs will have far-reaching effects in education.

DISCUSSION QUESTIONS

1. Reflect on a few early career teachers with whom you work. What knowledge of SEL did they have when they first started teaching? How did that prior knowledge help or hinder their approach to SEL in their classrooms?
2. In U.S. public schools, roughly 80% of teachers are White and 51% of students are students of color, so teachers need to be prepared to teach students who are different from them (Rimm-Kaufman & Thomas, 2021). SEL-Ready teachers need to have engaged in self-reflective work, so that they are prepared to counteract implicit bias and exercise strengths-based approaches. What are some successful practices that you have seen with preservice or inservice teachers that help teachers develop cultural competency, approach challenging situations using a strengths-based approach, and interrupt systemic racism? Were those practices successful or not? Do you think some people have more difficulty developing these skills than others? What conditions need to be present in the school or classroom to make those practices successful?
3. Take some time to read Tables 6.1, 6.2, and 6.3, which show varied SEL integration into teacher education programs ranging from SEL courses to SEL specialties and certifications, to full SEL program integration. Think about a teacher education program that is familiar to you. Identify where this teacher program fits in relation to these three categories (i.e., courses, specialties/certifications, or full integration). What changes would need to occur to take the teacher education program to the next higher level in SEL integration?
4. Reflect on the classroom of an SEL-Ready teacher. What would it look like? Sound like? Feel like? What would the students experience in this classroom?

REFERENCES

Abry, T., Rimm-Kaufman, S. E., Larsen, R. A., & Brewer, A. J. (2013). The influence of fidelity of implementation on teacher–student interaction quality in the context of a randomized controlled trial of the Responsive Classroom approach. *Journal of School Psychology, 51*(4), 437–453.

Aguilar, E. (2018). *Onward: Cultivating emotional resilience in educators*. Wiley.

Alim, H. S., & Paris, D. (2017). What is culturally sustaining pedagogy and why does it matter? In D. Paris & H. S. Alim (Eds.), *Culturally sustaining pedagogies: Teaching and learning for justice in a changing world* (pp. 1–21). Teachers College Press.

Anthony-Stevens, V., Mahfouz, J., & Bisbee, Y. (2020). Indigenous teacher education is nation building: Reflections of capacity building and capacity strengthening in Idaho. *Journal of School Leadership, 30*(6), 541–564.

Apple, M. W. (2011). *Education and power*. Routledge.

Bang, M., & Medin, D. (2010). Cultural processes in science education: Supporting the navigation of multiple epistemologies. *Science Education, 94*(6), 1008–1026.

Baroody, A. E., Rimm-Kaufman, S. E., Larsen, R. A., & Curby, T. W. (2013). The link between Responsive Classroom training and student–teacher relationship quality in the fifth grade: A study of fidelity of implementation. *School Psychology Review, 43*(1), 69–85.

British Columbia Ministry of Education. (n.d.). Vision for student success. Retrieved from *www2.gov.bc.ca/gov/content/education-training/k-12/administration/program-management/vision-for-student-success.*

Brittian-Loyd, A., & Williams, B. V. (2017). The potential for youth programs to promote African American youth's development of ethnic and racial identity. *Child Development Perspectives, 11*(1), 29–38.

Brown, J. L., Jones, S. M., LaRusso, M. D., & Aber, J. L. (2010). Improving classroom quality: Teacher influences and experimental impacts of the 4Rs program. *Journal of Educational Psychology, 102*(1), 153–167.

Carver-Thomas, D., & Darling-Hammond, L. (2019). The trouble with teacher turnover: How teacher attrition affects students and schools. *Education Policy Analysis Archives, 27,* Article 36.

CASEL. (2013). Effective social and emotional learning programs: Preschool and elementary school edition. Retrieved from *https://eric.ed.gov/?id=ed581699.*

CASEL. (2015). Effective social and emotional learning programs: Middle and high school edition. Retrieved from *https://static1.squarespace.com/static/5532b947e4b0edee99477d27/t/5d0948b6a78e0100015f652f/1560889545559/casel+secondary+guide+2015.pdf.*

Coalition for Psychology in Schools and Education. (2006). *Report on the teacher needs survey.* American Psychological Association.

Darling-Hammond, L., Flook, L., Cook-Harvey, C., Barron, B., & Osher, D. (2020). Implications for educational practice of the science of learning and development. *Applied Developmental Science, 24*(2), 97–140.

Devier, B. H. (2019). Teacher shortage and alternative licensure solutions for technical educators. *Journal of Technology Studies, 45*(2), 48–49.

Diliberti, M. K., Schwartz, H. L., & Grant, D. (2021). *Stress topped the reasons why public school teachers quit, even before COVID-19.* RAND Corporation.

Durlak, J. A., Weissberg, R. P., Dymnicki, A. B., Taylor, R. D., & Schellinger, K. B. (2011). The impact of enhancing students' social and emotional learning: A meta-analysis of school-based universal interventions. *Child Development, 82*(1), 405–432.

Eccles, J. S., & Roeser, R. W. (2003). Schools as developmental contexts. In G. R. Adams & M. D. Berzonsky (Eds.), *Blackwell handbook of adolescence* (pp. 129–148). Blackwell.

Fullard, J. (2021). *Teacher supply and COVID-19.* Education Policy Institute, University of Essex.

Gadermann, A. M., Warren, M. T., Gagné, M., Thomson, K. C., Schonert-Reichl, K. A., Guhn, M., . . . Oberle, E. (2021). *The impact of the COVID-19 pandemic on teacher well-being in British Columbia.* Human Early Learning Partnership.

Gee, G. C., Hing, A., Mohammed, S., Tabor, D. C., & Williams, D. R. (2019). Racism and the life course: Taking time seriously. *American Journal of Public Health, 109*(Suppl. 1), S43–S47.

Gray, L., & Taie, S. (2015). *Public school teacher attrition and mobility in the first five years: Results from the first through fifth waves of the 2007–08 Beginning Teacher Longitudinal*

Study (NCES 2015-337). U.S. Department of Education, National Center for Education Statistics.

Greenberg, M. T., Brown, J. L., & Abenavoli, R. M. (2016). *Teacher stress and health effects on teachers, students, and schools.* Edna Bennett Pierce Prevention Research Center, Pennsylvania State University.

Hamre, B. K., & Pianta, R. C. (2006). Student–teacher relationship. In G. G. Bear & K. M. Minke (Eds.), *Children's Needs III: Development, prevention, and intervention* (pp. 59–72). National Association of School Psychologists.

Hamre, B. K., & Pianta, R. C. (2010). Classroom environments and developmental processes: Conceptualization and measurement. In J. L. Meece & J. S. Eccles (Eds.), *Handbook of research on schools, schooling, and human development* (pp. 43–59). Routledge.

Humphrey, N. (2013). *Social and emotional learning: A critical appraisal.* SAGE.

Immordino-Yang, M. H., & Damasio, A. (2007). We feel, therefore we learn: The relevance of affective and social neuroscience to education. *Mind, Brain, and Education, 1*(1), 3–10.

Ingersoll, R. M. (2001). Teacher turnover and teacher shortages: An organizational analysis. *American Educational Research Journal, 38*(3), 499–534.

Ingersoll, R. M., & Strong, M. (2011). The impact of induction and mentoring programs for beginning teachers: A critical review of the research. *Review of Educational Research, 81*(2), 201–233.

Jagers, R. J., Rivas-Drake, D., & Williams, B. (2019). Transformative social and emotional learning (SEL): Toward SEL in service of educational equity and excellence. *Educational Psychologist, 54*(3), 162–184.

Jennings, P. A., Brown, J. L., Frank, J. L., Doyle, S., Oh, Y., Davis, R., . . . Greenberg, M. T. (2017). Impacts of the CARE for Teachers program on teachers' social and emotional competence and classroom interactions. *Journal of Educational Psychology, 109*(7), 1010–1028.

Jennings, P. A., & Greenberg, M. T. (2009). The prosocial classroom: Teacher social and emotional competence in relation to student and classroom outcomes. *Review of Educational Research, 79*(1), 491–525.

Jones, S. M., & Bouffard, S. M. (2012). Social and emotional learning in schools: From programs to strategies. *Society for Research on Child Development Social Policy Report, 26*(4), 1–33.

Jones, S. M., Bouffard, S. M., & Weissbourd, R. (2013). Educators' social and emotional skills vital to learning. *Phi Delta Kappan, 94*(8), 62–65.

Jones, S. M., & Kahn, J. (2017). *The evidence base for how we learn: Supporting students' social, emotional, and academic development. Consensus statements of evidence from the council of distinguished scientists.* Aspen Institute.

Katz, D. A., Greenberg, M. T., Jennings, P. A., & Cousino, L. (2016). Associations between the awakening responses of salivary a-amylase and cortisol with self-report indicators of health and wellbeing among educators. *Teaching and Teacher Education, 54*, 98–106.

Katz, D. A., Harris, A., Abenavoli, R., Greenberg, M. T., & Jennings, P. A. (2018). Educators' emotion regulation strategies and their physiological indicators of chronic stress over 1 year. *Stress and Health, 34*(2), 278–285.

Katz, D., Mahfouz, J., & Romas, S. (2020). Creating a foundation of well-being for teachers and students starts with SEL curriculum in teacher education programs. *Northwest Journal of Teacher Education, 15*(2), Article 5.

Koller, J. R., Osterlind, S. J., Paris, K., & Weston, K. J. (2004). Differences between novice and expert teachers' undergraduate preparation and ratings of importance in the area of children's mental health. *International Journal of Mental Health Promotion, 6*, 40–45.

Kyriacou, C. (2011). Teacher stress: From prevalence to resilience. In J. Langan-Fox & C. L. Cooper (Eds.), *Handbook of stress in the occupations* (pp. 161–176). Edward Elgar.

Ladson-Billings, G. (1995). Toward a theory of culturally relevant pedagogy. *American Educational Research Journal, 32*(3), 465–491.

Ladson-Billings, G. (2014). Culturally relevant pedagogy 2.0: a.k.a. the remix. *Harvard Educational Review, 84*(1), 74–84.

Mahfouz, J., & Anthony-Stevens, V. (2020). Why trouble SEL?: The need for cultural relevance in SEL. *Bank Street Occasional Paper Series, 43*, 1–14.

Mahoney, J. L., Weissberg, R. P., Greenberg, M. T., Dusenbury, L., Jagers, R. J., Niemi, K., . . . Yoder, N. (2021). Systemic social and emotional learning: Promoting educational success for all preschool to high school students. *American Psychologist, 76*(7), 1128–1142.

Markowitz, N., & Bouffard, S. (2020). *Teaching with a social, emotional, and cultural lens: A framework for educators and teacher educators*. Harvard Education Press.

Markowitz, N., Thowdis, W., & Gallagher, M. (2018). Sowing seeds of SEL. *Learning Professional, 39*(4), 30–34.

Montgomery, C., & Rupp, A. A. (2005). A meta-analysis for exploring the diverse causes and effects of stress in teachers. *Canadian Journal of Education, 28*(3), 458–486.

National Council on Teacher Quality. (2015). State Policy Yearbook Database: 2015. Retrieved February 13, 2018, from *www.nctq.org/yearbook/home*.

Pianta, R. C. (1997). Adult–child relationship processes and early schooling. *Early Education and Development, 8*(1), 11–26.

Rimm-Kaufman, S. E., & Hamre, B. K. (2010). The role of psychological and developmental science in efforts to improve teacher quality. *Teachers College Record, 112*(12), 2988–3023.

Rimm-Kaufman, S. E., & Sawyer, B. E. (2004). Primary-grade teachers' self-efficacy beliefs, attitudes toward teaching, and discipline and teaching practice priorities in relation to the "Responsive Classroom" approach. *Elementary School Journal, 104*(4), 321–341.

Rimm-Kaufman, S. E., & Thomas, K. (2021). How White middle class teachers can apply psychology to teach students who are different from them. Retrieved from *https://apadiv15.org/education-practice-briefs*.

Sauve, J. A., & Schonert-Reichl, K. A. (2019). Creating caring classroom and school communities: Lessons learned from social and emotional learning programs and practices. In J. Fredericks, A. L. Reschly, & S. L. Christenson (Eds.), *Handbook of student engagement interventions: Working with disengaged youth* (pp. 279–295). Elsevier.

Schonert-Reichl, K. A. (2017). Social and emotional learning and teachers. *The Future of Children, 27*(1), 137–155.

Schonert-Reichl, K. A. (2019). Advancements in the landscape of social and emotional learning and emerging topics on the horizon. *Educational Psychologist, 54*(3), 222–232.

Schonert-Reichl, K. A., Kitil, M. J., & Hanson-Peterson, J. (2017). *To reach the students, teach the teachers: A national scan of teacher preparation and social & emotional learning. A report prepared for CASEL*. Collaborative for Academic, Social, and Emotional Learning.

Shriver, T. P., & Weissberg, R. P. (2020). A response to constructive criticism of social and emotional learning. *Phi Delta Kappan, 101*(7), 52–57.

Sklad, M., Diekstra, R., Ritter, M. D., Ben, J., & Gravesteijn, C. (2012). Effectiveness of school-based universal social, emotional, and behavioral programs: Do they enhance students' development in the area of skill, behavior, and adjustment? *Psychology in the Schools, 49*(9), 892–909.

Stevenson, H., & Markowitz, N. L. (2019). Introduction: Social and emotional learning and culturally responsive and sustaining teaching practices. *Teacher Education Quarterly, 46*(4), 3+.

Taylor, R. D., Oberle, E., Durlak, J. A., & Weissberg, R. P. (2017). Promoting positive youth development through school-based social and emotional learning interventions: A meta-analysis of follow-up effects. *Child Development, 88*(4), 1156–1171.

Wertsch, J. V. (1985). *Vygotsky and the social formation of mind.* Harvard University Press.

Wiglesworth, M., Lendrum, A., Oldfield, J., Scott, A., ten Bokkel, I., Tate, K., & Emery, C. (2016). The impact of trial stage, developer involvement and international transferability on universal social and emotional learning programme outcomes: A meta-analysis. *Cambridge Journal of Education, 46*, 347–376.

Chapter 7

Creating Spaces for Adult Learning and Professional Development

SEL Skills for Facilitating Racial Equity Discussions

Shannon B. Wanless, Caitlin F. Spear, Jocelyn V. Artinger, and Jennifer O. Briggs

A superintendent at a medium-size, urban school district created a task force to map out a 5-year plan for increasing racial equity. We call this district "Westridge School District" and use it in this chapter to represent many real situations happening throughout the United States. As a result of the task force's recommendations, the district created an Office of Racial Equity (ORE) with two full-time staff members who planned a mandatory, districtwide, 3-day racial equity retreat for the week before the new school year. This retreat was to be facilitated by ORE staff members, one a White woman (who had worked elsewhere in the district for 10 years), and one Black woman (who had been hired 2 years earlier as part of a previous diversity initiative).

While planning, they met with administrators and sent an anonymous questionnaire to staff members to learn about their concerns and experiences. District staff members note that community members were raising questions about racial equity that they were not prepared to answer. Most had never discussed equity in their teacher preparation or professional development. Despite this need for more adult learning, many were resistant to the mandatory retreat. They were frustrated by the lack of action in previous initiatives, afraid to talk about race with colleagues, or knew that conversations about racial equity could often lead to conflict.

The retreat began on Day 1 with a whole-group session, then moved to breakout sessions. Later days began in racial affinity groups, and then the retreat closed with a

> discussion to generate action steps. In some cases, both women facilitated at the same time, and in others, they divided up or brought in guest speakers. They debriefed the retreat with participants, each other, and the superintendent. They reflected and considered how authentic conversations felt, how the group responded when something harmful was said, and whether or not group trust was present. The facilitators followed up 3 weeks later with a voluntary virtual session after school that continued monthly.

Calls for professional development about racial equity have increased as more businesses, schools, and organizations prioritize disrupting racial injustice (Beard et al., 2021; Devine & Ash, 2022). This is due, in part, to broader awareness of racial disparities brought to light during a global pandemic and to technological advances that make news about racism more visible. These patterns of racial inequity are not new, but what is new, perhaps, is increasing acknowledgment by White educational leaders, and growing interest in racial equity professional development as schools heed old calls to grapple with racism, and to state that *Black Lives Matter in Schools*. Many educators see that quality teaching cannot be color-evasive (a less ableist term for color-blind). Further, educators realize that bias is present in most classrooms and our schools continue to use instruction that reinforces historical inaccuracies. Much resistance remains and even acknowledging historically accurate information about racism is difficult to do. When leading racial equity professional development, facilitator social–emotional skills can disarm educator resistance and lead to open, honest, effective discussions.

Professional development includes a wide range of adult learning opportunities that vary in size, and that may be voluntary or mandatory, in-person or virtual, and may occur once or repeatedly and for different lengths of time. Facilitators are the people who design and conduct the professional development sessions. There may or may not be the formal leader (e.g., principal or school director) in the room, such as our example of facilitators at Westridge School District who do not have formal positions of authority in the district but are leading the sessions. Although there are different considerations for facilitating sessions that vary in all these ways, this chapter necessarily describes the social–emotional skills that facilitators use to facilitate across a range of professional development contexts. In fact, facilitators may engage in many different contexts within one event, and their social–emotional skills will help them navigate those shifts and nuances.

Despite increasing awareness and calls for racial equity professional development, recent reviews of research on racial equity training indicate mixed outcomes (e.g., Calanchini et al., 2021; Carter et al., 2020; Chang et al., 2019; Devine & Ash, 2022; Dobbin & Kalev, 2016; Paluck et al., 2021). In the worst cases, preexisting stereotypes are reinforced, and participants feel they are not treated fairly (Anand & Winters, 2008; Dobbin & Kalev, 2016, 2018). Given the increasing demand for racial equity professional development, and the critical need for shifts in educational systems, there is a need to focus on factors that make racial equity sessions effective, including an underexamined factor: facilitator social–emotional skills (brown, 2021; Elliott, 2021; Ieva et al., 2021). We propose that social and emotional learning (SEL) plays an important role in helping facilitators to be effective when leading discussions with adults about how to center racial equity in their educational practice.

We use the word *facilitator* to represent a broad range of formal roles (e.g., professor, professional development coach, principal/director, equity consultant) that are all represented by the authors of this chapter. It is important to note, however, that true social change calls for every person to see themselves as a racial equity facilitator across their own spheres of influence (Tatum, 2017), such as with their colleagues, neighbors, political representatives, and at the family dinner table. The SEL considerations in this chapter can support formal facilitators and might also nudge readers to think about their roles as informal "facilitators," too.

One of the primary responsibilities of racial equity facilitators is to "create the conditions for learning" (King, 2015) so participants can (1) unlearn a lifetime of living in a culture that does not value racial equity, (2) experience what it feels like to be in collective struggle to create an equitable space together, and (3) develop the skills to bring a lifelong, daily racial equity practice into their own personal and professional lives. To do this, we propose that facilitators need to attend to the social–emotional dynamics of the group space that they are creating, draw on their own social–emotional skills, and help participants focus on their own social–emotional development to sustain a lifelong racial equity commitment. As we describe the roles of SEL in racial equity facilitation, we draw from previous research and scholarship, the wisdom of racial equity facilitators from which we have learned, and experiences we have had in this role, most recently as part of the 3Rs Initiative (Reading, Racial Equity, Relationships) in Pittsburgh, PA.

What Is SEL?

As we grapple with the role of SEL in this context, it is necessary to describe how we are thinking about SEL given that the field is currently undergoing rapid critiques and reconceptualizations. The definition that has been most present in educational spaces in recent decades is from the Collaborative for Academic, Social, and Emotional Learning (CASEL) and includes self-awareness, self-management, social awareness, relationship skills, and responsible decision making, and its equity-based revisions called "Transformative SEL" (Jagers et al., 2019; Rivas-Drake et al., 2021). There is also an effort to expand intra- and interpersonal conceptualizations of SEL to include a systems perspective (e.g., Mahoney et al., 2020). This awareness of the way that systems contribute to or disrupt SEL is parallel to a similar growing awareness of the way that systems contribute to or disrupt racial equity.

Related to broader societal reckonings with the ways in which racial inequity perpetuates, a growing group of scholars is calling for more equity-focused changes in the conceptualization of SEL. These critiques of SEL inform our thinking and include a call for more awareness of context and history, less focus on individuals' skills as the primary driver of outcomes, and more intentionality to break free of harmful cultural norms, such as rigidity and conflict avoidance, and honor identities and groups that have been marginalized (Duchesneau, 2020; Higheagle Strong & McMain, 2020; Hoffman, 2009; Mahfouz & Anthony-Stevens, 2020; Simmons et al., 2021). Most are recommending changes to current SEL conceptualizations, but some suggest starting an entirely new field (e.g., "Humanization"; Camangian & Cariaga, 2021; Drake & Oglesby, 2020). In this chapter, we acknowledge the pressing need for further critique of current conceptualizations of SEL and situate the current discussion in CASEL's SEL framework.

Using Facilitator Social–Emotional Skills

There is no single way to facilitate a racial equity discussion. Styles and strategies vary across facilitators, and even within facilitators as they get to know each group of participants and decide how to be most responsive (Adams, 2016). Across all that variability, however, facilitators consistently draw on their SEL skills during professional development for teachers. This idea builds on research that has found that teacher SEL skills are important for creating productive learning environments (e.g., Jennings & Greenberg, 2009). Below we describe ways that five SEL skills may play a role in facilitation, although there are many more SEL skills and examples than we describe. Table 7.1 provides an overview of some of the ways each social–emotional skill might be used by a racial equity facilitator. We hope this initial framing will encourage further examination of the importance of facilitator SEL skills for generating productive racial equity learning and action.

Self-Awareness

Across the literature, authors consistently call for racial equity facilitators to be engaged in a lifelong practice of deep, ongoing reflection, so that they are aware of their own role in contributing to and disrupting systems of privilege and oppression, and are aware of their own racial identity, positionality, bias, and intersectionalities (Carpenter & Diem, 2013; Hackman, 2005; Kishimoto, 2018; Love et al., 2016; Miller & Donner, 2000; Sue, 2013; Sue et al., 2019). This foundational work requires self-awareness and is a part of everyday life, not just while facilitating. *Self-awareness* is an understanding of one's thoughts, beliefs, emotions, and how they relate to what you say and do (CASEL, 2020). When facilitating a racial equity discussion, facilitators must ask themselves, what am I conveying with my body language, facial expression, eye contact, tone, rhythm, choice of words? How am I seeing and interpreting this discussion based on my own identities and their

TABLE 7.1. Ways Facilitators Use SEL Skills for Discussions about Racial Equity

SEL skill	How facilitators use each SEL skill
Self-awareness	• Engaging in a lifelong practice of deep, critical self-reflection. • Recognizing one's own point of view and decentering it. • Balancing humility with asserting expertise and disrupting harm.
Self-management	• Noticing one's own biases and disrupting them. • Staying emotionally and cognitively present with the group. • Modeling comfort, vulnerability, and honesty. • Generating a collective feeling of energy and hope when the group seems complacent or defeated.
Social awareness	• Becoming aware of ever-changing group dynamics, power, and hierarchy and how they impact engagement. • Skillfully challenging oppressive social norms. • Seeing group interactions through the eyes of many participant identities (those that are visible and those that are not).
Relationship skills	• Managing the group process of grappling with racial equity content in a way that is productive for each person's learning. • Creating the collective experience of discourse in an equitable learning space. • Scaffolding the group's ability to welcome, withstand, and recover from strong emotions.
Responsible decision making	• Seeing when harm has occurred among participants and deciding to respond and to what degree. • Modeling an enhanced internal commitment to actively disrupting racism.

power? What do I need to do to see this discussion from the perspectives of people with other identities?

Facilitators need self-awareness to recognize their own point of view, to understand that theirs is just one perspective and not a universal truth, and to decenter their point of view (Hackman, 2005; Sue, 2017). Self-awareness also helps with explicitly naming the ways their own identities impact their ability to facilitate (Quaye, 2012). One way this awareness is useful is that it helps the facilitator decide on what "stance" they would like to take for each racial equity discussion. Do they want to take a didactic/expert stance to limit the number of challenges they get from participants who do not believe racism is a major issue in their setting, or take a teacher/co-learner stance to support participants in their own meaning making and understanding about racial equity, or do they want to focus on trust and relationship building if their positionality triggers distrust in this group? In some cases, the facilitator stance may shift fluidly, and in other cases there may be multiple facilitators who take different roles. When the facilitator is aware of their own positionality and power, they may approach racial equity discussions differently than in informal settings (with family members) where it may be different.

There is a delicate balance between the need to not only decenter one's own perspective and lead with humility but also know when to assert power to keep the group's focus on racial equity by challenging misinformation and addressing harm that is being caused to people with less power. As Gorski (2019) suggests, there are times when it is important for a facilitator to take a stance as "the expert" because they have knowledge that counters "detours" that participants may take to derail the group's focus on equity. Others, however, describe the need for facilitators to position themselves as co-learners with participants, rather than experts (Carpenter & Diem, 2013; Love et al., 2016; Smith et al., 2017; Swindall, 2021). These seemingly contradictory messages can both be true at the same time. The key is for facilitators to balance a stance of humility and being willing to consider a wide range of ideas, with the willingness to assert knowledge and power when racist narratives enter the discussion.

It is important to note that in educational settings for all ages in the United States, educators are most often White (National Center for Education Statistics [NCES], 2021), yet the burden for leading discussions about racial equity tends to fall to people of color. For widespread racial equity efforts to occur and sustain, these efforts must include adequate supports for facilitators of color to have the stamina for highly emotional and triggering discussions and seek out White facilitators who have enough self-awareness to reconceptualize their own identities as anti-racist (Smith et al., 2017).

Self-Management

Self-awareness helps facilitators see patterns in their own thoughts, emotions, assumptions, reactions, and behaviors. But once these patterns are visible to the facilitator, the next challenge is to manage them. In some cases, this means noticing one's own bias and deciding to let a thought go before it turns into words or behaviors. For example, as facilitators learn background information about the participants and the context before the first professional development session, they will likely notice their own biases and judgments forming about the group and will have to disrupt this tendency, while still using information about the group to make decisions about how to alter their stance, content, presentation style, and to meet the group where they are (Swindall, 2021). In other cases, it may mean keeping oneself present and emotionally engaged, not just cognitively engaged, which can be particularly challenging for White facilitators, because emotional detachment is a common protective reaction that White people have to race talk (Carpenter & Diem, 2013; Quaye, 2012; Sue, 2013). Self-management also is necessary when facilitators need to model comfort and vulnerability when sharing personal stories with the group (Miller & Donner, 2000; Sue, 2013; Swindall, 2021). Or self-management can help facilitators when they choose to stay silent and lessen control of the direction of the group in order to flatten the hierarchy dynamic and make more space for the voices of participants of color (Smith et al., 2017). This process of managing oneself to be responsive to what the group needs in the moment helps to create a trusting space for participants to do the same (Carpenter & Diem, 2013; Swindall, 2021).

A facilitator will use self-management skills to not only manage their own emotions about their own sharing, but also to manage their emotional responses to participant sharing (Smith et al., 2017; Sue, 2013). This may mean allowing oneself to visibly show sadness when a participant of color shares their experience with racism, anger when White participants express racist beliefs, or nervousness when it feels like the group discussion is getting heated and difficult to manage (Aguilar, 2020). As Aguilar (2016) said, to advance equity,

> we'll need to have some really hard conversations. We'll have to talk about racism and slavery, . . . about our own experiences as kids in school and about our own biases and misconceptions. There's no way we have these conversations without experiencing emotions. And there's no way we can transform . . . without having these conversations. The road to equity is paved with emotions.

In a case study of White faculty members facilitating discussions about racial equity in their courses, one faculty member extended Aguilar's sentiment to say that not only are emotions essential, but many of her peers actually advise her against bringing emotions into the classroom.

"Colleagues have said to me that this or that was risky. There's a lot of emotion in my classrooms. People want to keep it out. It has to be there. I just don't see how you can do this work without emotion" (in Quaye, 2012, p. 111). The challenge for a facilitator is to be ready to make space for their own emotions and participants' emotions, and use them to sustain engagement rather than end it.

Finally, facilitators' self-management skills also come into play when they must up-regulate to generate energy if the group is getting too complacent or comfortable (Hackman, 2005) and generate a sense of hope when particularly tragic and visible acts of racism are occurring in the world and the group is feeling defeated. The facilitator sets the tone of reengaging in racial equity work even when steps forward have been achieved, or steps back seem too daunting to overcome.

Social Awareness

Facilitators use a high level of social awareness to see group dynamics, power, and hierarchies among participants (Hackman, 2005; Miller & Donner, 2000; Sue, 2013) and to understand how these dynamics impact engagement and openness to learning. These dynamics constantly change based on who is in attendance, what is being discussed, and what is happening outside of the sessions (Love et al., 2016). Although one study suggests that engagement is not related to participant demographics (Kulik et al., 2007), another suggests that the racial composition of the group and other factors will play a role (Roberson et al., 2001). Gathering information about a new group, its history, power dynamics, and context will help the facilitator have some initial social awareness before they begin working together. The social dynamics in a group can vary greatly based on factors such as the racial composition of the group, whether group members are attending the session voluntarily (Kennedy, 2019), and (mis)match with the race of the facilitator. Particularly when the facilitator's race does not match the race of all of the group members, it can be beneficial to have a diverse team of facilitators to allow more participants to identify with a perspective of at least one of the facilitators, to ensure that facilitators have personally experienced some of the reactions that participants might be having, and make it less likely that participants have counterproductive emotional reactions to the content presented (DiAngelo & Flynn, 2010; Ngounou & Gutiérrez, 2019). A diverse team of facilitators also allows them to model trust and vulnerability with one another, and productive ways of challenging each other. Being a facilitator can, however, often feel like a lot of emotional labor, particularly for facilitators of color. For that reason, it is important to compensate facilitators, seek professional facilitators when possible, and not rely on staff of color to step into this role as a form of service. If a district or organization does not have a diverse team of facilitators, using first-authored sources (e.g., podcast interviews, readings, videos) by people of color can help bring diverse perspectives into the discussion until they are able to diversify their team.

Interestingly, facilitators also use their social awareness of group norms to figure out the most skillful ways to leverage and/or push against them (Sue, 2013). For example, different communities have different norms around race-based language (e.g., African Americans, people of color, people of the global majority, Black, Indigenous, and people of color [BIPOC]). Although facilitators may have their own ideas about nuances in terminology, they must also recognize that different communities and individuals may identify differently. Facilitators must use social awareness of these norms to determine whether they are rooted in identity or bias and be flexible enough to make space for terminology preferences, to shift their own language to support a group's identity-based language, or to challenge biases. Let us share an example from Westridge's racial equity retreat. Before the retreat began, the facilitators met with district administrators and heard them consistently use the term *African American*. At the retreat, however, the facilitators noticed that none of the teachers or staff members used the term *African American*, but instead referred to children, families, and their coworkers as "Black." So, as the facilitators began their opening session, they agreed that they would use the term *Black* to align with the majority of participants, particularly those who had less formal power.

In-the-moment decisions facilitators make as they have discussions with the group require them to see group dynamics through each participants' perspective (Miller & Donner, 2000; Sue, 2013). Does this moment show respect for participants who have visible and invisible identities that have been marginalized? What are the cues that participants may perceive as indicating being heard and valued versus being ignored or discounted? Although research suggests that participants of color are regularly reading the cues of group members to decide how to change their communication so it will be received in the way they intend it to be (Sue et al., 2009), the facilitator has an obligation to alleviate some of this burden. Specifically, facilitators can use their social awareness skills to be aware of these social dynamics and (1) intentionally center the voices of marginalized participants, (2) notice when White or privileged positions are doing harm, and (3) ensure that participants of color are not being asked to share their stories of trauma for the purpose of privileged participants' learning (e.g., Arao & Clemens, 2013). In other words, facilitators use social awareness to be alert to the group's power dynamics and to flatten the hierarchy by shifting more power to participants who have less.

Relationship Skills

A facilitator cannot be effective without strong relationship skills, because facilitation is not just about sharing content, it is about managing the group process of grappling with that content in a way that is productive for learning (Kuhar et al., 2019; Thomas & Thorpe, 2019). Facilitators face many challenges in racial equity conversations, including how to talk about a topic that many people do not want to talk about in a group that likely has highly varied knowledge and beliefs about that topic, how to challenge deep-seated beliefs, and how to build a strong enough sense of group trust that everyone will stay present, authentic, in relationship, and sustain their commitment to advancing racial equity despite inevitable challenges along the way. Relationship skills play an essential role in navigating these challenges, including communicating clearly, negotiating conflict, navigating power differences among participants, creating a sense of belonging, and being flexible enough to manage contexts with widely different social norms and expectations (Jagers et al., 2019). Below, we describe community agreements as one strategy for managing relationships in the group, but all these skills play a role in facilitating racial equity discussions.

Whereas self-management skills can help a facilitator regulate their own emotions, relationship skills can help a facilitator manage a group's ability to welcome, withstand, and recover from strong emotions (Sue, 2013). Sometimes this can be done with humor (although not sarcasm), so the group is more relaxed and trusting (Swindall, 2021), other times by pushing the conversation deeper (Welton et al., 2015), and still other times by acknowledging and validating emotions (Swindall, 2021) and helping participants to listen to one another (Sue et al., 2009). Although discerning which relationship skills to use in which moment with which participants can be challenging, it is rewarding when participants with widely varying beliefs begin to speak openly to each other and see from each other's perspectives.

Responsible Decision Making

A facilitator uses responsible decision making skills in two ways. First, challenging moments will occur in racial equity discussions, and facilitators must be able to use social awareness skills to see when harm has occurred and responsible decision-making skills to know when they need to respond and to what degree. A common example of harm is often called a *microaggression* (e.g., when a participant of color shares an example of racism and is dismissed by White participants, or when a White participant reinforces a stereotype or bias toward a participant of color; Sue et al., 2019). Is it necessary to stop and address a situation? Should someone be asked to explain their thinking? Asked to apologize? Does a facilitator need to step in and model how to respond when harm occurs? The answer to these questions likely relates to the positionality of the facilitator and participants involved. The facilitator's own core commitment to responsible decision making will help them decide when to prioritize addressing harm or debrief an act of racism that has occurred in the world, even if group time is running out, or if they are unsure how to address it.

Second, the facilitator needs to model an enhanced internal commitment to actively disrupting racism. This means emphasizing that each participant has a role in social change, and it is expected that they will act on it (Bensimon & Harris, 2007; Hackman, 2005). This may be particularly important for White facilitators, in that research suggests that even "good" White people do not typically disrupt racism when they see it (Sue, 2013). Facilitators can help disrupt complacency and redefine how participants hold themselves accountable for making responsible decisions even when it feels hard or clumsy (brown, 2020; Miller & Donner, 2000). This message has more strength when the facilitator is modeling responsible decision making in the group sessions, even when it is clearly challenging to do so. For an overview of some of the ways social–emotional skills might be used by racial equity facilitators, see Table 7.1.

Creating a Learning Community Grounded in Equity Values

All the facilitator's social–emotional skills work in concert to create a productive space for discussing racial equity and encouraging participants to act for change. This space is a community where everyone values relationships with each other, careful listening, and encourages everyone's participation (Adams, 2016; brown, 2021). If the goal of discussing racial equity is to help participants learn how to make communities more just and equitable, they must get firsthand experience of what a just and equitable community feels, sounds, and looks like (Ieva et al., 2021). For a facilitator, this means naming the values that underlie an equitable community, living within those values with regular group practices that reflect them, and addressing challenges to those values when they inevitably arise.

An example of creating a sense of community could be seen in the Westridge School District retreat. The importance of being able to question each other while maintaining strong relationships together was brought up in the first White affinity group session. Participants were unsure of how to question each other without damaging their relationships. They worried this would happen during their affinity group conversations and that their relationships would not be able to recover from confrontation. The White facilitator opened up a discussion about this, and the group came up with some starter phrases that the group agreed felt inviting rather than attacking, such as "Something you said caught my attention and I would like to ask more about it." Having this discussion helped the participants affirm that they all valued their relationships and wanted to keep them strong even when they felt compelled to question each other.

As Kishimoto (2018) describes in his review of anti-racist pedagogy, it is possible (yet highly problematic) to teach about anti-racism while employing facilitation practices that reinforce racist values such as centering authority, promoting competition and individualism, and emotionally distancing oneself from the content being taught. It is the facilitator's task to develop a sense of community that aligns with the racial equity values that are being discussed. Some of these values might include challenging assumptions, decentering authority so participants take responsibility for their own learning, collaborating and learning together, and valuing the process of learning rather than aiming to attain one set of knowledge that comes from one perspective (Kishimoto, 2018). Other values might include local contextualization of racial equity discussions in participants' own communities so they can connect with the reality of racism and see ways to disrupt it in their daily lives (Quaye, 2012) and so they can see value in the wisdom of local leaders who are outside of academia and formal authority roles (Alderman et al., 2021; Marshall, 2016). It is the facilitator's social awareness that helps them understand what values are present in the group's community, responsible decision making that will motivate the facilitator to constantly work to shift away from oppressive social norms, and relationship skills that will bolster their ability to create a new collective way of being together.

In Table 7.2, we provide an example set of values and practices that one of our authors (Shannon) uses, but these are by no means the definitive set. For more information, there are many frames that might help to inform what values would create the foundation for a just and equitable community (e.g., Fischer, 2020; Friere, 2018; hooks, 2014; King Center, n.d.; Urbach, 2017; in contrast, see Okun, 2000).

It is common for racial equity facilitators to establish community agreements that specify how a group will enact their values (e.g., Arao & Clemens, 2013; Singleton, 2014), although there are exceptions. There is limited research available about this practice, but it is somewhat reminiscent of the practice of co-creating classroom agreements that is part of some evidence-based SEL programs (e.g., Rimm-Kaufman et al., 2014). Community agreements often include statements about using talk space equitably, using "I statements," being present, and staying

TABLE 7.2. Example Equity Values and Associated Group Practices That Create the Conditions for Racial Equity Discussions

Equity values	Group practices that reflect equity values
Encouraging honest self-reflection and awareness	• Giving time for individual journaling in response to prompts, so everyone can become aware of deeper thoughts before sharing aloud. • Encouraging everyone to ask themselves how they contribute to and disrupt racism. • Providing activities that encourage everyone to think about how their identities shape their experience in the group. • Leading group mindfulness practices to encourage self-awareness.
Valuing relationships	• Taking time to ask about each other's news (e.g., new babies, birthdays, graduations, weddings) and find ways to celebrate together (e.g., making a photo collage, holding a party). • Acknowledging when a participant is having a hard time (e.g., illness) and creating opportunities to express care for each other (e.g., sending a group card or providing homemade meals). • Sharing personal stories and emotions, not just knowledge. • Practicing active listening to each other, so everyone knows what it feels like to be heard. • Co-creating a plan for how group members will confront each other, question each other, and have hard conversations while still maintaining relationships with each other (see description in text).
Seeking many ways of knowing and being	• Intentionally drawing from broad sources of knowledge (e.g., from multiple cultures, identities) and formats (e.g., storytelling, research findings, art and music). • Inviting local community members to share their experiences with the group. • Acknowledging all sources, whether they are peer reviewed and published, or spoken by a colleague or neighbor. • Inviting different perspectives on a topic and then not forcing the group to come to a consensus on them—because there is no one truth or perspective.
Responsiveness and transparency	• Seeking participant feedback often (e.g., one-word check-ins, online surveys), share it with the group, and make adjustments in the plan to reflect the feedback. • Letting go of the need to be rigid with agendas by making more time if a discussion becomes emotional and should not be cut off. • Reminding group members that they can suggest revisions of community agreements at any time.
Learning from each other and co-creating group members' experience	• Creating shared folders, collective vocabulary lists, or other ways to share resources and information so there is no insider knowledge or jargon. • Decentering facilitator authority by creating roles for group members to co-facilitate or have other jobs (e.g., group historian). • Being willing to listen to group members when they would like to spend more time on a topic or bring in new content.
Contextualizing group discussions in history and current events	• Acknowledging current events (e.g., local racial violence) and how they are impacting participants during the session. • Finding historical information (e.g., documentaries) that the group can learn together to understand the events that led to current racial inequities in their community, institution, or topic area.
Committing to an ongoing practice that aligns with our values	• Planning how the group will interact together and continually coming back to that plan (see description of community agreements in text). • Creating self- and collective care practices (e.g., going on walks together during lunch breaks; playing games together) to help sustain each other through challenging racial equity work. • Closing sessions with sharing "Ahas, Appreciations, and Apologies" with one another, to reiterate that learning is an ongoing practice of celebrating, taking feedback, and moving forward.

open to learning. Although community agreements may be helpful, they may also be problematic when they center participants with privilege or take substantial time away from other learning (Sensoy & DiAngelo, 2014). Sometimes community agreements overemphasize the need for White participants to feel comfortable, which can quickly derail equity initiatives. Participants of color have a long history of learning in a society that has not centered their comfort. So, to suggest that comfort is a prerequisite for learning is not accurate and dismisses their experiences (Miller & Donner, 2000). Also, prioritizing comfort of those with privilege reflects some of the problematic values in our society today, including avoidance of conflict and allowing space for defensiveness (Okun, 2000). Rather than creating safe spaces for discussing racial equity, Arao and Clemens (2013) propose creating brave spaces in which there is a need for courage, not safety. In a brave space, the facilitator acknowledges that learning about racial equity can feel unsafe because there are challenges to power and privilege, but that does not have to be a deterrent to learning. In fact, helping participants develop self-awareness to recognize when they are feeling unsafe, and self-management to stay engaged anyway, can be an important objective for racial equity facilitators.

In our example school district, Westridge facilitators presented three basic community agreements at the beginning of the 3-day racial equity retreat but did not give time to co-creating a more in-depth list. By offering three agreements, they described their expectations for the tone of the retreat, without getting derailed. Three weeks after the retreat, during the first voluntary virtual session after school, the facilitators decided to spend more time co-creating group agreements, to build collective expectations from this smaller, and more bought-in group. Their list of agreements became the first item on every meeting agenda and offered a moment to get regrounded in their intentions. The effectiveness of community agreements likely lies in facilitator implementation. Ultimately, racial equity discussion facilitators need to use their social awareness skills to read the group's dynamics and ensure that if used, community agreements are orienting the group toward equity by learning from voices that are often marginalized rather than making room for statements and ideas that are causing harm.

Key Takeaways

There is growing demand for racial equity discussions, and because research findings on their effectiveness are equivocal (e.g., Calanchini et al., 2021; Carter et al., 2020; Chang et al., 2019; Devine & Ash, 2022; Dobbin & Kalev, 2016; Paluck et al., 2021), it is important to identify what strategies are most promising and what factors could improve their impact. In this chapter, we have focused on the social–emotional skills of racial equity discussion facilitators, because resistance to racial equity discussion is often rooted in participants' feeling defensive and unwelcome, or in the inadvertent reinforcement of racial stereotypes (Anand & Winters, 2008; Dobbin & Kalev, 2016, 2018). As the authors of this chapter, we have collectively had experiences facilitating racial equity conversations across many contexts and demographics, and the success of those discussions seems to rely heavily on applying the facilitator's social–emotional skills in particular ways that we outlined earlier. We hear similar reflections from others with experience in racial equity facilitation (brown, 2021; Elliott, 2021; Ieva et al., 2021) and we offer readers key takeaways that could be put into practice today.

1. *Facilitator social–emotional skills are germane to almost every aspect of racial equity discussions.* Notice what moments in racial equity discussions seem to be happening with ease and those that are most challenging. You might ask a colleague to observe your facilitation and offer their perspectives on these moments. What social–emotional skills would a facilitator use in these situations? For example, one common challenge is skillfully speaking up when a participant is saying something that is causing harm or disengaging for another participant. If you find yourself letting a moment like this pass by and then regretting that you did not speak up, more self-awareness might be needed. Regretting not speaking up after the fact is a level of self-awareness that is too delayed. By studying your own thoughts, emotions, and body language in these moments, you can notice your own patterns (e.g., I always spend too long trying to decide whether harm is occurring and sorting through options for how to speak up) and recognize them more quickly in the future. In this example, seeing yourself mentally shuffle through responses would signal that you are caught in a pattern of silence and need to start speaking right away, before the moment passes. As a facilitator, ask yourself how you are investing time in building your own social–emotional skills (e.g., self-awareness) so that they will be ready when you need them.

2. *Every facilitation strategy reinforces or disrupts a value.* In racial equity discussions, it is essential for the facilitator to be aware of the link between their facilitation moves and the values they are prioritizing in the group. This requires a facilitator awareness practice that is constantly reflective from two different angles. First, from the values-to-practice angle, list three values that you believe define a racially just and equitable society, and continuously ask yourself how your facilitation efforts promote those values (or disrupt the opposite of those values). This could mean diversifying your sources of content because you want to help your participants strengthen their social awareness and practice respecting the points of view of a wide range of cultures. Second, from the practice-to-values angle, list facilitation practices that you use often and figure out what values are being reinforced or disrupted by them. For example, if all the sources you typically share with participants are findings from peer-reviewed research articles, even if your set of articles is written by White authors and by authors of color,

having one type of source reinforces the value that only people who use certain methods or have certain credentials should inform our thinking (e.g., epistemicide). How could you shift your facilitation practices to ensure they are grounded in racial equity values?

When facilitators are curious about their own social–emotional skills and how they intersect with their own racial identity, it is possible to spark a lifelong practice of awareness, reflection, and experimentation with new facilitation strategies. Using social–emotional skills to know yourself, understand group dynamics, build a trusting and honest discussion space, and commit to action will help facilitators see inequities, disrupt them, and create a more racially just world.

DISCUSSION QUESTIONS

1. This chapter states that "true social change calls for every person to see themselves as a racial equity facilitator across their own spheres of influence (Tatum, 2017), such as with their colleagues, neighbors, political representatives, and at the family dinner table." Identify one or two changes related to racial equity that you want to see in the world. Are there ways or settings in which you are currently acting as a racial equity facilitator? Are there ways that you can improve your facilitation efforts? What goals would you like to set for yourself in this area?
2. Consider some of the contemporary critiques of SEL that suggest the current conceptualization of SEL does not pay enough attention to history and context, places too much emphasis on individual social and emotional competencies, and perpetuates norms that are harmful to developing children and youth of color. What are examples of this problem that you have identified in SEL? Do you see that the field of SEL can shift to incorporate needs for greater racial equity or do we need an entirely new field to achieve these goals?
3. Think about moments when you have spoken up for racial equity, or wished you had. What patterns do you notice in your strengths and challenges in these moments? We suggest that you can study your own patterns to determine which of your social–emotional skills may be serving you well and which ones could use more practice. How will you lean into your strengths and continue to develop the social–emotional skills that are needed?
4. One of the takeaway messages from this chapter is that "every facilitation strategy reinforces or disrupts a value." Reflect on a PD session that you attended or facilitated. Think about how it was facilitated, who did most of the talking, and what sources or people were regarded as experts. What values did those facilitation strategies convey?

ACKNOWLEDGMENTS

This chapter was written by members of the 3Rs Initiative: Reading, Racial Equity, and Relationships (Principal Investigators: Wanless & Moye), housed at the University of Pittsburgh's Office of Child Development. The 3Rs Initiative is part of The Pittsburgh Study (Principal Investigators: Miller & Savage Friedman) and is funded by the University of Pittsburgh Medical Center (UPMC) Children's Hospital Foundation, the University of Pittsburgh's School of Education, The Grable Foundation, and Remake Learning. For more information about the 3Rs Initiative, contact *swanless@pitt.edu*. We are deeply grateful for our justice and equity mentors (including Meena Srinivasan and the Transformative Educational Leadership program team, Michelle King, Erika Gold Kestenberg, Felicia Savage Friedman, and Tina Raspanti) and to members of the American Education Research Association Social and Emotional Learning (SEL) Special Interest Group for their recent scholarship linking SEL to racial equity.

REFERENCES

Adams, M. (2016). Pedagogical foundations for social justice education. In M. Adams & L. A. Bell (Eds.), *Teaching for diversity and social justice* (pp. 27–54). Routledge.

Aguilar, E. (2016, March 3). The road to equity is paved with emotions. Retrieved from *www.edutopia.org/blog/road-equity-paved-emotions-elena-aguilar.*

Aguilar, E. (2020). *Coaching for equity: Conversations that change practice.* Wiley.

Alderman, D., Narro Perez, R., Eaves, L. E., Klein, P., & Muñoz, S. (2021). Reflections on operationalizing an anti-racism pedagogy: Teaching as regional storytelling. *Journal of Geography in Higher Education, 45*(2), 186–200.

Anand, R., & Winters, M. F. (2008). A retrospective view of corporate diversity training from 1964 to the present. *Academy of Management Learning & Education, 7*(3), 356–372.

Arao, B., & Clemens, K. (2013). From safe spaces to brave spaces. In L. M. Landrerman (Ed.), *The art of effective facilitation: Reflections from social justice educators* (pp. 135–150). Stylus.

Beard, K. S., Vakil, J. B., Chao, T., & Hilty, C. D. (2021). Time for change: Understanding teacher social–emotional learning supports for anti-racism and student well-being during COVID-19, and beyond. *Education and Urban Society.* [Epub ahead of print]

Bensimon, E. M., & Harris, F., III. (2007). Accountability, equity, and practitioner learning and change. *Metropolitan Universities, 18*(3), 28–45.

brown, a. m. (2020). *We will not cancel us: And other dreams of transformative justice.* AK Press.

brown, a. m. (2021). *Holding change: The way of emergent strategy facilitation and mediation.* AK Press.

Calanchini, J., Lai, C. K., & Klauer, K. C. (2021). Reducing implicit racial preferences: III. A process-level examination of changes in implicit preferences. *Journal of Personality and Social Psychology, 121*(4), 796–818.

Camangian, P., & Cariaga, S. (2021). Social and emotional learning is hegemonic miseducation: Students deserve humanization instead. *Race Ethnicity and Education, 25*(7), 1–21.

Carpenter, B. W., & Diem, S. (2013). Talking race: Facilitating critical conversations in educational leadership preparation programs. *Journal of School Leadership, 23*(6), 902–931.

Carter, E. R., Onyeador, I. N., & Lewis, N. A., Jr. (2020). Developing and delivering effective anti-bias training: Challenges and recommendations. *Behavioral Science & Policy, 6*(1), 57–70.

CASEL. (2020). CASEL's SEL framework: What are the core competence areas and where are they promoted? Retrieved from *https://casel.org/wp-content/uploads/2020/12/casel-sel-framework-11.2020.pdf.*

Chang, E. H., Milkman, K. L., Gromet, D. M., Rebele, R. W., Massey, C., Duckworth, A. L., & Grant, A. M. (2019). The mixed effects of online diversity training. *Proceedings of the National Academy of Sciences USA, 116*(16), 7778–7783.

Devine, P. G., & Ash, T. L. (2022). Diversity training goals, limitations, and promise: A review of the multidisciplinary literature. *Annual Review of Psychology, 73*, 403–429.

DiAngelo, R., & Flynn, D. (2010). Showing what we tell: Facilitating antiracist education in cross-racial teams. *Understanding and Dismantling Privilege, 1*(1), 1–24.

Dobbin, F., & Kalev, A. (2016). Why diversity programs fail. *Harvard Business Review, 94*(7), 2–10.

Dobbin, F., & Kalev, A. (2018). Why doesn't diversity training work?: The challenge for industry and academia. *Anthropology Now, 10*(2), 48–55.

Drake, R., & Oglesby, A. (2020). Humanity is not a thing: Disrupting white supremacy in K–12 social emotional learning. *Journal of Critical Thought and Praxis, 10*(1), 1–22.

Duchesneau, N. (2020). Social, emotional, and academic development through an equity lens. Retrieved from *https://edtrust.org/wpcontent/uploads/2014/09/social-emotional-and-academic-development-through-an-equity-lens-august-6–2020.pdf.*

Elliott, N. (2021). Using mind–body practices to uproot unconscious bias in the education profession. *AILACTE Journal, Special Issue*, 133–156.

Fischer, F. (2020, November 2). Leading liberated: Why liberation pedagogy is the heart and foundation of TAF's Network for Edwork. Retrieved from *https://techaccess.org/leading-liberated.*

Freire, P. (2018). *Pedagogy of the oppressed.* Bloomsbury.

Gorski, P. (2019). Avoiding racial equity detours. *Educational Leadership, 76*(7), 56–61.

Hackman, H. W. (2005). Five essential components for social justice education. *Equity & Excellence in Education, 38*(2), 103–109.

Higheagle Strong, Z., & McMain, E. M. (2020). Social emotional learning for social emotional justice: A conceptual framework for education in the midst of pandemics. *Northwest Journal of Teacher Education, 15*(2), 1–11.

Hoffman, D. M. (2009). Reflecting on social emotional learning: A critical perspective on trends in the United States. *Review of Educational Research, 79*(2), 533–556.

hooks, b. (2014). *Teaching to transgress.* Routledge.

Ieva, K. P., Beasley, J., & Steen, S. (2021). Equipping school counselors for antiracist healing centered groups: A critical examination of preparation, connected curricula, professional practice and oversight. *Teaching and Supervision in Counseling, 3*(2), 64–78.

Jagers, R. J., Rivas-Drake, D., & Williams, B. (2019). Transformative social and emotional learning (SEL): Toward SEL in service of educational equity and excellence. *Educational Psychologist, 54*(3), 162–184.

Jennings, P. A., & Greenberg, M. T. (2009). The prosocial classroom: Teacher social and emotional competence in relation to student and classroom outcomes. *Review of Educational Research, 79*(1), 491–525.

Kennedy, K. (2019). Centering equity and caring in leadership for social–emotional learning: Toward a conceptual framework for diverse learners. *Journal of School Leadership, 29*(6), 473–492.

King Center (n.d.). The King philosophy—Nonviolence365 (R): Beloved community. Retrieved from *https://thekingcenter.org/about-tkc/the-king-philosophy.*

King, M. (2015, July). Learning how to make a life [Video]. Retrieved from *www.youtube.com/watch?v=xg9ajtsxq4a.*

Kishimoto, K. (2018). Anti-racist pedagogy: From faculty's self-reflection to organizing within and beyond the classroom. *Race Ethnicity and Education, 21*(4), 540–554.

Kuhar, M., Krmelj, M., & Petrič, G. (2019). The impact of facilitation on the quality of deliberation and attitude change. *Small Group Research, 50*(5), 623–653.

Kulik, C. T., Pepper, M. B., Roberson, L., & Parker, S. K. (2007). The rich get richer: Predicting participation in voluntary diversity training. *Journal of Organizational Behavior, 28*(6), 753–769.

Love, J. M., Gaynor, T. S., & Blessett, B. (2016). Facilitating difficult dialogues in the classroom: A pedagogical imperative. *Administrative Theory & Praxis, 38*(4), 227–233.

Mahfouz, J., & Anthony-Stevens, V. (2020). Why trouble SEL?: The need for cultural relevance in SEL. *Occasional Paper Series, 43*(6), 58–70.

Mahoney, J. L., Weissberg, R. P., Greenberg, M. T., Dusenbury, L., Jagers, R. J., Niemi, K., . . . Yoder, N. (2020). Systemic social and emotional learning: Promoting educational success for all preschool to high school students. *American Psychologist, 76*(7), 1128–1142.

Marshall, G. S. (2016). The university in the knowledge economy: Academic capitalism and its implications for doctoral students in public administration. *Administrative Theory & Praxis, 38*(4), 296–304.

Miller, J., & Donner, S. (2000). More than just talk: The use of racial dialogues to combat racism. *Social Work with Groups, 23*(1), 31–53.

National Center for Education Statistics, U.S. Department of Education. (2021, May). Characteristics of public school teachers. Retrieved from *https://nces.ed.gov/programs/coe/indicator/clr#:~:text=in%202017%e2%80%9318%2c%20about%2079,1%20percent%20of%20public%20school.*

Ngounou, G. N., & Gutiérrez, N. B. (2019). The value of interracial facilitation of racial equity training. *Phi Delta Kappan, 100*(8), 56–61.

Okun, T. (2000). White supremacy culture. Retrieved from *www.dismantlingracism.org/uploads/4/3/5/7/43579015/okun_-_white_sup_culture.pdf.*

Paluck, E. L., Porat, R., Clark, C. S., & Green, D. P. (2021). Prejudice reduction: Progress and challenges. *Annual Review of Psychology, 72*, 533–560.

Quaye, S. J. (2012). White educators facilitating discussions about racial realities. *Equity & Excellence in Education, 45*(1), 100–119.

Rimm-Kaufman, S. E., Larsen, R. A., Baroody, A. E., Curby, T. W., Ko, M., Thomas, J. B., . . . DeCoster, J. (2014). Efficacy of the responsive classroom approach: Results from a 3-year, longitudinal randomized controlled trial. *American Educational Research Journal, 51*(3), 567–603.

Rivas-Drake, D., Rosario-Ramos, E., McGovern, G., & Jagers, R. J. (2021). Rising up together: Spotlighting transformative SEL in practice with Latinx youth. Brief by CASEL and University of Michigan. Retrieved from *https://casel.org/sel-rising-up-together*.

Roberson, L., Kulik, C. T., & Pepper, M. B. (2001). Designing effective diversity training: Influence of group composition and trainee experience. *Journal of Organizational Behavior, 22*(8), 871–885.

Sensoy, Ö., & DiAngelo, R. (2014). Respect differences?: Challenging the common guidelines in social justice education. *Democracy and Education, 22*(2), 1–10.

Simmons, D., Cariaga, S., Higheagle Strong, Z., & Martinez, L. (2021, April). *Decolonizing social emotional learning: Redefining and reclaiming SEL*. Chair: Daniel Soodjinda, Discussant: Lara Ervin-Kassab. Presented virtually at the American Educational Research Association Annual Conference. Retrieved from *www.youtube.com/watch?v=mrox_qo9mty*.

Singleton, G. E. (2014). *Courageous conversations about race: A field guide for achieving equity in schools*. Corwin Press.

Smith, L., Kashubeck-West, S., Payton, G., & Adams, E. (2017). White professors teaching about racism: Challenges and rewards. *Counseling Psychologist, 45*(5), 651–668.

Sue, D. W. (2013). Race talk: The psychology of racial dialogues. *American Psychologist, 68*(8), 663–672.

Sue, D. W. (2017). The challenges of becoming a White ally. *Counseling Psychologist, 45*(5), 706–716.

Sue, D. W., Alsaidi, S., Awad, M. N., Glaeser, E., Calle, C. Z., & Mendez, N. (2019). Disarming racial microaggressions: Microintervention strategies for targets, White allies, and bystanders. *American Psychologist, 74*(1), 128–142.

Sue, D. W., Lin, A. I., Torino, G. C., Capodilupo, C. M., & Rivera, D. P. (2009). Racial microaggressions and difficult dialogues on race in the classroom. *Cultural Diversity and Ethnic Minority Psychology, 15*(2), 183–190.

Swindall, L. R. (2021). Four ways to (re)consider facilitating discussions on race and social justice. *New Jersey Studies: An Interdisciplinary Journal, 7*(1), 373–382.

Tatum, B. (2017). *Why are all the Black kids sitting together in the cafeteria?: And other conversations about race*. Basic Books.

Thomas, G., & Thorpe, S. (2019). Enhancing the facilitation of online groups in higher education: A review of the literature on face-to-face and online group-facilitation. *Interactive Learning Environments, 27*(1), 62–71.

Urbach, M. (2017, May 28). Liberated spaces instead of "safe" spaces. Retrieved from *https://medium.com/@martinurbach/liberated-spaces-instead-of-safe-spaces-b94bbb146e6c*.

Welton, A. D., Harris, T. O., La Londe, P. G., & Moyer, R. T. (2015). Social justice education in a diverse classroom: Examining high school discussions about race, power, and privilege. *Equity & Excellence in Education, 48*(4), 549–570.

Part III Cultivating Student SEL

Creating School Conditions Conducive to Skill Development

Chapter 8

Cultivating Contexts of Interpersonal Skill Development among Diverse Students and Schools

Elise Cappella, Stacey Alicea, and Natalie May

Consider an elementary school with a student body that reflects a large city's public schoolchildren: approximately 73% from low-income families, and 41% Latine, 25% Black, 16% Asian, and 15% White students. The school has a small, open schoolyard, and strong family and community connections. After a school year in which the students experienced social challenges at recess, including physical fights and verbal aggression, school leaders developed a plan to address recess problems and create opportunities for social skill development.

Before the first day of school, leaders painted bright lines on the schoolyard to create quadrants for recess activities, and assigned supervisors to monitor one space and build relationships with students in that space. During workshops, recess supervisors and teachers discussed strengths-based, equitable behavioral strategies, and social and emotional learning (SEL) approaches, including consistent and positive reinforcement for prosocial behaviors, regulation breaks, redirection for minor misbehavior (e.g., calming activities), and restorative practices for resolving conflict. Recess supervisors visited classrooms to codevelop the recess rules (e.g., prosocial behaviors, language) and resolution strategies (e.g., "rock-paper-scissors" to see who goes first), posting rules with engaging, visual cues and demonstrating behaviors via classroom "fishbowl" activities (e.g., modeling in a circle of observers). School personnel invited families and neighborhood groups to bring cooperative games from various cultural traditions into Friday recess to enhance belonging, and games were extended into physical education and after-school programming. Throughout, data were gathered via weekly supervisor observations, postrecess classroom check-ins (feelings jar, community meeting), and incident monitoring (nurse visits, disciplinary infractions), and used to inform reflection and action as the year progressed.

This example demonstrates how schools with a commitment to systemic SEL (Mahoney et al., 2021) can create contexts that lead to interpersonal skill development for diverse students. Cultivating interpersonal skills is complex. The task involves multiple people (children, parents, peers, teachers, other adults), interconnected systems (school, home, neighborhood), and relationships across cultures and groups (social skills familiar to one culture or group may be unfamiliar to another). We argue that sustained development of interpersonal skills occurs within relationships and involves daily opportunities for effective, engaging, equitable, and strengths-based interactions (Figure 8.1). To create these opportunities, efforts to shift school structures, composition, routines, and activities must be guided by values and norms of equity, so that all students, particularly students from groups that are marginalized because of their race, ethnicity, language, income, (dis)ability,

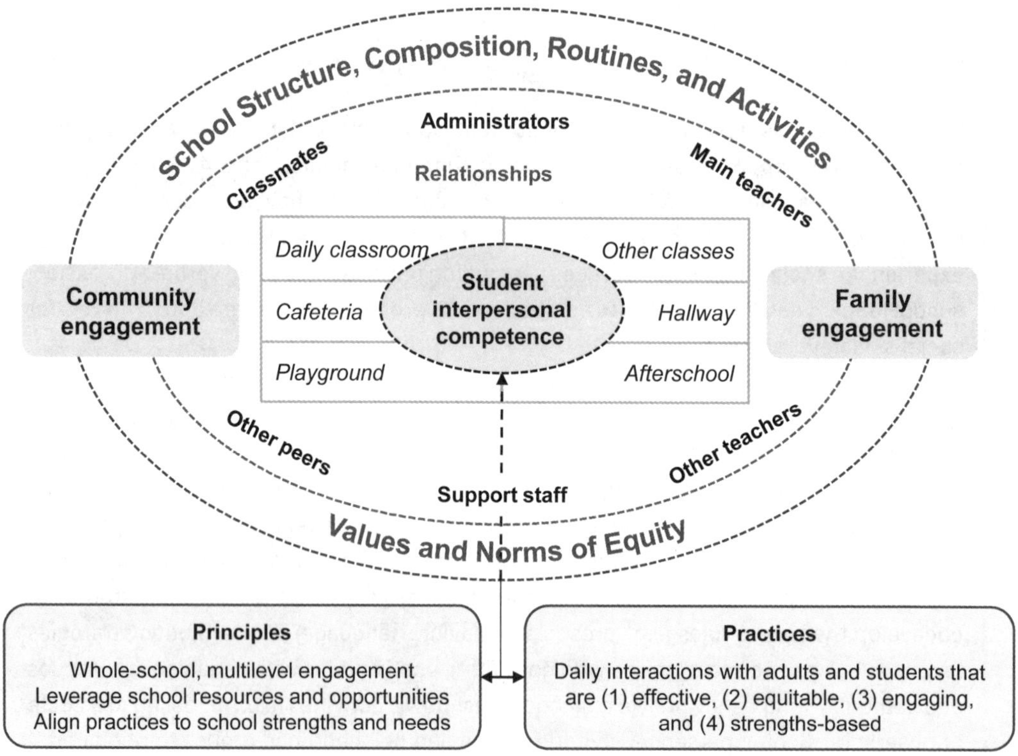

FIGURE 8.1. Opportunities for interpersonal skill development in schools.

or gender, benefit from skill development opportunities. Throughout, we emphasize three conditions of systemic SEL: (1) whole-school, multilevel engagement, (2) aligning practice with school strengths and needs, and (3) leveraging resources and opportunities within the school and community.

What to Expect in This Chapter

In this chapter, we integrate principles from SEL research (Simmons et al., 2018), theories of social capital (Coleman, 1988; Dika & Singh, 2002), social learning (Bandura, 1977) and social systems (Tseng & Seidman, 2007), and strengths-based equity initiatives (Jagers et al., 2019) to illuminate how to cultivate contexts of interpersonal skill development across students. We begin by defining interpersonal competence and synthesizing evidence on its development among students from varied backgrounds. We focus on early and middle childhood and early adolescence as key periods, and on schools as a critical developmental setting (National Academies of Sciences, Engineering, and Medicine, 2019a, 2019b). Then, we draw on theory and research to identify elements of schools that facilitate equitable interpersonal development. Finally, we propose recommendations to foster interpersonal competence through schools and classrooms, teaching strategies, and student and staff roles. Overall, we offer educators a roadmap for strengthening schools to improve interpersonal skills and enable success among all students.

What Is Interpersonal Competence?

Interpersonal competence represents the skills and behaviors that facilitate competent interaction with others (Spitzberg & Cupach, 2012), helping children to effectively navigate social situations to develop and maintain relationships with peers and adults (Jones et al., 2017). Although scholars and educators use various terms to describe interpersonal skills, all focus on building healthy relationships and navigating social settings with diverse individuals and groups (Denham, 2018). Given that SEL skills are interrelated (Eisenberg et al., 2005), *interpersonal skills* draw on a foundation of other skills, including self-awareness, self-management, and social awareness, and in turn support the development of these competencies.

How Does Interpersonal Competence Vary?

At the core of our definition of interpersonal competence is an understanding of the cultural and contextual differences in interpersonal development and practice.

Research on cultural differences in SEL is an emerging frontier (e.g., Aber et al., 2017; Torrente et al., 2015) and interpersonal competence is increasingly recognized as a culturally variable developmental process (Hecht & Shin, 2015). For example, children in more collectivist cultures may have different patterns of social interaction than those from more individualistic ones (Chen, 2000). Children from different racial and ethnic backgrounds may adopt different forms of interpersonal competence based on family, community, and societal norms. These intersecting backgrounds shape expectations for children's skills and behavior based on what is valued in their culture and context, leading to different manifestations of skills in the educational setting (Chen & French, 2008).

Take, as an example, a free-play period in a first-grade classroom. One pair of students is building a block tower together on the rug; they work, in tandem, to place blocks and create the structure, talking as they go. Beside them, two other students build their own structure, each taking turns to place their block, pausing for their partner to complete their turn before taking another turn. Not far away, a third group builds structures in parallel, side by side, while they offer advice and comment on each other's work. Students in each group are developing social skills, but their method of engagement varies. Although it may not be apparent at first glance, these students' sociocultural contexts contribute to patterns of interactions, leading to different ways of engaging even within the same classroom. Educators who recognize how interpersonal skills can be practiced in different ways and reflect on how their identities shape interpersonal competence will be better equipped to support students from varied backgrounds to develop.

Children recognize racial and gender differences as early as preschool (Aboud, 1984; Martin et al., 2002), which creates a natural opportunity for educators to help students understand and celebrate differences. Schools can capitalize on this existing variability by intentionally bringing students together from different communities and facilitating interactions, which exposes children to a variety of interpersonal styles throughout their schooling experience (e.g., see Schultz et al., 2001; Au, 2013). In diverse classrooms, students learn how to understand and interact with peers and adults who are embedded in families and communities with different values and norms than their own. Staff members also need to build a shared understanding of interpersonal competence as rooted in social and cultural contexts, including existing power differentials among staff and students that affect whose voices get heard and valued at school.

Individual children may also display these skills differently and/or develop them at different rates. Skill development varies, in part, according to student personality characteristics, such as agreeableness and conscientiousness (Jensen-Campbell et al., 2003). Students who experience internalizing problems, such as depression or anxiety, may refrain from engaging in some social interactions, resulting in fewer opportunities to practice and develop these skills (Rubin et al., 2003) or may face peer rejection, leading to further social withdrawal (Rudolph et al., 2000). Neurodiverse learners (i.e., students with learning-related differences from their neurotypical peers; Rentenbach et al., 2017) and students with emotional or behavioral difficulties may also face moderate or greater challenges in social interactions (Calero et al., 2015). To develop interpersonal competencies across the school community, and to address inequalities, schools need to provide developmentally appropriate support to students for whom social challenges lead to fewer opportunities for interpersonal skill development over time.

Why Does Interpersonal Competence Matter?

Across social and cultural contexts, interpersonal competence is critical for the development of healthy and supportive relationships, including relationships with peers and teachers (Chen & French, 2008; Graham & Echols, 2018; Spitzberg & Cupach, 2012). Students identified as having higher social skills are more likely to be accepted in their peer group and to have reciprocal friendships than their less-skilled peers (for a review, see Cillessen & Bellmore, 2002). Interpersonal skills also serve as a foundation for strong student–teacher relationships, which in turn affect students' engagement in and experiences of school (Wentzel et al., 2010).

Interpersonal skills are important for promoting school engagement and adjustment, and ultimately, academic success (Bierman et al., 2009; Denham & Brown, 2010). When students engage in interpersonally competent behaviors (e.g., collective problem solving), they receive greater support from and strengthen relationships with peers and teachers (Kiuru et al., 2015), which in turn facilitates their adjustment to school, creating a positive cycle of engagement (Spitzburg & Cupach, 2012). Indeed, these social skills partially account for gains in academic achievement in elementary school (DiPrete & Jennings, 2012) and middle school, although evidence is mixed in the later grades when children encounter greater academic and social challenges (Hall & DiPerna, 2017; January et al., 2011). Kindergarteners who develop strong interpersonal skills may also be more likely to thrive as adults (Jones et al., 2015).

Similarly, low interpersonal competence may have long-term consequences. Children with negative relationships with their kindergarten teachers exhibit lower levels of academic success through eighth grade, even after adjusting for gender, race, cognitive ability, and behaviors (Hamre & Pianta, 2001). Similarly, children who experience early peer problems (e.g., rejection, victimization) face more difficult adjustment in early adolescence (Pedersen et al., 2007). Interpersonal skills and relational challenges are a result of complex, interwoven factors at multiple levels, including the individual child, their intersecting social contexts, and the broader environment. Taken together, these findings suggest that interpersonal competence is important for students to develop relationships that support their adjustment to and performance in school.

How Do Interpersonal Skills Develop?

During the preschool years, children begin to initiate prosocial behaviors with their peers, learn how to ask for help when confronted with interpersonal problems, and work to follow social rules (e.g., sharing; Youngstrom et al., 2000). By elementary school, children cultivate reciprocal friendships, work to establish a positive reputation among peers, and try to prevent or resolve conflict as they navigate more complex peer dynamics (Bagwell & Bukowski, 2018). Toward middle school, peers typically become more influential, and youth gravitate toward "like" peer groups to shape and reinforce their identities (Cillessen & Bellmore, 2004). Students' developing ability to understand others' perspectives and communicate effectively allows them to solve interpersonal problems with less adult guidance. However, children may struggle to develop interpersonal skills as quickly when they are balancing more complex social demands (e.g., negotiating friend groups; Kokko et al., 2006; Reynolds et al., 2010).

As youth approach adolescence, new dynamics emerge. Adolescents are sensitive to hierarchy, status, and respect, and that plays out in friendship choices (Yeager, 2017). Highly skilled youth may apply their interpersonal skills toward goals that keep them engaged in school (i.e., sports, arts that require cooperation). Alternatively, students with strong social skills may turn to aggression or manipulation in order to gain or maintain social status with peers (Crick & Dodge, 1996). In summary, although interpersonal skills may not match social demands as children grow older, and skills are harnessed for varied goals, interpersonal skills build on each other and support children's need to navigate their social and academic worlds over time. As a critical context of development, schools have an opportunity to provide positive and consistent reinforcement of appropriate interpersonal behavior. Indeed, schools in which SEL is not embedded across the system (i.e., promotes interpersonal skills inconsistently or in a developmentally inappropriate way) can interfere with children's natural development.

How Can Schools Promote Interpersonal Competence?

We draw from three intersecting theories to offer guidance to schools. First, children's development of social competence occurs in the settings where they spend time, such as school. *Systems theory of social settings* (Tseng & Seidman, 2007) tells us that the resources available in the school, and the way those resources are organized, influence students. The influence occurs through the daily interpersonal interactions students have with adults and peers. School leaders may reorganize human resources in the school (e.g., have counselors spend time in classrooms) or adopt practices that change social processes in a particular space (e.g., use peer mediation at recess) and thereby increase opportunities for interpersonal skill development.

Second, educators often consider how to connect students or staff members to one another to promote learning and development. *Social capital theory* (Coleman, 1988; Dika & Singh, 2002) suggests these interpersonal connections provide access to resources that may deepen or expand interpersonal skills. *Bridging social capital* occurs when different students (or staff) have the chance to learn new skills and knowledge from each other. *Bonding social capital* occurs when similar students (or staff members) are linked, which deepens their skills and knowledge. A combination of bridging and bonding social capital promotes interpersonal competence through opportunities to develop new skills and knowledge, and deepen existing skills and knowledge.

Third, *social learning theory* (Bandura, 1977) suggests that students learn social skills by observing others and receiving reinforcement. Students learn most from the people they engage with regularly (classmates and primary teachers). However, they also learn from people they interact with less frequently if those interactions involve strong emotional content or individuals with high status (e.g., a school leader or student in a higher grade congratulates the student). Thus, a whole-school approach, where opportunities for prosocial modeling and reinforcement occur across the school day and its varied spaces and members, offers students many opportunities to develop interpersonal skills. Below, we apply these theories to practices schools can use.

Organize Classrooms to Support Relationships

Close relationships are ones in which each person in the pair experiences trust, safety, and belonging (Bagwell & Bukowski, 2018; Pianta et al., 2003). These relationships provide opportunities to take social risks, experience and resolve conflict, and increase communication skills (Ladd et al., 2014; Wentzel et al., 2010). Close relationships form when schools and classrooms have positive climates characterized by respect, trust, warmth, safety, belonging, and engagement (Thapa et al., 2013). When students feel safe and are embedded in a supportive environment, they open up to others and engage in positive interactions (Kim & Cappella, 2016).

Classroom structure and organization of resources are ways schools can create settings conducive to high-quality friendships and close relationships with teachers (Hallinan & Smith, 1989). Small classes with many peer interactions and consistent teachers are particularly helpful in early elementary school, when children benefit from strong attachment to teachers and close friendships form through shared activities. In early adolescence, students gravitate toward peers with similar identities (i.e., bonding social capital) and teachers with whom they feel connected, which may be more challenging for Black and Latine students, who are often underrepresented (Gershenson et al., 2021). Middle school leaders may want to create additional opportunities for students to engage in meaningful activities with a diversity of peers and teachers. The combination of a supportive climate and a stable, small classroom enables students to develop friendships, close relationships with teachers, and interpersonal skills (Ladd et al., 2014).

Create Opportunities for Peer Integration

Although the natural tendency of students is to choose friends who are similar to them, positive social interactions across ethnic, racial, linguistic, cultural, and (dis)ability identities create opportunities for bridging social capital (Killen et al., 2007). Schools can create situations in which students interact with others who are different from them (Hallinan & Teixeira, 1987; Simpkins et al., 2017). For instance, teachers can assign students to participate in a mixed group for an academic project (e.g., book group), bringing together students across differences to work toward a shared goal. However, the adult is critical to successful intergroup interactions (Cohen, 1994). When children are young, teachers must provide a clear set of activities and norms of engagement, and facilitate the interactions so students learn *how* to engage with peers with varying needs (e.g., different visual aids to understand a math problem) and to help students manage emotional experiences (e.g., frustration). As children grow older, adults' words and actions provide subtle information about how to treat students from different groups (Mikami & Mercer, 2017); in fact, teachers play an "invisible" role in how students treat peers (Farmer et al., 2011; Cappella et al., 2017). Positive intergroup interactions outside classrooms, such as recess and after-school programs, are facilitated by adults who model respectful communication and encourage inclusive and equitable interactions (Cappella et al., 2020). When students have the chance to develop relationships with dissimilar peers through sustained, structured, and cooperative interactions, these relationships can increase social and academic self-concept (Hwang et al., 2022), generate belonging (Hamm & Faircloth, 2005), and contribute to interpersonal skills (Kawabata & Crick, 2008).

Integrate Social Interaction into Instruction

Students thrive when they are given opportunities that meet both academic and social needs. Not only are they more engaged in school but they also develop positive relationships and stronger interpersonal skills (Hamre et al., 2013; Walberg & Paik, 2000; Yoder, 2014). Peer-assisted or cooperative learning (e.g., jigsaw classroom, peer tutoring) are example practices that engage students socially and academically, and lead to positive outcomes, including interpersonal competence in elementary and middle school (Gillies, 2014; Rohrbeck et al., 2003).

Take, as an example, think–pair–share, where students consider a question, discuss their ideas with a partner, and share back with the class. Think–pair–share provides a structure for students to practice skills in perspective taking and communication (Nastasi & Clements, 1991). Aligned with equity goals, youth who are uncomfortable or overlooked in a whole-class format get more time in academic conversation in a small group. Teachers can pair students who may not often work or play together, exposing students to new social ties or bridging social capital. As teachers use these approaches, students build more constructive, reciprocal relationships. As students get older, they can facilitate class discussions, allowing them agency in their learning.

Establish Positive Routines

Building familiar, predictable, and positive routines throughout the school day is critical for scaffolding interactions that foster social skills. Intentional classroom routines and practices, such as daily check-ins or opportunities to share, allow students to build relationships with peers through safe, regular communication (Jones et al., 2014; Dusenbury & Weissberg, 2017). The social processes developed through these routines create positive norms and sense of community (Tseng & Seidman, 2007), and offer the chance to build communication and perspective taking.

In early childhood and elementary school, effective and positive routines set the foundation for how to engage with others. During these years, staff members serve as models (e.g., by demonstrating equitable attention and asking open-ended questions). This provides students with a low-stakes space to engage in respectful, curious conversations about each other's lives and develops the facilitation skills of each student leading the "share" period.

In the middle grades, routines continue to be important as students encounter increasingly challenging social situations but must take on a different form to respect students' developing maturity and need for autonomy. Instead of engaging in a whole-class "share," adolescents might decide how they want to engage with each other (e.g., buddies, whole class) and what content is meaningful (e.g., moderating classroom disagreements, developing class activities). Students are able to dictate the terms of their own engagement, which communicates an environment of respect for their preferences and autonomy, while helping them practice a prosocial mind-set toward the classroom community. These approaches are more effective for middle and high school youth than a skills-based model, in which educators explicitly teach skills such as problem solving and communication, which is more appropriate for younger students (Yeager, 2017).

Embed Restorative Practices

Schools that take a restorative approach to building relationships and addressing challenges at school allow students, teachers, and staff members to engage in ways that give everyone a voice and are rooted in values of equity. Restorative practices reduce disproportionality in disciplinary practices and provide an opportunity to learn from mistakes rather than be punished for them (Boyes-Watson & Pranis, 2020; Gregory et al., 2016). *Proactive restorative practices* focus on community building and trust, which enables staff members and students to see, hear, and know each other better. *Responsive restorative practices* focus on understanding and addressing harm through nonpunitive conflict resolution to keep students and teachers connected to each other and the school community (Gregory et al., 2021).

Proactive restorative practices can be implemented across all grades. During the preschool and elementary school years, morning circles can be structured to support children in building a sense of community by learning the skills they need to positively interact with their peers and teachers. For example, a morning circle can be used to make cooperative decisions about how students will be assigned classroom jobs (e.g., lunch helper, line leader). This structured time provides students the opportunity to listen to the ideas and feelings of their peers, communicate their own ideas and feelings, and problem-solve. In upper elementary and middle school grades, community circles can also be used to create community agreements grounded in shared language that supports trust building and codesigning behavioral expectations among students and staff members. These circles can be increasingly led by students, in addition to teachers.

While regular community-building routines create a safe space for students to learn and engage with one another, conflict also provides a valuable opportunity to work on interpersonal skills. Responsive restorative practices, such as restorative conferences or community reentry circles, allow students, caregivers, and teachers to respond to harm that has happened among members of the classroom or school community. These practices give everyone involved in the incident an opportunity to share their perspective, reflect on how their actions affect others and themselves, and create a plan that can guide all parties involved should the conflict arise again.

One example combining both proactive and reactive restorative practices is a middle school that implemented a grade-level community circle period for all students. Circles used SEL activities that promoted the school's values, aligned activities with interpersonal skills central to positive community interactions, and provided opportunities to discuss and resolve conflicts. Teachers, paraprofessionals, guidance counselors, deans, parent coordinators, and leaders all took turns participating in community circles. Over the school year, students exhibited increased ownership over circles, teachers incorporated aspects of circle practices (e.g., prompts, student suggestions) into classrooms, and support staff members were better equipped to deescalate, mediate, and redirect peer-to-peer conflicts. Using restorative practices helped to shift the organization of social relationships (e.g., by promoting more horizontal communication and student leadership) and reorganize time and resources to focus on reparative dialogue over punishment.

The structure of restorative practices (e.g., passing a talking piece) and the overarching approach that supports interpersonal skill development (e.g., active listening, assuming good intentions) create a space of trust, while mitigating power differentials between youth and staff members, particularly youth from varied cultural backgrounds, who may have been socialized with different conflict management strategies. Over time, circles have the potential to develop both bridging capital, by allowing students and teachers to share different perspectives with each other, and bonding capital, in which participants can see themselves in others as they share.

Prepare Staff Members to Develop Students' Social Competencies

Educators experience a great deal of professional development (PD), and much has been written on best practices in teacher PD (Desimone, 2011). Here we highlight two aspects of PD central to improving students' social competencies. One is the *content,* such as learning specific strategies to promote students' interpersonal skills. The other is the *method,* such as discussing within- or across-role groups and providing opportunities for practice with formal feedback and informal support. Both provide meaningful opportunities for modeling and reinforcement (social learning) and capitalize on collaboration across staff members with dissimilar roles and similar roles (Johnson et al., 2011). Creating a sense of school community through collective PD builds an adult network that is equipped to cultivate skills among children. When staff members are asked to work together in interactive groups, to coach or mentor one another, or to provide support via informal networks, they have a chance to practice and develop their own interpersonal skills, which enhances their ability to promote students' skill development.

Consider a student conflict in a seventh-grade classroom in which the teacher calls the dean to remove the student from class. The dean feels the teacher has not done enough to address the conflict prior to removing the student; the teacher sees the handling of the conflict as the dean's responsibility. The student is removed and misses a lesson. How could this student conflict have been handled differently? If classroom teachers receive PD alongside school support staff members, they can engage in collective learning about common causes for and types of interpersonal conflict in their classroom, and learn together how to recognize, redirect, and resolve it. School leaders can further support teachers' development of skills to cultivate interpersonal competence and address conflicts by creating opportunities for teachers (and support staff members) to visit each other's classrooms, share expertise through exercises such as "watch one, do one, teach one," and seek and provide informal support via teacher networks. When staff members with different roles and responsibilities participate in PD *together*, they learn about one another's knowledge, skills, and strengths, and can co-create aligned practices to better model for students and operate as a team.

Leverage Family and Community Partnerships

When families and communities are engaged in the development of their children's interpersonal skills, it enables them to scaffold those skills at home, or in cases where beliefs about interpersonal skills in school differ from their cultural or contextual norms, aid their child in navigating those differences. The roles families play in their child's education are linked to a plethora of positive academic and social–emotional outcomes (Jeynes, 2012; Patrikakou et al., 2005). Research has also shown that family–school partnerships rooted in shared and equal responsibility, trusting relationships, and respect are central to the kinds of meaningful family engagement linked to positive student outcomes (Mapp & Kuttner, 2013). This is particularly important when teachers and families come from dissimilar cultures that may value different sets of interpersonal skills. Racially and culturally diverse schools can bolster alignment around interpersonal competence through intentional family engagement practices that build bonding and bridging capital and support the social learning necessary for such alignment to occur.

For example, lower elementary school grades can institute initiatives such as "Family Fridays," which invite caregivers into classrooms to spend one morning each month learning about their children's school. Teachers can use the time to inform caregivers what interpersonal skills are being taught and introduce activities (e.g., family games) that enable caregivers to share examples of interpersonal skills that are central to their family's culture. Participation in these activities provides families with the chance to observe in the classroom as they explore, model, and reinforce the interpersonal skills students are learning. They also promote meaningful exchanges that build trust by centering families' values and lived experiences (bonding capital) while bolstering efforts to diversify students' interpersonal skills (bridging capital).

At the community level, schools can reorganize resources that support students in and outside of school. For example, some schools use their after-school providers to support gym, health, or recess, which helps students to develop trusting relationships with after-school staff. After-school providers are often attached to larger, community-based organizations that provide community and family services, such as community centers, family support groups, enrichment classes, day camps, and more. In elementary school, students might see each other in class, at recess, and again in an after-school program, enabling them to become familiar with each other. Such interactions have the potential to extend outside of typical school and after-school hours through connections in other community spaces (Jones, Brush, et al., 2017). Schools that leverage relationships with community-based organizations increase the spaces where students and their families can continue to develop and deepen their interpersonal skills.

Putting It All Together

As schools target the interpersonal competencies they hope to build in their students and the broader school community, the work of organizing resources and supporting routines and practices requires a roadmap that will guide implementation, monitoring, and improvement. Below, we present an example of how this might happen in an elementary school that hopes to expand its use of cooperative learning practices (CLPs; i.e., small-group work centered around shared learning goals) in order to support interpersonal skills that enable students to maximize individual and collective learning, much of which is also applicable to middle school settings.

Imagine that several classroom teachers in a school have been using CLPs to support students' interpersonal skills. In order to achieve their goals, small groups of students work as a team, listen to each other, seek help from one another, and negotiate conflict. Students report enjoying this way of working and ask for more opportunities to do so. Teachers who use CLPs report seeing increased interpersonal competence in their classrooms. The school leadership team decides to use a systemic SEL approach to expand CLPs throughout the school in the upcoming year to actively build interpersonal competence for all community members. In planning for this initiative, they decide to incorporate the core features of implementation science, which seeks to systematically track and modify practices and policies related to an intervention, an approach that is highly complementary with systemic SEL, which can take years to actualize (Oberle et al., 2016). Core features involve (1) a whole-school approach; (2) aligning practices with the school's systems, processes, and resources; and (3) engaging in continuous improvement efforts.

Whole-School Approach

First, school leaders begin a process of ensuring that all school stakeholder groups—students, families, teachers, support staff, administrators, office personnel, school safety, and superintendents—inform how CLPs will be integrated into classrooms and shared spaces and activities (e.g., gym, recess, lunch, playgroups, class trips).

This includes mapping areas of the school where CLPs are already being used, spaces where it would take minimal effort to integrate CLPs into existing practices, and spaces where CLPs are not occurring. As part of this process, school leaders invite school community input around needs and existing strengths and resources the school can leverage through community forums, targeted surveys, and participatory planning activities. An inclusive resource-mapping and consensus-building approach helps a CLP school achieve community buy-in, provides multiple opportunities to communicate needs, and ensures equitable practices are selected that benefit all (and do not harm any) members of the school. Furthermore, it lays the groundwork for implementation, attending to sustainability over time.

Alignment of Practices to the School's Systems, Processes, and Resources

Next, the CLP school undergoes a process of aligning what is needed to implement and sustain CLPs based on its existing strengths, resources, needs, values, expectations, curriculum, and practices. The school creates a six- to eight-member whole-school CLP implementation team, which includes individuals who participated in resource mapping, feedback, and planning. This group conducts a comprehensive assessment that considers how practices could be embedded within and across systems (e.g., operations, administration), spaces (e.g., classrooms, hallways), and times of day (e.g., arrival, dismissal). The school implementation team uses assessment learnings to reallocate resources, leverage community strengths, and develop solutions for challenge areas. For example, the team proposes an action plan that extends turn-and-talk and small-group challenges, successful in classrooms using CLPs, to the common spaces of lunch, recess, and physical education. They also propose embedding more targeted CLPs that involve collaborative problem solving (e.g., elaborate puzzles) in classrooms and school day routines.

Support from school leadership is essential to achieve such alignment. Administrators at the CLP school establish systems that enable change in practice to evolve over time. For example, school leaders support the development of implementation working groups (e.g., teacher teams, recess support staff) to holistically integrate CLPs into the school. Each team is responsible for supporting systems change and implementation within its purview, while meeting shared goals across teams. Teams come together routinely to share learnings and discuss challenges that should be addressed. Teachers focus on curricula and instructional practices with students, family engagement specialists work to increase opportunities to practice interpersonal skills at home, and after-school staff members support recess and lunch activities and connect those to after-school programming. The school leadership team ensures that each group has the resources necessary to achieve its respective goals, and feedback loops are in place so that community stakeholders can continue to inform and support adoption, progress, and sustainability of CLPs.

Continuous Improvement

As the CLP school embarks on its multiyear journey to expand its CLP practices, it recognizes the importance of putting continuous improvement (CI) processes in place at the outset to support its endeavor. CI processes involve the routinization of data collection, management, and analysis, time for reflection on the aggregate and subgroup data, and continuous refinement of plans and actions to ensure that practices are in alignment with whole-school systems, needs, and resources (Bryk et al., 2015). School leadership and the CLP implementation team create a comprehensive schedule that "bakes in" all of the CI activities for the school year, which ensures that dedicated time and resources are set aside for these activities.

CI cycles are most likely to affect change when grounded in a strong culture of collaboration. School leadership and the CLP implementation team routinely review data, expand on areas of strength and identify improvement opportunities, including potential inequities in subgroup experience, and implement changes to improve social competencies for all students. To do this, the team uses multiple data forms that provide information about school processes, practices, and outcomes, community stakeholder behavior and attitudes, and their alignment. They conduct focus groups with school community subgroups (caregivers, students, teachers, support staff), observe classrooms and out-of-classroom spaces for CLPs, collect data about student and teacher experiences with CLPs via opinion polls and self-report surveys, and review archival data (e.g., policy and operational documents). Then, they triangulate these data to identify fidelity to the implementation process as originally designed, "bright spots" where they are experiencing success in achieving their goals, and areas that need course correction.

Finally, the school implementation team and related work groups ensure equitable experiences, practices, and outcomes by reviewing all data through an equity lens to identify and explore any emerging opportunity or outcome gaps. For example, data disaggregated by demographic groups (e.g., gender, race, multilingual learners, disability) can shed light on subgroups within the school that may benefit most or least from CLPs. Perhaps CLPs work best for girls in lower grades, but markers of success diminish as girls age. Or, perhaps Black and Brown boys are excluded more often from activities that afford them opportunities to deepen their interpersonal skills with students of other racial groups. As inequities are discovered, the implementation team works together to find solutions that align with both CLPs and existing school strengths, resources, needs, and practices, creating equitable opportunities for interpersonal relationships and skill development for all members of the school community.

Conclusion and Recommendations

Schools play a key role in creating opportunities for productive, positive relationships among students and their peers, families and community partners, and school staff, and it is through these relationships that students develop interpersonal skills. Figure 8.1 depicts opportunities for relationships and skill development to occur across two broad areas. First, school leaders must examine and shift *structures, composition, routines*, and *activities* to ensure that each student experiences productive and positive relationships with teachers, other students, and school staff members. Second, assessment and action must be grounded in *values and norms of inclusion and equity*, so that all school members, particularly those who have been marginalized, are acknowledged for their skills and benefit from opportunities for skill development. Ultimately, the goal is to embed effective and equitable strategies in schools committed to systemic SEL and to use an inclusive, data-based process to create and improve opportunities for interpersonal relationships and skill development. For educators engaged in this important work, we recommend the following set of actionable strategies.

Shifting School Structure, Composition, Routines, and Activities

- Set up physical school spaces that are safe, organized, and warm. For example, make sure students and staff members know where to access materials, and that materials are represented in visual displays so everyone feels like they belong and can participate in the community.

- Build familiar, predictable, and positive routines to scaffold interactions that foster interpersonal skills. In the classroom, intentional routines and practices, such as daily check-ins and community shares, allow students to build relationships with their peers.

- Set up class sizes and compositions that provide small, stable communities for younger children and exposure to more peers as children grow older. Use inclusive grouping in shared school spaces to provide exposure to diverse perspectives, skills, and strengths.

- Offer engaging and appropriately challenging instructional methods that support interpersonal skill development for students from all cultural and linguistic backgrounds, racial/ethnic identities, and abilities.

- Provide many and varied opportunities for students to practice skills with adult support and supervision across the school day and throughout the school building.

Grounding Interpersonal Skill Development in Values and Norms of Equity

- Build a shared vision and language that supports interpersonal skill development, and communicate openly with the community. Take the time to ensure that a variety of voices, lived experiences, and suggestions are included.

- Provide many and varied opportunities for adults to reflect on, understand, and grow their interpersonal skills, including reflection on how their beliefs and behaviors may or may not align with their students and colleagues. Bring school staff members together in PD across and within roles.

- Ensure that students and educators are aware of and have experience with varied interpersonal skills and expectations from all cultural groups that make up the school community. Integrate the strengths and experiences of families and community partners.

- Embed culturally responsive, restorative approaches into daily classroom practices, name and shift relational power dynamics, and use nonpunitive disciplinary actions. Create and champion opportunities for youth to maximize their own skill development.

- Continuously assess and adjust values to align with whole-school practices and approaches for interpersonal development for all. Ask, "Do our practices work for *all* students and educators, or only for some subgroups?" Address emerging disparities.

DISCUSSION QUESTIONS

1. Developing interpersonal skills requires practice, practice, and more practice. Yet this means that children and youth who are most enthusiastic about time spent with others get the most practice and those who prefer to be alone or have less well-developed social skills get the least practice. What can educators do to counteract that tendency?
2. Think about the goal of creating equitable opportunities for children and youth to develop friendships and interpersonal skills in schools. What does this mean? What is currently being done? What challenges come up? What are ideas for addressing these challenges?
3. We have talked in this chapter about opportunities for students to engage with peers as part of academic work. There are a lot of forms this can take:

cooperative learning, peer-assisted learning, peer tutoring, service learning, and more. What are some of the challenges we anticipate, and how might we solve these challenges to make engagement with peers successful in academic work?

4. After a school has identified and begun to use practices to support interpersonal development, it is important to monitor what is happening and how it is going for different members of the school community. How might you engage and learn from families? How could staff in various roles contribute? How could students' perspectives be included?

REFERENCES

Aber, J. L., Tubbs, C., Torrente, C., Halpin, P. F., Johnston, B., Starkey, L., . . . Wolf, S. (2017). Promoting children's learning and development in conflict-affected countries: Testing change process in the Democratic Republic of the Congo. *Development and Psychopathology, 29*(1), 53–67.

Aboud, F. E. (1984). Social and cognitive bases of ethnic identity constancy. *Journal of Genetic Psychology, 145*(2), 217–229.

Au, K. H. (2013). A sociocultural model of reading instruction: The Kamehameha Elementary Education Program. In S. A. Stahl & D. A. Hayes (Eds.), *Instructional models in reading* (pp. 191–212). Routledge.

Bagwell, C. L., & Bukowski, W. M. (2018). Friendship in childhood and adolescence: Features, effects, and processes. In W. M. Bukowski, B. Laursen, & K. H. Rubin (Eds.), *Handbook of peer interactions, relationships, and groups* (pp. 371–390). Guilford Press.

Bandura, A. (1977). Self-efficacy: Toward a unifying theory of behavioral change. *Psychological Review, 84*(2), 191–215.

Bierman, K. L., Torres, M. M., Domitrovich, C. E., Welsh, J. A., & Gest, S. D. (2009). Behavioral and cognitive readiness for school: Cross-domain associations for children attending Head Start. *Social Development, 18*(2), 305–323.

Boyes-Watson, C., & Pranis, K. (2020). *Circle forward: Building a restorative school community.* Living Justice Press.

Bryk, A. S., Gomez, L. M., Grunow, A., & LeMahieu, P. G. (2015). *Learning to improve: How America's schools can get better at getting better.* Harvard Education Press.

Calero, M. D., Mata, S., Bonete, S., Molinero, C., & Gómez-Pérez, M. M. (2015). Relations between learning potential, cognitive and interpersonal skills in Asperger children. *Learning and Individual Differences, 44*, 53–60.

Cappella, E., Frazier, S. L., Smith, E. P., & Hwang, S. H. (2020). Strengthening social processes to support youth with emotional and behavioral difficulties: An ecological, public health approach in afterschool programs. In T. W. Farmer, M. Conroy, E. M. Z. Farmer, & K. Sutherland (Eds.), *Handbook of research on emotional and behavioral disorders: Interdisciplinary developmental perspectives on children and youth* (pp. 167–182). Routledge.

Cappella, E., Hughes, D. L., & McCormick, M. P. (2017). The hidden role of teachers: Child and classroom predictors of change in interracial friendships. *Journal of Early Adolescence, 37*(8), 1093–1124.

Chen, X. (2000). Social and emotional development in Chinese children and adolescents: A contextual cross-cultural perspective. In F. Columbus (Ed.), *Advances in psychology research* (Vol. 1, pp. 229–251). Nova Science.

Chen, X., & French, D. C. (2008). Children's social competence in cultural context. *Annual Review of Psychology, 59*, 591–616.

Cillessen, A. H., & Bellmore, A. D. (2004). Social skills and interpersonal perception in early and middle childhood. In P. K. Smith & C. H. Hart (Eds.), *Blackwell handbook of childhood social development* (pp. 355–374). Blackwell.

Cohen, E. G. (1994). Restructuring the classroom: Conditions for productive small groups. *Review of Educational Research, 64*, 1–35.

Coleman, J. S. (1988). Social capital in the creation of human capital. *American Journal of Sociology, 94*, S95–S120.

Crick, N. R., & Dodge, K. A. (1996). Social information-processing mechanisms in reactive and proactive aggression. *Child Development, 67*(3), 993–1002.

Denham, S. (2018). *Keeping SEL developmental: The importance of a developmental lens for fostering and assessing SEL competencies.* Frameworks Briefs, Special Issues Series, Establishing Practical Social Emotional Competence Assessments Work Group.

Denham, S. A., & Brown, C. (2010). "Plays nice with others": Social–emotional learning and academic success. *Early Education and Development, 21*(5), 652–680.

Desimone, L. M. (2011). A primer on effective professional development. *Phi Delta Kappan, 92*(6), 68–71.

Dika, S. L., & Singh, K. (2002). Applications of social capital in educational literature: A critical synthesis. *Review of Educational Research, 72*(1), 31–60.

DiPrete, T. A., & Jennings, J. L. (2012). Social and behavioral skills and the gender gap in early educational achievement. *Social Science Research, 41*(1), 1–15.

Dusenbury, L., & Weissberg, R. P. (2017). *Social emotional learning in elementary school: Preparation for success.* Penn State University/Robert Wood Johnson Foundation.

Eisenberg, N., Sadovsky, A., & Spinrad, T. L. (2005, Fall). Associations of emotion-related regulation with language skills, emotion knowledge, and academic outcomes. *New Directions for Child and Adolescent Development, 109*, 109–118.

Farmer, T. W., Lines, M. M., & Hamm, J. V. (2011). Revealing the invisible hand: The role of teachers in children's peer experiences. *Journal of Applied Developmental Psychology, 32*(5), 247–256.

Gershenson, S., Hansen, M., & Lindsay, C. A. (2021). *Teacher diversity and student success: Why racial representation matters in the classroom.* Harvard Education Press.

Gillies, R. M. (2014). Cooperative learning: Developments in research. *International Journal of Educational Psychology, 3*(2), 125–140.

Graham, S., & Echols, L. (2018). Race and ethnicity in peer relations research. In W. M. Bukowski, B. Laursen, & K. H. Rubin (Eds.), *Handbook of peer interactions, relationships, and groups* (pp. 590–614). Guilford Press.

Gregory, A., Clawson, K., Davis, A., & Gerewitz, J. (2016). The promise of restorative practices to transform teacher–student relationships and achieve equity in school discipline. *Journal of Educational and Psychological Consultation, 26*(4), 325–353.

Gregory, A., Ward-Seidel, A. R., & Carter, K. V. (2021). Twelve indicators of restorative practices implementation: A framework for educational leaders. *Journal of Educational and Psychological Consultation, 31*(2), 147–179.

Hall, G. E., & DiPerna, J. C. (2017). Childhood social skills as predictors of middle school academic adjustment. *Journal of Early Adolescence, 37*(6), 825–851.

Hallinan, M. T., & Smith, S. S. (1989). Classroom characteristics and student friendship cliques. *Social Forces, 67*(4), 898–919.

Hallinan, M. T., & Teixeira, R. A. (1987). Students' interracial friendships: Individual characteristics, structural effects, and racial differences. *American Journal of Education, 95*(4), 563–583.

Hamm, J. V., & Faircloth, B. S. (2005). The role of friendship in adolescents' sense of school belonging. *New Directions for Child and Adolescent Development, 107*, 61–78.

Hamre, B. K., & Pianta, R. C. (2001). Early teacher–child relationships and the trajectory of children's school outcomes through eighth grade. *Child Development, 72*(2), 625–638.

Hamre, B. K., Pianta, R. C., Downer, J. T., DeCoster, J., Mashburn, A. J., Jones, S. M., . . . Hamagami, A. (2013). Teaching through interactions: Testing a developmental framework of teacher effectiveness in over 4,000 classrooms. *Elementary School Journal, 113*(4), 461–487.

Hecht, M. L., & Shin, Y. (2015). Culture and social and emotional competencies. In J. A. Durlak, C. E. Domitrovich, R. P. Weissberg, & T. P. Gullotta (Eds.), *Handbook of social and emotional learning: Research and practice* (pp. 50–64). Guilford Press.

Hwang, S. H. J., Cappella, E., Kieffer, M. J., & Yates, M. (2022). "Let's hang out!": Understanding social ties among linguistically diverse youth in urban afterschool programs. *Social Development, 31*, 52–68.

Jagers, R. J., Rivas-Drake, D., & Williams, B. (2019). Transformative social and emotional learning (SEL): Toward SEL in service of educational equity and excellence. *Educational Psychologist, 54*(3), 162–184.

January, A. M., Casey, R. J., & Paulson, D. (2011). A meta-analysis of classroom-wide interventions to build social skills: Do they work? *School Psychology Review, 40*(2), 242–256.

Jensen-Campbell, L. A., Gleason, K. A., Adams, R., & Malcolm, K. T. (2003). Interpersonal conflict, agreeableness, and personality development. *Journal of Personality, 71*(6), 1059–1086.

Jeynes, W. (2012). A meta-analysis of the efficacy of different types of parental involvement programs for urban students. *Urban Education, 47*(4), 706–742.

Johnson, W., Lustick, D., & Kim, M. (2011). Teacher professional learning as the growth of social capital. *Current Issues in Education, 14*(3), Article EJ945437.

Jones, D. E., Greenberg, M., & Crowley, M. (2015). Early social–emotional functioning and public health: The relationship between kindergarten social competence and future wellness. *American Journal of Public Health, 105*(11), 2283–2290.

Jones, S. M., Bailey, R., & Jacob, R. (2014). Social–emotional learning is essential to classroom management. *Phi Delta Kappan, 96*(2), 19–24.

Jones, S. M., Barnes, S. P., Bailey, R., & Doolittle, E. J. (2017). Promoting social and emotional competencies in elementary school. *Future of Children, 27*, 49–72.

Jones, S. M., Brush, K., Bailey, R., Brion-Meisels, G., McIntyre, J., Kahn, J., . . . Stickle, L. (2017). *Navigating SEL from the inside out: Looking inside and across 25 leading SEL programs: A practical resource for schools and OST providers (Elementary School Focus).* Wallace Foundation.

Kawabata, Y., & Crick, N. R. (2008). The role of cross-racial/ethnic friendships in social adjustment. *Developmental Psychology, 44*(4), 1177–1183.

Killen, M., Crystal, D. S., & Ruck, M. (2007). The social developmental benefits of intergroup contact among children and adolescents. In E. Frankenberg & G. Orfield (Eds.), *Lessons in integration: Realizing the promise of racial diversity in American schools* (pp. 31–56). University of Virginia Press.

Kim, H. Y., & Cappella, E. (2016). Mapping the social world of urban classrooms: A multi-level, multi-reporter approach to social processes and behavioral engagement. *American Journal of Community Psychology, 57*(1–2), 20–35.

Kiuru, N., Aunola, K., Lerkkanen, M. K., Pakarinen, E., Poskiparta, E., Ahonen, T., . . . Nurmi, J. E. (2015). Positive teacher and peer relations combine to predict primary school students' academic skill development. *Developmental Psychology, 51*(4), 434–446.

Kokko, K., Tremblay, R. E., Lacourse, E., Nagin, D. S., & Vitaro, F. (2006). Trajectories of prosocial behavior and physical aggression in middle childhood: Links to adolescent school dropout and physical violence. *Journal of Research on Adolescence, 16*(3), 403–428.

Ladd, G. W., Kochenderfer-Ladd, B., & Rydell, A.-M. (2014). Children's interpersonal skills and school-based relationships. In P. K. Smith & C. H. Hart (Eds.), *The Wiley-Blackwell handbook of childhood social development* (2nd ed., pp. 181–206). Wiley-Blackwell.

Mahoney, J. L., Weissberg, R. P., Greenberg, M. T., Dusenbury, L., Jagers, R. J., Niemi, K., . . . Yoder, N. (2021). Systemic social and emotional learning: Promoting educational success for all preschool to high school students. *American Psychologist, 76*(7), 1128–1142.

Mapp, K. L., & Kuttner, P. J. (2013). *Partners in education: A dual capacity-building framework for family–school partnerships.* Southwest Educational Development Laboratory & U.S. Department of Education.

Martin, C. L., Ruble, D. N., & Szkrybalo, J. (2002). Cognitive theories of early gender development. *Psychological Bulletin, 128*(6), 903–933.

Mikami, A. Y., & Mercer, S. H. (2017). Teacher behaviors toward children with attention-deficit/hyperactivity disorder predict peers' initial liking and disliking impressions in a summer camp setting. *Journal of Social and Clinical Psychology, 36*(6), 506–534.

Nastasi, B. K., & Clements, D. H. (1991). Research on cooperative learning: Implications for practice. *School Psychology Review, 20*(1), 110–131.

National Academies of Sciences, Engineering, and Medicine. (2019a). *The promise of adolescence: Realizing opportunity for all youth.* National Academies Press.

National Academies of Sciences, Engineering, and Medicine. (2019b). *Fostering healthy mental, emotional, and behavioral development in children and youth: A national agenda.* National Academies Press.

Oberle, E., Domitrovich, C. E., Meyers, D. C., & Weissberg, R. P. (2016). Establishing systemic social and emotional learning approaches in schools: A framework for schoolwide implementation. *Cambridge Journal of Education, 46*(3), 277–297.

Patrikakou, E. N., Weissberg, R. P., Redding, S., & Walberg, H. J. (2005). School–family partnerships: Enhancing the academic, social, and emotional learning of children. In E. N.

Patrikakou, R. P. Weissberg, S. Redding, & H. J. Walberg, (Eds.), *School–family partnerships for children's success* (pp. 1–17). Teachers College Press.

Pedersen, S., Vitaro, F., Barker, E. D., & Borge, A. I. (2007). The timing of middle-childhood peer rejection and friendship: Linking early behavior to early-adolescent adjustment. *Child Development, 78*(4), 1037–1051.

Pianta, R. C., Hamre, B., & Stuhlman, M. (2003). Relationships between teachers and children. In W. M. Reynolds & G. E. Miller (Eds.), *Handbook of psychology: Vol. 7. Educational psychology* (pp. 199–234). Wiley.

Rentenbach, B., Prislovsky, L., & Gabriel, R. (2017). Valuing differences: Neurodiversity in the classroom. *Phi Delta Kappan, 98*(8), 59–63.

Reynolds, M. R., Sander, J. B., & Irvin, M. J. (2010). Latent curve modeling of internalizing behaviors and interpersonal skills through elementary school. *School Psychology Quarterly, 25*(4), 189–201.

Rohrbeck, C. A., Ginsburg-Block, M. D., Fantuzzo, J. W., & Miller, T. R. (2003). Peer-assisted learning interventions with elementary school students: A meta-analytic review. *Journal of Educational Psychology, 95*(2), 240–257.

Rubin, K. H., Burgess, K. B., Kennedy, A. E., & Stewart, S. L. (2003). Social withdrawal in childhood. In E. J. Mash & R. A. Barkley (Eds.), *Child psychopathology* (pp. 372–406). Guilford Press.

Rudolph, K. D., Hammen, C., Burge, D., Lindberg, N., Herzberg, D., & Daley, S. E. (2000). Toward an interpersonal life-stress model of depression: The developmental context of stress generation. *Development and Psychopathology, 12*(2), 215–234.

Schultz, L. H., Barr, D. J., & Selman, R. L. (2001). The value of a developmental approach to evaluating character development programmes: An outcome study of Facing History and Ourselves. *Journal of Moral Education, 30*(1), 3–27.

Simmons, D. N., Brackett, M. A., & Adler, N. (2018). *Applying an equity lens to social, emotional, and academic development.* Edna Bennett Pierce Prevention Research Center, Pennsylvania State University.

Simpkins, S. D., Riggs, N. R., Ngo, B., Vest Ettekal, A., & Okamoto, D. (2017). Designing culturally responsive organized after-school activities. *Journal of Adolescent Research, 32*(1), 11–36.

Spitzberg, B. H., & Cupach, W. R. (2012). *Handbook of interpersonal competence research.* Springer Science & Business Media.

Thapa, A., Cohen, J., Guffey, S., & Higgins-D'Alessandro, A. (2013). A review of school climate research. *Review of Educational Research, 83*(3), 357–385.

Torrente, C., Alimchandani, A., & Aber, J. L. (2015). International perspectives on SEL. In J. A. Durlak, C. E. Domitrovich, R. P. Weissberg, & T. P. Gullotta (Eds.), *Handbook of social and emotional learning: Research and practice* (pp. 566–587). Guilford Press.

Tseng, V., & Seidman, E. (2007). A systems framework for understanding social settings. *American Journal of Community Psychology, 39*(3–4), 217–228.

Walberg, H. J., & Paik, S. J. (2000). *Effective educational practices.* International Academy of Education.

Wentzel, K. R., Battle, A., Russell, S. L., & Looney, L. B. (2010). Social support from teachers and peers as predictors of academic and social motivation. *Contemporary Educational Psychology, 35*, 193–202.

Yeager, D. S. (2017). Social and emotional learning programs for adolescents. *Future of Children, 27,* 73–94.

Yoder, N. (2014). *Teaching the whole child: Instructional practices that support social–emotional learning in three teacher evaluation frameworks.* American Institutes for Research.

Youngstrom, E., Wolpaw, J. M., Kogos, J. L., Schoff, K., Ackerman, B., & Izard, C. (2000). Interpersonal problem solving in preschool and first grade: Developmental change and ecological validity. *Journal of Clinical Child Psychology, 29*(4), 589–602.

Chapter 9

Cultivating Students' Intrapersonal SEL Skills

Tyralynn Frazier and Brendan Ozawa-de Silva

In 2009, a small team of compassion scientists at Emory University, led by Drs. Lobsang Tenzin Negi and Charles Raison, began a multiyear project working to bring a compassion-based meditation training program called Cognitively-Based Compassion Training (CBCT®) to children in foster care. This program targeted the intrapersonal skill of self-compassion, and the critical interpersonal skill of compassion for others that can stem from the development of self-compassion. CBCT was later adapted for educational settings and developed into a program that would grow to reach children in schools around the world. One of the first steps of this adaptation was a short, 2-month pilot focusing on six girls, ages 13–16, who lived together at a group foster home.

The girls quickly began to express that the compassion-based meditation practices they were learning made them feel calmer and helped them deal with stress. They looked forward to the sessions and reported feeling noticeably less anxious afterward. However, as the program progressed from a focus on mindfulness to self-compassion to compassion for others, they began to see that the purpose of meditation was not simply about reducing stress. Rather, it was also about exploring how their emotions connect with their relationships to others—what we might call the interdependence of the personal and the interpersonal.

Shortly after the program's conclusion, one of the participants in the program was called to appear alongside her adopted mother for a court hearing to finalize her placement with the family. The young girl had a complex relationship with her mother. In front of everyone, the young girl told the judge that through the compassion meditation practices, she learned that although she could not control the behavior of others, she could decide how to respond to her own thoughts and emotions with positive behaviors. She said that her ability to make her own decisions about how to treat others, rather than waiting for others to prove themselves and earn her trust, was the only way she felt she could ever have genuine relationships and be happy. Impressed, the judge said that the foster care system should promote such programs more widely. Staff members with social services, in Atlanta, continued to work with the Emory research team, and over 200 foster children in Atlanta were offered the program within a few years. It became the basis for a published research study on the efficacy of CBCT with adolescents and its potential benefits for decreasing generalized anxiety (Reddy et al., 2013). Mainstream educational systems are increasingly bringing specialized initiatives like the one described earlier to their students and teachers through social and emotional learning (SEL). This is an exciting development, because translating specialized knowledge into practical and accessible tools for educators benefits children on a wide scale. In this chapter, we discuss intrapersonal skills development. What are intrapersonal skills? Why are they important? How can they be cultivated with equity? We answer each of these questions and provide examples based on our experiences with educational systems around the world. There are many ways to engage in intrapersonal development. SEE Learning is one of a number of programs that focuses on the development of intrapersonal skills. One unique facet of SEE Learning is the emphasis on compassion and self-compassion. One thing that is universally clear is that the development of intrapersonal skills effectively supports children and teachers in cultivating resilience, compassion, and engagement, thus making educators feel supported, students feel seen, and leadership more dedicated to a systemic approach to social and emotional development.

What Are Intrapersonal Skills?

Intrapersonal means "within yourself." As described by the *APA Dictionary of Psychology*, *intrapersonal skills* refer to "factors operating or constructs occurring within the person, such as attitudes, decisions, self-concept, self-esteem, or self-regulation" (American Psychological Association, n.d.). Intrapersonal skills differ from interpersonal skills, which emphasize interactions "between people" (Oleś et al., 2020). Identifying your emotions is an *intra*personal skill, because it focuses inner dialogue or self-talk, self-assessment, and self-management (Oleś et al., 2020). In contrast, active listening is an *inter*personal skill, because it focuses on a social interaction. Intrapersonal and interpersonal skills are inextricably related and often mutually supportive. Developing intrapersonal skills when you are a child decreases your risk of anxiety and contributes to your learning ability (Valenzuela et al., 2022; Valosek et al., 2021).

The Two Roots of Intrapersonal Skills Development

Intrapersonal skills are rooted in two main traditions—contemplative frameworks and SEL frameworks. The Center for Contemplative Mind in Society (CMind; 2021) defines *contemplative traditions* as practices that cultivate an individual's awareness and support them in developing a stronger connection with a divine source or inner wisdom. These can include many different types of practices. Figure 9.1 is a summary of contemplative intrapersonal practices that derive from various traditions. The Collaborative for Academic, Social, and Emotional Learning (CASEL, 2022) has developed an SEL framework that includes self-awareness, self-management, social awareness, relationship skills, and responsible decision making. The intrapersonal skills include *self-awareness* and *self-management* (CASEL, 2022).

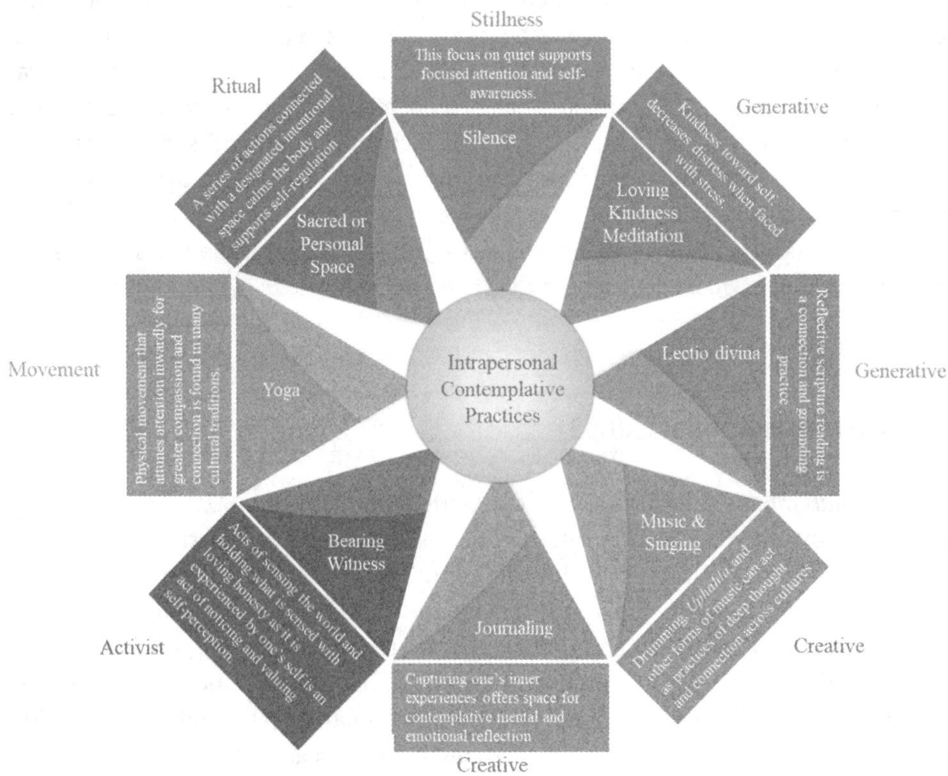

FIGURE 9.1. Summary of intrapersonal contemplative practices found on the Tree of Contemplative Practices (CMind, 2021), illustrating a range of religious, secular, or cultural traditions.

The Contemplative Approach to Intrapersonal Development

Contemplative traditions exist in many religions and cultures, and are much older than SEL, but they have only recently been integrated into SEL programs (Mind and Life Education Research Network [MLERN], 2012; Lawlor, 2016; Schonert-Reichl & Roeser, 2016). The practices from contemplative traditions include forms of mindfulness and compassion practices. Bishop et al. (2004) define *mindfulness* as "a mode of awareness that is evoked when attention is regulated" (p. 234). *Compassion* is generally defined as a perception of or sensitivity toward suffering and the nonjudgmental motivation to help (Straus et al., 2016). Mindful and compassionate practices include meditation, yoga, tai chi, and many others from diverse cultural, religious, and secular origins. When brought into schools, the practices summarized in Figure 9.1 take a secular form. They are not bound to a religion; rather, they are practices that can be applied across diverse secular or religious educational contexts. Although many of the most popular intrapersonal practices are secular forms that derive from Eastern traditions (meditation, yoga, tai chi, etc.), these practices can be found across cultures and religions (Figure 9.1). One of the common features of virtually all contemplative practices is the idea that self-awareness is grounded in understanding one's own emotions, thoughts, and values. Contemplative practices have become attractive to schools not only for child well-being but also because these practices can help students or teachers direct their focus internally, which directly benefits academic performance (Caballero et al., 2019). In short, these contemplative practices focus on the skills of mindfulness, attention, and self-compassion from a secular lens, which together with SEL, can work to support intrapersonal development.

The SEL Approach to Intrapersonal Development

Self-awareness refers to understanding one's emotions and recognizing that emotions affect behavior (CASEL, 2022). Recognizing this link between emotions and behaviors can provide an opportunity to see one's strengths and limitations with a well-grounded sense of confidence and purpose (Jones et al., 2017). This ability depends on one's patterns of thinking (growth or strengths-based vs. deficit-focused) and beliefs about oneself (self-efficacy). Self-management extends from self-awareness toward regulation of "emotions, thoughts, and behaviors" through that awareness, for the purpose of working toward and achieving goals (CASEL, 2022). Characteristics of self-awareness and self-management are valuable for psychological well-being and the development of perspective taking and empathy, two capacities that are critical for positive relationships (Taylor et al., 2020). They also have an important influence on how one's academic goal orientation, stress management, self-discipline, self-efficacy, and executive function foster academic success (Duckworth & Seligman, 2005; Elliot & Dweck, 2005).

Self-management is sometimes referred to as *self-regulation,* and here we use these terms synonymously. The importance of self-regulation and self-management is rooted, in part, in work done in the 1960s examining young children's abilities to delay gratification. Specifically, Metcalfe and Mischel (1999) conducted a series of experiments with young children in studies commonly referred to as the "marshmallow test." In this classic work, preschool children were presented with the option of having one small treat (a marshmallow or a pretzel) right away or waiting for about 15 minutes to receive two treats. There were two conditions: For some children the small treat was in the room with them while they waited, and for others the treat was not in the room with them while they waited. For both conditions, children were instructed to ring a bell if they wanted the treat. Some children were told how to redirect their thoughts to help them delay eating the delicious treat. Results showed that the children who delayed eating the marshmallow scored higher on academic tests, stress and coping tests, and other measures when they were older (Mischel et al., 1989). The act of redirecting one's attention starts with awareness of one's thoughts. This self-awareness can then be used to manage one's own thoughts by choosing to think about something else. In these studies, choosing to think about something other than the treat helped children delay eating the treat and receive the larger quantity after the 15 minutes was up. This work links to a growing body of evidence that self-awareness and self-management help children succeed in school (Kidd et al., 2013; Lamm et al., 2018).

Why Are Intrapersonal Skills Important?

The research on the "marshmallow test" is interesting for many reasons. It points to a cluster of skills that work together—self-awareness, self-regulation, inhibitory control, and, ultimately, delayed gratification. This cluster of skills tends to be highly valued in schools in the United States, and existing work describes classroom practices that can contribute to the development of these skills. In this chapter, we present a few examples of tools that support this cluster of skills, but there are many others out there (Brock et al., 2009; Brock et al., 2014; Merritt et al., 2012) that could be described.

Why Does Intrapersonal Skills Development Help with Academics?

In the context of education and through contemplative practices, intrapersonal skills can enhance self-awareness, self-regulation, and inhibitory control to help students learn better (Panadero, 2017). Psychologist, Olivier Houde (2019) describes the intrapersonal skills of SEL as enabling a child to try, fail, feel regret and curiosity, try again, and move toward success. Contemplative training in practices, such as mindfulness, builds a student's ability to achieve the following:

- Present-moment awareness of an experience without reacting with harmful behaviors.
- Present-moment awareness of strong emotions without being entangled or overtaken by those emotions.
- A balance between emotional avoidance and excessive preoccupation with thoughts.

These new skills create the ability for "distress tolerance" in the presence of difficulty (Broderick & Jennings, 2012), and prevents the self-judgment and anxiety that might come with the fixation on negative rumination, which can lead to poor outcomes (Berkowitz, 2008). Developing greater awareness of one's patterns of thoughts and feelings enables one to disrupt these patterns and access greater regulatory control over one's own mind (Derryberry & Rothbart, 1997; Zelazo & Cunningham, 2007).

There is no question that stress is part of learning and life (Houde, 2019). Learning to manage stress is a part of learning to navigate the world. As children grow, they discover how to handle relationships and academics, and come to understand that they have a choice about their place in the world. In childhood, behaviors such as sharing or self-control can be difficult. The parts of a child's brain that control emotion are still developing, and these areas also help interpersonal relationship behaviors (Miller et al., 2015). Changes in the nervous system, with age, transform children's ability to regulate their emotions (Eisenberg, 2000). Early childhood is a time when learning skills to help with these regulation processes can support long-term emotional control. In turn, this learning can influence relationships, because children are better able to manage frustration and anger in their interactions with the people around them. The young girl in foster care presented in the story at the beginning of this chapter connected with the compassion meditation practice. This resonance shifted how she perceived and related to her world first by helping her develop self-awareness without distress or judgment. On the surface, the approach she learned was simple—she followed a series of guided reflections about directing compassion to herself and to others. On the inside, the effect of that practice was helping her develop the critical skills of noticing, choosing to calm, and beginning to regulate her body and mind to create space for exploring emotions. Through this, she could relate what she learned about her own inner life to others, such as her mother, based on their common humanity.

Why Does Intrapersonal Skills Development Matter beyond Academics?: The Whole Child

A *whole-child approach* in schools means that educators are acutely aware of the connections between children's emotional, social, physical, and academic development. For example, if students are unable to manage intense experiences of frustration, they will be unable to engage in the process of learning, regardless of the quality of instruction (Darling-Hammond et al., 2020). Aspiring to a whole-child approach fits well with the contemplative practices previously discussed (Figure 9.1) in that meditative practices provide a compendium of opportunities that help individuals bridge their inner processes with their outer experiences. For example, loving kindness meditation is a generative practice in that it allows an individual to cultivate an ability to be kind toward oneself even when a mistake is made, a failure is encountered, or stressful situation is occurring (Lea et al., 2015). In other words, these practices allow children to learn how to navigate challenges while also holding themselves with love. For example, if we teach a child to approach a math test while holding themselves with loving kindness, then that child's zone of proximal development expands and they are more likely to show a higher level of independent performance (Vygotsky, 1978). As another example, a child who can experience self-compassion can then turn this sentiment toward others to reduce judgment and increase understanding. Yet another example comes from efforts to use singing and playing music to enhance focused attention, which in turn can then give students a pathway to connect with their own and others' cultures. Engaging in inner work and cultivating awareness then becomes a bridge to connect meaningfully with others and attend to and engage with classroom learning opportunities.

Contemplative practices provide strong tools that are hypothesized to grow the heart, the soul, and the way one lives with value and purpose through the habits of thought and action (Ash et al., 2021). These practices support abilities for sustained concentration (Dweck, 2017), which in turn allows for greater mastery and goal attainment (Maehr & Braskamp, 1986) that can lead to enhanced stress regulation, subject-matter learning, and improved classroom behavior (Boekaerts, 1993; Valosek et al., 2021; Valenzuela et al., 2022). Bridging these capacities that are highly valued in education with tenderness and loving kindness enhances the quality of a child's whole well-being, not simply academic performance. Traditionally, these contemplative practices have occurred within cultural framings that reinforce and extend the meaningfulness of the practices through opportunities to develop one's abilities with supportive guidance through this process of mastery. The outcomes of such mastery directly influence abilities that are relevant to academic achievement, while also situating the child within a caring and supportive environment. Thus, contemplative practices can be foundational to a whole-child approach to education.

How Are Intrapersonal Skills Developed?: What We Have Learned from the Field

While it is true that intrapersonal skills exist across diverse cultures and religious traditions, sometimes people are resistant to contemplative practices because they do not see themselves, their culture, or their religion in the practice. They may fear that the practices are a way of bringing other religions or cultural practices into schools and ignoring the practices that are locally valued. There are diverse ways of bringing the practices into classrooms, and many programs exist to support the integration of intrapersonal skills development in schools. Some of these programs focus more directly on SEL intrapersonal skills such as self-management for goal setting (Lion's Quest, 2022) or emotional intelligence cultivation (Yale Center for Emotional Intelligence, 2022). The CASEL program guide describes MindUP and Second Step as examples of programs that focus on internal emotional states and contemplative practices. Here, we describe SEE Learning as an example of a program that brings contemplative practices into schools with a focus on cultivating compassionate awareness of self, others, and the systems in which children are embedded to support compassionate engagement in the world. Common themes exist across programs that build on both SEL and contemplative practices, namely, cultivation of internal state awareness and aspects of kindness or compassion development (Jones et al., 2017).

In developing SEE Learning, we recognized the need for more diverse representations of practices, as well as the need to integrate practices across religious, secular, and cultural settings. The work grew from the first step with just a few young girls in foster care and pilots at local elementary classrooms in Atlanta, described at the beginning of this chapter. SEE Learning, which was adapted from CBCT to work in a school-based setting, was launched internationally in 2019 and is currently being used in more than 25 countries (SEE Learning, 2022). Work with thousands of teachers and students around the world, has taught the SEE Learning team about challenges and key considerations that impact SEL programs within diverse local contexts. For example, in Kenya and in the United States, resistance to practices is explicitly linked to the local traditions, religions, or cultures that bring distrust and skepticism. In Nairobi, one group invited participants to adapt the practices by using examples that were specific to themselves, and to find models of practices within their local culture that reflect the contemplative practice they were learning. This led to more engagement from participants. Within the United States, we have worked with Christian and Jewish schools on integration into their existing traditions. Similar work has occurred with our Muslim affiliates within the Middle East. The purpose is to take an integrated approach, so that communities have agency to align their beliefs, traditions, and cultural knowledge with the practices, so that the practices exist in a contextually relevant way.

Across the many settings that use meditative practices to contribute to intrapersonal skills, we see a few critical components that need to be present to ensure success. First, the skills themselves are taught with opportunities for practice—for example, just like music instruction, teaching compassion meditation takes time and occurs over many weeks. Second, the meditative practices need to be connected to the immediate school context. For instance, meditative practices and the learning of intrapersonal skills need to be integrated into content through culturally relevant examples that show when and how they might be used. Third, for the practices to contribute meaningfully to intrapersonal growth, teachers and students need to know *why* they work. They need to understand answers to questions: How has music been used to foster connection through history? Why do humans connect with rituals through psychology? And, what are ways that journaling to capture inner experiences can generate creative written expression through language arts? Fourth, we know to expect diversity of practice. So, for instance, it is important to have alignment between cultural and religious traditions and contemplative practice in educational settings for these meditative practices to make sense and be effective. Yet schools also need flexibility in implementation to allow for growth of the SEL practices. SEL instruction and SEL program implementation can get stale unless they are allowed to evolve and shift in ways that match teacher and student interests, needs, and local issues.

Conditions Needed for Intrapersonal Skills Development: Safety, Supportive Settings, and Compassionate Systemic SEL

In the previous section, we defined intrapersonal skills, why they are important, and how they develop. This section focuses on the conditions needed within schools to support intrapersonal development. Individual intrapersonal growth can only happen when the school conditions support this process. We have observed many challenges in schools across diverse contexts as they work to bring intrapersonal skills development to their students. Three critical factors—safety, setting, and systems—need to be present for intrapersonal skills to develop. Next, we describe the meaning of these conditions in school and classroom life, and identify ways intrapersonal development practices are influenced by their context.

Safety

Young people need to feel physically and psychologically safe to thrive. From a developmental perspective, the perception of a safe environment is a product of both current and past experiences that shape how current experiences are interpreted. In the very young, security, caring interactions, and predictability are essential to feeling psychologically safe. Elementary-age children need a secure, caring, and stable connection with teachers as they navigate peer relationships that are more complex (Baker, 2006; Roorda et al., 2011). Adolescents are developing more autonomy and independent agency (Beyers et al., 2003). They need the space and opportunities to do this while continuing to have safe harbors or anchoring adults with whom they can have authentic connections (National Academies of Sciences, Engineering, and Medicine, 2019). These anchors provide a secure base as they navigate their boundaries of agency and independence (Bath, 2008; Erikson, 1963; Siegel, 2015).

A lack of psychological safety might be something carried into the classroom. From very young children to the oldest adolescents, psychological safety might mean entering into trauma- and resilience-informed spaces. Nearly half of the children in the United States have experienced at least one of the traumatic experiences listed on Adverse Childhood Experiences (ACEs) Inventory, and more than 20% have experienced two or more (Merrick et al., 2018). Research suggests a direct correlation between one's ACEs score (the number of such ACEs one had) and a number of negative health outcomes, including diabetes, heart disease, and obesity (Dube et al., 2003). According to the Centers for Disease Control and Prevention (CDC; 2022), *trauma-informed* refers to practices that are informed by the recognition that there are many behaviors resulting from past traumatic experiences. Practices, particularly those that employ contemplative approaches such as mindfulness, work best when they are trauma- and resilience-informed. This means that they are supporting the psychological safety of the space. This includes recognition that childhood adversities exist across many groups of people.

We also know that children and youth show resiliency when they experience adversity, and this can be viewed as a remarkable strength. Individuals who have never faced adversity have not had opportunities to demonstrate resilience (Masten, 2001; Luthar & Cushing, 2002; Rutter, 2012). *Resilience* is defined as the ability to "withstand or recover from significant disturbances that threaten its adaptive function, viability, or development" (Denckla et al., 2020, p. 8). Given that trauma and resilience often go hand-in-hand, we use the terms *trauma-* and *resilience-informed practices* to emphasize the strengths present in children and youth. This trauma- and resilience-informed approach moves beyond the problem-focused question, "What is wrong with you?" and beyond the trauma-informed question, "What happened to you?" toward the resilience- and strengths-based question, "What is right with you, and how can we build on that to help one another?" One example is body- and sensory-based resilience practices to regulate the nervous system, which can be integrated into contemplative protocols (Miller-Karas, 2015). Within the scope of these practices, individuals should be empowered with choices in a kind and respectful manner, so that they can navigate their experiences with the goal of psychological safety and healing.

Contemplative practices used across the trauma exposure spectrum, when combined with body- and sensory-based resilience practices, help prepare students for safe and productive engagement (Bornemann & Singer, 2017; Farb et al., 2015; Grabbe et al., 2021). For example, in SEE Learning, the doorway toward self-awareness starts with simply guiding students in noticing their own body sensations and how to identify sensations that feel pleasant or neutral. This body literacy then supports students in identifying for themselves which practices are most helpful for them, and how to handle thoughts or experiences when they threaten to become overwhelming. This guidance works best when the space is equipped with the broader context elements that, from a psychological and developmental perspective, promote safety.

Let us recall the earlier discussion about children's development of self-control (as assessed by the marshmallow test). More recent work indicates that performance on this test depends on how the child perceives their environment—whether it is reliable or unreliable (Kidd et al., 2013). A child perceiving that they can rely on and predict what will happen in their environment helps them to feel like their environment is safe. In turn, this helps the child feel like the people in their environment will take care of them and can be trusted (Andresen et al., 2019). A child's general feeling and perceptions of safety are shaped by experiences that happen over the course of development, including adversity, which is a part of the human condition.

This relationship between intrapersonal skills and environment is bidirectional and mutually supportive. Trauma- and resilience-informed intrapersonal practices can help children play a more active role in regulating their own nervous system and compassionately supporting the regulation of their peers when they themselves are involved in supportive relationships with adults (Weir, 2017). While adversity is both part and parcel of the human condition, it is not destiny, but spaces must intentionally endorse psychological safety by supporting trauma- and resilience-informed approaches. It is important for SEL programs to take a trauma- and resilience-informed approach that supports both the students and adults within the environment (Kim et al., 2021; MacLochlainn et al., 2022).

These resilience skills, developed by the Trauma and Resilience Institute and embedded within SEE Learning, include sensory- and body-based skills such as tracking the nervous system (recognizing pleasant, neutral, and unpleasant sensations in the body in order to cultivate body awareness or body literacy); grounding (making contact with a surface for self-regulation); and resourcing (bringing to mind a resource, real or imagined, that makes one feel better, more safe, or happier). They also include simple "Help Now!" strategies such as looking at colors, listening for sounds, or pushing or leaning against a wall. Importantly, students also learn some basic knowledge about sympathetic and parasympathetic nervous system activation and a simple model of the "high zone," "low zone," and "resilient zone." This helps them understand how these practices can help them monitor their state of well-being and return to their resilient zone if they get "bumped out" into the high zone or low zone. These methods have been used with children in some very high-trauma settings with significant and positive impacts on their intrapersonal skills development (Grabbe & Miller-Karas, 2018). Empowering students with such skills alongside other intrapersonal practices can create a foundation of psychological safety.

From a resilience-informed perspective, the fidgety student struggling to connect with the practices is not acting "bad"; rather, they are having trouble connecting. This might be an indication of dysregulation. The goal of the resilience-informed practice is to provide students with tools to help them build their own self-awareness and sense of self-directedness. On one occasion, we visited a K–8 public school, in Atlanta, Georgia, while personnel were beginning to pilot SEE Learning. An experienced educator was teaching yoga poses to her class, but the students were laughing, falling over, and having a hard time concentrating. It was clear that the students wanted to learn, but their energy wasn't quite matching the activity. At this point, one of our visiting SEE Learning facilitators, who was working with the teacher on that day, guided the class though a Help Now! experience that invited the students to take a moment to try pushing, leaning, or sitting against the wall. The students tried out different actions until each found a pose they liked. Within minutes, the classroom energy shifted, and the students settled. When asked how they were feeling, they reported feeling calmer and better able to concentrate. They were ready to go back to yoga or do whatever other activities were in store.

In this example, students were given options and agency to find what works for them. Giving students a menu of options is itself an act of kindness. It can not only destigmatize those whose experiences do not match an educator's expectations—due to past adversity, disability, neurodiversity, or a variety of other factors—but it can also increase participation. Most importantly, when students have choices and are guided on how to evaluate what does work best for them (e.g., by learning to monitor their own state of regulation or dysregulation through paying attention to sensations and emotions), the resulting agency and autonomy they develop becomes the basis for further learning on their own.

The realization that choice and body-based practices like this can help prepare children for contemplative practice only came to our group after almost a decade of trying to teach mindfulness and compassion meditation practices to children with varying results. By establishing safety and autonomy, self-chosen, body-based practices provide a simple foundation for both self-awareness and interpersonal skills. Globally, these practices shift the stigma of trauma for students and communities. Specifically, communities dealing with extreme trauma have expressed the need to bring in resilience-informed and strength-based supports for parents and teachers to understand the power trauma can have on students and communities, along with the even greater power resilience-informed practices can have when a shared language and understanding exists.

According to Nanook Smildiger, Director of Fundacion Levapan in Tuluá, Colombia, an organization that supports bringing SEL to schools across Tuluá, programs that support resilience can be of great value in postconflict countries that have seen a great deal of violence, such as Colombia. A few educators in Tuluá felt skepticism toward SEL, she says, but became convinced when they saw children who had been externalizing a lot of distress using the skills to take a moment, count to 10, breathe, and beneficially self-regulate their emotions. "It's going to take time, but it doesn't mean you don't see small victories along the process. But this is what society needs—worldwide," she said. As a result of their positive experiences with SEE Learning, the Foundation has hired a full-time staff person, a former teacher, Miller Aponte, and two successive Mayors of Tuluá have supported citywide implementation, with all schools in the city electing to participate.

Setting

The ideal setting for the cultivation of intrapersonal skills within the classroom is guided by the developmental needs of students. Very young children need a setting that fosters security, belonging, inclusion, and overall well-being (Sumsion et al., 2009). Elementary-age children have the same needs as very young children but also need space to deepen their developing skills of complex social navigation. Adolescents continue to need security, inclusion, and belonging, while also needing time and space for autonomous social navigation, knowing that they are supported by the adults around them (National Academies of Sciences, Engineering, and Medicine, 2019). Across the developmental spectrum, the notions of inclusion and belonging are critical. The way teachers teach (pedagogy), and the way children feel seen (representation and authentic interactions) impact a student's sense of belonging in the classroom. These are areas that must be considered as SEL programs enter diverse spaces around the world. Research on SEL integration in international settings, educator skills development for student impact, and educational equity on culturally relevant adaptation are the evidence-based foundations for this focus (Cressey, 2019).

Setting includes to the cultural relevance of the curriculum, including both the translation of materials and the incorporation of culturally relevant content and strategies that align with the norms and values of the culture and the school (Castro-Olivo, 2014; Cramer & Castro-Olivo, 2016). While cultural relevance is recognized in the literature as essential to realizing SEL programs' full potential, existing methodologies are lacking and in need of development (Jagers et al., 2018). This alignment requires an understanding of three primary domains: (1) broader cultural references within the curriculum content (i.e., stories, examples, and characters), (2) contextual factors that are unique to a given school, and (3) the educator's pedagogical ability to create a student-centered and culturally responsive classroom environment.

SEL programs need to have broader cultural references or flexibility for educators to include local and diverse cultural references in the curriculum content. Cultural references in the SEL curriculum determine how accessible it is to the students. If they do not understand or relate to the images and stories used to support their skills acquisition, then they will not see how the skills are relevant to them. *Nihil de nobis, sine nobis* is a Latin phrase that means "nothing about us without us" is for us. This phrase has been used in school-based interventions to reference the importance of centering the voice of those who are the target of the intervention into the intervention process (Charlton, 1998). SEL programs have more recently worked to respond to criticisms within the educational equity literature for not giving enough space for the voices of those who are the target of adaptation (Hoffman 2009; Jagers et al., 2018). Doing this well can be very difficult, but it is a critical step toward the sustained effectiveness of a program. This means using student voices during a program development or adaptation phase to make sure the student feels seen and represented within the program. The lesson for educators is to listen to students and be on the lookout for ways to connect SEL materials to the concerns of students' lives, and to feel empowered to adapt such materials as and when necessary.

This leads to the next critical consideration—school culture and climate. Schools have their own contextually unique elements even when they are embedded within the same cultural context. We often use the term *school culture and climate*, which refers to the norms, values, and teaching and learning practices that permeate across the school or school system (Thapa et al., 2013). Classroom climate refers to emotional and relational dynamics within the class. Culture and climate can support the work of intrapersonal skills development or it can hinder intrapersonal skills development. For example, school climate can decrease the negative impact of self-criticism (Kuperminic et al., 2001) and support student behavioral and mental health (Way et al., 2007), including decreases in substance abuse, depression, and anxiety (Shochet et al., 2006). In many of the schools with whom the SEE Learning program works, teachers have said that if there is a mismatch between the SEL intrapersonal skills development being supported in the classroom and the climate of the school outside the classroom, then the SEL classroom becomes a safe harbor, but it can also become the only place where those skills are used. The solution to this mismatch is for leadership to think about a whole-school approach to the integration of these skills and programs into their communities.

The final critical consideration regarding setting is the educator's pedagogical ability to create a student-centered and culturally responsive classroom, which is called a *teacher's pedagogical orientation* and means the way educators support student autonomy and voice. Constructivist orientations and strengths-based engagement support students in fostering intrapersonal skills (Schreiber & Valle, 2013; Waajid et al., 2013). Such strategies include active approaches that decenter the teacher from giving information and repositioning them toward facilitators "on the side" who provide meaning-making opportunities through classroom experiences (Brooks & Brooks, 1999). A culturally responsive pedagogical orientation means the teacher is able to know and understand their students through authentic engagement and culturally relevant context. This aspect of setting is informed by culturally responsive pedagogy (Hammond, 2014), which is an approach that uses the student's cultural strengths as entry to nurturing student success and well-being. It includes the following processes: (1) self-inquiry about one's own culture and biases, (2) curiosity about other cultures, and (3) authentic learning about the students and their cultures (Hammond, 2014; Ladson-Billings, 2004). In the context of intrapersonal development, this looks like skills development programs that explicitly integrate examples and case studies that reflect the context and diversity of the students and cultures represented within the classroom.

Another aspect of the educator's pedagogical orientation has to do with their own well-being. What we know about this dynamic is that teacher well-being has a disproportionally high impact on students' emotional regulation (Buchanan et al., 2009; Oberle et al., 2020). In general, emotions are contagious (Hatfield et al., 1993). Therefore, it is important for educators to support themselves and to cultivate their own self-regulation and self-management. By doing this, they model behavior for their students. Teachers' well-being matters!

Systems

Schools are complex systems that have policies, procedures, and practices that influence students and teachers in ways they have no control over. These schools are embedded within broader social systems that both affect and are impacted by individuals within those systems. A systemic approach to SEL implementation means aligning conditions to support the cultivation of SEL competencies across schools, school systems, and the communities they serve (Mahoney et al., 2021). Creating compassionate systems also means cultivating systems thinking within students. When intrapersonal skills are introduced, students need to understand that these skills are not being developed to simply put the burden on students to address issues that are the product of the larger systems in which they are embedded. This is *systems thinking,* which can inform both students' understanding of their intrapersonal skills development and educators' teaching of this material (Senge, 1996).

There are two ways of thinking about the importance of systems. First, there is the way we teach children to think about systems. Second, there is the awareness adults have about the systems they inhabit as they are teaching intrapersonal skills.

Systems thinking is a way of understanding, thinking, and speaking that expresses the "interrelationships that shape the behavior of systems" (Senge, 1996, p. 15).

Student Learning about Systems

Even young children can learn to see that they are part of complex, dynamic, and interconnected systems that shape the patterns they see in their environment. The reason to integrate this thinking into intrapersonal skills development is that we do not want to put the weight of fixing the problem of an inequitable social system on the shoulders of the individual child. An example of this can be seen in the way "grit" has been misused (Tewell, 2022). For example, mindfulness and contemplative practices without a critical consideration and awareness of the inequities a system may be creating can unintentionally hinder, rather than foster, the equity intentions of SEL programming by signaling that students' cultivation of "grit" matters more than the transformation of systems. It can reinforce the inequities of the system.

Through the perspective of educational equity, the "intra," or work within, can be used to guide and motivate action with wisdom and discernment. This is more difficult to foster if the language of self-regulation ignores systems dynamics or seems to reinforce oppression. Systems awareness means being able to see the system, and hold whatever anger or pain that sight may bring, while remaining within our zone of well-being, so that students can compassionately act for change. For example, within SEE Learning, anger is a part of the "OK" zone where students can hold that anger and think productively. In this way, SEE Learning is not anesthesia but regulation for right action.

Adult Awareness of Systems

In order to support systems thinking, teachers also need some awareness of the ways in which the educational system they inhabit might be generating and sustaining inequities within their institution and society. The educational equity literature provides a few consistent areas of consideration of systemic issues found within educational systems, globally, that can impact the way intrapersonal skills might be received. Through a review of the literature, along with an evaluation of our experiences with educational systems around the world, we developed a summary of key areas of systems-level considerations that can act as a checklist when thinking about conditions at the level of systems that supports individual intrapersonal growth. Table 9.1 defines these considerations. We have summarized these into a model called the PRICES, an acronym for (1) Preparation and access, (2) Restoration, (3) Integration, (4) Connection and community, (5) Educator support, and (6) Strengths-based cultivation. We describe each of these ideas in Table 9.1, along with questions educators can ask themselves about their students and classrooms.

TABLE 9.1. The PRICES Model

PRICES component	Definition
Preparation and access	This includes access to quality education, access to authentic connections at school, and access to developmentally matched supports. Question: *Am I, the student, prepared, and do I have access to the supports I need in preparation for long-term academic and personal success?*
Restoration	This includes rebuilding or integrating restorative practices into school community to support rebuilding relationships when past or present harm is experienced. Question: *Can you, the teacher and the school, authentically see me, the student, and can you see the past harm that has been done, so that we can build the trust needed to repair and grow together?*
Integration	This includes taking a whole-school approach to the integration of social and emotional development practices. Question: *Is school leadership involved in or aware of the work we, the student and the teacher, are doing together in the classroom, and is this work being integrated into policies, or whole-school goals within the school?*
Connection and community	This includes building communication and authentic connections across groups of students, parents, staff, and the broader school community. Question: *Is there authentic connection between the adults in the school and with me, the student, and the people that make up my school community?*
Educator support	This includes supporting educators during the implementation process of social and emotional learning programs. It also includes providing support for educators to develop their own SEL skills. Question: *Is there professional development and training support to enable you, the teacher, to support your classrooms in building spaces for transformational change?*
Strengths-based cultivation	This includes the ways in which strengths-based approaches are integrated into the communications and teaching practices across the school community. Question: *Are you, the teacher, focusing on what is working in the classroom and with each student, and are we, the teacher and the student, building on these strengths for meaningful shifts to occur?*

Note. This is a summary of the PRICES model, along with questions that teachers and administrators can ask themselves as they are working to support their school communities in cultivating intrapersonal skills.

Full Definition of the PRICES

Preparation and Access

Preparation and access are linked, because a student's ability to be prepared to succeed beyond school depends on the access they have to material and psychological resources. Who has access to the high-quality schools? Unfortunately, this material access is often more available to wealthier heterosexual students of "normal" ability than to students from marginalized groups. The notion of "high quality" is often defined by wealth; that is, schools with more money tend to be rated as being of higher quality. Access to psychological resources is another type of access to consider. Not all students have access to experiences in which they are seen authentically for who they are and want to be. Important questions about equity in terms of psychological access include the following: Who is seen? Who is known? Who is nurtured in building their capacities for positive academic and personal development? Psychological access needs to be equitable to promote intrapersonal skills and whole-child development.

As children move through the education system, material and psychological access and preparation also have to do with the courses that are offered to them, the educational and counseling supports available to them, the ways in which those supports are made available, and the developmental stage at which they have access to such supports. This is important for intrapersonal skills development, because it impacts how children will come to see and know themselves.

Restoration

Restoration means repairing a relationship after a harm. It also refers to rebuilding oneself after experiencing harm. Many schools and school systems replicate societal inequities that are products of historical conditions. In the United States and around the world, racial, gender, cast, ethnicity, and many other disparities originated from past systems and have been carried forward into present systems. Some youth have experienced harm or intergenerational harm more than others and this needs to be acknowledged and discussed in schools. Attempts at supporting a child's inner qualities while ignoring these social injustices can lead to blindness—color blindness, gender blindness, ability blindness—in all forms. This does harm even when the intention is not one of harm (McCluskey et al., 2008) because it inhibits an authentic understanding of the social context in which children will come to know themselves.

Integration

SEL programs that support intrapersonal skills development should be systemically implemented (Oberle & Schonert-Reichl, 2016). This implementation process should support ongoing professional learning for educators (Borko et al., 2005; Hammond, 2014). It should also include continuous cycles of inquiry for program improvement (Copland, 2003; Hodges & Wotring, 2004). The conditions that leaders need to focus on for this integration are fostering a caring environment, offering dedicated time for students and educators to support their social and emotional development, providing space to use tools for personal and classroom practice, and supporting opportunities to build resilient peer networks as teachers are learning how to support their students and themselves.

Connection and Community

This domain refers to building an authentic connection and relationship with students, staff, and parents. The goal is to foster authenticity among all of the connections that make up the school community. This also includes embedding the curriculum with stories and voices from the school communities and families (Wang & Degol, 2016).

Educator Support

Educator development is important for the implementation of SEL programs that support intrapersonal development. This is well documented and defines much of the established literature supporting educator trainings (Gimbert et al., 2021). This includes supporting educators in developing pedagogical or teaching skills to create a compassionate and equitable classroom environment. Teachers learn by doing. While short training promotes professional development, educator support also means building communities of practice that offer ongoing support, in which teachers try things out and work to integrate principles and practices into their classroom spaces (Patton & Parker, 2017). Educators should feel empowered and need not wait for mastery, but can learn and build confidence alongside their students. Meanwhile, administrators should commit to ongoing support of educator development that includes both dedicated trainings and ongoing support and community building. Educator support and professional development is a key component in successfully bringing intrapersonal development into the classroom. By building educator learning communities, teachers can both learn and do in a way that will eventually support both student and educator mastery.

Strengths-Based Cultivation

In education, a strengths-based teaching approach is a learner-centered way of helping students identify the skills that they have and how they might apply those to their learning needs. A strengths-based approach destigmatizes difference and shifts the focus of attention from what is wrong with a child to what is working for a child and how the classroom, educator, and curriculum might be responsive to a child's strengths. For the educator, this means being able to come into the classroom with a flexible mentality—being able to see and uplift the good while holding space for edges of growth. Practically, it also means providing choices for students in a way that, as we have discussed, respects the diversity of learners and creates a foundation for autonomy and agency—rather than, for example, mandating that students engage in a single practice in a single way with the expectation of a single result. At the classroom level, this means integrating policies and practices that are developed through this strengths-based perspective (Waters, 2017).

The PRICES Model in Action

Lina Moreno, principal of the Guillermo Ponce de Leon school in Tuluá, Colombia, decided early on to tackle SEL implementation by taking a culturally responsive, whole-school approach through trying to establish a culture within the entire school and staff by having everyone trained in their SEL program of choice (SEE Learning, 2022), including work with parents. As a result, in just 2 years of implementation, she feels that the school has established a culture in which the value of compassion and the school's commitment to compassion, as well as the intrapersonal skills of grounding, resourcing, tracking, and mindfulness, are commonly understood. The benefits of this shared understanding and shared vocabulary can be seen, she said, even when a parent calls in upset about something that happened with their child. Even staff members who are not teachers can help respond to such situations in a positive way. Lina's approach shows the complementarity of paying attention to the culture of a larger system, with the goal of implementing practices that enhance intrapersonal skills. She reported that increasingly parents were asking to transfer their children to her school, because their children were telling them that they had learned from peers that it was a school free from bullying.

While intrapersonal skills can infuse the entire culture, this does not mean they should not be taught as a stand-alone subject or curriculum. In this school in Colombia, SEE Learning is taught across all primary and elementary school grades, 1 hour per week for all students. As our SEE Learning affiliate in Colombia noted, "When people see this as a transversal competency that should be taught across subject areas, then the result can be that no one actually does it." Lina feels, therefore, that both the 1-hour per week focused instruction and the training of all teachers and staff in the schools for transversal implementation have been very helpful. Again, this supports the complementarity of supporting transformation on an intrapersonal and systems level in conjunction, rather than simply one or the other.

When we consider the context in which intrapersonal skills are brought into a school, they can have a powerful and life-changing impact on the students. We end this chapter with the voice of one, Kitty Graham, who experienced one of the very first pilots of what became SEE Learning in 2009 when she was in first grade. She wrote this letter to us years after participating in the Emory program.

> Hello! I hope you are well. You may remember me from John and Christy's kindergarten/first grade class many years ago! I wanted to reach out to you to thank you for introducing me to compassion meditation and mindfulness at such a young age. I'm

> 17 now and just finishing up high school while taking a few college classes this fall, including Intro to Religions of Asia. After revisiting your work through articles and old conference videos, I realized that the introduction to meditation at such a young age has had a lifelong impact on how I work, train, and appreciate the world around me. While I've maintained a meditation practice on and off for the last 12 years, I recently started a daily practice again and it has changed my outlook on life and the future drastically. I remember every day, through this incredible amount of change, to never obsess over the "what if?" questions and to be appreciative of everything around me.

Conclusion

In this chapter, we have defined *intrapersonal skills* as the way children, youth, and adults develop internal-focused attention and emotional awareness. It is this awareness and attention that are antecedents for the development of self-regulation. Seen through the lens of contemplative practices, these skills reflect mindfulness and self-compassion gained through repeated introspection and reflective practice. Seen from the point of view of SEL, these skills map onto self-awareness and self-management. Together, contemplative and SEL intrapersonal practices support the development of inner awareness. Once a student is aware of their inner dynamics they can begin to choose how to respond. This response can be described as self-management, self-compassion, and self-regulation. All of these capacities have measurable impact on student well-being, if the context supports this development. In this chapter, we have discussed three critical areas within school contexts that can support or become barriers to intrapersonal skills development: (1) safety, (2) settings, and (3) systems. First, students need physical and psychological safety. They need to feel as if they are seen and heard within the SEL curriculum and pedagogical practices brought into the classroom. Second, they need settings that match their developmental needs and cultural background. Third, they need systems—systems that support intrapersonal growth and development, so that children, youth, and adults develop self-compassion, as well as compassion for others. In this chapter, we have introduced the PRICES model that describes six key features educators need to think about as they strive to support their school communities in cultivating intrapersonal skills: (1) Preparation and access, (2) Restoration, (3) Integration, (4) Connection and community, (5) Educator support, and (6) Strength-based cultivation. Without these contextual elements, the environment will not be ready to support intrapersonal skills development. Taken together, we conclude that contemplative practices have remarkable promise to cultivate intrapersonal skills. Yet to achieve positive, meaningful, and long-lasting effects, such practices must be carefully integrated with the contexts and cultures in which children, youth, and educators dwell and learn.

DISCUSSION QUESTIONS

1. Consider the chapter opening case study of the young girls in foster care who participated in compassion training. Taking the perspective of the girls, what are some of the reasons that they might have found the compassion training particularly useful? What sorts of questions would you want to ask them about their experiences with the training? How might this sort of training lead to changes in their classroom behaviors? In what ways might the classroom context influence the success or failure of such an approach?
2. In this chapter, the authors distinguish between SEL approaches and contemplative approaches to intrapersonal development. What are some of the ways these two approaches are similar? In what ways are these two approaches different? How would you describe a secular approach to contemplative approaches? How would you rationalize the connection to SEL? How would you present these approaches to colleagues? To principals? To parents? And to students?
3. We have stated that intrapersonal skills—self-awareness, self-regulation, inhibitory control, and the ability to delay gratification—are particularly important in schools in the United States. Would you agree with statement? Why or why not?
4. We have described the SEE Learning program and how it has been adapted for other countries. We discussed how the approaches in the program had to be designed with the flexibility needed to align with local customs and contexts. Why might such adaptions be necessary? How is the teaching of intrapersonal skills in your school aligned with the cultures and specific needs of your students, and how might this be done better?
5. We discussed the importance of creating a safe, supportive, and caring context that is trauma-informed and one in which students have a sense of agency to develop their own resilience. Why would this be important? And how might teachers be supported to create such a context? What factors might impede such an approach? How can educators create a context that is trauma-informed and in which student agency is at the core? What challenges might be encountered?

REFERENCES

American Psychological Association. (n.d.). APA dictionary of psychology. Retrieved July 25, 2022, from *https://dictionary.apa.org/intrapersonal.*

Andresen, S., Bradshaw, J., & Kosher, H. (2019). Young children's perceptions of their lives and well-being. *Child Indicators Research, 12*(1), 1–7.

Ash, M., Harrison, T., Pinto, M., DiClemente, R., & Negi, L. T. (2021). A model for cognitively-based compassion training: Theoretical underpinnings and proposed mechanisms. *Social Theory and Health, 19*(1), 43–67.

Baker, J. A. (2006). Contributions of teacher–child relationships to positive school adjustment during elementary school. *Journal of School Psychology, 44*(3), 211–229.

Bath, H. (2008). The three pillars of trauma-informed care. *Reclaiming Children and Youth, 17*(3), 17–21.

Berkowitz, L. (2008). On the consideration of automatic as well as controlled psychological processes in aggression. *Aggressive Behavior, 34*, 117–129.

Beyers, W., Goossens, L., Vansant, I., & Moors, E. (2003). A structural model of autonomy in middle and late adolescence: Connectedness, separation, detachment, and agency. *Journal of Youth and Adolescence, 32*(5), 351–365.

Bishop, S. R., Lau, M., Shapiro, S., Carlson, L., Anderson, N. D., Carmody, J., & Devins, G. (2004). Mindfulness: A proposed operational definition. *Clinical Psychology: Science and Practice, 11*, 230–241.

Boekaerts, M. (1993). Being concerned with well-being and with learning. *Educational Psychologist, 28*(2), 149–167.

Borko, H., Stecher, B. M., Alonzo, A. C., Moncure, S., & McClam, S. (2005). Artifact packages for characterizing classroom practice: A pilot study. *Educational Assessment, 10*(2), 73–104.

Bornemann, B., & Singer, T. (2017). Taking time to feel our body: Steady increases in heartbeat perception accuracy and decreases in alexithymia over 9 months of contemplative mental training. *Psychophysiology, 54*(3), 469–482.

Brock, L. L., Rimm-Kaufman, S. E., Nathanson, L., & Grimm, K. J. (2009). The contributions of "hot" and "cool" executive function to children's academic achievement, learning-related behaviors, and engagement in kindergarten. *Early Childhood Research Quarterly, 24*(3), 337–349.

Brock, L. L., Rimm-Kaufman, S. E., & Wanless, S. B. (2014). Delay of gratification in first grade: The role of instructional context. *Learning and Individual Differences, 29*, 81–88.

Broderick, P. C., & Jennings, P. A. (2012). Mindfulness for adolescents: A promising approach to supporting emotion regulation and preventing risky behavior. *New Directions for Youth Development, 136*, 111–126.

Brooks, J. G., & Brooks, M. G. (1999). *In search of understanding: The case for constructivist classrooms.* Association for Supervision and Curriculum Development.

Buchanan, R., Gueldner, B. A., Tran, O. K., & Merrell, K. W. (2009). Social and emotional learning in classrooms: A survey of teachers' knowledge, perceptions, and practices. *Journal of Applied School Psychology, 25*(2), 187–203.

Caballero, C., Scherer, E., West, M. R., Mrazek, M. D., Gabrieli, C. F., & Gabrieli, J. D. (2019). Greater mindfulness is associated with better academic achievement in middle school. *Mind, Brain, and Education, 13*(3), 157–166.

CASEL. (2022, January 19). Advancing social and emotional learning. Retrieved from *https://casel.org.*

Castro-Olivo, S. M. (2014). Promoting social–emotional learning in adolescent Latino ELLs: A study of the culturally adapted Strong Teens program. *School Psychology Quarterly, 29*(4), 567–577.

Centers for Disease Control and Prevention. (2022, January 19). The six guiding principles to a trauma-informed approach. Retrieved from *www.cdc.gov/cpr/infographics/6_principles_trauma_info.htm.*

Charlton, T. (1998). Experiencing school effectiveness though using peer support strategies with pupils and teachers. *Support for Learning, 13*(2), 50–53.

CMind. (2021). The Tree of Contemplative Practices [Illustration]. Retrieved from *www.contemplativemind.org/practices/tree.*

Copland, M. A. (2003). Leadership of inquiry: Building and sustaining capacity for school improvement. *Educational Evaluation and Policy Analysis, 25*(4), 375–395.

Cramer, K. M., & Castro-Olivo, S. (2016). Effects of a culturally adapted social–emotional learning intervention program on students' mental health. *Contemporary School Psychology, 20*(2), 118–129.

Cressey, J. (2019). Developing culturally responsive social, emotional, and behavioral supports. *Journal of Research in Innovative Teaching and Learning, 12*, 53–67.

Darling-Hammond, L., Flook, L., Cook-Harvey, C., Barron, B., & Osher, D. (2020). Implications for educational practice of the science of learning and development. *Applied Developmental Science, 24*(2), 97–140.

Denckla, C. A., Cicchetti, D., Kubzansky, L. D., Seedat, S., Teicher, M. H., Williams, D. R., & Koenen, K. C. (2020). Psychological resilience: An update on definitions, a critical appraisal, and research recommendations. *European Journal of Psychotraumatology, 11*(1), Article 1822064.

Derryberry, D., & Rothbart, M. K. (1997). Reactive and effortful processes in the organization of temperament. *Development and Psychopathology, 9*(4), 633–652.

Dube, S. R., Felitti, V. J., Dong, M., Chapman, D. P., Giles, W. H., & Anda, R. F. (2003). Childhood abuse, neglect, and household dysfunction and the risk of illicit drug use: The adverse childhood experiences study. *Pediatrics, 111*(3), 564–572.

Duckworth, A. L., & Seligman, M. E. (2005). Self-discipline outdoes IQ in predicting academic performance of adolescents. *Psychological Science, 16*(12), 939–944.

Dweck, C. S. (2017). From needs to goals and representations: Foundations for a unified theory of motivation, personality, and development. *Psychological Review, 124*(6), 689–719.

Eisenberg, N. (2000). Emotion, regulation, and moral development. *Annual Review of Psychology, 51*(1), 665–697.

Elliot, A. J., & Dweck, C. S. (2005). Competence and motivation: Competence as the core of achievement motivation. In A. J. Elliot & C. S. Dweck (Eds.), *Handbook of competence and motivation* (pp. 3–12). Guilford Press.

Erikson, E. H. (1963). *Youth: Change and challenge.* Basic Books.

Farb, N., Daubenmier, J., Price, C. J., Gard, T., Kerr, C., Dunn, B. D., . . . Mehling, W. E. (2015). Interoception, contemplative practice, and health. *Frontiers in Psychology, 6*, Article 763.

Gimbert, B. G., Miller, D., Herman, E., Breedlove, M., & Molina, C. E. (2021, May 24). Social emotional learning in schools: The importance of educator competence. *Journal of Research on Leadership Education.* [Epub ahead of print]

Grabbe, L., Higgins, M., Jordan, D., Noxsel, L., Gibson, B., & Murphy, J. (2021). The Community Resiliency Model®: A pilot of an interoception intervention to increase the emotional self-regulation of women in addiction treatment. *International Journal of Mental Health and Addiction, 19*(3), 793–808.

Grabbe, L., & Miller-Karas, E. (2018). The trauma resiliency model: A "bottom-up" intervention for trauma psychotherapy. *Journal of the American Psychiatric Nurses Association, 24*(1), 76–84.

Hammond, Z. (2014). *Culturally responsive teaching and the brain: Promoting authentic engagement and rigor among culturally and linguistically diverse students.* Corwin Press.

Hatfield, E., Cacioppo, J. T., & Rapson, R. L. (1993). Emotional contagion. *Current Directions in Psychological Science, 2*(3), 96–100.

Hodges, K., & Wotring, J. (2004). The role of monitoring outcomes in initiating implementation of evidence-based treatments at the state level. *Psychiatric Services, 55*(4), 396–400.

Hoffman, D. M. (2009). Reflecting on social emotional learning: A critical perspective on trends in the United States. *Review of Educational Research, 79*(2), 533–556.

Houde, O. (2019, December). *The social and emotional brain and its role in learning.* Presented at TECH 2019, Vishakapatnam, India.

Jagers, R. J., Rivas-Drake, D., & Borowski, T. (2018). *Equity and social and emotional learning: A cultural analysis.* CASEL Assessment Work Group Brief series.

Jones, S., Brush, K., Bailey, R., Brion-Meisels, G., McIntyre, J., Kahn, J., . . . Stickle, L. (2017). *Navigating SEL from the inside out: Looking inside and across.* Harvard Graduate School of Education.

Kidd, C., Palmeri, H., & Aslin, R. N. (2013). Rational snacking: Young children's decision-making on the marshmallow task is moderated by beliefs about environmental reliability. *Cognition, 126*(1), 109–114.

Kim, S., Crooks, C. V., Bax, K., & Shokoohi, M. (2021). Impact of trauma-informed training and mindfulness-based social–emotional learning program on teacher attitudes and burnout: A mixed-methods study. *School Mental Health, 13*(1), 55–68.

Kuperminic, G. P., Leadbeater, B. J., & Blatt, S. J. (2001). School social climate and individual differences in vulnerability to psychopathology among middle school students. *Journal of School Psychology, 39*, 141–159.

Ladson-Billings, G. (2004). *Crossing over to Canaan: The journey of new teachers in diverse classrooms.* Wiley.

Lamm, B., Keller, H., Teiser, J., Gudi, H., Yovsi, R. D., Freitag, C., & Lohaus, A. (2018). Waiting for the second treat: Developing culture-specific modes of self-regulation. *Child Development, 89*(3), e261–e277.

Lawlor, M. S. (2016). Mindfulness and social emotional learning (SEL): A conceptual framework. In K. A. Schonert-Reichl & R. W. Roeser (Eds.), *Handbook of mindfulness in education* (pp. 65–80). Springer.

Lea, J., Cadman, L., & Philo, C. (2015). Changing the habits of a lifetime?: Mindfulness meditation and habitual geographies. *Cultural Geographies, 22*(1), 49–65.

Lions Quest. (2022). The Choose Kindness Project. Retrieved July 25, 2022, from *www.lions-quest.org*.

Luthar, S. S., & Cushing, G. (2002). Measurement issues in the empirical study of resilience. In M. D. Glantz & J. L. Johnson (Eds.), *Resilience and development* (pp. 129–160). Springer.

MacLochlainn, J., Kirby, K., McFadden, P., & Mallett, J. (2022). An evaluation of whole-school trauma-informed training intervention among post-primary school personnel: A mixed methods study. *Journal of Child and Adolescent Trauma, 15*, 925–941.

Maehr, M. L., & Braskamp, L. A. (1986). *The motivation factor: A theory of personal investment.* Lexington Books/D. C. Heath.

Mahoney, J. L., Weissberg, R. P., Greenberg, M. T., Dusenbury, L., Jagers, R. J., Niemi, K., . . . Yoder, N. (2021). Systemic social and emotional learning: Promoting educational success for all preschool to high school students. *American Psychologist, 76*, 1128–1142.

Masten, A. S. (2001). Ordinary magic: Resilience processes in development. *American Psychologist, 56*(3), 227–238.

McCluskey, G., Lloyd, G., Kane, J., Riddell, S., Stead, J., & Weedon, E. (2008). Can restorative practices in schools make a difference? *Educational Review, 60*(4), 405–417.

Merrick, M. T., Ford, D. C., Ports, K. A., & Guinn, A. S. (2018). Prevalence of adverse childhood experiences from the 2011–2014 behavioral risk factor surveillance system in 23 states. *JAMA Pediatrics, 172*(11), 1038–1044.

Merritt, E. G., Wanless, S. B., Rimm-Kaufman, S. E., Cameron, C., & Peugh, J. L. (2012). The contribution of teachers' emotional support to children's social behaviors and self-regulatory skills in first grade. *School Psychology Review, 41*(2), 141–159.

Metcalfe, J., & Mischel, W. (1999). A hot/cool-system analysis of delay of gratification: Dynamics of willpower. *Psychological Review, 106*, 3–19.

Miller, J. G., Kahle, S., & Hastings, P. D. (2015). Roots and benefits of costly giving: Children who are more altruistic have greater autonomic flexibility and less family wealth. *Psychological Science, 26*(7), 1038–1045.

Miller-Karas, E. (2015). *Building resilience to trauma: The trauma and community resiliency models.* Routledge.

Mind and Life Education Research Network. (2012). Contemplative practices and mental training: Prospects for American education. *Child Development Perspectives, 6*(2), 146–153.

Mischel, W., Shoda, Y., & Rodriguez, M. L. (1989). Delay of gratification in children. *Science, 244*, 933–938.

National Academies of Sciences, Engineering, and Medicine. (2019). *The promise of adolescence: Realizing opportunity for all youth.* Author.

Oberle, E., Gist, A., Cooray, M. S., & Pinto, J. B. (2020). Do students notice stress in teachers?: Associations between classroom teacher burnout and students' perceptions of teacher social–emotional competence. *Psychology in the Schools, 57*(11), 1741–1756.

Oberle, E., & Schonert-Reichl, K. A. (2016). Stress contagion in the classroom?: The link between classroom teacher burnout and morning cortisol in elementary school students. *Social Science and Medicine, 159*, 30–37.

Oleś, P. K., Brinthaupt, T. M., Dier, R., & Polak, D. (2020). Types of inner dialogues and functions of self-talk: Comparisons and implications. *Frontiers in Psychology, 11*, Article 227.

Panadero, E. (2017). A review of self-regulated learning: Six models and four directions for research. *Frontiers in Psychology, 8*, Article 422.

Patton, K., & Parker, M. (2017). Teacher education communities of practice: More than a culture of collaboration. *Teaching and Teacher Education, 67*, 351–360.

Reddy, S. D., Negi, L. T., Dodson-Lavelle, B., Ozawa-de Silva, B., Pace, T. W., Cole, S. P., . . .

Craighead, L. W. (2013). Cognitive-based compassion training: A promising prevention strategy for at-risk adolescents. *Journal of Child and Family Studies, 22*(2), 219–230.

Rimm-Kaufman, S. E., Curby, T. W., Grimm, K. J., Nathanson, L., & Brock, L. L. (2009). The contribution of children's self-regulation and classroom quality to children's adaptive behaviors in the kindergarten classroom. *Developmental Psychology, 45*(4), 958–972.

Roorda, D. L., Koomen, H. M., Spilt, J. L., & Oort, F. J. (2011). The influence of affective teacher–student relationships on students' school engagement and achievement: A meta-analytic approach. *Review of Educational Research, 81*(4), 493–529.

Rutter, M. (2012). Resilience as a dynamic concept. *Development and Psychopathology, 24*(2), 335–344.

Schonert-Reichl, K. A., & Roeser, R. W. (Eds.). (2016). *Handbook of mindfulness in education: Integrating theory and research into practice.* Springer.

Schreiber, L. M., & Valle, B. E. (2013). Social constructivist teaching strategies in the small group classroom. *Small Group Research, 44*(4), 395–411.

SEE Learning. (2022, January 19). Social, emotional, and ethical learning. Retrieved from *https://seelearning.emory.edu.*

Senge, P. (1996). Systems thinking. *Executive Excellence, 13*(1), 15–16.

Shochet, I. M., Dadds, M. R., Ham, D., & Montague, R. (2006). School connectedness is an underemphasized parameter in adolescent mental health: Results of a community prediction study. *Journal of Clinical Child and Adolescent Psychology, 35*, 170–179.

Siegel, D. J. (2015). *Brainstorm: The power and purpose of the teenage brain.* Penguin.

Strauss, C., Taylor, B. L., Gu, J., Kuyken, W., Baer, R., Jones, F., & Cavanagh, K. (2016). What is compassion and how can we measure it? A review of definitions and measures. *Clinical Psychology Review, 47*, 15–27.

Sumsion, J., Barnes, S., Cheeseman, S., Harrison, L., Kennedy, A., & Stonehouse, A. (2009). Insider perspectives on developing belonging, being and becoming: The early years learning framework for Australia. *Australasian Journal of Early Childhood, 34*(4), 4–13.

Taylor, L. K., O'Driscoll, D., Dautel, J. B., & McKeown, S. (2020). Empathy to action: Child and adolescent out-group attitudes and prosocial behaviors in a setting of intergroup conflict. *Social Development, 29*(2), 461–477.

Tewell, E. (2020). The problem with grit: Dismantling deficit thinking in library instruction. *Portal: Libraries and the Academy, 20*(1), 137–159.

Thapa, A., Cohen, J., Guffey, S., & Higgins-D'Alessandro, A. (2013). A review of school climate research. *Review of Educational Research, 83*(3), 357–385.

Valenzuela, L., Dillbeck, M., & Sacristán Rock, A. (2022). The effects of the transcendental meditation technique on intellectual ability, personal well-being, and academic performance among Mexican high school students. *Education, 142*(2), 102–110.

Valosek, L., Nidich, S., Grant, J., Peterson, M., & Nidich, R. (2021). Effect of meditation on psychological stress and academic achievement in high school students: A randomized controlled study. *Education, 141*(4), 192–200.

Vygotsky, L. (1978). Interaction between learning and development. *Readings on the Development of Children, 23*(3), 34–41.

Waajid, B., Garner, P. W., & Owen, J. E. (2013). Infusing social emotional learning into the teacher education curriculum. *International Journal of Emotional Education, 5*(2), 31–48.

Wang, M. T., & Degol, J. L. (2016). School climate: A review of the construct, measurement, and impact on student outcomes. *Educational Psychology Review, 28*(2), 315–352.

Waters, L. (2017). *The strength switch: How the new science of strength-based parenting can help your child and your teen to flourish*. Penguin.

Way, N., Reddy, R., & Rhodes, J. (2007). Students' perceptions of school climate during the middle school years: Associations with trajectories of psychological and behavioral adjustment. *American Journal of Community Psychology, 40*, 194–213.

Weir, K. (2017). Maximizing children's resilience. *Monitor on Psychology, 48*(8), Article 40.

Yale Center for Emotional Intelligence. (n.d.). RULER. Retrieved July 25, 2022, from *https://ycei.org/ruler.*

Zelazo, P. D., & Cunningham, W. A. (2007). Executive function: Mechanisms underlying emotion regulation. In J. J. Gross (Ed.), *Handbook of emotion regulation* (pp. 135–158). Guilford Press.

Part IV Identifying Roadmaps for SEL in Action

Chapter 10

The SEL Roadmap

Avoiding the Roadblocks, Ruts, and Dead Ends

Sheldon Berman, Jacqueline Jodl, and Joyce Barnes

My (Sheldon's) experience in leading four school districts' social and emotional learning (SEL) initiatives leads me to believe that each district's roadmap to SEL implementation will take a different course, reflecting the history of SEL in the district, the conditions in the district, and the opportunities that present themselves for making progress. In my first superintendency—in the Hudson Public Schools in Massachusetts, a district of 3,000 students in six schools—SEL began with a small $2,000 state grant to support service learning. Believing that service experiences would enable students to grow their self-confidence, improve their self-image, and extend their social skills, teachers interested in service learning gathered to launch projects across the districts. The projects ranged from cross-age buddy programs to environmental protection efforts to partnerships with senior citizens. As these projects took hold and expanded to other teachers in each school, teachers began to talk about how best to promote social development in a consistent way, leading to a committee of teachers and administrators who visited other schools, interviewed program service providers, and piloted various programs. Their work led to adopting Responsive Classroom as a vehicle for promoting social skill development through building community in the classroom, which later led to the integration of weekly lessons from the Committee for Children's social skill curriculum, Second Step, into Responsive Classroom's daily morning meeting structure. The initiative moved to the middle school, where Responsive Classroom was adopted, and to the high school, where several initiatives supported social skill development. The development of SEL was strengthened by its alignment with instructional initiatives focused on inquiry-based instruction and by the district's efforts to provide an inclusive approach for students with special needs, so that both instruction and the classroom environment promoted personalization, voice, and agency among students. The service-learning program remained as an essential opportunity for students to demonstrate their social skills and concern for the good of the community, but it was now grounded in SEL and instructional practices that strengthened its impact on students. Over an extended period of years, Hudson put together the puzzle pieces for a holistic and comprehensive PreK–12 approach.

The development of SEL programming in the Jefferson County Public Schools (JCPS) in Louisville, Kentucky, took a very different course. In this urban district of 100,000 students in 155 schools, a long-serving superintendent had focused on raising state test scores; SEL skills were not part of the curriculum. However, prior to his tenure, the district had been the pilot site for an exceptionally comprehensive SEL approach entitled the Child Development Program, created by the Developmental Studies Center (now the Center for the Collaborative Classroom). Teachers and administrators who had implemented the program not only gained skills in fostering students' social skills but were enthusiastic advocates of the program. Many of those teachers and administrators had since moved to key principal and central office administrative roles. When I arrived as the superintendent and raised the question of whether the district would benefit from a focus on SEL, they enthusiastically responded, pursuing the reestablishment of their prior program. Based on their leadership, the district was able to implement a strong "Caring for Kids" K–8 program grounded in the practices they had learned so many years before. In addition, in the intervening years, curricular and instructional changes that promoted inquiry-based instruction and inclusion of students with disabilities gave greater meaning to the need for and productivity of SEL. Because of the readiness level of school and district leaders, relaunching the SEL program simply required reestablishing a relationship with the Developmental Studies Center and funding professional development in SEL instructional practices.

The Eugene 4J Public Schools in Eugene, Oregon, a district of 16,000 students, faced a very different situation. Teachers and district leaders were steeped in a behaviorist model of instruction and discipline, stemming from the fact that many had completed their degrees at the University of Oregon, which was the national leader in Positive Behavioral Interventions and Supports (PBIS) and Direct Instruction. However, some of Eugene's administrators and teachers chafed under this model, believing that these practices led to compliance rather than intrinsic motivation arising from a sense of community in the classroom and strong positive relationships between adults and students, and among students. Working with a small group of interested schools, the district piloted the Caring Schools Community program from the Developmental Studies Center. The permission to pursue a different course based on the interest of teachers and school administrators stimulated enthusiasm and expansion of the program to other schools and eventually to districtwide dissemination. However, the challenge of transitioning away from behaviorist practices and aligning instructional practices with SEL practices required an equal emphasis on a different model of instruction and moving away from direct instruction, which entailed a significant commitment to professional development over a period of years.

The Andover Public Schools, a district of 6,000 students in Andover, Massachusetts, had implemented an elementary social skills program mandated by administration many years in the past. However, enthusiasm had faded, and implementation had become inconsistent at best. As an instructional program in social skills, it felt to teachers like a separate curriculum to be taught, and the program's class meetings had generally devolved into a way to manage class discipline issues. Yet the program had fostered a sense that social skill development was important and that SEL was of value to students. When, as their new superintendent, I engaged the administrative team in beginning to articulate the next strategic plan for the district, SEL emerged as the most significant need, along with a desire to abandon the current program and seek programs that created a sense of community within the classroom and school. Inquiry-based instruction, personalization, and inclusion had become core to Andover's instruction. However, the district's focus on equity added a need to ensure that SEL provided a culturally inclusive and identity-safe approach to SEL. Through the district's agile strategic planning process, teachers and administrators formed a strong "SEL Sprint" to lead the work. Their enthusiasm led to systemwide implementation of the Responsive Classroom program at the elementary level and the creation of advisory programs at the secondary level.

Although each of these four districts took different routes, all were able to move toward a comprehensive program over time. Each put the puzzle pieces together through different processes to fit their own context. Professional development over time was critical, as was alignment with instruction and discipline. Because I came to the superintendency from a decade of work with an organization focused on the development of social skills and social responsibility in students, I understood what a comprehensive approach looked like and could articulate a vision and rationale to district and school leaders, as well as to teachers. However, because I understood that each context was different, I recognized the wisdom in allowing each district to find its own path to that vision. The puzzle pieces could be assembled in different ways, but the final picture would still be a holistic one.

As with many initiatives in education, the road to systemic implementation of SEL is embarked upon with good intentions—and then the obstacles come into view around the bend. The field of SEL has grown dramatically as districts' SEL programming expanded in the United States (Weissberg et al., 2015). What we know from observing this expansion is that districts begin at very different points and set off down this path motivated by widely divergent rationales. Some districts start by formulating well-intentioned and well-designed strategic plans; others choose opportunistic moments that catch the imagination and interest of faculty and administrators; and still others seize upon SEL as a vehicle to address an urgent crisis. Each district follows a unique path based on the context of its cultural and political environment. It is clear that there is no one best path, or one best program; rather, for those who would make progress, there is a layering of program development and a gradual deepening of fidelity to a vision. This chapter, then, is intended not so much to provide a uniform roadmap as it is to let those who have chosen this road know where the obstacles, ruts, and roadblocks may lie, so that strategies can be put in place to effectively avoid or work through them.

Pathways to Implementation

Research and experience offer a number of insights into successful implementation. Employing an observational rather than investigative approach, Berman (2018) reported on lessons learned in implementing SEL in four districts across an almost 30-year career as superintendent. He cited a number of key factors that contribute to the effectiveness of SEL implementation, starting with the acknowledgment that the social curriculum is as important as the academic curriculum and requires the same attention and planning. Despite the ease of adopting ready-made curricula, weekly 30-minute lessons are not sufficient; rather, it is the integration of SEL into the classroom environment and into academics that provides consistency and coherence in social skill development—and those SEL skills are further solidified by repeated opportunities for service learning. Berman noted that SEL requires cultural inclusivity, ensuring that all children experience an identity-safe school and classroom community. Successful SEL implementation requires administrative vision and leadership, and professional development for all—teachers, administrators, support staff. And finally, success is built on the understanding that progress in modifying such a foundational aspect of school culture and instruction will be gradual and incremental.

Similar findings were presented by The Aspen Institute National Commission on Social, Emotional and Academic Development (Berman et al., 2018) which convened researchers, policymakers, and educators to forge a consensus for the field. The Commission's Council of Distinguished Educators, made up of experienced practitioners from around the country, posed several guiding principles to support effective and high-quality SEL practice, including that SEL is for all students, but it starts with adults; that explicit and embedded instruction plus a caring classroom and school climate combine to develop social, emotional, and academic competencies; that home–school–community partnerships matter; and that strong leadership is central.

In 2010, the Collaborative for Academic, Social, and Emotional Learning (CASEL) launched a project entitled the Collaborating District Initiative (CDI) to "study and scale high-quality, evidence-based academic, social, and emotional learning" in eight urban districts. CASEL worked with the American Institutes for Research (AIR) to collect data and evaluate progress. Among its findings about successful implementation, AIR identified that SEL ideally is integrated into every aspect of the district's work, from the strategic plan and budgets to human resources and operations, and into every aspect of the school, from classroom instruction to school climate and culture to community–family partnerships. In addition, adult

SEL matters, too, and the engagement and commitment of both school and district leadership are essential. AIR found that data are essential for continuous improvement, and districts benefit from collaborating with each other. Encouragingly, AIR noted that systemic SEL is possible even with leadership changes and relatively small budgets. Finally, and of particular relevance to this discussion, AIR found that successful implementation can follow multiple pathways, based on each district's unique needs and strengths (CASEL, 2017).

A number of common themes run through these reports and studies on implementation and SEL practice. First, SEL has to serve all students and be inclusive of cultural and racial diversity. It is not just for those who require behavioral or emotional support. Second, SEL is most effectively implemented when a parallel emphasis is placed on the professional development of adults. Third, SEL initiatives work best when they are multifaceted, involving explicit instruction, integration with academic curricula, a focus on the culture and climate of classroom and school as caring communities, and application in real-world settings through service learning and community service. Fourth, clear administrative support and leadership in articulating a vision are essential, as is building SEL into strategic planning, budgeting, personnel, and other elements of administrative leadership. Fifth, partnerships with parents, the community, out-of-school-time providers, and other districts support successful implementation.

As with any educational initiative, the implementation of SEL is a complicated process. Most districts find that progress is incremental, at best, and the usual lessons apply. Start small and pursue early and modest successes. Build buy-in and investment slowly but strategically, including key groups of stakeholders along the way. While articulating a larger vision, invest in the success of each step before leaping ahead to the next. Invest most in high-quality professional development to build a strong knowledge base and the capacity to deliver SEL programming with fidelity, meaningfulness, and sincerity.

Changing the mind-sets and instructional practices of teachers and administrators is challenging. It takes time, ongoing effort, and follow-through. While the process is under way, reflecting on how implementation is going, dissecting its strengths and weaknesses, and monitoring progress through data will support thoughtful decisions about next steps.

Given that change is hard, requiring courage and commitment, even modest steps forward deserve recognition and acknowledgment. Those who undertake the challenge of leading SEL implementation are fortunate, in that teachers and administrators are drawn to the field of education because they care deeply about children and their development, making them receptive to the need for and value of SEL. Because SEL strengthens relationships between teachers and students, and because students' acquisition of social and emotional skills makes teaching and leading easier, a commitment to a developmental approach to learning that embraces SEL can generate its own enthusiasm and investment. For example, in our experience, once elementary teachers adopt the simple strategy of a daily morning meeting to build community (e.g., Responsive Classroom Morning Meeting; Kriete & Davis, 2014), they rarely abandon it as the preferred way to start their day.

If an SEL program (or programs) is part of the implementation plan, the identification and selection of a program that is high quality becomes crucial. Given the current popularity of SEL and the numerous programs emerging on the market, it is vital to ensure the program is evidence-based and effective in delivering results; otherwise, the initiative will fizzle when teachers don't see results.

One caution we feel compelled to reiterate is that there is no one best path to achieving effective SEL implementation. As reflected in the different paths described in the introductory case, understanding the context and environment of the school or district is vitally important, and the essential findings from research and experience cited earlier are valuable considerations as a school or district creates plans to move forward. Once that movement is under way, it is wise to be aware of five potential obstacles—often overlooked in the SEL literature—that can limit or undermine implementation efforts. As school and district leaders open the door to understanding what promotes SEL and the building of caring classroom and school communities, they begin to see the larger implications for instruction, discipline, professional development, cultural responsiveness, and community engagement. Each is challenging in its own right. We offer our thoughts about aligning them with SEL, because that alignment or misalignment can either enhance or compromise implementation. With planning, these foreseeable bumps in the road need not be inevitable obstacles in a school's or district's journey to success.

Removing Roadblocks, Steering Clear of Ruts, and Avoiding Dead Ends

The guideposts to effective practice are clear and consistent across the various studies and the experience of educators. However, not as clear are the obstacles that districts face and the inconsistencies that may be present, undermining both the essential principles behind SEL and the ability to support genuine development in children's social–emotional skills and behavior.

Aligning Instructional Practices

The *first obstacle* is the potential lack of alignment between instructional practices and the core principles of SEL. Philip Jackson, in his groundbreaking 1968 book *Life in Classrooms,* pointed to the power of the hidden curriculum in the interpersonal environment of the classroom—through its didactic and teacher-directed methods of instruction, behaviorist disciplinary approaches, and rigid classroom social structure—to teach passivity and compliance rather than meaningful engagement and authentic presence. By definition, the "hidden curriculum" comprises the implicit norms, values, and beliefs transmitted to students through the underlying rules, routines, and social structure of the classroom and school (Giroux, 1983). Studies of classrooms and teaching by Goodlad (1984), Sirotnik (1988), and Cuban (1984) showed little change from teacher-directed instruction in the decades following Jackson's study. That same pattern continues today, particularly in urban settings (Darling-Hammond, 2001; Pianta et al., 2001, 2012). While instruction in more affluent communities, states Schaps (2021, p. 121), has shifted to include some learner-centered approaches, "one fundamental inequity remains overlooked: the heavy diet of didactic instruction that prevails in most urban schools. Lecturing predominates across grade levels and content areas. Teachers do most of the modeling and questioning as well as the talking. Students are put in passive sit-and-get roles. And reward-and-punish discipline systems such as PBIS are used to keep them in line."

The core instructional tenets of SEL are learner-centered, focusing on authentic relationships, voice, and choice. Schaps (2021, p. 122) defines *learner-centered instruction* as

> the use of *multiple* teaching methods that are simultaneously attuned to: academic goals, content, and skills; social, emotional, and ethical goals and skills; students' personal interests and questions as well as the essential elements of the subject matter at hand; the current state of students' knowledge and skills (which may vary widely within any given classroom); the goal of evoking and strengthening students' intrinsic motivation to learn; the goal of building an inclusive learning community in the classroom; and the goal of involving students in assessing their own growth; as well as the particular pedagogies that enable students to learn best.

Accordingly, one of the primary roadblocks to effective SEL implementation is a misalignment between the classroom instruction that is actually occurring and the type of instruction that is required to effectively foster students' social–emotional skills. This misalignment was evident in both JCPS and Eugene, two urban systems where traditional instructional approaches had long been dominant and the movement toward more constructivist and inquiry approaches to teaching had just begun. In contrast, in those schools and classrooms where constructivist and learner-centered approaches had been adopted in each of the four districts described in the case, the path to implementing SEL was smoother. Teachers understood the vital importance of student voice and agency in helping students make meaning of the curriculum and building a sense of community in the classroom through open dialogue and problem solving that encouraged growth in SEL skills. On the other hand, as long as teaching takes the form of telling rather than engaging, the message behind SEL instruction remains one of passivity and compliance rather than intrinsic motivation and independent judgment (Schaps, 2021).

Students may be able to parrot the words of SEL, yet not exhibit the social skills that embody them.

At its heart, both learner-centered instruction and SEL shift the focus from what the teacher is doing to what the students are experiencing. The classroom moves away from lecture, worksheets, and teacher-directed questioning to pedagogies involving small-group discussions, collaborative problem solving, investigations and experimentation, brainstorming, and the posing of alternative explanations and methods. Student voice, embodied in the ability to express personal perspectives, and student choice, exemplified by the ability to pursue individual questions and interests, represent key elements in learner-centered instruction that enable and encourage students to be present and engaged in the classroom. Learner-centered approaches require students to engage with each other in meaningful dialogue and to build authentic relationships founded on careful listening and perspective taking that promote learning.

As we found in the work on SEL in JCPS and Eugene, removing this potential roadblock requires parallel professional development on instruction and SEL, so that teachers feel comfortable letting go of some control, facilitating students' building on each other's thinking, asking open-ended questions that extend students' thinking, and enabling students to have voice and presence in the classroom. A simple example in the SEL arena is engaging students in a dialogue at the beginning of the year about the classroom conditions they believe will help them learn best and the co-creation of guiding norms for the classroom to best support learning. In the academic arena, a simple example can involve students' choice of books for their independent reading time in an elementary classroom and multiple ways of sharing their reading with the class.

Learner-centered instruction is more complex than didactic instruction. It requires teachers to master a more diverse set of skills in observation, listening, and facilitation, and to utilize a wider range of teaching strategies that engage students in inquiry and exploration (Schaps, 2021). These same skills are required to effectively lead classrooms in SEL. Therefore, alignment of professional development in both SEL and instruction is mutually supportive and synergistic.

Aligning Discipline Systems

The same issue of alignment emerges in the discipline systems utilized in the classroom and the school at large, potentially raising a *second obstacle* to the effective implementation of SEL. Too often, discipline systems are behaviorist in approach, focusing on control of behavior through rewards and punishments rather than through learning and relationships. Behaviorist systems of discipline can be somewhat effective at controlling behavior (Bierman & Motamedi, 2015; Hart, 2010; Levy et al., 2018). Wanting to be appreciated by the teacher, children tend to respond to rewards and praise. They also want to avoid both the humiliation and the consequences of punishment for a violation.

However, this approach has several essential problems. First, it promotes extrinsic rather than intrinsic motivation. The student is oriented toward obedience to rules established by an external authority rather than mastering self-control, self-motivation, and ownership and responsibility for their actions. In addition, it tends to be divorced from learning from the experience, because the reward or punishment is usually not aligned with logical consequences of the action. Although most teachers and administrators make sincere efforts in disciplinary situations to help students appreciate the rationale for the rule that was violated and to facilitate students' taking ownership of the consequences of their actions, the disciplinary consequence is often unrelated to the violation. For example, receiving a detention for cutting a class is a punishment, but is not a logical consequence, in that it does not lead to solving the triggering problem or reconnecting the student with the teacher or the material. A logical consequence is one that is directly related to the misbehavior, realistic for the child to achieve, and respectful, in that it focuses on the behavior and not the child's character. For example, if a child writes on a desk, cleaning the desk is a logical consequence, while missing recess or staying after school has no connection to the offense.

In a behaviorist system, if the disciplinary issue involves negative interactions with other students or teachers, the consequence is often removal from the relationship with those who were violated. A problematic interaction between two students, for example, can result in the requirement that both students stay away from each other, with one or both receiving a temporary or even permanent removal from the classroom through a suspension or time spent in the principal's office. Little effort is expended to repair and restore the relationship. Consequences such as these serve as extrinsic reinforcement focused on controlling the behavior. Not only do they fail to solve the underlying problem, but they may also actually subvert development and growth of social and emotional skills by not providing the students with an opportunity to understand their own motivations and to problem-solve solutions that will address the incident or infraction.

If we are to effectively foster students' social–emotional development and growth, we need to apply systems of discipline that are better aligned with goals that focus on relationships over control and on understanding the motivation behind the behavior and responding empathically. Systems such as developmental discipline (Ellsworth & Monahan, 1987; Watson, 2003, 2014) and restorative practices (Amstutz & Mullet, 2015) are based on promoting intrinsic motivation through learning from the experience, and through repairing and restoring relationships. They are grounded on the principle that classrooms and schools should become caring and just communities and that teacher–child relationships should be characterized by nurturing and trusting relationships (Watson, 2014). Misbehaviors are viewed as communication to adults that something is wrong, and as mistakes and opportunities for learning. According to Watson (2014), rather than promote motivations "to avoid punishment, gain pleasure, emulate a powerful model, or please authority," developmental discipline seeks to foster "students' empathic caring, moral awareness, and moral understanding" (p. 179).

Therefore, in a problematic situation between two students, facilitating dialogue between them about the conflict and about how they can restore their relationship teaches students that resolving conflicts is possible, and it provides them with a lived experience of accomplishing that goal. In the case of damage to property, reparation and restitution represent ways to repair situations and restore relationships. In developmental discipline or restorative practice approaches, the consequences are directly related to the situation, the focus is on addressing the harm done, and the desired outcome is learning from the experience of repairing the situation and being accepted back into the community.

Another example is a situation in which one child teases another who has special needs. Often the solution is to impose a consequence or remove the offending student and send them to an administrator to address the issue. Alternatively, the teacher can join with the student in understanding the impact of that action on the other child, encourage an empathic response on the part of the student, and join with the student in an effort to solve the problem and redress the wrong. Engaging the student in a problem-solving discussion, with the teacher and/or with the child who has been impacted, of what action the student could take to repair the relationship and what consequences are appropriate to address the behavior enables the student to learn, grow, and assume responsibility. Rather than simply imposing a disciplinary consequence, the problem-solving dialogue between the teacher and the student helps to uncover ways to restore the relationship between the students. Restorative practices, in particular, focus attention on those harmed by including them in the dialogue and giving them voice about both solutions and consequences, with the goal of repairing the relationship.

The fact that teachers and administrators respond with empathy and curiosity about why a conflict happened does not minimize the violation. Empathy doesn't mean letting go of accountability. Neither restorative practices nor developmental discipline denies consequences for misbehavior; instead, both place an emphasis on addressing the harm done and finding solutions that repair that harm. Clarity and honesty about the violation are critical elements of feedback for the student. Still, these approaches enable the teacher to preserve the dignity of the student and to join with the student, or students, in an effort to find the best path to right a wrong.

Approaches such as developmental discipline and restorative practices are consistent with the goals of SEL in terms of resolving conflicts, building strong relationships, and making responsible decisions. Such strategies place students in a position of responsibility and inspire meaningful ways to learn from mistakes and retain connection with their peers and teachers. Conflicts are a natural part of community life, and these models of discipline support the effort to create a caring community within the classroom while respecting each child's need for autonomy, competence, and affection. They foster belonging over exclusion, mutual resolution of problems over control, and individual accountability over punishment. Fundamentally, because they view misbehavior as communication about something of concern to the student, they are teaching strategies that help students experience success and learn new behaviors. When discipline is aligned with SEL practices and principles, the consistency strengthens students' social and emotional growth as they experience it in real situations.

Given the deep-seated patterns of discipline in America's schools, adopting these SEL-consistent approaches is not easy. In each of the four districts in the introductory case, discipline systems were the hardest and slowest to change. It takes professional development and, most important, ongoing reflection on the part of the teacher and administrator. However, setting goals of creating an inclusive, connected, and caring classroom community and teaching social and emotional skills within the context of the daily life of the classroom is a strong and positive way to begin walking a different path in addressing behavior and discipline issues.

Aligning Professional Capacity

High-quality professional development is essential for effective SEL implementation. Thus, the *third obstacle* entails the inadequate attention devoted to building professional capacity. Schools often fail to provide the professional development support required of SEL programs and initiatives, assuming that the brief professional development provided by vendors is sufficient. To execute programming in SEL, educators need help in their own social–emotional development as well as in-depth training to support classroom implementation. This assistance includes training adults to reconstruct their relationships with students. It also includes how educators approach discipline, how they use language, and how they structure their instruction and classroom environment to create an inclusive, caring, and respectful classroom community.

One of the troubling areas of vulnerability in SEL implementation is that districts too often select a specific commercial program and view that package as having taken care of what's needed to support SEL. Professional development to teach these programs is often cursory and time-constrained. Districts generally have very limited time built into their school year for professional development, and the demand on this time tends to give priority to core content in reading and math. Therefore, vendors and district staff members have to force-fit SEL program professional development into limited half-day or full-day trainings, even though much more depth is required for teachers both to master the content of the program and develop their own SEL skills in order to model them effectively in the classroom. In fact, the latter component is the more difficult of the two, because it entails unlearning long-established behaviors, as well as developing new practices of adult–student and even adult–adult interaction.

What district and school administrators sometimes fail to realize is that, as adults, teachers have their own social–emotional vulnerabilities that project themselves onto the classroom. How adults traditionally deal with anger, disruption, conflict, and trauma in their personal lives becomes reflected in how they respond to situations in the classroom. Teaching social and emotional skills, and responding in the moment to social and emotional situations inevitably surfaces the patterns and habits we've honed and nurtured since our own childhood days. It takes conscious reflection and effort to observe our own behavior and overcome negative patterns in order to teach students positive approaches and coach them in how to transform patterns in their own response to situations. For example, to effectively teach conflict resolution skills to children and model those skills in the classroom, teachers must understand their own response to conflict and apply effective conflict-resolving strategies as incidents emerge in the classroom, particularly when a conflict develops between the student and the teacher.

Similarly, teacher language and tone of voice are powerful influences on not only the relationships constructed between teacher and student but also the culture of the classroom itself (Denton, 2007). Sarcasm, judgmental comments, labeling, accusatory language, threats and warnings, and even praise that is used to control can constitute painful microaggressions that make a deep impression on students, causing them to withdraw trust and be reluctant to risk. Such adult behaviors undermine learning, while creating a climate that counters the very SEL lessons a teacher is attempting to transmit. Applying effective teacher language requires not only knowledge of constructive communication strategies but also reflection on the language we use, plus the self-control to find alternatives when we observe ourselves relying on unproductive strategies.

These language skills are critical for building a sense of community in the classroom. We know that direct instruction in SEL is insufficient; the classroom must also model these lessons daily and create a sense of community in which students are able to better understand how their actions and failures to act impact others in the community. Creating community in the classroom requires conscious and well-planned attention and entails more than classic community-building activities. It requires facilitating connections among students, modeling and promoting respect and appreciation for individual perspectives, and restoring relationships when there is a conflict or transgression. Building community requires active teacher coaching of students, helping students learn to collaborate and problem-solve in order to move beyond points at which small groups may be stuck. Teachers need to help students identify and affirm their strengths and assets. And teachers need to intervene with reflective questioning that deepens student understanding of the social dynamics within the classroom. For example, a fourth-grade student may feel frustrated because his math problem-solving partner uses different strategies than he does. To promote understanding between the two students, the teacher can ask questions that help the student appreciate that there is more than one way to solve problems, and that each partner offers a valuable approach.

Some teachers possess these skills coming into teaching and/or had them strengthened in teacher preparation programs (see Johnson, Barthelus, Skoog-Hoffman, Nwafor, & Jagers, Chapter 5, this volume, for a discussion of SEL in teacher preparation). However, most benefit from in-depth professional development experiences and ongoing coaching in order to master them and bring them to the level of second nature. While the necessary training in SEL program implementation provides a base, this deeper level of professional development enables teachers to be effective in moving beyond the SEL program to create an environment that embodies the very traits the program is designed to teach. In fact, the professional development programs implemented by the four districts in the introductory case provided depth through both multiple levels of workshops and job-embedded coaching by peers and instructional coaches.

We would never just give teachers a brief workshop in a new reading or math program, hand them the teaching manual, and expect them to provide quality instruction in reading or math. The same is true for SEL. Programs such as Responsive Classroom (*www.responsiveclassroom.org*) provide weeklong trainings, with multiple levels of depth, in order to give teachers the time and feedback to master these skills. Districts that provide ongoing coaching substantially improve the effectiveness of their SEL programming. Because quality SEL instruction has a direct and positive impact on instruction (Durlak, Weissberg, Dymnicki, Taylor, & Schellinger, 2011), devoting time to quality professional development in SEL has the ancillary impact of improving students' academic performance.

Reflecting Diversity, Equity, and Inclusion

Most teachers and administrators enter into the implementation of SEL with the best of intentions, seeking to transform schools and classrooms in ways that improve the present and future lives of students. Yet this goodwill is destined to fall far short of its intended goal if it does not encompass an unswerving and actionable devotion to equity. For generations, the racial and economic injustices of society have been reflected in the way students are pre-judged and sorted in academic settings, where skin color and socioeconomic status are strong determinants of the coursework, resources, and discipline that a child encounters (Allen et al., 2013; Darling-Hammond et al., 2018). Providing equitable opportunities requires differentiating for individual student needs and at the same time addressing systemic disparities in school settings. It is also important to guard against SEL approaches that reinforce inequities, such that students with the least need benefit the most while students with the most need are not given the necessary resources and support to fully benefit from SEL. This cautionary statement leads to the *fourth obstacle* to quality SEL implementation—falling into the rut of accepting and projecting the dominant social values, norms, and mores of our culture, without fully recognizing the diversity of cultural norms and cultural and racial heritages of students in the classroom.

Students bring with them a wide range of rich cultural traditions and lived experiences that may be strikingly different from the norms of White, Western, middle-class culture. Because so many teachers come from White and middle-class backgrounds, they frequently have little personal familiarity with and awareness of the cultural nuances of many of the children in their care (Meckler & Rabinowitz, 2019). For example, the individualistic and competitive norms that pervade White, middle-class American culture may be strikingly different from the collectivist cultures that children from other races and ethnicities may experience in their family circles, thereby leaving these children feeling isolated, unsupported, and unrecognized in the classroom.

Research (Aronson & Laughter, 2016) is beginning to shed light on how SEL-based learning settings can most effectively capture the intersection of SEL skill building with race and ethnicity. Based on evidence that suggests meaningful and sustainable change requires transformations in the ways in which those experiencing relative privilege understand themselves and their role in ameliorating inequities in interpersonal and institutional contexts, transformative SEL expands the focus from historically disenfranchised groups to include those who experience relative privilege (Jost, 2015; Seider, 2008; Jagers et al., 2019). Referred to as *transformative SEL,* the approach recognizes that the classroom needs to be a mirror in which students see themselves reflected in the material they are studying and the educational settings they experience. The classroom also needs to serve as a window on the larger world, revealing to students a wealth of experiences and insights that broaden their horizons.

The SEL-based classroom provides both windows and mirrors by enabling students to bring their cultures into the classroom, see those cultures reflected in the reading and other curricular work they are pursuing, and experience norms that make them feel comfortable and present. The effective SEL classroom is, in essence, a community that is identity-safe and culturally, as well as socially and emotionally, responsive.

Cultural perspectives and different ways of knowing can be powerful instructional tools both for SEL and for the academic curriculum. The introduction of diverse cultural perspectives stimulates students' questions, validates their experiences, and expands their ways of knowing and seeing. It can also raise students' consciousness about bias, prejudice, and perspective, and reveal problems of inequity (Jagers et al., 2019). As we discuss in the next section, surfacing the issues of inequity can help students find ways to take action and strive for a more equitable and just world.

Achieving this goal requires professional development in culturally responsive pedagogy. It also requires teachers to be curious about the cultures and experiences of their students, to continually self-reflect on the norms of the classroom, and to have an ongoing dialogue with students about their experiences. Curricular resources in SEL tend to focus on a specific set of strategies for recognizing emotions, building relationships, solving problems, and resolving conflict. When teaching from these resources, teachers need to continually ask students for alternatives and options that may reflect other cultural traditions and are equally effective in addressing issues. "Are there other ways to think about this?" and "Are there other solutions that may be helpful?" are important questions for teachers to ask to enable students to pose ways of thinking and acting that provide inclusive options while broadening students' perspectives. The teacher doesn't need to know upfront everything about students' cultural backgrounds, but by using this kind of open-ended questioning, the teacher encourages students to present options based in their experiences, then weigh these options alongside others.

For effective SEL implementation, it is essential to avoid the trap of projecting SEL as middle-class cultural uniformity. Ensuring that SEL professional development integrates with professional development in culturally responsive pedagogy is critical.

Connecting the Classroom to the Community

The *fifth obstacle* is the tendency to limit the lessons of SEL to the interpersonal relationships within the classroom and students' immediate social circles. For students to anchor the key concepts of SEL in their own development, they must be able to practice their developing skills through real-world experiences outside the classroom. This link between SEL and service learning gave the Hudson Public Schools program a vitality and depth that significantly enhanced students' social skill development.

In addition, both Hudson and JCPS implemented at the high school level a program entitled Facing History and Ourselves that linked the study of intolerance with service experiences that enhanced social justice and care for others. Facing History and Ourselves—an approach to teaching history and literature that addresses racism, critical thinking, and ethical decisionmaking—is designed to stretch students to be comfortable with people different from themselves. The organization uses the term "universe of obligation," coined by sociologist Helen Fein (1979), to denote the individuals or groups toward whom we feel an obligation to extend our care and protection (Facing History and Ourselves, 2017). The extent of that circle of individuals and groups is often defined by the attitudes and beliefs of a child's family and the social consciousness of the family (Berman, 1997). One of the vulnerabilities of the typical practice of SEL is that its lessons are confined to the dynamics between individuals; the SEL programming fails to be applied to the larger social area, thereby constraining children's universe of obligation. On the flip side, one of the significant assets of SEL is that it is applicable to how we think about and behave in the larger social and political arena.

The principles of SEL, from active listening and perspective taking to collaborative problem solving and finding common ground, apply just as well to problems and conflicts within our communities, states, nation, and across nations as they do to our interpersonal issues and concerns. Yet few commercial SEL programs build in extensions to those larger social and political issues or engage students in thinking about the ethical considerations that ground their social and emotional understandings. Although core to the CASEL framework are processes that enable young people to achieve collective goals and make responsible and caring decisions (*https://casel.org/fundamentals-of-sel*), the activities and lessons commonly employed to achieve these goals are primarily focused on interpersonal interactions within the classroom and school. While students are given ample opportunity within classrooms that implement SEL to discuss and find solutions that help students "develop healthy identities, manage emotions and achieve personal and collective goals, feel and show empathy for others, establish and maintain supportive relationships, and make responsible and caring decisions," little is done to expand students' universe of obligation and apply this skill set to the broader social and political context around them where it will meet the real test of application (CASEL, n.d.).

There is great potential in teachers' engaging students in dialogue about the application of the positive social and emotional lessons to social and political issues. There is also much to be gained in the use of excellent curricula such as Facing History and Ourselves' *Holocaust and Human Behavior.* Both of these strategies enable students to apply their newly acquired social and emotional skills, engage in experiences in which those skills are practiced, and expand their universe of obligation. The most effective way to do this is through service learning and community service.

Community service is simply volunteer work, such as collecting canned goods, with little connection to the classroom curriculum. Operating at a more educational level, *service learning* is a pedagogical approach that combines learning objectives with community service opportunities and engages students in experiential learning, reflection, and action to make a difference in their communities, state, and nation (Berman, 2000). By engaging with others in efforts to make a difference, students apply the social and emotional skills they have been acquiring in the classroom to their actions in the real world. And by identifying and selecting areas of concern where they can make a difference in their community or in the broader social and political world, they extend their universe of obligation beyond their friends and family, their classroom, and their school.

The avenues for potential community service and service-learning opportunities are diverse. They can be environmental in protecting and preserving the earth's ecosystems; educational in supporting the academic development of others; humanitarian in providing aid to those who have been impacted by disaster, disease, or other circumstances; intergenerational in providing support and companionship to senior citizens; or legislative and political in advocating changes in law, policy, or funding. Examples abound, from buddy programs in which older students read to and engage in projects with younger students, to Special Olympics Unified Sports® programs in which regular education and students with disabilities play together on teams, to environmental reclamation efforts tied to the science curriculum, to working with local nonprofit organizations as part of a civics course (Berman, 2000).

Service learning engages students in meeting real community needs, integrates with and strengthens curricular lessons, and provides students with the opportunity to reflect on the significance of their service and the application of social and emotional skills. Also, when students have the opportunity to engage with local service and nongovernmental organizations, they interact with individuals who model social and emotional skills as they work to make a difference. These experiences, if regularly integrated into the curriculum, as we did in Hudson, expand not only students' universe of obligation but also their social consciousness and sense of social responsibility.

The work we do in SEL is essential to give students the attitudes and skills to improve their lives and their relationships with others. However, there is a larger mission to this work. When we create caring classroom communities and engage students in opportunities to serve others, we provide our students with a vision of the way the world could be, the skills to help realize that vision, and the inspiration to move that vision forward. The potential of SEL is to help students develop a personal investment in the well-being of others and of the planet, be concerned about the world around them, and be engaged in its improvement.

Developing a Roadmap for Success

As we stated in our introduction, what is clear about SEL implementation is that there is no one best path, or one best program; rather—for those who would make progress—there is a layering of successful elements of change that lead to a deepening of fidelity to a vision. We recognize that different communities need different entry points for this work. Some communities may prefer to start by building adult capacity; others may view community partnerships as a critical first step. With the exception of beginning by setting a clear vision for students' need for SEL, we do not present the recommendations in sequential order.

So where does one start? Varying contexts and needs require different solutions. One of the most empowering approaches is to bring together a group of inspired educators. Charged with finding the starting point for launching the work, the process begins by understanding the context within which the plan for transformation will unfold. Understanding the context requires an assessment of the critical conditions that the district or school is facing relative to broader strengths and weaknesses. In the business world, this process is referred to as a *landscape analysis.* In the world of education, the key is to honestly assess the most critical issues or challenges within the broader backdrop of district or school strengths and weaknesses. Once context is understood, the group members may choose to take the first step in the journey by targeting a strength or by correcting a problem. For some, the place to start may be in program review or professional development. Many believe climate and culture is the place to begin, especially at the elementary school level. While the high school level is much harder to approach because the student and teacher experience is more fragmented, creating an advisory program—that is, a regularly scheduled time to support small-group learning and social connection—may offer an ideal starting point. Sometimes, a discipline issue is the obvious first step. And for still others, dissatisfaction with a specific program triggers a general sense of the need for change, so a refresh or reboot starts with a program review.

Wherever a district starts, two factors are essential to building an achievable plan. First, it is vital that the first step is successful, because that initial work forms the foundation for the next phase of the transformation plan. Success begets success. The second point is to understand how all the elements or components of a plan will intersect and build on each other. For some districts, the components may interlock equally, while for other districts, certain elements must be emphasized over others. Understanding the connections helps to identify the potential paths, as well as the sequencing and scaffolding among the various elements that, taken together, define the roadmap. Many routes can lead to the same destination.

Conclusion

Clearly, these five obstacles are not the only ruts and roadblocks to avoid on the path to successful implementation. All the effective implementation principles identified by CASEL and others, as outlined at the beginning of this chapter, have their inverse, which can create circumstances that limit or undermine implementation and become dead ends to well-intentioned SEL efforts. Two good examples are clear vision and administrative leadership. Without these elements, it is difficult to sustain systemic implementation. Without inclusion of SEL in a strategic plan, and without implementation planning for SEL in particular, programs suffer from episodic and haphazard implementation. Without adequate buy-in of faculty and building administrators, SEL is left to those who can make their way independently, without institutional support. Without data to monitor progress, it is difficult to make just-in-time adjustments to plans and focus on areas that need attention. These issues impact implementation of any new initiative, and the literature on addressing them is rich and elaborate.

Throughout this chapter, we have attempted to pay close attention to the issues that may compromise the implementation of SEL in specific ways. Ensuring that instructional and disciplinary practices reflect and embody the core principles of SEL, providing depth in professional development that addresses adult as well as student skill development, bridging the work in SEL with culturally responsive practice so that all students feel known and included, and extending student skill development by means of realistic and experiential practice through service learning are particularly important aspects of systemic and effective implementation that often don't receive the attention they require. The best answer to overcoming these obstacles is to collaboratively develop a roadmap with a clear and honest understanding of context—the ruts, the roadblocks, and the dead ends, as well as the strengths and opportunities.

Each of the districts in the introductory case confronted these ruts, roadblocks, and dead ends as they progressed through implementation. However, it was the ability to assess their own context, chart an individual implementation course, and pursue incremental successes that gave them the ability to avoid or overcome these obstacles. Also, having a vision of what success could look like enabled the districts to address the obstacles and allow the incremental steps and puzzle pieces to come together over time.

By calling attention to these issues, we hope to expand the vision of those leading SEL implementation efforts. We believe that a larger vision enables school and district leaders to take small and incremental steps to implement effective SEL programming, while being intentional about aligning other curricular and instructional initiatives in the district with the core principles embodied in SEL. This work is not simple, easy, or quickly accomplished; however, by spotlighting these key components, we hope to assist district and school leaders, teachers, and policymakers to become more effective in creating powerful SEL learning experiences for students and adults.

DISCUSSION QUESTIONS

1. This chapter identifies five common obstacles to full SEL implementation:
   a. Aligning of instructional practices
   b. Aligning of discipline systems
   c. Aligning of professional capacity
   d. Reflecting diversity, equity, and inclusion
   e. Connecting the classroom to the community
2. Think about a district or school with which you have worked closely and reflect on their SEL implementation in relation to these five common obstacles. Which of these obstacles has the district/school navigated successfully? Which of these

obstacles have been roadblocks? Are there lessons learned from successful navigation experiences that can be used to respond to other roadblocks?

3. We have discussed the idea that each district needs to make choices about SEL and that the process of integration and implementation needs to be customized to the district or school. Reflect on your experiences with a district or school with which you have worked. Generate an example of when that customization and implementation process was successful. What were the roles different people played in that successful customization process? What expertise and skills did those people have that made that possible? What actions were taken during the process of implementation that led to its success?
4. SEL takes different forms in classrooms depending on the age of the students involved. That means key values are consistent across PreK–12, but the practices that follow from those key values change depending on the age of the students.
    a. Providing equitable opportunities for students and guarding against SEL approaches that reinforce inequities are critical goals. Specifically, as expressed earlier in this chapter, "Meaningful and sustainable change requires transformations in the ways in which those experiencing relative privilege understand themselves and their role in ameliorating inequities in interpersonal and institutional contexts." How will advancement of this idea look different in elementary, middle, and high school contexts?
    b. Connecting the classroom to the community is an important goal of schools. How will this idea take shape differently in elementary, middle, and high school students?

REFERENCES

Allen, A., Scott, L. A., & Lewis, C. W. (2013). Racial microaggressions and African American and Hispanic students in urban schools: A call for culturally affirming education. *Interdisciplinary Journal of Teaching and Learning, 3*(2), 117–129.

Amstutz, L. S., & Mullet, J. H. (2015). *Restorative discipline for schools: Teaching responsibility; Creating caring climates.* Good Books.

Aronson, B., & Laughter, J. (2016). The theory and practice of culturally relevant education: A synthesis of research across content areas. *Review of Educational Research, 86*(1), 163–206.

Berman, S. (1997). *Children's social consciousness and the development of social responsibility.* State University of New York Press.

Berman, S. (2000). Service as systemic reform. *School Administrator, 57*(7), 20–24.

Berman, S. (2018). What we've learned about implementing social–emotional learning. *School Administrator, 75*(8), 32–36.

Berman, S., Chaffee, S., & Sarmiento, J. (2018). *The practice base for how we learn: Supporting students' social, emotional, and academic development* (Consensus statements of evidence from the Council of Distinguished Educators of the National Commission on Social, Emotional and Academic Development). The Aspen Institute.

Bierman, K. L., & Motamedi, M. (2015). Social and emotional learning programs for preschool children. In J. A. Durlak, C. E. Domitrovich, R. P. Weissberg, & T. P. Gullotta (Eds.), *Handbook of social and emotional learning: Research and practice* (pp. 135–150). Guilford Press.

Collaborative for Academic, Social, and Emotional Learning. (2017). *Key insights from the Collaborating Districts Initiative*. Author.

Collaborative for Academic, Social, and Emotional Learning. (n.d.). Fundamentals of SEL. Retrieved from *https://casel.org/fundamentals-of-sel.*

Cuban, L. (1984). *How teachers taught: Constancy and change in American classrooms*. Longman.

Darling-Hammond, L. (2001). Inequality in teaching and schooling: How opportunity is rationed to students of color in America. In B. Smedley, A. Stith, L. Colburn, & C. Evans (Eds.), *The right thing to do, the smart thing to do: Enhancing diversity in the health professions: Summary of the symposium on diversity in health professions in honor of Herbert W. Nickens, M.D.* (pp. 208–233). National Academies Press.

Darling-Hammond, L., Cook-Harvey, C., Flook, L., Gardner, M., & Melnick, H. (2018). *With the whole child in mind: Insights from the Comer School Development Program*. Association for Supervision and Curriculum Development.

Denton, P. (2007). *The power of our words*. Northeast Foundation for Children.

Durlak, J., Weissberg, R., Dymnicki, A., Taylor, R., & Schellinger, K. (2011). The impact of enhancing students' social and emotional learning: A meta-analysis of school-based universal interventions. *Child Development, 82*(1), 405–432.

Ellsworth, J. D., & Monahan, A. K. (1987). *A humanistic approach to teaching/learning through developmental discipline*. Irvington.

Facing History and Ourselves. (2017). *Holocaust and human behavior.* Author.

Fein, H. (1979). *Accounting for genocide*. Free Press.

Giroux, H. (1983). *Theory and resistance in education*. Bergin & Garvey.

Goodlad, J. (1984). *A place called school*. McGraw-Hill.

Hart, R. (2010). Classroom behaviour management: Educational psychologists' views on effective practice. *Emotional and Behavioural Difficulties, 15*(4), 353–371.

Jackson, P. W. (1968). *Life in classrooms*. Teachers College Press.

Jagers, R., Rivas-Drake, D., & Williams, B. (2019). Transformative social and emotional learning (SEL): Toward SEL in service of educational equity and excellence. *Educational Psychologist, 54*(3), 162–184.

Jost, J. (2015). Resistance to change: A social psychological perspective. *Social Research, 82*(3), 607–636.

Kriete, R., & Davis, C. (2014). *The morning meeting book*. Northeast Foundation for Children.

Levy, R., Naff, D. B., Terry, M., & Coffee, M. (2018). *A review of disciplinary interventions in K–12 public education*. Metropolitan Educational Research Consortium.

Meckler, L., & Rabinowitz, K. (2019, December 27). America's schools are more diverse than ever: But the teachers are still mostly white. Retrieved from *www.washingtonpost.com/graphics/2019/local/education/teacher-diversity.*

Pianta, R., Pianta, R. C., Hamre, B. K., & Allen, J. P. (2012). Teacher–student relationships and engagement: Conceptualizing, measuring, and improving the capacity of classroom interactions. In S. L. Christenson, A. L. Reschly, & C. Wylie (Eds.), *Handbook of research on student engagement* (pp. 365–386). Springer.

Pianta, R. C., Belsky, J., Houts, R., & Morrison, F. (2007). Opportunities to learn in America's elementary classrooms. *Science, 315*(5820), 1795–1796.

Schaps, E. (2021). The overlooked inequity. *Journal of Character Education, 17*(1), 121–124.

Seider, S. (2008). Resisting obligation: How privileged adolescents conceive of their social responsibility to others. *Journal of Research on Character Education, 6*(1), 3–19.

Sirotnik, K. A. (1988). What goes on in classrooms? Is this the way we want it? In L. E. Beyer & M. W. Apple (Eds.), *The curriculum: Problems, politics, and possibilities* (pp. 56–74). State University of New York Press.

Watson, M. (2003). *Learning to trust: Transforming difficult elementary classrooms through developmental discipline.* Wiley.

Watson, M. (2014). Developmental discipline and moral education. In L. Nucci, D. Narvaez, & T. Krettenauer (Eds.), *Handbook of moral and character education* (pp. 159–179). Routledge.

Weissberg, R. P., Durlak, J. A., Domitrovich, C. E., & Gullotta, T. P. (2015). Social and emotional learning: Past, present and future. In J. A. Durlak, C. E. Domitrovich, R. P. Weissberg, & T. P. Gullotta (Eds.), *Handbook of social and emotional learning: Research and practice* (pp. 3–19). Guilford Press.

Chapter 11

Supporting Transformative SEL Implementation through a Collaboratory for Inclusion

Christina Cipriano, Gabrielle Rappolt-Schlichtmann, Julie Riley, Lauren H. Naples, and Abigail Eveleigh

If we *want* something *different*, we need to *do* something *differently*. Over the last 5 years we have witnessed a seismic shift in how efforts to address diversity, equity, access, and inclusion in social and emotional learning (SEL) are conceptualized. Termed *transformative SEL*, Jagers et al. (2019) extended the five-competency model of SEL to articulate the necessary conditions for building the skills central to enabling SEL as a lever for educational equity (see discussion in Johnson et al., Chapter 5, this volume; Collaborative for Academic, Social, and Emotional Learning [CASEL], 2020). A transformative SEL approach embraces learner cultural identity, agency, belonging, and engagement—and we add diverse ways of knowing, perceiving, and navigating the world (Hehir, 2002; Rappolt-Schlichtmann et al., 2020)—as central tenants of intervention programming (Jagers et al., 2019; Williams & Jagers, 2020). But how exactly can schools go about doing transformative SEL well? Currently, the field lacks specific strategies and evidence to inform its approach (Cipriano et al., 2022; Jagers et al., 2019; Williams & Jagers, 2020).

We contend that transformative SEL will require active perspective taking in the service of the students most marginalized within school communities—including, explicitly, students with disabilities (SWDs)—to achieve robust outcomes for all. SWDs include those who qualify for special education under the Every Student Succeeds Act (2015) and have individualized education plans (IEPs), those with a formal disability diagnosis, and students with 504 Plans. SWD identifiers can include those who are sensorially or perceptually diverse or have sensory processing challenges. SWDs also include the 1 in 5 students with specific learning disabilities, such as dyslexia, or attention issues, such as attention-deficit/hyperactivity disorder, as well as social processing differences, such as autism or emotional and behavioral disorders (U.S. Department of Education, 2018). Identified SWDs collectively make up an estimated 14–18% of the student population (National Center for Education Statistics, 2021). SWDs are not the only marginalized students in public education, as we discuss further on in this chapter, but SWDs are currently the least represented in SEL studies, pedagogies, and practice (Cipriano et al., 2022; Rappolt-Schlichtmann et al., in press). Through working to build rich and meaningful understandings of SWDs and their intersectional identities, educators and administrators are able to run a more informed, iterative, and data-based decision-making process to derive a strategy for SEL implementation. And, resulting SEL implementation will better represent the needs and strengths of the SWD community and be inclusive of all those therein.

Toward this end, in this chapter, we present a process that school communities can leverage to enable and implement SEL that is transformative. We begin by describing this process—the "Collaboratory for Inclusion"—an intentional approach to transformative SEL implementation that has two phases: (1) *discovery*, focused on *critical self- and social awareness through effortful and scaffolded perspective taking*, and (2) *exploration*, which is *data-driven decision making rooted in empathy and fueled by data literacy and availability in schools*. We illustrate the approach with real examples from a recent case study exploring one district's experience supporting SEL implementation for all learners.

The Collaboratory for Inclusion

Evidence-based interventions in education have a long and complex history that precedes them. More often than not, new and innovative practices feel like "just another thing" that teachers have to do and leaders have to enforce (Osher et al., 2016). For this reason, new evidence-based practices run the risk of being the next buzzy big thing in one year and a thing of the past in the next. A rush to implementation that fails to be systematic may shoulder much of the blame (Cipriano et al., 2021; Jagers et al., 2019). When it comes to transformative SEL, there is considerable and mounting research, especially in the past decade, that describes what systemic and successful SEL implementation looks like (Blewitt et al., 2018; Durlak et al., 2011; Rimm-Kaufman & Hulleman, 2015; Taylor et al., 2017), yet there has been little explicit attention to or guidance about *how exactly* school communities can work to build SEL implementation that honors a school community in its full, rich complexity and successfully promotes educational equity that is inclusive of SWDs (for a full review, see Cipriano et al., in press).

To respond to this challenge, we developed a practical approach to transformative SEL that leans into the perspective-taking work of adults in school communities. Termed a *Collaboratory for Inclusion*, the approach is an intentional and iterative process that allows school communities to create the conditions necessary for the implementation of transformative SEL. The Collaboratory for Inclusion *requires the adults in school communities to commit to ongoing work that continuously improves learning conditions, components, and culture to better reflect the needs, strengths, and preferences of marginalized students.*[1] This work has two phases: one focused on discovery and therefore the development of adult self and social awareness through perspective taking, and the other focused on responsible decision making in the exploration and design of learning environments that are equitable and inclusive. Figure 11.1 illustrates the components of each phase and their overall, iterative relationship.

If the aim is to provide all students equitable access to meaningful opportunities for learning and thriving, then we must begin by working together to listen to and understand students who are made most vulnerable by our education system, communities, or society at large. While schools may not always create these vulnerabilities on their own, serving students and creating school climates that protect and uphold students will require much from adults within school communities. Building a strong foundation for the implementation of transformative SEL—one that is focused on perspective taking to build understanding—will need adults who work together with intention, purpose, and humility to be inclusive of everyone.

The work of the collaboratory is a means to honor the experiences and support the equitable inclusion of learners who have been most marginalized within a

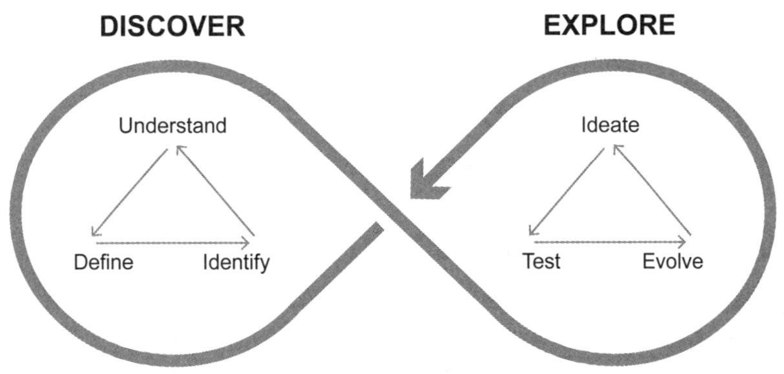

FIGURE 11.1. The Collaboratory for Inclusion.

[1]To learn more about key universal design for learning SEL practices identified through this work, see Rappolt-Schlichtmann et al. (2023).

school community, so that everyone will be able to see themselves in, interact with, customize or modify, and implement SEL. In this way, the experiences of learners and educators are in fact critical assets that inform and lead decision making as SEL is implemented. We define *equity* as the assurance that everyone has access to the same opportunities. Equity begins by acknowledging the unequal starting place of each individual in the school community and making a commitment to correct and address the imbalance through immediate, intentional, and preventive actions, policies, and practices. We define *inclusion* as the practice or policy of providing equitable access to opportunities and resources for people who might otherwise be excluded or marginalized. Inclusive learning environments value, welcome, and consider learner diversity and variability as the norm.

Importantly, reaching fully inclusive and equitable solutions to SEL implementation is more than an issue of learner differences related to ability and disability. There is overwhelming evidence that when learning experiences and environments provide for access and equity in learning and create supportive conditions in which marginalized students feel safe and belong, the benefits for all members of the school community are positive and palpable (Berger & Fisher, 2013; Greenstone et al., 2012; Ladson-Billings, 1995, 2021; Mitra, 2011; Treviranus, 2019).

Every school is diverse in unique and distinct ways, with student populations that vary along multiple dimensions of identity, including disability, race, culture, ethnicity, sexuality, and socioeconomic status (SES). *Think about which students, families, staff members, and others might be or currently are marginalized by SEL in your school.* You might consider the following:

Who are the five students in this school community who most need SEL to work for them?

Which teachers, aides, and support staff members work most closely with those students?

Which educators have given input on relevant challenges in the past?

Which educators have not traditionally been engaged, and why?

The Collaboratory for Inclusion: From Theory to Practice

The Collaboratory for Inclusion was conceived to better understand the relationship between culturally responsive pedagogy (Barnes & McCallops, 2019; Gay, 2018) and universal design for learning (Center for Applied Special Technology [CAST], 2018) in the service of transformative SEL. *Culturally responsive pedagogy*, or CRP, recognizes students' cultural characteristics, experiences, and perspectives in all aspects of instruction to motivate learning and engage students effectively with optimal relevance across contexts. *Universal design for learning*, or UDL, recognizes students' variability in how they are engaged and motivated to learn, perceive, and comprehend information, as well as navigate the learning environment and express what they know. The UDL framework and guidelines support educators to proactively design the learning environment and learning experiences, so that all people can meaningfully access and participate in challenging learning opportunities.

These two frameworks for equity have been siloed from each other in the research literature—the first dealing with issues of discrimination related to race, culture, and ethnicity, and the second dealing with issues of discrimination related to disability (e.g., having a learning disability, cerebral palsy, or being Autistic, Blind, or Deaf). Of course, in reality, disability is experienced across racial, ethnic, and cultural boundaries. And, in fact, students with disabilities who are also members of a minoritized race or ethnicity comprise the most underserved group within the American public school system (U.S. Department of Education Office for Civil Rights, 2019). For example, students with disabilities are the least likely group to graduate high school with a diploma at just 76%, with Black students with disabilities being 1.5 times more likely to drop out of school than white students with disabilities (National Center for Education Statistics, 2021). There are also discrepancies in how and whether racially minoritized students are identified for and receive supportive services. In comparison to their white peers, students of color and those who have experienced poverty are more likely to be identified as having a learning-related disability at school, and Black students with disabilities are more likely to be identified with intellectual disability or emotional disturbance (U.S. Department of Education, 2015). Once identified, students of color, English language learners, and those with experiences of poverty are less likely to receive services when warranted and more likely to spend time in restrictive rather than general education environments (Artiles, Dorn, & Bal, 2016; Hibel et al., 2010).

When it comes to SEL, students who are minoritized racially, linguistically, sexually, and/or in terms of ability report higher rates of anxiety, feelings of stigmatization, social isolation, depression, and low self-esteem (Cipriano et al., 2021; Horowitz et al., 2017; Mahfouz & Anthony-Stevens, 2020; Rappolt-Schlichtmann et al., 2020; Umaña-Taylor et al., 2018). These same students evidence academic disengagement, including low motivation for in-school learning, as well as higher rates of skipping school and dropping out (Brown & Rodriguez, 2009; Mireles-Rios et al., 2020). Students with disabilities, those growing up in economically disadvantaged communities, and those with experiences of trauma also lag in both intra- and interpersonal skills, including social relationships, recognizing and managing emotions, and awareness of strengths and needs (Cipriano et al., 2021). These are skills explicitly targeted by most SEL programs and interventions (Grant et al., 2017; Lawson et al., 2019), yet the outcomes fall short of expectations for all students (Cipriano et al., 2021; Rowe & Trickett, 2018).

In our work, we have catalogued and described where SEL falls short, so that we might better support educators to create flexible solutions to meet student needs for a more inclusive SEL (Rappolt-Schlichtmann et al., 2020). For example, we have found that typical learning activities included in SEL require skills with which students with disabilities and students who have not had access to adequate instruction tend to struggle, including reading and writing. As another example, students who have experienced bullying or peer rejection because of their disability or other aspects of their identity may feel uncomfortable with activities that require them to interact directly with peers or express themselves in front of a group—common activities found in SEL programming (Cipriano et al., 2021). In still other cases, students with disabilities may struggle because of their disability with core skills being targeted by SEL. For example, identifying one's emotions (a foundational SEL skill) can present challenges for students with disabilities including Autistic youth who may have difficulty recognizing emotions or those with a learning or attention-related disability who may have difficulty with emotion vocabulary or self-awareness related to emotion.

To move toward effective solutions, it is critical that school leaders and practitioners learn how to better understand both the experiences and perspectives of students with disabilities, and those who may be multiply marginalized at the intersection of race, ethnicity, culture, and disability, and apply such understanding to ethical decision making around the implementation of SEL. Leaders and educators must identify the failings of the current system by using empathy-anchored practices (e.g., empathy interviewing, journey mapping, shadowing, collaborative portraiture) to better understand those who are struggling under its weight and why.

For example, empathy interviewing is an approach to eliciting and receiving feedback when a student is interviewed by an educator using questions that explore that student's experience of a classroom, classroom practice, or curricular materials. Questions are posed with openness, and feedback is received without judgment or reaction. The interaction is supportive and leans into the interviewer accepting the interviewees perspective of the classroom as valid. There are no negative repercussions for sharing critical feedback, and the interviewer commits to being responsive to the student's concerns. In our experience, the practice of empathy interviewing often begins for educators in an intensive way, as many teachers are not practiced at or used to receiving feedback from students about their teaching. But the practice of empathy interviewing can be developed into a routine over time in which whole classrooms of students regularly provide feedback on activities, practices, routines, and materials. In soliciting students' thoughts and feedback on their classroom experiences, then responding with meaningful and visible change, educators are able to make their classrooms more accessible to all students and build classroom communities in which students know that they are seen, heard, and belong (Cipriano & Pape, 2022).

This approach to inclusion is an improvement over the more commonly used deficit-oriented thinking that often dominates practices in school settings in which educators tend to focus on identifying students as "problems" to be addressed, remediated, or solved (Bradshaw et al., 2014; Darling-Hammond et al., 2020; Doyle, 2006; Gay, 2018; Osher et al., 2010). Instead, the focus of the collaboratory should move toward identifying the ways in which school environments are disabling to marginalized students, then remediate or redesign the aspects of the learning environment (goals, materials, methods, assessments, and culture) that are problematic. School leaders and educators must work to take the perspective of and understand students better and implement SEL that enables school communities to be inclusive by design. This means that practitioners move to embrace the diversity and variability of all learners and implement SEL that directly reflects and supports such diversity and variability. As Treviranus (2019) explains, if you design for those who are marginalized as a result of their disability, "you create a system that is better for everyone. It is inevitably more innovative, responsive, agile, and generous."

For example, even though most educators would place their students' well-being at the very top of their list of concerns, most have less awareness of and knowledge about exactly how to create emotionally supportive conditions for diverse students (see Hon, Sauve, Mahfouz, & Schonert-Reichl, Chapter 6, this volume, for discussion of preservice educators' SEL training). Students' emotional responses to the learning environment can be wildly diverse and vary based on personal and sociocultural influences. Cultural norms for individual or collective experiences might make some learners feel negatively about solo, peer-to-peer, or large-group experiences. Students with difficulty reading might feel significant and overwhelming stress in response to a text that is above their current reading level. Or students might feel uncomfortable about an activity if the materials used do not reflect personally important aspects that may include gender, racial, ethnic, or other identities, resulting in reduced engagement, comprehension, and/or participation. Cultural differences may shape the likelihood of attending to different emotional cues and the strategies used to regulate emotions (e.g., Doan & Wang, 2010; Matsumoto et al., 2008). For these reasons and more, lack of attention to the emotional accessibility of SEL experiences can introduce unintentional and negative bias, reinforcing the separation and isolation many marginalized students already feel at school (Rappolt-Schlichtmann et al., in press).

The Collaboratory for Inclusion Process

The Collaboratory for Inclusion process begins with the formation of SEL leadership teams that reflect the diverse range of roles in building across all levels of hierarchy. The key to forming a leadership team is to work deeply and transparently toward building a team that is representative of the school community. In placing students and teachers at the center of decision making, solutions can be derived that more equitably address and support the wellness and positive development of all community members. It is essential that intentions and assumptions are clear to the entire school—this team will be empowered to guide the process and support the entire school community toward building capacity for transformative SEL. Within this context, reflection is critical to supporting reevaluation and adjustment as conditions change. Decisions should reflect the diverse needs and circumstances of the larger school community whenever possible, and the collaboratory provides the space for all voices to be reflected in decision making. When voices are absent from the decision-making process, equitable decision making is obscured. For this reason, the work of the collaboratory is to deeply understand the school experiences of those impacted by SEL implementation, and to derive solutions that are iteratively developed, informed by empathy, systematically tested, and carefully evolved to better reflect needs specific to the school community

Phase 1: Discovery

Now that the leadership team is in place, the collaboratory work can begin. The first phase is focused on *discovery,* in which schools work to better *understand* the strengths, needs, and experiences of all learners and educators in their community, *define* clear and specific goals as a collective, and *identify* barriers to learning or participation that learners and educators may experience that are inherent in the educational system and SEL program they are implementing. In the discovery phase, the collaboratory intentionally and effortfully builds self- and social awareness to support perspective taking, and the emergence of a better and deeper understanding of those who may be or have historically been marginalized by the educational system and SEL approach as designed.

In her recent TED talk, Harvard Medical School psychologist Susan David describes the gift and power of emotional courage. She notes, "*Sawubona* is the Zulu word for 'hello.' " There is a beautiful and powerful intention behind the word, because *Sawubona* translated means "I see you and by seeing you I bring you into being" (David, 2017).[2] This is the intention of the discovery phase of work within the collaboratory. We effortfully and intentionally work without judgment to see and authentically take the perspective of those whom we intend to serve as educators.

But why is effortful and supported perspective taking so important to implementing inclusive and equitable SEL? Many educators do not have personal experience with disability, and most general educators have very limited training as to how to think about or teach youth with disabilities (Horowitz et al., 2017; Malone & Horowitz, n.d.). It is hard to truly understand something and do it well (e.g., teaching SWDs) when you have little or no background knowledge. And worse, in the absence of experience and background knowledge we are more likely to adopt implicit bias and deficit-based thinking about marginalized youth, such as those with disabilities that can be harmful to students and school communities alike (Daley & Rappolt-Schlichtmann, 2018; Whitford & Emerson, 2019).

---

[2]Available at *www.ted.com/talks/susan_david_the_gift_and_power_of_emotional_courage?language=ku.*

For example, imagine a fourth-grade teacher preparing an SEL lesson in which students will listen to different musical compositions meant to evoke a range of different feelings. The educator plans to have students listen to the music, then share how they feel and what emotions they experience in response. But the educator is concerned because they have a Deaf student[3] in their class—what should they do? Because the educator has never had the experience of being Deaf, limited interactions with Deaf people, and limited training about how to teach youth who are Deaf, the educator might assume that the student cannot experience, would not enjoy, or cannot learn through music.

Over time, with experience and the development of expertise in our professional careers, we become more and more inwardly leaning into what is known and comfortable, while paying less attention to information in the external world. This is a fact of human consciousness and development (Brownstein, 2019; Byyny, 2017; Mayfield, 2020). Thus, without effortful perspective taking, the educator may misidentify the barrier to learning as their student not being able to hear the music, and so the educator might decide to provide an alternative experience where the Deaf student looks at images instead. This misidentification of the barrier to learning leads to a solution that excludes and separates, increasing social isolation and feelings of stigmatization, with negative impacts to well-being and learning for the student, as well as negative impacts to the cohesiveness of the community within the classroom as a whole.

With effortful perspective taking, the educator will *discover* that Deaf people can and do enjoy music in its full capacity, but *understand* that they experience music differently from those who are hearing. When listening to music, Deaf people garner emotional meaning from the tactile experience in the bass, beat, and sound vibration, while in comparison, people who are hearing may take more emotional meaning from the melody. Deaf people also use the lyrics to take emotional meaning from music, but the lyrics need to be made accessible via captions, signing, or lip reading, which may also include emotional interpretation through gesture or facial expression. It is important to note that Deafness varies from person to person—some people are fully Deaf while others hear some aspect of sound to different degrees, and some Deaf people use assistive devices such as hearing aids and cochlear implants, that change how they experience sound. There is also variation in how Deaf people communicate with others, for example, not all Deaf people

[3]How people with disabilities describe themselves is personal and varied. In this example, we describe a hypothetical Deaf student and, as such, had to make choices about how the student identifies. In this case, we use identity-first language (a Deaf student) rather than person-first language (a student who is Deaf) and capitalize the word Deaf to indicate that the student identifies with the Deaf community and culture, and sees their Deafness as an important part of their identity. Others may identify differently. For example, a student might prefer person-first language (a person who is Deaf or hard of hearing) without capitalization, which indicates a mild, moderate, or profound hearing difference, and that the student does not identify as being a part of Deaf community or culture. The term *hearing impaired* should never be used, as it is considered offensive and inappropriate to many in the Deaf community. In general, if you are unsure how a student identifies, ask them!

sign. The educator will have to work to *understand* their Deaf student's particular strengths, needs, and ways of perceiving the world, because not all Deaf students are the same.

With this new knowledge the teacher *defines clear and specific goals*. The educator can *identify* barriers to learning or participation that learners and educators may strategically build options, support, and scaffolding into the lesson for a more inclusive and equitable experience. The educator can decide to use music as the medium for the lesson for all their students by using music that can play in multiple ways—audio, video, American sign language (ASL) interpretation and captions. The educator intentionally selects music that has a pronounced beat for easily discernable tactile interpretation. The educator orients to all ouavr senses as strengths and in the lesson asks students to consider different aspects of the sound as it relates to their feelings rather than leaning exclusively on the melody, which the educator might have been inclined to do in the past as a hearing person. In thinking about their students' differences more broadly, the educator considers the content, tenor, and history of the music. Further considerations include the following:

Are my selections representing a diverse array of musical genres, composers, and musicians? Can I find ways to have students bring music into the lesson that they are interested in or have personal and cultural relevance?

Can I design my lesson to emphasize how diverse ways of perceiving, sensing, and knowing the world inform our emotional experience?

From this example you can see how effortful perspective taking can transform educators' understandings of students to inform strategies for equitable inclusion in SEL. Therein, SEL becomes more accessible and meaningfully complex, while also enhancing interpersonal connections within our classrooms. In this way, and through the discovery phase of work, we can move to a SEL design and implementation in which all students are seen and embraced for who they actually are rather than who we imagine they might be.

Phase 2: Exploration

Whereas the discovery phase of work focuses on building self- and social awareness, the exploration phase moves to the generation of solutions that are responsive to and restorative of school communities. In the *exploration* phase, collaboratories work to *ideate* a suite of potential solutions, systematically *test* potential solutions through appropriate quantitative and qualitative methods in their learning community, and *evolve* their team, thinking, and approach to better reflect the experiences, variability, and diversity of intended learners. This phase of work is about intentionally and effortfully working toward making responsible and inclusive decisions about dismantling, rebuilding, and creating SEL goals, methods, materials, and assessments that will best work in your school community.

Through this process, and with increased awareness of the systems that perpetuate subconscious bias, ableism, and racism, comes new and urgent opportunities to restore our collective humanity and commitments to each other (Cipriano et al., 2020; Rappolt-Schlichtmann et al., 2020). During this phase, schools reorient themselves to shift away from deficit thinking and toward the identification of strengths—where we stop asking questions that focus on the ways in which we see students as problems to be solved ("How are individuals disabled?"), to questions that consider the flaws in the system ("How are our learning environments disabling?"), and finally to questions that proactively support the development of more inclusive systems ("How can we design learning environments that enable, give means, and give power?"). These shifts move educators, approaches, and schools to a more strengths- and assets-based design of learning environments and experiences. During this phase of work, the inclusion of representative and diverse learners on the collaborative team (as advisors and participants in ideation, testing, and the evolution of the SEL approach) is critical to the mindful analysis of data and the generation of reasoned judgments about potential competing solutions.

To ensure that outcomes of the exploration phase reflect evidence-based practice moving forward, exploration will require data-driven decision making, rooted in empathy and fueled by increased data and data literacy. Early in 2019, a National Commission Report, "From a Nation at Risk to a Nation at Hope," highlighted the urgency for the use of data to drive social, emotional, and academic learning. When done well, data can empower teachers' autonomous and authentic instruction, center in and accelerate student voice, and foster the continuous improvement of school culture. Simultaneously, advancing the methodologies for collecting, understanding, and using data also promotes the sustainability of effective SEL practices throughout the school community. Data that accurately capture the impact of SEL for students, their teachers, parents, and the school community can drive systemic and sustainable change and have an enduring impact on both policy and practice (Cipriano et al., 2020; McKown, 2019)

However, the *what*, *why*, *how*, and *who* of data collection and use in education has a long and complicated history rooted in racism and ableism, and has been used to promote and foster structural inequities rather than dismantle them (Annamma et al., 2013; Blanchett, 2010; Cubberley, 1909; Du Bois, 2007; Dunn, 1968; Ferri & Connor, 2006; Harry & Klingner, 2006; Losen & Orfield, 2002; Menchaca, 1997; Valencia, 2012). Consider the following:

Do your school policies reflect the diversity of students in your classrooms?

How and who gets to define what is "best" for students and teachers?

Which students and teachers are held up as the "best" in your school community?

Do school leaders understand their responsibilities as primary change agents in the context of crafting an inclusive educational environment?

Do leaders inspire in others a genuine value of diversity and acknowledge its role in building communities of excellence for generations to come?

Are leaders committed to advancing policies and practices centered on diversity with intentionality and conviction to serve the whole school community?

For a school system to grow into a culture of inclusion, its leaders must recognize, understand, and embrace the unique heterogeneity and intersectionality of its members' identities. A commitment to diversity is a commitment to the celebration of all human variance reflected in each school's organizational landscape—both vertically, through open engagement within the departments of the institution—and horizontally, through cross-campus collaboration and cooperation. Use the collaboratory to verify standards as culturally affirming and dismantling of deficit narratives. Work to design measures of knowledge and skills to evaluate the competency of standards and ground measurement in local knowledge, values, and understanding that focus on the strengths and assets of the school community. Consider the use of engagement practices including family or community surveys to understand which competencies and skills are most important to the community and how those connect to national standards. Designing with the learner in mind means honoring the unique heritage of the school community through active involvement and consideration of all learners and their support systems to be truly effective as a collaboratory.

The Collaboratory for Inclusion: An Illustration

In this final section, we illustrate the Collaboratory for Inclusion with examples from one district's experience—Manchester Essex Regional School District (MERSD)—during the implementation of a universal school-based SEL intervention—RULER.

MERSD is a public school district located on Cape Ann in Essex County, Massachusetts. In 2000, Manchester and Essex voted to regionalize, bringing two similar, yet unique towns together in one school district. The MERSD school district includes two towns, four schools, and a total student population of approximately 1,270 students, of which 27% of students are considered high needs and 18% of students are students with disabilities. Eighty-eight percent of the teaching staff have been working in the district for more than 3 years. As a result of district strategic planning in 2009, MERSD established a school system Core Values initiative and identified the Whole Child as one of the district's five core values. Whole Child core values included "establishing a safe environment conducive to the development of the whole child, which extended beyond the academic core to include experiential learning, the arts, cultural awareness, and physical and emotional well-being" (MERSD Strategic Plan, 2009).

RULER is a fully developed set of universal interventions with strong theoretical grounding in developmental and educational psychology. It begins with training for staff and continues with classroom curricula, family engagement, and implementation support through coaching and an online platform (*rulerapproach.org*). RULER curricula include four offerings specific to the developmental needs of early childhood, elementary, middle, and high school students. RULER prioritizes skill building for educators and emphasizes their roles as agents of change in the promotion of student SEL (Brackett et al., 2019). Core to RULER's philosophy is that adults will be more effective at teaching and students at learning when they are able to recognize, understand, label, express, and regulate emotions and apply these RULER skills in their daily lives (Brackett, Rivers, & Salovey, 2011; Brackett et al., 2019). Since 2005, RULER has been introduced to over 1 million students in over 3,000 K–12 schools (65% serving low SES students, 70% public). RULER has demonstrated cultural responsivity and matches the developmental level of students in grades K–8 (Torrente et al., 2016), and preliminary research shows promise for RULER's impact on classroom climate and student academic, social, and education outcomes (Brackett et al., 2012; Cipriano et al., 2019; learn more at *rulerapproach.org*).

Reflecting this core value, the MERSD school system began RULER implementation in Summer 2019 as part of their strategic plan to invest in whole-child development at the district level. Work is ongoing to develop school- and district-based practices for staff, students, and families to best support a robust SEL mindset throughout the district. In an effort to rethink the school experience for all students, MERSD developed a vision for student SEL success and goals for student learning experiences, as well as faculty learning that would be necessary to support student success and the creation of inclusive and equitable learning experiences for all students.

The collaboratory's process begins with forming the team. MERSD's collaboratory consisted of their entire district administrative team and all members of their School Committees—including district and school leaders, parents, and community stakeholders.

The discovery phase of work is to better *understand* the strengths, needs, and experiences of all learners and educators in their community, *define* clear and specific goals as a collective, and *identify* barriers to learning or participation that learners and educators may experience that are inherent in the educational system and SEL program they are implementing. The MERSD collaboratory began by establishing norms as a collective and developing a MERSD Charter, with each school and several district committees also developing their own Charters. An emotional intelligence Charter—one of the four RULER tools—is a contract that reflects the agreed-upon feelings and behaviors of the members of a learning community. District leaders created Charters with the School Committee and the Administrative Leadership Team to build community and participation norms for each group member. The Administrative Team analyzed how each member wanted to feel "coming to work every day" and participated as part of a district- and school-based leadership team. School leaders shared their feelings and engaged in creating a collective vision for successful work as an individual and as part of a team. Across the district, schools created Charters to support community building and level-setting practices for educators.

This work was not one of convenience. Throughout, leaders and educators delved deeply and shared vulnerabilities surrounding feelings about their work to build a collective vision and collaborative practice for engaging in high-level and productive work. At times, various leaders and educators expressed concerns about sharing vulnerabilities with fears of being marginalized and excluded from the group should they voice unpopular beliefs. By doing the work together across one whole school year and uncovering and expressing hopeful goals for best practices and future work together, leaders and educators built a safe space where all feelings were validated and supported. Discussions of feelings and goals, despite their difficulties at times, made way for productive conversation defining what creating a school community meant to the group, and the steps the district would have to take to create that ideal through the development of Charters.

Continuing in their *discovery* work, the MERSD collaboratory looked to their special education students, teachers, and systems. MERSD's robust special education program serviced nearly one-fifth of the district's students; however it was structured not unlike most other public schools in the United States, with special educators being assigned primary instructional roles in the education and servicing of students designated in need of special education services. These traditional distinctions in role differences between special and general educators create a false dichotomy in the service of students with disabilities: Most students with learning differences spend most (80%) of their time in general education classrooms. The district faced many problems due to this false dichotomy. For instance, teacher preparation programs were highly variable, and some teachers in the schools had no training or prior experience working with students with special education needs (Horowitz et al., 2017; Malone & Horowitz, n.d.; Rappolt-Schlichtmann et al., 2020). Furthermore, student designations in administrative records for IEPs or 504 plans (documentation of student identified needs per Individuals with Disabilities Education Act; 2015), focus on areas of need, struggle, and challenge—often without reference to specific diagnoses. This is dually problematic given that students with and without disabilities who are not struggling in school will not have an IEP, such as students who are in the cultural or linguistic minority in their classroom community;

thus, these records undoubtedly represent incomplete descriptors of classroom composition and may result in unintentional overlooking, and in some cases, barriers to the education of diverse students. As a result of the collaboratory identifying these challenges, MERSD administration directed attention to identifying how its school structures and the interactions among teachers and students may have been unintentionally further marginalizing youth with disabilities. This review further amplified special educators' influence and voice in the district policies and practices.

Developing supports for students with disabilities—especially historically marginalized students and those with experiences of trauma and chronic poverty—is critical to allow for the emotional investment of youth in a school community. Students are supported through this work through the development of relationships with a trusted adult and learning in a trusted school community. At MERSD, district leaders engage in outreach and intake of students' voices as they become enlisted champions in the fight to develop supports that will truly honor students' experiences and further enhance connections for all students. MERSD found that when its students across all grade levels were given the opportunity to define what *school* means to them and respond to how they ultimately want to feel at school and in the world, they were immediately more invested and engaged. During small, student-led discussions at the school level, MERSD leaders learned about the school experience through their students' eyes. School leaders provided varied and repeated opportunities for students to safely respond to their lived school experiences by inviting participation of all students in structured discussion sessions and through schoolwide surveys. This process looked different at each school building in MERSD, and varied as a function of student age, school-building needs and climate, educator and leader availability, and student engagement.

The district leaned on RULER tools to support this work. RULER embeds analysis and discussion of relationships throughout its interventions. As one example, students are given opportunities to analyze what makes relationships healthy versus unhealthy, how emotional expression and social display rules may influence their relationships with others, and how analyzing their "best self" can promote healthy conflict resolution or coping. At MERSD, educators leveraged the practice of building a Charter to support students' individual understanding of relationship skill building as essential to the foundation of a healthy classroom climate across subject areas and throughout the school day. For example, one middle-school teacher prompted students to "Identify a Charter emotion you think a presenter would like to feel and tell me how you, as an audience member can help?" Furthermore, student-led Family Connections activities about each RULER tool reinforce self-awareness about how students and their family members are feeling and want to feel. Student-led School–Home Partnership Worksheets help students and their families connect and build a shared emotion vocabulary at home. Students and families consider their strengths and triggers within the context of their best selves as child and parent or caregiver. Activities like these create opportunities to explore the influence of family and cultural values in the home and connect these values to the school community. Throughout RULER implementation, each school and the district as a whole gained valuable insight to the often-unspoken needs of students and faculty—allowing members to communicate in a shared language and develop a collective understanding of each member of the school community as unique individuals contributing to a strong and supportive classroom, school, and district culture.

The exploration phase of work suggests the collaboratory *ideate* a suite of potential solutions, systematically *test* potential solutions through appropriate quantitative and qualitative methods in their learning community, and *evolve* their team, thinking, and approach to better reflect the experiences, variability, and diversity of intended learners.

For example, over these first years of RULER implementation at MERSD, both formal and informal data reflected the needs of each school community, including faculty and schoolwide meetings devoted to RULER, feedback surveys, and RULER focus group meetings with diverse school constituents (i.e., general and special educators, specialists and paraprofessionals, students, and caregivers). While each school in MERSD had a different approach to data collection, all schools thoughtfully and systematically utilized data and feedback to inform decision making about RULER implementation and planning at the school level. Importantly, at each school, intentional subgroup analyses were completed on the data sources to elevate and examine the experiences of ability-, racially, gender, linguistically, and sexually minoritized students in the district. Across the district, students and staff members were invited to respond to surveys on the different aspects of RULER implementation and staff members' and students' comfort with each aspect of RULER. Some sample questions include asking students the following:

How can RULER help your classmates to feel included at school?

How does RULER help you to understand people who are different than you?

and asking teachers the following:

How does RULER help you promote Diversity, Equity, and Inclusion (DEI) in your classroom?

How does RULER support you in navigating conflict with your colleagues?

Students and staff members who engaged in survey feedback allowed school leaders to adjust implementation and engage in specific supports, ultimately allowing for the creation of supports, such as quiet rooms, conflict resolution supports for both staff and students, the creation of small-group trainings on trauma-informed schools, personalized leadership coaching, additional staff counseling, and the development of school-based supports designed to address specific needs emerging from the data for both students and staff.

Additionally, schools can work intentionally with youth to identify measures that align to standards, build upon interests and foundations of knowledge, and perhaps most importantly, schools can enable these data to be what counts as evidence of meeting the standards. As MERSD teachers implemented RULER strategies and lessons, there were many school-wide opportunities for collaboration and feedback with students. General and special education teachers worked in small collaborative teams with students to develop lessons and formative assessments that reflected how students were feeling, whether or not they understood the elements of RULER, and the ways in which RULER might be creating barriers for student SEL by design. For example, in working together with their students, general and special education teachers were able to define the needs of students in their own words through collaborative discussions about the types of intentional supports students benefited from to access RULER effectively. For example, the collaboratory supported all students in one schools to consider how they wanted to use emotions as information to support their learning. Students chose to use the Mood Meter, a RULER tool, and apply their own innovations to it through the use of graphics (from stock images, to student drawings, to photographs of the students themselves) and tactiles (e.g., felt, magnets, Velcro, glitter and beads, among others) to design systems that aligned with their own interests in strengths. In another school, the students opted to have mini-Mood Meters at the top of and bottom of each assignment block—so students would plot themselves before and after a lesson to support the teacher in recalibrating the learning experience to meet the strengths and needs of their classroom. And in another school, leaders enlisted the school adjustment counselor and guidance staff to create small-group meeting times with specific students throughout the semester to support the most challenging aspects for each individual within RULER implementation (i.e., one counselor held a group for elementary school students with autism, where they worked together to unpack identifying their "Best Self" through application of the "Meta-Moment,"—an SEL tool that supports individuals to pause when experiencing a challenging emotion to identify and change their behavior productively for the situation.

Schools used surveys codesigned by students to elicit feedback from students to determine what supports and changes to RULER were needed to meet the needs of each school community. For example, administrators at the middle school surveyed students to determine their level of knowledge and understanding of RULER components. The middle school students pointed out that they didn't like taking a break for a "meta-moment" because there wasn't a place to actually go that was private and comfortable, where they could pause and reset. Administrators then used this data to design and explore more opportunities for student engagement and to create more usable and flexible spaces for students and staff to take a break for a Meta-Moment. Some teachers created these spaces in their classrooms, while others were developed by students, for students only. These spaces were open on a sign-out basis and offered comfortable seating, lighting, puzzles, music, and opportunities for meditation and writing. Additionally, deeper and more specific professional development around RULER supported staff with advancing their social and emotional practices.

Looking ahead, each collaboratory intends to collect further data and feedback from staff members and students about their experiences with all of the RULER SEL tools, with emphasis on building understanding of the implementation of RULER as it connects to students' emotional lives, as well as their coursework. There is no doubt that much has changed in the school community during the COVID-19 pandemic, and MERSD personnel feel confident they are equipped with the tools and strategies to continue to evolve to better support learners and educators moving forward.[4]

Conclusion

> One of the main critiques I've heard from other providers who have gone to SEL is that it doesn't reflect everyone in community.
>
> —ELEMENTARY SCHOOL SPECIAL EDUCATOR, MERSD

In this chapter we have described the Collaboratory for Inclusion—an intentional and iterative process for school communities to create the conditions necessary for transformative SEL implementation. We have added that in addition to embracing learner cultural identity, agency, belonging, and engagement, there must be an intentional effort to embrace diverse ways of knowing, perceiving, and navigating the world (Hehir, 2002; Rappolt-Schlichtmann et al., 2020) as central tenants of transformative SEL programming (Jagers et al., 2019; Williams & Jagers, 2020). Toward the end of providing all students with equitable access to meaningful opportunities for learning and thriving, we must begin by working together to listen to and understand students who are made most vulnerable by our education system—students with disabilities. This process will be best enabled by district policy structures that allocate sustainable funding mechanisms for the continual implementation of evidence-based SEL programming and encourage the intentional breakdown of silos of practice that reinforce deficit thinking—silos such as general and special education. As discussed in this chapter, the collaboratory for inclusion process will take time—the iterative two phases of discovery and experimentation are evergreen and intended to continue across school years to support school communities to learn and evolve SEL alongside the changing needs of their school communities.

[4]To learn more about how MERSD educators innovated with RULER during the COVID-19 pandemic, see Eveleigh et al. (2021).

DISCUSSION QUESTIONS

1. This chapter defines *equity* as "the assurance that everyone has access to the same opportunities" and *inclusion* as "the practice or policy of providing equitable access to opportunities and resources for people who might otherwise be excluded or marginalized." Thinking about your school, are there any groups of students for whom equity and inclusion may be improved? Which ones, and what might be some of the reasons for these needs?
2. Again considering your school, how may "traditional" SEL practices may need to be adapted to support the inclusion of SWDs?
3. Drawing from some of the key concepts of the Collaboratory for Inclusion, what might the "discovery" and "exploration" phases look like at your school if you were to adopt this approach?
4. The authors invite readers to consider, "What is held up as 'best' in your school community and why?" How would you address this question in relation to your school? Specifically, what practices are prioritized, and what kinds of data are emphasized to measure them?

NOTE AND ACKNOWLEDGMENTS

Drs. Cipriano and Rappolt-Schlichtmann contributed equally to this chapter, and our suggested in-text citation is Cipriano, Rappolt-Schlichtmann, et al. We thank the students, educators, and administrators at MERSD for learning with us and colleagues Amanda Cook, Michael McCarthy, Nikki Elbertson, Tia Barnes, Shivohn Garcia, and Alyssa Boucher. This research was funded by a grant to Drs. Cipriano and Rappolt-Schlichtmann from the Oak Foundation (OCAY-19-407). The content presented in this chapter explicitly builds on an approach to professional learning developed by EdTogether (*edtogether.org*) to support the implementation of universal design for learning for equity and inclusion.

REFERENCES

Annamma, S. A., Connor, D., & Ferri, B. (2013). Dis/ability critical race studies (DisCrit): Theorizing at the intersections of race and dis/ability. *Race, Ethnicity, and Education, 16*(1), 1–31.

Artiles, A. J., Dorn, S., & Bal, A. (2016). Objects of protection, enduring nodes of difference: Disability intersections with "other" differences, 1916 to 2016. *Review of Research in Education, 40*(1), 777–820.

Barnes, T. N., & McCallops, K. (2019). Perceptions of culturally responsive pedagogy in teaching SEL. *Journal for Multicultural Education, 13*(1), 70–81.

Berger, N., & Fisher, P. (2013, August). A well-educated workforce is key to state prosperity. Retrieved from *www.epi.org/files/2013/A%20well-educated%20workforce%20is%20key%20 to%20state%20prosperity.pdf.*

Blanchett, W. J. (2010). Telling it like it is: The role of race, class, and culture in the perpetuation of learning disability as a privileged category for the white middle class. *Disability Studies Quarterly, 30*(2), 1230–1277.

Blewitt, C., Fuller-Tyszkiewicz, M., Nolan, A., Bergmeier, H., Vicary, D., Huang, T., . . . Skouteris, H. (2018). Social and emotional learning associated with universal curriculum-based interventions in early childhood education and care centers: A systematic review and meta-analysis. *JAMA Network Open, 1*(8), Article e185727.

Brackett, M. A., Bailey, C. S., Hoffmann, J. D., & Simmons, D. N. (2019). RULER: A theory-driven, systemic approach to social, emotional, and academic learning. *Educational Psychologist, 54*(3), 144–161.

Brackett, M. A., Rivers, S. E., Reyes, M. R., & Salovey, P. (2012). Enhancing academic performance and social and emotional competence with the RULER feeling words curriculum. *Learning and Individual Differences, 22*(2), 218–224.

Brackett, M. A., Rivers, S. E., & Salovey, P. (2011). Emotional intelligence: Implications for personal, social, academic, and workplace success. *Social and Personality Psychology Compass, 5*(1), 88–103.

Bradshaw, C. P., Bottiani, J. H., Osher, D., & Sugai, G. (2014). The integration of positive behavioral interventions and supports and social and emotional learning. In M. D. Weist, N. A. Lever, C. P. Bradshaw, & J. S. Owens (Eds.), *Handbook of school mental health* (pp. 101–118). Springer.

Brownstein, M. (2019, Winter). Implicit bias. Retrieved from *https://stanford.library.sydney.edu.au/archives/win2019/entries/implicit-bias.*

Byyny, R. L. (2017). Cognitive bias: Recognizing and managing our unconscious biases. *Pharos of Alpha Omega Alpha Honor Medical Society, 80*(1), 2–6.

Center for Applied Special Technology (CAST). (2018). Universal Design for Learning Guidelines version 2.2. Retrieved from *http://udlguidelines.cast.org.*

Cipriano, C., Barnes, T., Rivers, S., & Brackett, M. A. (2019). Exploring changes in student engagement through the RULER approach: An examination of students at risk of academic failure. *Journal of Education for Students Placed at Risk, 24*(1), 1–19.

Cipriano, C., Naples, L. H., Eveleigh, A., Funaro, M., Cook, A., Cassidy, C., . . . Schlichtmann, G. (2022). A systematic review of student disability and race representation in universal school-based SEL interventions for elementary school students. *Review of Educational Research.* [Epub ahead of print] doi/10.3102/00346543221094079

Cipriano, C., Naples, L. H., Eveleigh, A., Rappolt-Schlichtmann, G., & Cook, A. (2021). *Whose emotions matter: Student disability and race representation in universal school based social and emotional learning by the numbers.* National Center for Learning Disabilities.

Cipriano, C., & Pape, B. (2022, May 16). Building a climate of belonging in schools opens the door for robust—and joyful—teaching and learning. The 74 million. Retrieved from *www.the74million.org/article/cipriano-pape-building-a-climate-of-belonging-in-schools-opens-the-door-for-robust-and-joyful-teaching-and-learning.*

Cipriano, C., Rappolt-Schlichtmann, G., & Brackett, M. A. (2020). *Supporting school community wellness with social and emotional learning (SEL) during and after a pandemic.* Edna Bennet Pierce Prevention Research Center, Pennsylvania State University.

Cipriano, C., Strambler, M., Naples, L. H., Ha, C., Chang, M., Wood, M., . . . Durlak, J. (in press). The state of evidence for social and emotional learning: A contemporary meta-analysis of universal school-based SEL interventions. *Child Developement*. Available at *https://osf.io/r246m*.

Cipriano, C., Taylor, J. J., Weissberg, R., Blyth, D., & McKown, C. (2020). *Catalyzing future directions of SEL assessment*. Collaborative for Academic, Social, and Emotional Learning.

Collaborative for Academic, Social, and Emotional Learning. (2020, May). What is SEL? Retrieved from *https://casel.org/what-is-sel*.

Cubberley, E. (1909). *Changing conceptions of education*. Houghton Mifflin.

Daley, S. G., & Rappolt-Schlichtmann, G. (2018). Stigma consciousness among adolescents with learning disabilities: Considering individual experiences of being stereotyped. *Learning Disability Quarterly, 41*(4), 200–212.

Darling-Hammond, L., Flook, L., Cook-Harvey, C., Barron, B., & Osher, D. (2020). Implications for educational practice of the science of learning and development. *Applied Developmental Science, 24*(2), 97–140.

David, S. (2017, November). The gift and power of emotional courage [Video]. Retrieved from *www.ted.com/talks/susan_david_the_gift_and_power_of_emotional_courage?language=en*.

Doan, S. N., & Wang, Q. (2010). Maternal discussions of mental states and behaviors: Relations to emotion situation knowledge in European American and immigrant Chinese children. *Child Development, 81*(5), 1490–1503.

Doyle, W. (2006). Ecological approaches to classroom management. In C. Evertson & C. Weinstein (Eds.), *Handbook of classroom management: Research, practice, and contemporary issues* (pp. 97–125). Erlbaum.

Du Bois, W. E. B. (2007). *Black folk then and now: An essay in the history and sociology of the Negro race*. Oxford University Press.

Dunn, L. M. (1968). Special education for the mildly retarded—Is much of it justifiable? *Exceptional Children, 35*(1), 5–22.

Durlak, J. A., Weissberg, R. P., Dymnicki, A. B., Taylor, R. D., & Schellinger, K. B. (2011). The impact of enhancing students' social and emotional learning: A meta-analysis of school-based universal interventions. *Child Development, 82*(1), 405–432.

Eveleigh, A., Cook, A., Naples, L. H., & Cipriano, C. (2021). How did educators of students with learning differences use social and emotional learning to support their students and themselves early in the COVID-19 pandemic. *Children and Schools, 44*(1), 27–38.

Ferri, B. A., & Connor, D. J. (2006). *Reading resistance: Discourses of exclusion in desegregation and inclusion debates*. Peter Lang.

Gay, G. (2018). *Culturally responsive teaching: Theory, research, and practice* (3rd ed.). Teachers College Press.

Greenstone, M., Harris, M., Li, K., Looney, A., & Patashnik, J. (2012, September). A dozen economic facts about K–12 education. Retrieved from *www.hamiltonproject.org/assets/legacy/files/downloads_and_links/thp_12edfacts_2.pdf*.

Hehir, T. (2002). Eliminating ableism in education. *Harvard Educational Review, 72*(1), 1–33.

Horowitz, S. H., Rawe, J., & Whittaker, M. C. (2017). *The state of learning disabilities: Understanding the 1 in 5*. National Center for Learning Disabilities.

Individuals with Disabilities Education Act, 20 U.S. Code § 1400 (2015).

Jagers, R. J., Rivas-Drake, D., & Williams, B. V. (2019). Transformative social and emotional learning (SEL): Toward SEL in service of educational equity and excellence. *Educational Psychologist, 53*(3), 162–184.

Klingner, J. K., & Harry, B. (2006). The special education referral and decision-making process for English language learners: Child study team meetings and placement conferences. *Teachers College Record, 108*(11), 2247–2281.

Ladson-Billings, G. (1995). But that's just good teaching!: The case for culturally relevant pedagogy. *Theory Into Practice, 34*(3), 159–165.

Ladson-Billings, G. (2021). I'm here for the hard re-set: Post pandemic pedagogy to preserve our culture. *Equity and Excellence in Education, 54*(1), 68–78.

Losen, D. J., & Orfield, G. (Eds.). (2002). *Racial inequity in special education.* Harvard Education Press.

Mahfouz, J., & Anthony-Stevens, V. (2020). Why trouble SEL?: The need for cultural relevance in SEL. Retrieved from *www.bankstreet.edu/research-publications-policy/occasional-paper-series/archive/ops-43/why-trouble-sel.*

Malone, A. S., & Horowitz, S. (n.d.). *The state of learning disabilities: Inspiring innovation.* Unpublished manuscript, National Center for Learning Disabilities.

Manchester Essex Regional School District (MERSD) Strategic Plan (2009). *MERSD Strategic Plan.* Author.

Matsumoto, D., Yoo, S. H., & Nakagawa, S. (2008). Culture, emotion regulation, and adjustment. *Journal of Personality and Social Psychology, 94*(6), 925.

Mayfield, V. (2020). *Cultural competence now: 56 exercises to help educators understand and challenge bias, racism, and privilege.* Association for Supervision and Curriculum Development.

McKown, C. (2019). *Student social and emotional competence assessment: The current state of the field and a vision for its future.* Collaborative for Academic, Social, and Emotional Learning.

Menchaca, M. (1997). Early racist discourses: Roots of deficit thinking. In R. R. Valencia (Ed.), *The evolution of deficit thinking: Educational thought and practice* (pp. 13–40). Routledge Falmer.

Mireles-Rios, R., Simon, O., & Nylund-Gibson, K. (2020). The critical role of teacher Emotional support for Latinx students. *Teachers College Record, 122*(12), 1–32.

Mitra, D. (2011, June). Pennsylvania's best investment: The social and economic benefits of public education. Retrieved from *www.elc-pa.org/wp-content/uploads/2011/06/bestinvestment_full_report_6.27.11.pdf.*

Naples, L. H., Riley, J., McCarthy, M., Rappolt-Schlichtmann, G., Cipriano, C., & Eveleigh, A. (2020, October 15). A collaboratory for inclusion: Serving student diversity through district-wide social emotional learning implementation. *Social and Emotional Learning Research Abstracts.* Retrieved from *https://bit.ly/selabstracts.*

National Center for Education Statistics. (2021, May). Students with disabilities. Retrieved from *https://nces.ed.gov/programs/coe/indicator/cgg.*

National Commission on Social, Emotional, and Academic Development. (2019). From a nation at risk to a nation at hope. Retrieved from *https://nationathope.org/wp-content/uploads/2018_aspen_final-report_full_webversion.pdf.*

Osher, D., Bear, G. G., Sprague, J. R., & Doyle, W. (2010). How can we improve school discipline? *Educational Researcher, 39*(1), 48–58.

Osher, D., Kidron, Y., Brackett, M., Dymnicki, A., Jones, S., & Weissberg, R. P. (2016). Advancing the science and practice of social and emotional learning: Looking back and moving forward. *Review of Research in Education, 40*(1), 644–681.

Rappolt-Schlichtmann, G., Cipriano, C., Robinson, K., & Boucher, A. (in press). Universal design for social and emotional learning. In K. R. Harris & K. H. Robinson (Eds.), *Universal design for learning in the classroom: Practical applications* (2nd ed.). Guilford Press.

Rappolt-Schlichtmann, G., Lovelace, T., Kruse, L., & Tucker, E. (2020, July 16). How we move forward: Practicing three inclusive, anti-racist mindsets for reopening schools. Retrieved from *www.gettingsmart.com/2020/07/how-we-move-forward-practicing-three-inclusive-anti-racist-mindsets-for-reopening-schools.*

Rimm-Kaufman, S. E., & Hulleman, C. S. (2015). Social and emotional learning in elementary school settings: Identifying mechanisms that matter. In J. A. Durlak, C. E. Domitrovich, R. P. Weissberg, & T. P. Gullotta (Eds.), *Handbook of social and emotional learning: Research and practice* (pp. 151–166). Guilford Press.

Rodríguez, L. F., & Brown, T. M. (2009). From voice to agency: Guiding principles for participatory action research with youth. *New Directions for Youth Development, 2009*(123), 19–34.

Rowe, H. L., & Trickett, E. J. (2018). Student diversity representation and reporting in universal school-based social and emotional learning programs: Implications for generalizability. *Educational Psychology Review, 30*(2), 559–583.

Taylor, R. D., Oberle, E., Durlak, J. A., & Weissberg, R. P. (2017). Promoting positive youth development through school-based social and emotional learning interventions: A meta-analysis of follow-up effects. *Child Development, 88*(4), 1156–1171.

Torrente, C., Rivers, S. E., & Brackett, M. A. (2016). Teaching emotional intelligence in schools: an evidence-based approach. In A. A. Lipnevich, F. Preckel, & R. D. Roberts (Eds.), *Psychosocial skills and school systems in the 21st century* (pp. 325–346). Springer.

Treviranus, J. (2019). Inclusive design: The bell curve, the starburst and the virtuous tornado. Retrieved from *https://medium.com/@jutta.trevira/inclusive-design-the-bell-curve-the-starburst-and-the-virtuous-tornado-6094f797b1bf.*

Umaña-Taylor, A. J., Kornienko, O., Douglass Bayless, S., & Updegraff, K. A. (2018). A universal intervention program increases ethnic–racial identity exploration and resolution to predict adolescent psychosocial functioning one year later. *Journal of Youth and Adolescence, 47*(1), 1–15.

U.S. Department of Education. (2015). IDEA Section 618 Data, for students ages 6–21 in 2015–2016. In T. F. Boat & J. T. Wu (Eds.), *Mental disorders and disabilities among low-income children.* National Academies Press.

U.S. Department of Education. (2018). Individuals with Disabilities Education Act: Sec. 300.8 child with a disability. Retrieved from *https://sites.ed.gov/idea/regs/b/a/300.8.*

U.S. Department of Education Office for Civil Rights. (2019, July). *Beyond suspensions: Examining school discipline policies and connections to the school-to-prison pipeline for students of color with disabilities* (Briefing report). Author.

Valencia, R. R. (2012). *The evolution of deficit thinking: Educational thought and practice.* Routledge.

Whitford, D. K., & Emerson, A. M. (2019). Empathy intervention to reduce implicit bias in pre-service teachers. *Psychological Reports, 122*(2), 670–688.

Williams, B., & Jagers, R. (2020). Transformative social and emotional learning: Work notes on an action research agenda. *Urban Education, 57*(2), 191–197.

Yoder, N. (2014). *Teaching the whole child: Instructional practices that support social–emotional learning in three teacher evaluation frameworks* (Research-to-Practice Brief). Center on Great Teachers and Leaders.

Chapter 12

Using Measurement and Continuous Improvement to Support SEL at the Classroom, School, District, and State Levels

Pilar Alamos, Jenna Conway, Tamilah Richardson, and Amanda P. Williford

> I (Amanda) had been interested in children's emotions and behaviors since I was a high school student working as a teacher's assistant at the early childhood education program that my mom directed. I studied child development as an undergraduate student, and went to graduate school to study how young children develop self-regulation skills and how to support those children who display difficulties inhibiting impulsive behavior, managing strong emotions, and/or shifting and maintaining attention in the classroom at developmentally expected levels (e.g., have a hard time sitting quietly during a 15-minute group lesson, invade other children's personal space, become easily frustrated when faced with challenging tasks). Frequently, teachers find these behaviors "challenging" and "disruptive" because they interfere with their capacity to provide effective interactions and instruction in the classroom. As a clinical psychologist and research professor at the University of Virginia, I designed and evaluated strategies and interventions to help teachers support these children. We know young children vary widely in their self-regulation skills. When faced with a new, challenging task, some children are overwhelmed and frustrated, and may give up easily, while others calmly consider how they can approach this new puzzle and ask for help if they need it. Some children can sit quietly and listen to a book reading for an hour and other children need to get up and move after a few minutes. Given this variation, I thought it was obvious that if we were going to expand school readiness assessments in Virginia, it would be balanced between academic and social and emotional skills. I was completely unprepared for my first interactions with

> Virginia legislators who did not understand the term "self-regulation" or what it had to do with reading and math. Social and emotional learning (SEL) was not going to be the "easy sell" that I assumed it would be when advocating for a statewide school readiness assessment.

We describe in this chapter the process of incorporating assessments of children's social and emotional skills when establishing a statewide school readiness assessment system in Virginia. This statewide assessment provides families, teachers, and leaders with useful information at the student, classroom, school, district, and state levels to support children's SEL. Virginia serves over 100,000 students in Pre-K and kindergarten. According to the state's enrollment data, about 43% of students are White, 24% are Black, 19% are Hispanic,[1] 7% are Multiracial, and 7% are Asian. Approximately 38% of students meet the state's low-income criteria,[2] 7% are English language learners, and 14% have a diagnosed disability. Using Virginia as a case study, we describe the process for choosing an SEL measure; describe the guidance provided in completing and interpreting the data; delineate how the system reports data from this measure to families, teachers, and leaders; and detail how the data are tied to instructional resources.

SEL includes young children's skills to form stable, positive relationships with peers and adults, to regulate and express emotions in culturally and socially appropriate ways, and to demonstrate self-regulatory behaviors (Halle & Darling-Churchill, 2016; Houri & Miller, 2020; Jones & Bouffard, 2012). Children who are better able to follow directions, regulate their emotions, take turns, and play cooperatively with others engage more positively in the classroom, and teachers perceive them as more academically and socially competent (Bulotsky-Shearer et al., 2012; Denham, 2006; Rimm-Kaufman et al., 2009). Conversely, when children show difficulty getting along with peers, working through strong emotions, or following classroom expectations, they tend to engage less positively in the classroom and teachers report more conflict interacting with them (Doumen et al., 2008; Searle et al., 2014).

SEL skills are best supported when using a systemic approach, with coordinated efforts at the state, district, school, and classroom levels (Weissberg et al., 2015), along with embracing the primary role of families in children's development. One key aspect to systemic SEL is to establish an ongoing process to collect and use children's SEL outcome data to inform decisions and drive improvements across levels (Mahoney et al., 2021). For example, families may use information about their

---

[1]We acknowledge the ongoing debate about the use of Hispanic rather than Latino, Latine, or Latinx (e.g., Melzi, Curenton, Harris, & Jarquin, 2021). We use the word *Hispanic* because it is used by the Virginia Department of Education.

[2]Defined as student is eligible for free/reduced meals, receives Temporary Assistance for Needy Families [TANF], or is eligible for Medicaid.

child's SEL to reinforce a certain skill at home through everyday moments and interactions. Teachers and families can use a child's SEL data to partner around ways to build continuity in SEL supports between the home and the classroom. Teachers may use the information to make instructional SEL decisions for all children in their classroom or to individualize their interactions and instruction according to individual children's needs (McKown, 2019). Principals or school district leaders can use the assessment results to target SEL supports such as professional development or programs (Taylor et al., 2018). Policymakers may use the data to allocate resources and to create equitable learning opportunities focused on children's social and emotional growth.

In this chapter, we describe the development of the Virginia Kindergarten Readiness Program (VKRP), Virginia's statewide school readiness assessment system. Over a period of 6 years, Virginia established an ongoing process to collect and use children's SEL outcome data to support SEL at the student, classroom, school, district, and state levels. Currently, this process is being conducted in kindergarten and expanded into preschool to understand children's SEL growth over time. Below we provide some background about VKRP and how this initiative measures two specific SEL skills: self-regulation and social skills.

Virginia Kindergarten Readiness Program

VKRP History

In 2018, the Virginia General Assembly passed legislation requiring all children enrolled in public kindergarten in the state to be assessed using VKRP in the fall and spring of the 2019–2020 academic year and annually thereafter. To provide a more comprehensive understanding of children's school readiness skills in Virginia, VKRP added measures of children's math, self-regulation, and social skills to the existing and long-standing statewide assessment of literacy skills, the Phonological Awareness Literacy Screening (PALS), operating in the state since 1997. As an initiative, VKRP was originally advocated for by Elevate Early Education (E^3)—a statewide bipartisan issue-advocacy organization devoted to early childhood education—and made possible through a research–practice partnership between E^3, the Virginia Department of Education (VDOE), and the University of Virginia's Center for Advanced Study of Teaching and Learning (CASTL) (for more information, see Williford et al., 2021).

The development of VKRP spanned 7 years (2013–2019) and occurred in four phases: (1) research and selection of assessment tools that could be used statewide to accurately capture children's readiness skills (2013–2014); (2) a pilot study of VKRP in a sample of children who were representative of the state kindergarten population (2014–2015); (3) expansion of VKRP through a gradual voluntary rollout to school divisions that allowed for frequent iterations to incorporate practitioners' feedback (2015–2019); and (4) universal implementation of VKRP (2019–present), meaning that every kindergarten student enrolled in public education in the state is assessed in the fall and spring of kindergarten in the areas of literacy, math, self-regulation, and social skills (for more information, visit *www.vkrponline.org*).

Methods for Assessing Children's SEL Skills at Scale

Three methods are commonly used to capture children's SEL within kindergarten readiness assessments: (1) teacher ratings, (2) direct assessments, and (3) naturalistic observations (Regenstein et al., 2017). Teacher ratings and direct assessments are typically recommended for use at scale, whereas naturalistic observations of children's SEL tend to be costly and time-consuming (McKown, 2019; Taylor et al., 2018). Teacher ratings and direct assessments have advantages and limitations that are typically in tension with one another. Teacher ratings are cost-efficient, and teachers are one of the most important sources of ecologically valid, summative data about children's SEL as displayed in the classroom (Brownell et al., 2015). A preschool or early elementary teacher spends approximately 5 hours a day, 5 days a week in direct contact with their students and as such are valuable informants who have intuitive knowledge of what is expected and what skills students typically display in the classroom. However, teacher ratings are susceptible to rater bias, including teachers' racial and cultural bias influencing the way they perceive and rate children (Mason et al., 2014). Conversely, direct assessments—child performs various tasks and/or answers questions as directed by an adult who is trained to deliver the assessment in a standardized manner (i.e., deliver the assessment the same way to each student)—are less prone to bias but are more time consuming. Even when direct assessments are conducted in a school-based setting, typical procedures involve removing the child from the classroom context and administering assessments in a quiet space with an attentive data collector or teacher. By removing the child from the classroom context, direct assessments can provide less ecologically valid data than teacher ratings, because they may not be accurate indicators of the skills children demonstrate within the actual classroom, particularly skills in the social–emotional domain. The early childhood and elementary classroom context places demands on students (e.g., complete tasks independently, take turns, stop a desired activity such as playing with blocks to start a less-desired activity like cleaning up) that do not exist outside of the classroom or during a direct assessment. In the context of assessing children's self-regulatory and social school readiness, one needs to be able to measure students' skills as they are expressed in the classroom—the context where skill demonstration matters for learning.

Why VKRP Selected a Teacher Rating Scale

During the first phase of VKRP's development, we piloted two SEL assessment tools that could be used statewide: (1) a teacher rating, the Child Behavior Rating Scale (CBRS; Bronson et al., 1990), and (2) selected subtests (social problem-solving and self-control modules) from a computer-based direct assessment, SELweb (McKown et al., 2016). These measures were selected because they had demonstrated acceptable reliability (consistency when administered across a range of settings) and validity (provide meaningful information about the skills being measured) when used in large, racially and ethnically diverse samples of children in grades K–3. The CBRS was selected as the measure to assess self-regulation and social skills for a number of reasons: SELweb did not outperform the CBRS in terms of its reliability and validity; the CBRS took much less time to administer; it was strongly preferred by teachers, who reported it to be more face valid in terms of more comprehensively assessing the skills children displayed in the classroom (critical for buy-in); and it was substantially less expensive to administer (Williford et al., 2014). However, the selection of the CBRS was not without limitations (see below, "Teacher Bias in SEL Rating Scales").

The CBRS

VKRP uses the CBRS to assess SEL. The CBRS is a teacher rating scale of children's self-regulation and social skills in the classroom. The CBRS is a brief screening measure that includes 17 items (Matthews et al., 2009); 10 for self-regulation (e.g., "concentrates when working on a task; is not easily distracted by surrounding activities") and seven for social skills (e.g., "willing to share toys or other things with other children when playing; does not fight or argue with playmates in disputes over property"). The CBRS is an accessible measure (does not require a high level of inference) that asks teachers to rate specific classroom behaviors versus behaviors out of context (e.g., shares, hits, cries). Teachers apply a 5-point frequency scale (1 = *never*; 5 = *always*) to rate how often they see a child demonstrating a specific behavior. The CBRS focuses on positive or strengths-based behaviors rather than using a deficit lens in screening for behavior problem. Such focus on strengths advances equity by considering students' assets (rather than only needs), informs teachers and program leaders where they need to provide instruction and support to develop student skills, and gauges progress over time, aligning with the SEL essence of fostering social and emotional skills through explicit instruction.

In terms of reliability, the CBRS Self-Regulation and Social Skills subscales have demonstrated good internal consistency (e.g., Kim et al., 2016; Sung, 2014) and several studies have replicated the two-factor structure (Ponitz et al., 2009; Von Suchodoletz et al., 2013; Wanless et al., 2013). Regarding validity, the CBRS has been linked to children's directly assessed self-regulation (e.g., Cameron Ponitz et al., 2008; Wanless et al., 2011) and has been found to predict children's preacademic school readiness skills, including math and literacy outcomes (Birgisdotter et al., 2020; Gestsdottir et al., 2014; Schmitt et al., 2014). For more detailed information on the CBRS, see VKRP (2020).

Statewide Assessment of Children's SEL Skills Brings Attention to SEL across Levels

Within VKRP, the CBRS is meant to bring teachers, families, leaders, and policymakers' attention to SEL as being of equal importance to children's early reading and math skills. As emphasis on early academics is accelerating in the country, so are concerns that children's social and emotional needs are not being met adequately in the classroom. Indeed, school administrators are less likely to report screening students for social and emotional versus academic needs (Bruhn et al., 2014), and kindergarten classrooms have become increasingly academic in focus in the past 15 years (Bassok et al., 2016). In such context, measuring SEL statewide serves to assert that SEL skills are an integral part of children's school readiness. For example, asking teachers to complete the CBRS sends the message that observing children's SEL behaviors in the classroom is important. Kindergarten teachers shared feedback on how completing the CBRS has brought their attention to SEL:

> "Shows these behaviors can play a part in a student's academic progress."
>
> "I like that while processing all the students through this assessment, I have time to reflect on and about the student and how does the behavior hurt or help the students' academic success."
>
> "Sometimes we consider mostly the behavior of struggling students. This let me take a closer look at the behavior of all my students."

Similarly, providing leaders and policymakers with information about children's self-regulation and social skills, along with math and literacy, communicates a vision of school readiness that balances academic and SEL skills. Leaders shared how the CBRS data have served to reinforce their commitment to SEL:

> "This screening tool has given our K teachers important information for their instruction in mathematics and has brought the socio-emotional learning piece to light in our K classrooms."
>
> "I agree students' social–emotional readiness has a significant impact on

academic readiness in a classroom setting. VKRP help teachers understand individual and class needs."

"The CBRS is a wonderful tool and honestly something that our teachers are not used to having as a SEL data point. We will need to continue to support their skills in data analysis in the social–emotional frame and most importantly the resources to leverage in terms of 'now what.'"

VKRP in Action

VKRP aims to press on the role that adults, particularly teachers, can play in kindergarten readiness. To that end, VKRP produces reports that provide the adults in a child's life with readiness data, including SEL. Plus, there are instructional resources to create a shared language around what SEL is and how it develops, and offer teachers and families a window into how to best support SEL.

Reports

Data reports provide adults with a common language around what self-regulation and social skills look like in the classroom, serving to reinforce self-regulation and social skills as two important skills that children need to develop. VKRP provides a snapshot of children's school readiness—including self-regulation and social skills—in the fall and spring. Reports offer detailed, actionable information for adults to leverage children's strengths and meet their needs, and a snapshot of how students' skills have changed across the year. For teachers, VKRP provides four reports: (1) classroom-level report that provides data on all children in a classroom (see Figure 12.1); (2) student-level report that provides detailed information about a child's skills (see Figure 12.2); (3) a family report that can be shared or used to communicate information with families; and (4) a growth report that provides data on how children's skills have changed from fall to spring. For leaders, VKRP generates school- and district-level reports that provide data on all children in a school and district, respectively.

VKRP reports provide benchmarks to assist when interpreting the data. These benchmarks were established using developmental expectations in conjunction with data collected across Virginia over the 2015–2019 expansion phase. The benchmarks offer a quick, first-pass means of making meaning of a child's scores. For instance, when a teacher rates a child as well above the benchmark in social skills, that child likely possesses a strength in that area that could be leveraged. Conversely, children whose teachers perceive them to be falling well below the self-regulation benchmark may benefit from additional supports to meet their regulatory needs. In addition to benchmarks, VKRP offers suggestions on how to use the data to reflect on interactions and instruction, and on how to utilize the linked instructional resources.

CBRS Classroom Summary

Teacher:	Example Teacher	Class:	Example Class 1	School:	*Example School 1	Date:	5/17/2021	Spring 2020-2021

Self-Regulation

Student	Average Score	1. Observes rules, follows directions	2. Completes multi-step tasks	3. Completes tasks successfully	4. Attempts new challenging tasks	5. Concentrates when working	6. Responds to instructions	7. Takes time to do his/her best	8. Finds and organizes materials	9. Sees, corrects own errors	10. Returns to unfinished tasks	Resources Recommended
Banks, Daisy	2.80	3	4	2	3	2	3	3	4	2	2	☑
Cantrell, Sean	4.00	4	4	3	4	5	4	4	3	4	5	☐
Davidson, Jerry	NT	-	-	-	-	-	-	-	-	-	-	
Elliott, Alivia	2.40	2	2	3	3	3	2	1	2	3	3	☑
Ferguson, Riya	NT	-	-	-	-	-	-	-	-	-	-	
Hughes, Carlos	2.90	3	3	3	2	3	4	3	3	3	2	☑
Hunter, Valentino	3.70	3	4	3	4	3	4	4	4	4	4	☐
Jacobs, Eugene	NT	-	-	-	-	-	-	-	-	-	-	
Larsen, Alena	NT	-	-	-	-	-	-	-	-	-	-	
Mckee, Kennedi	NT	-	-	-	-	-	-	-	-	-	-	
Page, Kelton	1.90	2	2	2	1	1	2	2	3	2	2	☑
Richards, George	NT	-	-	-	-	-	-	-	-	-	-	
Romero, April	E	-	-	-	-	-	-	-	-	-	-	
Sherman, Charles	NT	-	-	-	-	-	-	-	-	-	-	
Stephens, Carly	NT	-	-	-	-	-	-	-	-	-	-	
Valencia, Diego	NT	-	-	-	-	-	-	-	-	-	-	
Wood, Geovanni	NT	-	-	-	-	-	-	-	-	-	-	

Social Skills

Student	Average Score	11. Willing to share	12. Expresses hostility verbally	13. Expresses hostility physically	14. Cooperative in group play	15. Takes turns without being told to do so	16. Complies with adult directions	17. Does not fuss when he/she has to wait	Resources Recommended
Banks, Daisy	4.57	5	5	5	4	4	5	4	☐
Cantrell, Sean	4.00	3	5	5	4	4	3	4	☐
Davidson, Jerry	NT	-	-	-	-	-	-	-	
Elliott, Alivia	4.43	4	5	5	5	4	4	4	☐
Ferguson, Riya	NT	-	-	-	-	-	-	-	
Hughes, Carlos	3.00	3	3	4	3	3	2	3	☑
Hunter, Valentino	2.86	3	3	3	3	3	2	3	☑
Jacobs, Eugene	NT	-	-	-	-	-	-	-	
Larsen, Alena	NT	-	-	-	-	-	-	-	
Mckee, Kennedi	NT	-	-	-	-	-	-	-	
Page, Kelton	3.00	3	3	4	3	3	2	3	☑
Richards, George	NT	-	-	-	-	-	-	-	
Romero, April	E	-	-	-	-	-	-	-	
Sherman, Charles	NT	-	-	-	-	-	-	-	
Stephens, Carly	NT	-	-	-	-	-	-	-	
Valencia, Diego	NT	-	-	-	-	-	-	-	
Wood, Geovanni	NT	-	-	-	-	-	-	-	

Interpreting This Report

In keeping with best practices for student assessment, we recommend that you use the information in this report in conjunction with other sources of information about each student as you plan instruction.

At or Above Benchmark

Below Benchmark

E Exempt

NT Not Tested

Scoring: 1 (Never), 2 (Rarely), 3 (Sometimes), 4 (Frequently), 5 (Always). Items 12 and 13 are reverse-scored.

Interpreting Your VKRP Reports

Summary of Results

Self-Regulation		
Class Average	*Benchmark*	*Max*
2.95	3.20	5.00
Social Skills		
Class Average	*Benchmark*	*Max*
3.64	4.00	5.00

Instructional Resources

Resources are recommended below if a majority of students in the class fall below the benchmark:

Self-Regulation ☑

Social Skills ☑

FIGURE 12.1. VKRP classroom-level report. (The actual report is color coded.) Copyright © 2021 the Rector and Visitors of the University of Virginia. Reprinted by permission from *vkrponline.org*. To see a report example, visit the VKRP webpage (*www.vkrponline.org*), go to the Resources tab, and download the presentation slides from the Administrator ToolKit.

Instructional Resources

VKRP links results from the assessments to a set of instructional resources. For SEL, instructional resources include a skill overview and a set of evidence-based strategies that teachers can use in the classroom to support children's self-regulation and social skills, respectively (see Table 12.1 for a summary of VKRP resources for SEL).

Teacher resources consist of a brief document that describes what the strategy is, how it looks when implemented in the classroom, its importance, and resources, activities, or practices to implement the strategy (see Figure 12.3). Similarly, the family information report includes a link to a family resources packet. For SEL, this packet provides information about social and emotional skills that typically developing children will continue to work on in kindergarten, including suggested at-home activities for families to try (see Figure 12.4). These resources are focused on meeting students where they are and providing scaffolding to help children adjust to the classroom. For example, one strategy provided to support children's self-regulation skills is to offer cues and visuals to reduce the self-regulatory demands in the classroom. When a student is provided a visual reminder of what to do in the moment, this reduces the cognitive load for a student (e.g., they do not have to

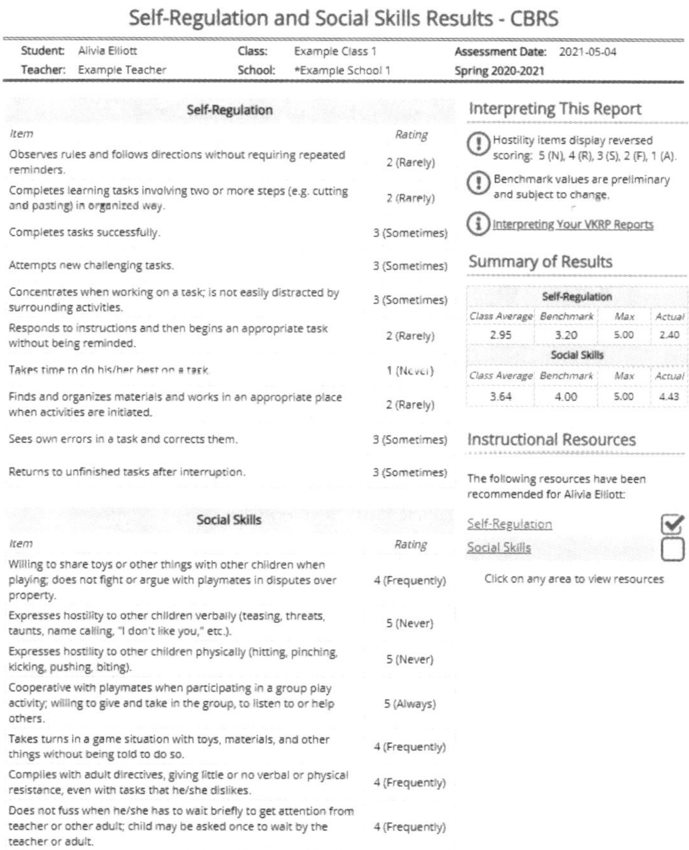

Self-Regulation and Social Skills Results - CBRS

Student: Alivia Elliott **Class:** Example Class 1 **Assessment Date:** 2021-05-04
Teacher: Example Teacher **School:** *Example School 1 **Spring 2020-2021**

Self-Regulation

Item	*Rating*
Observes rules and follows directions without requiring repeated reminders.	2 (Rarely)
Completes learning tasks involving two or more steps (e.g. cutting and pasting) in organized way.	2 (Rarely)
Completes tasks successfully.	3 (Sometimes)
Attempts new challenging tasks.	3 (Sometimes)
Concentrates when working on a task; is not easily distracted by surrounding activities.	3 (Sometimes)
Responds to instructions and then begins an appropriate task without being reminded.	2 (Rarely)
Takes time to do his/her best on a task.	1 (Never)
Finds and organizes materials and works in an appropriate place when activities are initiated.	2 (Rarely)
Sees own errors in a task and corrects them.	3 (Sometimes)
Returns to unfinished tasks after interruption.	3 (Sometimes)

Social Skills

Item	*Rating*
Willing to share toys or other things with other children when playing; does not fight or argue with playmates in disputes over property.	4 (Frequently)
Expresses hostility to other children verbally (teasing, threats, taunts, name calling, "I don't like you," etc.).	5 (Never)
Expresses hostility to other children physically (hitting, pinching, kicking, pushing, biting).	5 (Never)
Cooperative with playmates when participating in a group play activity; willing to give and take in the group, to listen to or help others.	5 (Always)
Takes turns in a game situation with toys, materials, and other things without being told to do so.	4 (Frequently)
Complies with adult directives, giving little or no verbal or physical resistance, even with tasks that he/she dislikes.	4 (Frequently)
Does not fuss when he/she has to wait briefly to get attention from teacher or other adult; child may be asked once to wait by the teacher or adult.	4 (Frequently)

Interpreting This Report

Hostility items display reversed scoring: 5 (N), 4 (R), 3 (S), 2 (F), 1 (A).

Benchmark values are preliminary and subject to change.

Interpreting Your VKRP Reports

Summary of Results

Self-Regulation			
Class Average	*Benchmark*	*Max*	*Actual*
2.95	3.20	5.00	2.40
Social Skills			
Class Average	*Benchmark*	*Max*	*Actual*
3.64	4.00	5.00	4.43

Instructional Resources

The following resources have been recommended for Alivia Elliott:

Self-Regulation ☑
Social Skills ☐

Click on any area to view resources

FIGURE 12.2. VKRP student-level report. Copyright © 2021 the Rector and Visitors of the University of Virginia. Reprinted by permission from *vkrponline.org*. For more information or reports, visit the VKRP website (*www.vkrponline.org*), go to the "How It Works" tab, and click on "Using and Intepreting Reports."

TABLE 12.1. VKRP Resources for Self-Regulation and Social Skills

Strategy	Some key foci	Self-regulation	Social skills
Observing behavior	• Observe students' regulatory or social behavior in context. • Better understand why and under what circumstances a behavior occurs.	x	x
Using reinforcement	• Focus on appreciating students' positive behaviors. • Individualize reinforcers options based upon students' linguistic, racial/ethnic, and cultural backgrounds.	x	x
Providing effective instructions	• Give instructions about a behavioral expectation that gets the student's attention; include one step at a time; and state specifically, assertively, and positively.	x	x
Allowing choice	• Give students the chance to have a say, allowing them to feel included and part of the decision. • Individualize choice options based upon students' linguistic, racial/ethnic, and cultural backgrounds.	x	x
Using cues and visuals	• Provide student with support and gentle reminders of classroom expectations. • Establish and maintain realistic behavioral expectations.	x	
Modifying activities and environment	• Plan developmentally and culturally relevant activities. • Adapt and modify tasks to maximize engagement. • Organize the classroom to minimize distraction.	x	
Playing games	• Incorporate games and activities throughout the day that encourage the use of self-regulation skills.	x	
Peer pairing	• Provide students with opportunities to learn from and with peers. • Purposely set up interactions between student with different levels of social skills development.		x
Supporting friendship skills	• Provide explicit instruction in social skills. • Build a safe space with repeated opportunities for students to practice social skills.		x
Promote problem solving	• Provide explicit instruction in specific steps to resolve small social problems. • Provide repeated opportunities to practice solving small social problems with peers.		x
Working through emotions	• Provide explicit instruction in emotion regulation. • Guide students through recognizing and describing emotions and choosing how to respond.		x
Using a social skills curriculum	• Implement a social skills curriculum. • Consider students' backgrounds (e.g., linguistic, racial/ethnic, and cultural) and school culture when choosing a curriculum.		x

Self-Regulation Guide to
MODIFYING ACTIVITIES AND ENVIRONMENTS

VKRP
Virginia Kindergarten Readiness Program

WHAT IS IT?

Modifying Activities and Environments (MAE) is a set of techniques to increase students' on-task, classroom behaviors by:

- Planning activities to meet each students' learning needs
- Adapting and modifying tasks to maximize active engagement
- Organizing the classroom to minimize distractions

WHAT DOES IT LOOK LIKE?

Jason's teacher notices that the task may be too difficult for his current skill level (e.g., he is doodling in his math notebook while others work on patterning). The teacher adapts the task to meet Jason's needs by giving him concrete manipulatives to use to duplicate the pattern.

Students are playing with one another's shoelaces and elbowing each other during whole group time on the rug. The teacher moves the adjacent shelves back and encourages students to spread out to better keep hands to themselves.

WHY IS IT IMPORTANT?

When students are in well-organized classrooms and participating in interesting and culturally-relevant activities, they are more likely to engage, learn, and feel comfortable in the classroom! This is especially important for students who demonstrate more challenging behaviors – teachers can support these students by individualizing activities and/or environments to meet their specific needs!

Tips for Modifying Activities and Environments

Make sure activities are developmentally and culturally appropriate by incorporating...

- ☑ **Movement.** Kindergartners cannot be expected to stay seated for more than 20 minutes.
- ☑ **Student Interest.** Consider the unique needs and interests of your students in choosing content.
- ☑ **Student Culture.** Be mindful of the rituals and traditions, mannerisms, interactions, or communication styles of your students when choosing content and instruction type. Do not make assumptions about your students' culture when making classroom considerations.
- ☑ **Choice.** Allow choice whenever possible to increase feelings of autonomy and help students feel included and part of the decision making.

Be ready to adjust the activity to meet students' needs by...

- ☑ **Adapting.** Add more support and guidance for students who may struggle, and greater challenge for those who are more advanced or get bored easily.
- ☑ **Engaging.** Keep students engaged by staying close by and asking open-ended questions.

Minimize distraction in your classroom by...

- ☑ **Organizing.** Make sure classroom materials are well-organized, appropriately labeled, and easy to reach. Remove or cover materials that may be distracting.
- ☑ **Rearranging.** Reduce wide-open spaces, and redirect "traffic patterns." Clearly define boundaries and off-limit spaces.

FIGURE 12.3. VKRP teacher resources document. Copyright © 2021 the Rector and Visitors of the University of Virginia. Reprinted by permission from *vkrponline.org*.

Helping Your Kindergartner Get Ready for 1st Grade

SELF-REGULATION

VKRP
Virginia Kindergarten Readiness Program

WHAT WAS MY CHILD LEARNING IN KINDERGARTEN?

In kindergarten, your child worked on...

- ☑ Paying attention to the teacher, following directions, and waiting patiently
- ☑ Identifying, expressing, and managing emotions
- ☑ Establishing healthy physical boundaries and respecting the personal space of others
- ☑ Persisting on difficult tasks and transitioning smoothly to new activities
- ☑ Connecting actions to consequences
- ☑ Taking turns and making compromises

WHAT WILL MY CHILD BE LEARNING IN FIRST GRADE?

In first grade, your child will continue to build upon these skills by working on...

- ☑ Comparing and contrasting emotions
- ☑ Expressing emotions appropriately
- ☑ Identifying ways to cope with new and difficult emotions
- ☑ Recognizing the purpose of rules and practicing self-control
- ☑ Taking responsibility for one's own actions

How can I help my child continue to build their self-regulation over the summer?

You can help your child practice these skills by providing opportunities to learn and use them through story time and play! Below are a few fun ideas to help you get started.

To practice comparing, contrasting, and expressing emotions, try: Feelings Charades!
On small pieces of paper, write down the names of different feelings or different situations that would make someone feel happy, sad, scared, etc. You may need to read the slips to your child, or to print out images to go along with the words. Place the papers in a bag or container and have players take turns pulling out a piece to act out while the rest of the players guess the feeling! Together, discuss situations in which a person might feel that way. (Source: PBS Parents; http://www.pbs.org/parents/adventures-in-learning/2013/10/feelings-charades/)

To practice managing emotions, try: Deep Breathing and Shared Readings!
One fun and easy way for children to learn and remember to take deep, calming breaths when they are experiencing difficult emotions is blowing bubbles! Start by talking with your child about taking deep breaths while blowing real bubbles, reminding them to fill their lungs with lots of air before taking a slow, careful breath out and directing their breath through the bubble wand so that the bubble grows big and doesn't pop. When they need help calming down, have them pretend they are blowing five big bubbles. For more creative and engaging ways to teach coping skills, check out these books: *Breathe Like a Bear* by Kira Willey, *When I Feel Angry* and *When I Feel Worried* by Cornelia Maude Spelman, and *The Most Magnificent Thing* by Ashley Spires.

To practice self-control, try: Red Light, Green Light!
The goal of this game is to get from a designated starting line to a designated finish line. When the leader says "Green Light," everyone can walk towards the finish line, but when the leader says "Red Light," children must freeze. If children are still moving when the leader says "Red Light," they must go back to the starting line. The first person to the finish line becomes the new leader. To make things more challenging, try adding "Yellow Light," where children must walk very slowly. Once they get the hang of it, try creating funny names together for new commands that require players to take tiny steps, big steps, walk in a pattern (like switching from backward to forward every 3 steps), hop, or dance toward the finish line!

FIGURE 12.4. VKRP family resources document focusing on SEL skills. Copyright © 2021 the Rector and Visitors of the University of Virginia. Reprinted by permission from *vkrponline.org.*

remember, they can quickly look, see, and be reminded of what is expected). As can be seen from this example, the strategy is designed to support a student where they are rather than expect more from a student who is still developing these skills.

Statewide Assessment of Children's SEL Is Critical to Monitor Equity in Children's SEL Outcomes

> As a former preschool teacher, I (Tamilah) came to know the names and faces of far too many of the children included in Virginia's harsh discipline and preschool expulsion data over the past two decades. And as state and national data have shown, most of these children would be Black, Hispanic, and American Indian/Alaska Native, have an identified disability, or were boys (and most often Black boys). Without policy and a widely accessible system of support in place to help change adult behaviors and practice, this negative trend has persisted over time. Fast forward to today: Virginia is addressing these inequities by heavily investing in efforts to ensure all children have equitable opportunity to enter kindergarten ready to thrive.

In 2020, the VDOE published the state's roadmap to advance equity in education. This document defines *education equity* as the inability to predict student outcomes based on race, gender, zip code, ability, socioeconomic status, or languages spoken at home. Based on this definition, a statewide assessment of children's SEL skills is the basis to provide empirical grounding for conversations about SEL and education equity in the state. These conversations involve reflective and critical discussion about the ways schools and classrooms may be contributing to create or perpetuate existing educational inequities, along with taking data-informed action (Carter et al., 2017). A system like VKRP allows for ongoing disaggregated data collection and analysis to identify, bring awareness to, and address disparities.

A district leader could use VKRP data to ascertain that children who are multilingual and may have limited English proficiency are being rated by teachers as displaying lower levels of social skills than their English-dominant peers. Bringing awareness to such disparity could start discussions about the extent to which teachers are providing these children with opportunities to develop social skills or explore false or harmful assumptions that educators may hold about English language learners (e.g., seeing a native language that is not English as a barrier instead of a difference). Such discussion could then lead to advancing equity by, for example, allocating resources for teacher professional development around social skills development in dual or multilanguage learners or about culturally responsive teaching, including helping teachers and families embrace the benefits of supporting children's home language to support SEL. Furthermore, continued examination of disaggregated data could be used to monitor whether this or other interventions are effective in reducing disparities in children's SEL outcomes.

However, the opportunity to examine disaggregated data is necessary but not sufficient to advance equity. Rather, it could serve to perpetuate stereotypes of children from particular groups (Carter et al., 2017). For instance, data showing that Black boys are rated by teachers as displaying lower self-regulation than their non-Black peers could lead to continuing the stereotype that Black boys *are* more aggressive or hyperactive, rather than educators and leaders critically reflecting on their own assumptions, biases, and practices when working with Black boys (Iruka et al., 2020). When thinking about Virginia's SEL assessment, the risk of using and interpreting the data in ways that perpetuate stereotypes has been a challenge, especially considering that the teachers completing the CBRS are predominantly White women, even in classrooms serving mostly Black, Indigenous, and people of color (BIPOC) children.

Teacher Bias in SEL Rating Scales

In the context of heightened awareness of racial inequities in the country, apprehensions have been raised about using a teacher rating scale to capture children's social and emotional skills. Particularly, that teacher racial biases may affect the validity of CBRS scores because racial biases affect how teachers perceive and interpret Black children's behavior in the classroom. For example, early childhood teachers tend to watch Black boys more closely than White boys when expecting challenging behaviors, despite no such behaviors occurring (Gilliam et al., 2016), middle school teachers perceive a "stroll" walking style—considered a Black walking style—as aggressive (Neal et al., 2003), and Black boys are perceived as significantly older and less innocent than their same-age White peers (Goff et al., 2014). As a result, racial biases likely affect how teachers rate children using the CBRS, or any other teacher-reported measure. Indeed, a proportion of the variability in teacher ratings of children's SEL skills (typically around 12%) is due to teacher biases, mood, or other teacher factors (An et al., 2019; Mason et al., 2014; Waterman et al., 2012). Yet teacher bias is typically not enough to compromise the validity of the data when the rating scales have demonstrated adequate psychometric properties and are being used with formative purposes (McKown, 2021). The question then is how to ensure that the CBRS data are interpreted and used in ways that account for how teacher bias may have affected children's scores.

At least two actionable steps have been valuable in our work in Virginia: First, using precise language by explicitly stating that these data measure teachers' perceptions of children's SEL skills, as opposed to students' actual skills. The use of precise language has served to maintain awareness that teachers are the ones having the power to rate children's skills. It has also served to acknowledge that part of the differences in the CBRS data are due to how teachers perceive children, based on their cultural background and experiences. For example, instead of saying "Black and American Indian children display weaker self-regulation skills than their White or Asian peers," we intentionally say, "*teachers reported* that Black and American Indian children display weaker self-regulation skills than their White or Asian peers." This subtle language difference allows us to include in our conversations that teachers may be perceiving Black and American Indian children's regulatory behavior more negatively than that of White and Asian children. Understanding ratings of children's SEL as perceptions opens the door to discuss how teachers' own assumptions and practice play out in those perceptions, rather than on what is "the problem" with Black and American Indian children when compared to their White and Asian peers.

Second, explicitly acknowledging teacher bias in CBRS ratings and providing concrete steps to mitigate it. VKRP has gradually worked to incorporate this content in the teacher trainings and user manual that now includes a section entitled "Understanding the CBRS as a Teaching Rating Scale: Recognizing and Reducing the Impact of Teacher Bias." This section of the manual discusses how teachers' reports of student behavior on the CBRS are influenced by their explicit and implicit biases—related to gender, race/ethnicity, culture, disability, religion, language, or socioeconomic status. It also highlights that without a commitment to reflect and take action to counteract these negative automatic thoughts or assumptions, a teacher's biases will be reflected in how they interpret student behaviors. One strategy to counteract bias when completing CBRS ratings is to encourage educators to observe children across settings to obtain a more complete picture of students' average behaviors, avoiding biased overgeneralizations. Another strategy is instructing teachers to take notes about specific, concrete behaviors that relate to the CBRS items during observations to increase rating accuracy. Describing specific behaviors allows teachers to move away from interpretation and evaluation—both of which are influenced by their own biases and cultural values.

Statewide Assessment of Children's Social and Emotional Skills Should Focus on Growth over Time

We argue that to truly support SEL, statewide SEL assessment should focus on growth over time. When we assess children's SEL skills at one time point only, we are limited to a snapshot of children's skills at that moment. For example, when we were gradually rolling out VKRP, children's CBRS data were only collected at kindergarten entry. These data were valuable to learn about students' SEL at the beginning of the year, providing a snapshot of children's social and emotional strengths and needs as perceived by teachers. These data were also informative of how teachers' ratings of children's SEL skills varied across districts and schools, and to examine disparities in SEL outcomes that need to be addressed. However, without several time points, we know very little about whether children's SEL skills improve over time. For instance, we could not know to what extent children's SEL skills grow from preschool to kindergarten, which students show the greatest or the least growth, or how growth trends vary across classrooms, schools, and districts.

Developmentally, the early childhood years are a crucial time to support children's SEL. Between ages 3 and 6, children are gradually transitioning from being self-centered to socially integrated, and from relying on the external regulatory supports provided by others to internally regulating themselves (Bierman & Motamedi, 2015). Early childhood classrooms can play a key role in supporting children during this process. Particularly, teachers model how to express emotions and can explicitly teach children emotion regulation (Denham et al., 2012). Teachers can also provide children with opportunities and scaffolding to learn how to share, solve problems, and collaborate with peers.

We are learning at least two lessons from our work in Virginia. First, a consistent statewide assessment that captures growth in children's SEL skills is needed to work toward supporting SEL development over the early childhood years. A consistent SEL assessment can help advance the alignment of children's classroom experiences from preschool to kindergarten. For example, a consistent SEL assessment can further promote school districts and the state to prioritize children's SEL development, countering the push down of developmentally inappropriate instruction from upper elementary grades (Markowitz & Ansari, 2020), instruction that offers children limited opportunities for the kind of culturally affirming exploration and play that support their social and emotional development. As schools work to support SEL across the early childhood years, leaders may benefit from growth data when attempting to evaluate the effects and future of SEL interventions. Similarly, policymakers need growth data to equitably allocate resources and weigh the returns of current initiatives on children's SEL. The lack of data tracking children's SEL growth over time creates a substantial evidence gap, particularly for leaders and policymakers.

Second, communicating SEL growth data is challenging. SEL growth looks different than growth in literacy and math, which typically increases over time in a somewhat linear way. However, SEL skills tend to oscillate over time in ways that are less straightforward to make meaning of, when compared to academic skills. Particularly, we have seen that CBRS scores go up from fall to spring of preschool, go down at kindergarten entry, and then go up again by the end of kindergarten. This pattern observed with the VKRP data is consistent with work examining SEL trajectories from preschool to kindergarten (Barbarin, 2013) or with SEL measurement on several occasions in the kindergarten to first grade transition (e.g., An et al., 2019). One way to make meaning of this pattern is to recognize that SEL skills are more context dependent (Chan et al., 2000) when compared to academic skills. For example, children might need to become familiar with their peers to play cooperatively with them, whereas they may be able to count to 20 regardless of context. Therefore, when children change classrooms during the preschool to kindergarten transition (e.g., new peers and teachers) their SEL skills go down, while their academic skills stay the same or grow slightly. The preschool-to-kindergarten transition also creates an issue that researchers call *cross-classification*—children belong to more than one classroom—when modeling longitudinal data, a methodological challenge that is important to consider when understanding SEL growth.

Future Directions

In this chapter, we have described how social and emotional skills are a crucial part of Virginia's statewide school readiness assessment system, VKRP. Over time, the continued commitment to SEL through VKRP has been instrumental in advancing discussions from *why* teach SEL skills at school to *how* to best support children's social and emotional needs in the classroom. We end this chapter by considering two areas that we continue to strengthen as part of the VKRP system—equity and family engagement.

We continue to work toward ensuring that the information from VKRP supports equity—that we stress that children are complex and to be aware of and to prevent a single moment of data to become the story of a young child's potential or that data are used punitively for any student, or group of students. Rather, we have worked to situate the information coming from VKRP as information for teachers, program leaders, and families to support a child's learning and development rather than the child needing to be "ready" for school. To address this issue, Virginia is implementing an equity-centered professional development and coaching model that will help inform appropriate data use and data interpretation, including data from VKRP. In addition, CASTL and VDOE have worked together to explore how biases—related to gender, race/ethnicity, culture, disability, religion, language, or socioeconomic status—are reflected within our own materials and messaging. We have acted intentionally to deepen the knowledge of our staff members and to audit work to ensure that we are promoting diversity, inclusion, and equity.

To date, VKRP has placed more emphasis on reaching teachers, and school and state level leaders as compared to connecting to families. However, family engagement is a critical element of school readiness. We have seen the overfocus on academics in early childhood in our conversations with families.

> The importance of SEL was a hard sell to parents as something to focus on above and beyond early mathematics and literacy for the families (mostly Black and from low-income backgrounds) that I (Tamilah) served. There was limited understanding of developmental expectations from both families and teachers, particularly those teachers who were shifted into Pre-K classrooms because of perceived upper grade teaching incompetence. I also noticed a great divide on teaching philosophy and the importance of play and SEL between teachers and school leaders (many who do not have access to early childhood backgrounds).

Part of our ongoing equity work is making sure everyone who is part of a child's life, particularly parents/families as first and forever teachers, are involved in and are supported to foster their child's learning and development. Too often, BIPOC children, children with disabilities, and multilingual/English learners' first lessons are why they are not valuable and what is "wrong" about them. One area we continue to work on is how to message the information from VKRP and the family resources to promote student's strengths and not solely where they may need more support.

DISCUSSION QUESTIONS

1. We have discussed the importance of SEL assessment as a central aspect to systemic SEL. Why do you think it would be important to assess students' SEL? What are the potential benefits and challenges when assessing students' SEL? What are your experiences in using data on students' SEL to inform decisions and drive improvements across levels of the SEL? Why would it be important to have a statewide approach to the assessment of SEL? Why is it important to examine SEL growth over time?
2. In this chapter, we have discussed three types of methods often used to assess children's SEL within kindergarten readiness assessments. Discuss each of these methods and the pros and cons of each approach. Following this, discuss your experiences with different types of SEL assessments and reflect on what you learned.
3. As described in the chapter, we were part of the VKRP, in which we worked collaboratively to identify SEL tools. The VKRP now uses the CBRS. What is the CBRS and what dimensions of children's SEL does it assess? Why was the CBRS chosen, and what do you see as its strengths and potential challenges?
4. As outlined in this chapter, in moving the assessment of SEL to action, VKRP provides reports to both teachers and school leaders. Examples of these reports are provided in the figures. Look through these reports and identify some of the key elements presented on children's SEL. What do you see as the most important aspects of the reports that you would want to use in the classroom? How might you use the benchmarks? Also examine the teachers' resources provided in Table 12.1 and Figure 12.3. How would you use these resources in the classroom?
5. As we have noted, teacher bias in rating SEL in their students can escalate racial inequities. Discuss some of the research we have described in which this has occurred. What are the actionable steps have been taken in Virginia to address these issues to reduce inequities?

REFERENCES

An, X., Curby, T. W., & Brock, L. L. (2019). Is the child really what's being rated?: Sources of variance in teacher ratings of socioemotional skills. *Journal of Psychoeducational Assessment, 37*(7), 899–910.

Barbarin, O. (2013). A longitudinal examination of socioemotional learning in African American and Latino boys across the transition from Pre-K to kindergarten. *American Journal of Orthopsychiatry, 83*(2–3), 156–164.

Bassok, D., Latham, S., & Rorem, A. (2016). Is kindergarten the new first grade? *AERA Open, 1*(4), 1–31.

Bierman, K. L., & Motamedi, M. (2015). SEL programs for preschool children. In J. Durlak, C. E. Domitrovich, R. P. Weissberg, & T. P. Gullotta (Eds.), *Handbook of social and emotional learning: Research and practice* (pp. 135–150). Guilford Press.

Birgisdottir, F., Gestsdottir, S., & Geldhof, G. J. (2020). Early predictors of first and fourth grade reading and math: The role of self-regulation and early literacy skills. *Early Childhood Research Quarterly, 53*, 507–519.

Bronson, M. B., Goodson, B. D., Layzer, J. I., & Love, J. M. (1990). *Child Behavior Rating Scale.* Abt Associates.

Brownell, C. A., Lemerise, E. A., Pelphrey, K. A., & Roisman, G. I. (2015). Measuring socioemotional development. In M. E. Lamb (Vol. Ed.) & R. M. Lerner (Series Ed.), *Handbook of child psychology and developmental science: Socioemotional processes* (pp. 11–54). Wiley.

Bruhn, A., Woods-Groves, S., & Huddle, S. (2014). A preliminary investigation of emotional and behavioral screening practices in K–12 schools. *Education and Treatment of Children, 37*(4), 611–634.

Bulotsky-Shearer, R. J., Manz, P. H., Mendez, J. L., McWayne, C. M., Sekino, Y., & Fantuzzo, J. W. (2012). Peer play interactions and readiness to learn: A protective influence for African American preschool children from low-income households. *Child Development Perspectives, 6*(3), 225–231.

Cameron Ponitz, C. E., McClelland, M. M., Jewkes, A. M., Connor, C. M., Farris, C. L., & Morrison, F. J. (2008). Touch your toes!: Developing a direct measure of behavioral regulation in early childhood. *Early Childhood Research Quarterly, 23*(2), 141–158.

Carter, P. L., Skiba, R., Arredondo, M. I., & Pollock, M. (2017). You can't fix what you don't look at: Acknowledging race in addressing racial discipline disparities. *Urban Education, 52*(2), 207–235.

Chan, D., Ramey, S., Ramey, C., & Schmitt, N. (2000). Modeling intraindividual changes in children's social skills at home and at school: A multivariate latent growth approach to understanding between-settings differences in children's social skill development. *Multivariate Behavioral Research, 35*(3), 365–396.

Denham, S. A. (2006). Social–emotional competence as support for school readiness: What is it and how do we assess it? *Early Education and Development, 17*(1), 57–89.

Denham, S. A., Bassett, H. H., & Zinsser, K. (2012). Early childhood teachers as socializers of young children's emotional competence. *Early Childhood Education Journal, 40*, 137–143.

Doumen, S., Verschueren, K., Buyse, E., Germeijs, V., Luyckx, K., & Soenens, B. (2008). Reciprocal relations between teacher–child conflict and aggressive behavior in kindergarten: A three-wave longitudinal study. *Journal of Clinical Child and Adolescent Psychology, 37,* 588–599.

Gestsdottir, S., von Suchodoletz, A., Wanless, S. B., Hubert, B., Guimard, P., Birgisdottir, F., & McClelland M. (2014). Early behavioral self-regulation, academic achievement, and gender: Longitudinal findings from France, Germany, and Iceland. *Applied Developmental Science, 18*(2), 90–109.

Gilliam, W. S., Maupin, A. N., Reyes, C. R., Accavitti, M., & Shic, F. (2016). Do early educators' implicit biases regarding sex and race relate to behavior expectations and recommendations of preschool expulsions and suspensions? Retrieved from *https://medicine.yale.edu/childstudy/zigler/publications/preschool%20implicit%20bias%20policy%20brief_final_9_26_276766_5379_v1.pdf.*

Goff, P. A., Jackson, M. C., Di Leone, B. A. L., Culotta, C. M., & DiTomasso, N. A. (2014). The essence of innocence: Consequences of dehumanizing Black children. *Journal of Personality and Social Psychology, 106*(4), 526–545.

Halle, T. G., & Darling-Churchill, K. E. (2016). Review of measures of social and emotional development. *Journal of Applied Developmental Psychology, 45,* 8–18.

Houri, A. K., & Miller, F. G. (2020). A systematic review of universal screeners used to evaluate social–emotional and behavioral aspects of kindergarten readiness. *Early Education and Development, 31*(5), 653–675.

Iruka, I. U., Currenton, S. M., Durden, T. R., & Escayg, K. A. (2020). *Don't look away: Embracing anti-bias classrooms.* Gryphon House.

Jones, S. M., & Bouffard, S. M. (2012). Social and emotional learning in schools: From programs to strategies. *Social Policy Report, 26*(4), 1–33.

Kim, H., Byers, A. I., Cameron, C. E., Brock, L. L., Cottone, E. A., & Grissmer, D. W. (2016). Unique contributions of attentional control and visuomotor integration on concurrent teacher-reported classroom functioning in early elementary students. *Early Childhood Research Quarterly, 36,* 379–390.

Mahoney, J. L., Weissberg, R. P., Greenberg, M. T., Dusenbury, L., Jagers, R. J., Niemi, K., . . . Yoder, N. (2021). Systemic social and emotional learning: Promoting educational success for all preschool to high school students. *American Psychologist, 76,* 1128–1142.

Markowitz, A. J., & Ansari, A. (2020). Changes in academic instructional experiences in Head Start classrooms from 2001–2015. *Early Childhood Research Quarterly, 53,* 534–550.

Mason, B. A., Gunersel, A. B., & Ney, E. A. (2014). Cultural and ethnic bias in teacher ratings of behavior: A criterion-focused review. *Psychology in the Schools, 51*(10), 1017–1030.

Matthews, J. S., Ponitz, C. C., & Morrison, F. J. (2009). Early gender differences in self-regulation and academic achievement. *Journal of Educational Psychology, 101*(3), 689–704.

McKown, C. (2019). Challenges and opportunities in the applied assessment of student social and emotional learning. *Educational Psychology, 54*(3), 205–221.

McKown, C. (2021). In defense of teacher rating scales for SEL assessment. Retrieved from *https://xsel-labs.com/blog/in-defense-of-teacher-rating-scales-for-sel-assessment.*

McKown, C., Russo-Ponsaran, N. M., Johnson, J. K., Russo, J., & Allen, A. (2016). Web-based assessment of children's social-emotional comprehension. *Journal of Psychoeducational Assessment, 34*(4), 322–338.

Melzi, G., Curenton, S., Harris, K., & Jarquin, C. (2021). CEED is embracing "Latine." Retrieved from *www.bu-ceed.org/community-blog/ceed-is-embracing-latine.*

Neal, L. V. I., McCray, A. D., Webb-Johnson, G., & Bridgest, S. T. (2003). The effects of African American movement styles on teachers' perceptions and reactions. *Journal of Special Education, 37*(1), 49–57.

Ponitz, C. C., McClelland, M. M., Matthew, J. S., & Morrison, F. J. (2009). A structured observation of behavioral self-regulation and its contribution to kindergarten outcomes. *Developmental Psychology, 45*(3), 605–619.

Regenstein, E., Connors, M., Romero-Jurado, R., & Weiner, J. (2017). Uses and misuses of kindergarten readiness assessment results. Retrieved from *https://startearly.org/app/uploads/pdf/policyconversationkra2017.pdf.*

Rimm-Kaufman, S. E., Curby, T. W., Grimm, K. J., Nathanson, L., & Brock, L. L. (2009). The contribution of children's self-regulation and classroom quality to children's adaptive behaviors in the kindergarten classroom. *Developmental Psychology, 45*(4), 958–972.

Schmitt, S. A., Pratt, M. E., & McClelland, M. M. (2014). Examining the validity of behavioral self-regulation tools in predicting preschoolers' academic achievement. *Early Education and Development, 25*(5), 641–660.

Searle, A. K., Sawyer, M. G., Miller-Lewis, L. R., & Baghurst, P. A. (2014). Prospective associations between children's preschool emotional and behavioral problems and kindergarten classroom engagement, and the role of gender. *Elementary School Journal, 114*(3), 380–405.

Sung, M. Y. (2014). Effects of behavioral and emotional regulation on preschool children's peer play behavior: Focusing on gender differences. *Family and Environment Research, 52*, 541–549.

Taylor, J. J., Buckley, K., Hamilton, L. S., Stecher, B. M., Read, L., & Schweig, J. (2018). Choosing and using SEL competency assessments: What schools and districts need to know. Retrieved from *https://measuringsel.casel.org/pdf/choosing-and-using-sel-competency-assessments_what-schools-and-districts-need-to-know.pdf.*

Virginia Department of Education. (2020). Navigating EdEquityVA: Virginia's roadmap to equity. Retrieved from *www.doe.virginia.gov/edequityva/navigating-equity-book.pdf.*

Virginia Kindergarten Readiness Program. (2020). Overview of the Child Behavior Rating Scale. Retrieved from *https://vkrponline.org/wp-content/uploads/sites/3/2020/03/cbrs_overview.pdf.*

Von Suchodoletz, A., Gestsdottir, S., Wanless, S. B., McClelland, M. M., Birgisdottir, F., & Ragnarsdottir, H. (2013). Behavioral self-regulation and relations to emergent academic skills among children in Germany and Iceland. *Early Childhood Research Quarterly, 28*, 62–73.

Wanless, S. B., McClelland, M. M., Acock, A. C., Ponitz, C. C., Son, S., Lan, X., & Li, S. (2011). Measuring behavioral regulation in four societies. *Psychological Assessment, 23*, 364–378.

Wanless, S. B., McClelland, M. M., Lan, X., Son, S., Cameron, C. E., Morrison, F. J., & Sung, M. (2013). Gender differences in behavioral regulation in four societies: The United States, Taiwan, South Korea, and China. *Early Childhood Research Quarterly, 28*, 621–633.

Waterman, C., McDermott, P. A., Fantuzzo, J. W., & Gadsden, V. L. (2012). The matter of assessor variance in early childhood education—Or whose score is it anyway? *Early Childhood Research Quarterly, 27*(1), 46–54.

Weissberg, R. P., Durlak, J. A., Domitrovich, C. E., & Gullotta, T. P. (2015). Social and emotional learning: Past, present, and future. In J. A. Durlak, C. E. Domitrovich, R. P. Weissberg,

& T. P. Gullotta (Eds.), *Handbook of social and emotional learning: Research and practice* (pp. 3–19). Guilford Press.

Williford, A. P., Downer, J. T., Hamre, B. K., & Pianta, R. C. (2014). The Virginia Kindergarten Readiness Project: Executive summary Fall 2014, Phase II. Retrieved from *https://vkrponline.org/wp-content/uploads/sites/3/2020/03/VKRP_executive_summary.pdf.*

Williford, A. P., Downer, J. T., Miller-Bains, K., Howard, L., & Conway, J. (2021). Developing decision-making tools through partnerships. *Future of Children, 31*(1), 39–56.

Chapter 13

Conclusion

Trends, Challenges, and Future Directions in SEL

Michael J. Strambler, Kimberly A. Schonert-Reichl,
and Sara E. Rimm-Kaufman

In our introductory chapter, we noted that our intent in this book was to provide readers with insights about the conditions needed to support social and emotional learning (SEL) and the steps that can be taken to create those conditions. In this concluding chapter, we take a more macro view and consider some of challenges and promises of some of the current trends we have observed in the SEL field that have important implications for systemic SEL. In contrast to the rest of the book, where we have aimed to provide some strategies for implementing systemic SEL, our intent in this chapter is to offer more questions than answers; that is, we aim to highlight issues for researchers and practitioners to examine that are important for extending and deepening the well-established benefits of SEL. Just as we asked our chapter contributors to do, we also strive to make our discussion relatable and concrete by providing examples, some of which are based on our own personal experiences, and others which come from the voices of youth given that youth voice and engagement is a critical component of any SEL approach. On this latter point, we thought it would be particularly important to bring the voices of students into this picture, so we held five separate informal discussions with students in which we asked them about their experiences with SEL and other, related school experiences.

Here is an introduction to our five student contributors. In each case, we use the students' descriptions of how they define themselves and their identity. With the exception of Rowan, who requested we use their actual name, all names are pseudonyms.

1. Miguel is a fourth-grade, Black and Latine boy at a public school in Connecticut.
2. Sarah is a fourth-grade girl who attends a private Jewish day school in New Jersey.
3. Anthony is a fifth-grade boy who also attends a private Jewish day school in New Jersey.
4. Lisa is a 12th-grade girl who attends a private college preparatory school in New Jersey.
5. Rowan is an eighth-grade student who identifies as nonbinary, prefers pronouns of they/them, and attends a public middle school in British Columbia, Canada.

Throughout the chapter, we share parts of our conversations with these students to illustrate points in our discussion of three topics. We begin with a discussion of the growing trend of the inclusion of mindsets in SEL programming. We then move to exploring how SEL has addressed issues of individual and group differences in SEL, as well as alternative perspectives on these issues. Then, we end with discussing the role of teachers' own social and emotional skill set in relation to supporting students' SEL.

SEL and Mindsets

Traditionally, SEL has focused on principles and practices for developing the social and emotional skills of students. This is reflected in many of the theoretical frameworks, including that of the Collaborative for Academic, Social, and Emotional Learning (CASEL), which focus on the specific outcomes that practices are aimed to produce, such as self-regulation, interpersonal skills, and self-awareness. However, one of the growing trends in SEL has been to give more attention to outcomes such as attitudes that go beyond skills. A mindset, or a set of beliefs that shapes one's worldview and perceptions of self, is one such factor. Carol Dweck's concept of *theories of intelligence* (Dweck, 2006; Dweck & Yeager, 2019), also commonly referred to as fixed versus growth mindsets, is a very popular example of this concept. The idea is that having or cultivating a *growth mindset*—a belief that intelligence is malleable and can be grown rather than innate and fixed—allows a person to be more effective in responding to failure. If a student fails at a task but believes that they can perform better next time if they change their strategy and/or try harder, they are more likely to be successful next time than if they believe that they failed because they "just don't have the smarts." Dweck and others have studied this concept many times and have found compelling evidence to this effect. She and others have also developed programming to foster the development of growth mindsets (Yeager et al., 2019), of which a core feature of these approaches involves teaching students about the science of the brain and its malleability.

Mindsets are likely to be equally important in supporting SEL and the development of effective social–emotional skills, not just achievement. For example, research on a program to reduce youth aggression and improve prosocial skills provides a terrific example of growth mindset applied to social, emotional, and behavioral learning. Ninth- and tenth-grade students were assigned randomly into one of three conditions. In the treatment condition, students were taught information on incremental theories of behavior (growth mindset) for 3 weeks. For instance, students experienced instruction on how brains can be changed and that motivations for behaviors can shift over time (and are not predetermined based on their personalities). Students in this group had a chance to practice growth mindset approaches in response to hypothetical interpersonal conflicts and peer rejection situations. In contrast, students assigned to the other two groups experienced either a coping skills intervention that did not teach a growth mindset toward aggression or no treatment at all. One month after the completion of the program, students played a computer game that created situations in which students experienced victimization or exclusion. Students in the treatment group responded with lower aggression and higher prosocial behavior than those in the other two groups. Three months after the program, teachers (who did not know which condition students experienced) reported on students' conduct problems. Students who experienced the growth mindset intervention showed fewer conduct problems than the other two groups, and these findings were the largest for students who were frequently victimized at school and thus needed the intervention the most (Yeager et al., 2013).

In theory, we can apply the idea of mindsets to our emotional lives as well. Consider the experience of anxiety—imagine that a person notices the onset of anxiety, feels their body get tense, and realizes their mind is distracted from the task at hand. Then, one of at least two possibilities may occur. One possibly is that the person may think, "I hate this feeling and hate even more that there's nothing I can do about this." This may even lead to a very common anxiety spiral in which they become anxious, angry, and/or depressed about the anxiety itself, thereby further worsening the situation. Alternatively, one may take the perspective of "I'm anxious because I really care about the issue at hand, and now I need to try a few strategies to calm myself down before I can go back to the task." In the second response, the person believes that emotional states are malleable rather than unalterable, and they are more likely to persist at developing skills related to the awareness of their emotions and their ability to regulate them. However, if the person believes that emotional states are fixed, as in the first example, they are less likely to persist at the development of those skills.

The growth and fixed mindset idea that has been explored so deeply related to student achievement is also an important and relevant idea in our emotional lives and the lives of our students. Miguel shared how this showed up in his life. He was feeling nervous about performing in his martial arts school and had skipped classes because of that anxiety. He reflected on what helped eventually get him back on track to going more consistently. He explained how he reminded himself about how anxiety dissipated during prior experiences of anxiety in classes. Reminding himself of this helped give him the confidence to return to class. This may seem like a rather mundane strategy, but it required him to have a perspective, a mindset, that his emotions—in this case, his anxious feelings—were manageable.

In fact, there may be an even more fundamental application of mindset approaches related to understanding and appreciating the value of social–emotional skills in our lives. Unfortunately, as a function of us moving through the world, focused on our responsibilities and their associated tasks, we can easily lose sight of and implicitly come to devalue the importance of, our inner experiences. For instance, we may follow identical routines each morning without checking in on ourselves about our emotional states that signal that we need a few extra moments of quiet in our home, some social connection with people who love us, or a few minutes to notice the beauty around us. Applied to our students, a middle schooler may come to school feeling tense or anxious but may have developed a belief that there is nothing they can do about that feeling state, so they should just ignore it. Then, they may show up at school ready to check out or pick a fight rather than looking for ways to engage in what lies ahead.

Thus, for individuals to truly engage in SEL, it may be necessary to first see its value and importance in one's own life. The RULER approach discussed by Cipriano, Rappolt-Schlichtmann, Riley, Naples, and Eveleigh (Chapter 11, this volume) is one program that includes such a component, with their "emotions matter" mindsets component. Similar to the intelligence mindset programs, RULER orients teachers and students to the evidence around the ways in which emotions play important roles in our daily lives and the goals we are trying to achieve. To the extent that these types of ways of thinking about the world and oneself can enhance individuals use of health and effective social–emotional practices, the integration of these mindset approaches into SEL shows great promise for the field.

What other kinds of SEL-related mindsets might be important to foster? One direction some approaches take is developing mindsets around the value of civic engagement and social justice. Civic engagement tends to focus on "individual and collective actions designed to identify and address issues of public concern" (American Psychological Association, 2022). *Social justice* as defined by the National Education Association is about "distributing resources fairly and treating all students equitably so that they feel safe and secure—physically and psychologically" (Alvarez, 2019). These approaches also have great potential to enhance SEL programming, especially as youth become aware of the problems in their community and our world. Imagine that youth regularly hear about poverty through the news, social media, and social studies and start to wrap their minds around the idea that hundreds of millions of people in the world suffer from poverty. The students know that this is unjust, which can lead to a feeling of helplessness and anxiety. (We adults may easily be able to relate to those negative feelings as we listen to the news.) However, there are ways to counter this anxiety with action. With support from a skilled teacher, students can absorb these facts and the teacher can provide insight into what steps youth can take to focus in on one problem that matters to them, then work toward a solution for that problem. In doing so, the teacher is developing a growth mindset about youth's ability to work with others and create change. Certainly, one of the goals of education is to produce individuals who will serve as the leaders of tomorrow and make value contributions to society that will ultimately make the world a better place for us all. Focusing on developing mindsets oriented toward civics and justice/fairness can be one way of supporting these goals.

However, the road of civics and justice can lead us down some thorny paths that are not as straightforward as the intelligence and emotions-focused mindsets discussed earlier. Since perspectives of civics and justice are often associated with political orientations, there may be a risk of "mindsets" bleeding into ideology influenced by where certain SEL program developers, schools, or communities fall along a liberal–conservative continuum. The last thing we should want for our schools is for them to become sites of ideological indoctrination, as this would violate core principles of free speech and freedom of thought. Furthermore, if we believe that social–emotional skills are important for *all* individuals, we should want to make opportunities for skill development available to youth and adults of all political persuasions.

Therefore, the field of SEL needs to contend with a challenging issue. With any effort to develop student and adult mindsets, educators need to ensure that the process of mindset development is relatable to a wide range of viewpoints. This requires SEL program developers to practice an important social–emotional skill themselves—*perspective taking* or stepping outside of one's own worldview and imagining how individuals on the "other side" may view it. Importantly, this also requires communicating the value and purpose of these mindsets in terms that are understandable and acceptable to a diverse set of people.

Whether we like it or not, SEL has become a political flashpoint. (Recall we had a similar situation with character education in the 1990s, so this is not new terrain [Skinner, 2004].) This means that to the extent that SEL continues to move in the direction of fostering mindsets that intersect with politics, our hope is that it does so in a way that embraces the core social–emotional skills that we aim to instill in all our students. To do so, we need to take seriously the values of perspective taking, civil discourse, and learning how to work with others even if we do not agree with them. Above all, we need to respect each person's humanity. Educators can help our society by asking students to stretch, learn from people who are different from them, and value (or at least manage) disagreement.

The Varieties of Diversity

Many of the chapters in this book touch on the issue of diversity and how SEL connects to individual differences in culture, identity, language, ability, and viewpoint, and promotes (or does not promote) appreciation of difference. While these issues have always been a topic of interest within SEL, they have become more prominent over the past several years, largely driven by greater attention being paid to racial issues following a number of police killings of Black citizens that were widely covered by the press. Increases in race-based attacks on Asian Americans in some cities such as New York City have also contributed to this trend of addressing racial problems. Additionally, a great deal of attention has recently been directed toward diversity in gender and sexual orientation, with transsexualism and nonbinary identities being of particular interest. We cannot ignore that we live in a highly politically and ideologically polarized society to the point that it seems to be more difficult than ever to engage others with differing points of view. Youth appear to be keenly aware of this polarization as well. For example, Lisa shared the following statement with us:

> "During COVID and during election season everything became very polarized, and in that way friend groups, especially within my school, became polarized . . . people I was friends with during Freshmen year, I wasn't so close to after last year. And the only reason for that is because of everything that happened and how we both portrayed our own belief sets regarding certain things like Black Lives Matter, COVID, and things like that."

Schools however can also make a difference in creating a context of belonging and inclusion for all students. Examples related to youth in the lesbian, gay, bisexual, transgender, and queer (LGBTQ) community present this reality in stark relief. Several studies now show that having a Gay–Straight Alliance (GSA) in the school or being a member of GSA improved students' perception of safety and led to students' perception of less homophobic bullying in their school (Ioverno et al., 2016). Retrospective studies of young adults showed that GSAs in their high schools was linked to improved adult well-being and educational attainment (Toomey et al., 2011). Rowan, a nonbinary 13-year-old, described their experiences at two different schools—one school in which they did not feel seen because the school did not explicitly provide programs and practices that supported LGBTQ youth and the other to which they transferred that did. When asked about their experiences, Rowan provided us with their experiences when asked how teachers and their school helped them feel they belong:

> "Right from the start my new school felt like that, but my old school not really. At my old school the LGBTQ community was never talked about—and there was

no awareness. We didn't really have anything where people in the [LGBTQ] community could just go and meet other people. It just was not the same as my new school where they have a Gay Straight Alliance (GSA) club."

Centering and Inclusion

In this section, we focus on issues of diversity and disparities, and highlight some areas where we see some challenges and promise. One important challenge in this area concerns the extent to which one leans more toward focusing on certain groups to accomplish these goals or focusing on more universal concepts. For example, one might focus on "centering" certain groups or taking a more universal approach in which no one's group or identity is a focus. One early example of this from the 1980s was the Afrocentric movement, which argued for educational practices that centered around African history, principles, and values. This was, in part, in response to what was argued to be a Eurocentric education system. More modern representations of this approach have called for centering the history, literature, and other perspectives of underrepresented groups in education. This idea is important and means we first need to acknowledge that the "default setting" in schools often excludes the histories, perspectives, and/or values of certain identity groups.

As I (Michael) have pointed out in an op-ed (Strambler, 2021) there can be some tensions between concepts of centering and inclusiveness in that the more one prioritizes a certain group, the less inclusive the overall setting can become as a result. The solution may be somewhere between these two concepts, but striking the right balance between them can be tricky. On the one hand, it is essential for students from all backgrounds to feel welcome at their school and to be able to personally connect with the learning material. On the other hand, an important goal of education is to help students develop a perspective that extends beyond their immediate experiences and perspectives. One approach to addressing such issues is through relying on universal concepts to address the specific group subjects. This is the idea behind approaches such as targeted universalism, or "setting universal goals pursued by targeted processes to achieve those goals" (Powell et al., 2019). The term *universal* may feel off-putting to some because in some cases what is presented as universal may actually be group norms that members of those groups believe to be universal but are not. However, we believe there are three good reasons to value universalism.

First, in academic learning and SEL alike, we should aim for identifying and teaching skills (and potentially mindsets) that are most likely to benefit the largest number of individuals—which is to say, we should be aiming to promote *universal* skills. Second, while definitely there are cultural differences in the value and expression of emotions, it is undeniable that the experience of a core set of emotions is a universal phenomenon. The project of better understanding these common emotions *and* their diverse presentations seems to be essential for creating effective SEL programming and for arguing for its importance. Last, as we discussed earlier in the context of mindsets, being able to make a case for oneself, one's identity group, or for society at large is most successful when one can appeal to values shared among the largest number of individuals. So, while skepticism may be warranted when some use the term *universal,* we view this concept as an essential component to the study, implementation, and advocacy of SEL. In other words, how can we stick together and create productive change in our society if we do not recognize our commonalities and believe in our collective ability to create positive change?

Diversity and Social–Emotional Skills

The diversity present in the United States and (some of) its schools is one of our greatest assets. The mix of race, ethnicity, language, gender, political beliefs, sexual orientation, and religion all bring value for cultivating social and emotional skills in youth and the adults around them. Diversity also presents real challenges for education and society at large. When an institution or society is culturally and ideologically homogenous, it is easier for individuals to agree, work together, and make decisions than individuals with diverse views, values, attitudes, and behaviors. Additionally, when one is designing and/or implementing new practices or policies in a diverse setting, they need to attend to the myriad of ways diverse factors play a role in the effectiveness of such practices or policies. SEL is no exception. While we have a strong evidence base for the effectiveness of SEL on a wide range of academic and well-being outcomes, we know less about the conditions under which SEL is more or less effective—or even harmful.

A personal example may help illustrate this point. When I (Michael) was growing up in South Jersey, I played a lot of pickup basketball in the outdoor courts in my neighborhood. The courts provided excellent opportunities for kids like me to be occupied after school and during the summers. They also were sites where it was common for kids test each other. "Trash talking," teasing, and some bullying were common experiences. We also all implicitly knew who was higher and lower on the social hierarchy of the courts, and the last thing anyone wanted was to be at the bottom. In this setting, you avoided that through basketball skill, humor, and/or toughness. I was a good enough player to play on the court where the good players played (nowhere near the best), but was rather serious and could not hang when it came to teasing and joking. I knew that toughness was an area in which I needed to excel. So I played physically and learned to brush off hard fouls. The same was true when we boxed on the court and went "hard to the body"—punching at full force but only to the body. I would act like I wasn't hurt even when I was and would always make sure to get in some hard shots myself. When I once overheard some say, "Don't mess with him, he hits hard!" I knew I had accomplished the level of protection again being bullied that I had hoped for.

The point of this example is that the behaviors described were very adaptive for the setting I was in. And while it definitely required some social–emotional skills, like social awareness and self-regulation to navigate the courts, the use of those skills looked very different from how they look in schools. In fact, those very same behaviors that were essential to me outside of school would have been harmful to my success if applied in the same ways in school. Big questions for our field to address are the varieties of ways in which children socially and emotionally code switch as I did. Are kids able to switch naturally in these behavioral ways as they do across Black English and Standard English? Or is this unnatural, in which case we may inadvertently be doing these children a disservice when providing SEL that does not take this variability into account. We do not have the answers to these big and important questions, but we urge researchers to take them up and encourage educators to be open to these possibilities.

Equity

Over the past 10 to 20 years, the concept of equity has become central to the field of education and more recently it has become an imperative in the field of SEL. As mentioned in the first chapter, in its simplest sense, equity as a practice can be characterized by treating others fairly. This sometimes means treating everyone equally, but when some individuals have greater needs, it means providing more resources to them than to those who have fewer needs. When considering equitable *outcomes,* there are two prevailing views. One view focuses on equal outcomes for all, where equity would mean no gaps in indicators in areas such as wealth, achievement, and health. Another view focuses on opportunity, where equity would mean everyone having equal opportunity to success regardless of their lot in life. One thorny issue regarding the outcomes perspective is that individuals and groups will always differ, sometimes because of unfair differential treatment and sometimes not. Since, by definition, social groups will differ from each other across attitudes, beliefs, customs, and behaviors, sometimes these differences will result in different outcomes. What may be less obvious is that opportunity is also often influenced by similar group differences that are not easily classified as "good" or "bad." As a hypothetical example, let's say immigrant families at a given school place higher demands on their children to study and have higher academic expectations than nonimmigrant families. Effectively, these families provide more "opportunities" for learning that may result in higher academic performance. But a high emphasis on academics may mean fewer opportunities for SEL development. Ultimately, these family-derived practices may result in higher academic performance and lower SEL outcomes. To truly create equal opportunities and outcomes in such a case would require intrusively micromanaging family practices in a way that would be antithetical to any democratic society.

If truly equal or equitable opportunity and outcomes are unattainable, what can or should we do to create a more fair education system that provides the greatest range of opportunities for students with diverse backgrounds and needs? One proposal by Joseph Fishkin (2016) is to pursue opportunity pluralism with a focus on what he refers to as "anti-bottleneck" practices. According to this theory, a great deal of the problem with unfair disparities concerns the lack of various opportunities for students to thrive. Instead, society tends to direct students to very similar pathways with strict and narrow selection criteria for getting there. The more severe the funneling and the stricter the criteria, the more it creates "bottlenecks" that allow only a limited number of individuals to pass through and access opportunities that greatly increase the chances of upward mobility. And students are very aware of these strict criteria even when educators profess otherwise and urge students to become more well-rounded individuals. Lisa shares some relevant perspectives on this issue:

> "One thing that I find that is contradictory is that when you go to a college preparatory school and if you're trying to get into a good college . . . they always talk about a holistic approach, but also one of the main factors in that holistic approach is your grades . . . like that is the primary factor . . . so when a teacher comes up to me and tells me to not place that much emphasis on the grade . . . I feel like, you can't really tell me that . . . that's not what I'm here for. It becomes kind of contradictory."

What this quote communicates is that if opportunities are to be offered, they must be linked to real chances of success. Developing a "holistic" approach should result in skills that open up real opportunities for social mobility and productive engagement in adult society.

While it may be impossible to eliminate sorting and strict selection criteria, just as it is impossible to eliminate groups difference, Fishkin (2016) argues that we should direct our efforts toward loosening bottlenecks by providing diverse opportunities for individuals to thrive. What might such a concept look like for SEL? Potentially the same way it looks regarding "traditional" academic outcomes. We offer another personal example to illustrate how this may play out. I (Michael) was once a spin instructor as a way to make some money during graduate school. But being introverted and reserved, I lacked the social and emotional qualities of the typical fitness instructor, who is usually outgoing with high energy. I'm convinced that had the fitness industry only used these criteria of instructor selection then I would never been certified or hired at a gym. And while going through the instructor certification process, I wondered whether this venture into the fitness world would be a total failure, with no one showing up for my classes and me eventually being fired. It turned out to be quite the opposite. Soon after I started teaching at a local gym, my classes became regularly full—usually with a waiting list. What I came to learn was that there was an alternative path to success at this job. It turned out I was able to attract two main types of gym members—those with similar personalities as mine, many of whom avoided high-energy instructors, and those who liked the different type of music I played. Drawing on this example, it is possible that students who have social–emotional profiles that deviate from the norm, can still thrive in "traditional" settings so long as more than a single door of opportunity is open to them. This requires more than just educators, policymakers, researchers, or activists to make it happen. Loosening bottlenecks requires a collaborative and *systemic* effort of all of these individuals to ensure that we create real and attainable diverse pathways in society for individuals with diverse social-emotional profiles.

It's Possible

While there is still a lot of work to be done regarding SEL, diversity, and equity, we have high confidence that schools can be places where children from all different backgrounds can experience the sense of belongingness and connection that is needed for them to thrive in school and beyond. We have observed plenty of such settings, and more importantly, we've heard from youth who have *experienced* such schools. Here is what Sarah said about her school experience:

> "I feel like I belong here, I've made great connections and I feel like if I left the school . . . I feel like I still belong to them, I feel like they are still in my heart. And I feel like I've learned so much from the school and nothing can make me forget about it."

Miguel also expressed similar sentiments about his school experience:

> "I feel like I belong. Like, 10 out of 10 most of the time. I think most people feel like they belong [at my school] because most people are treated fairly."

Lisa's experience suggests that even when one initially feels left out, that schools can turn these situations around for the better:

> "I am one of the only Muslim people at my school and one of the things that I was never able to do was talk about my experiences with other people, because they didn't understand what it was like to be Muslim. But at the end of the day, people from different minority groups, were often pitted against each other to see who like . . . who can reach the top. And that is how I felt in previous years of the school, but last year in particular, we had a lot of conversations about our identity and we went into topics that I didn't [previously] talk about so much and as a result I got really close to some other people at my school."

It seems important to organize ourselves around one of the goals of systemic SEL. We strive to see alignment in policies and approaches at the state, district, school levels so classrooms create an equitable space in which all students have opportunities for social and emotional development, expecting that students will vary in the outcomes derived from those opportunities.

SEL for Educators

The field of SEL began with a focus primarily on students. Increasingly, the focus has expanded to include teachers. Indeed, there is increasing recognition that teachers are the engine that drives SEL (Schonert-Reichl, 2017). This means that if teachers not knowledgeable and skilled enough regarding SEL, they will be more likely to apply their social and emotional skills to everyday interactions with their students and provide high-quality SEL instruction to them (Schonert-Reichl, 2017). Here is an example quote from (Anthony) describing a time when a teacher with strong social and emotional competencies intervened and helped him stop his negative self-talk and got him unstuck and refocused on his writing:

> "Once I was really upset at myself because I couldn't get anything done . . . we had to do this Google Doc . . . and I was really upset because there was nothing to write about . . . and I couldn't find any connections to write about, so I was really stumped and didn't know what to do. I told myself, 'I'm the worst at this, I can't find anything.' And my teacher said, 'Don't talk to my student that way, he's a really smart kid.' And she really encouraged me and made me want to keep going and she really makes you feel good about yourself."

In this brief exchange, this teacher used their relationship skills and social awareness to interrupt the student's negative thinking pattern, convey caring toward the student, and guide the student toward productive work.

The link between teachers' social and emotional competencies and their ability to apply those skills to the classroom and teach SEL is amplified given teachers' high rates of stress and burnout, which means that even if teachers *have* good social and emotional skills, the strained conditions make it hard for them to use these skills in their classrooms. This was especially the case during the COVID-19 pandemic when teachers, especially teachers of color, were found to experience high job-related stress and were leaving their jobs due to poor working conditions and stress (Diliberti et al., 2021; Steiner & Woo, 2021). As a result, there is a growing effort not only to train teachers to deliver SEL practices but also to help teachers develop social–emotional experiences themselves. Such efforts are theorized to serve two mutually reinforcing goals—to help teachers reduce stress and more effectively implement SEL in the classroom.

My work (Kim) on SEL and my recognition of the importance of SEL for teachers originated from my time as a middle school teacher and as a teacher at an alternative high school for youth deemed "at risk" during the 1980s. My students inspired me, taught me, and coached me to learn from them about what it takes to create an educational context in which they could learn and flourish. What was missing at that time was the field of SEL and the science behind it. I worked on instinct and had little from which to draw from my teacher training or support from the educators in my school context.

Two particular lessons stand out for me in my work as a beginning teacher. First, at the foundation of learning is the creation of a context that is nurturing, participatory, safe, and caring. Indeed, creating supportive, safe and respectful school environments in which all children feel they belong is foundational to teaching and learning. As a new teacher at an alternative high school in my early 20s—this was a hard lesson to learn. The first months at the school were trying to say the least. My students essentially seemed to hate me (this may have been something to do with the fact that I was the reading teacher, a subject with which many of the students struggled). At first, I was devastated. I worked so hard—how could they dislike me so much? It was not until I saw this as their strength—their resilience. They had created an "armor" to protect their vulnerability—they pushed me away so that I could not hurt them. It was not until I developed my own self-awareness and social awareness that I understood that I could move past my own hurt feelings and recognize that I needed to see the world through the eyes of my students, that I could find ways to engage them in creating the learning context that included them helping decide on classroom rules, decorate the classroom, have a voice in assignments, and find the strengths they each possessed. I learned the simple lesson that "students don't care how much you know, until they know how much you care."

My second lesson is one that is gaining increasing traction in the SEL field and the larger education field in general—the importance of teacher social and emotional competence and well-being. What we know from current research is that teachers play a central role in promoting the social and emotional competencies of their students. Yet, until recently, the role and influence of teachers in the implementation of SEL has been given scant attention, as have discussions about teachers' own social and emotional competence and well-being in relation to SEL. As a new teacher working with students with a number of emotional and behavioral problems, I absorbed it all and soon experienced empathy fatigue, as well as "stress contagion" that manifested in a series of somatic problems, including hives, stomach problems, and headaches. At that time, there was no acknowledgment of the stress that teachers encounter. Today's teachers have some support from research. For example, a Gallup Poll on U.S. burnout rates showed that K–12 educators ranked on the top of all industries for feeling burned out at work, with 44% of educators saying they felt burned out "very often" or "always" (Gallup, 2022). I had nowhere to turn for my own stress, and hence joined the ranks of the between 23 and 43% of new teachers who leave the profession in the first 5 years of teaching—a figure that costs schools an estimated $7 billion a year (National Commission on Teaching and America's Future, 2007).

If teachers are not skilled in SEL and lack social and emotional skills themselves, there may be a risk of them hindering the development skills themselves and/or worsening as situation. Miguel described a situation in his classroom when the teacher decided to lead a discussion on anxiety because the psychologist, who usually led such discussions, was absent. The teacher asked students to share their anxieties with the class, to which students responded with concerns that ranged from performance anxiety to fear of death. Miguel shared that since there was no processing of these responses that included skillful responses, the exercise led to anxiety contagion whereby some students were becoming anxious about things that were previously not concerning to them or which they had not previously considered.

Similarly, Rowan shared a concern about a physical education teacher who was teaching SEL. When asked how much they were learning about SEL at their school, Rowan commented that they were learning about how to deal with stress and anxiety in school:

> "In gym, we are doing kind of that, but it's like can you help with positive thinking?—something I think doesn't help at all. Well, it's like how's your emotional and mental health? Like, are you worried about finances in the future? and stuff like that. Which I found put a lot more stress on to me. It made me think about those things more, and we are not actually learning about it, it's just we are not actually learning about it . . . it's just like this is what it is—they're not explaining it that much. Yeah—it's just goal setting for positive thinking—which I don't think it helps a lot of people. I am sure that some things [the teachers] are doing, such as teaching students about setting their goals are helping, but I am pretty sure no one is actually doing it. My friends would find it a lot more helpful having a professional come in, because most of my friends find that we are not actually learning in the gym class—they [the friends] are finding it very stressful and it's not helping. My gym teacher is really nice, but [we feel] she does not teach social and emotional learning—well she teaches it, but she does not know a lot about it."

On a more positive note, research also suggests that when teachers receive training in the behavioral and emotional factors that impact teaching and learning in the classroom, they feel better equipped to propose and implement positive, active classroom management strategies that deter students' aggressive behaviors and promote a positive classroom learning climate (Alvarez, 2007). How much does this training and support take place during preservice teacher preparation? A recent scan of SEL in teacher preparation shows that the answer is very little (Schonert-Reichl et al., 2017). Therefore, an important issue to address in education reform is to ensure that preservice teacher education provides the necessary information, coursework, and/or experiences that prepare teachers to address dimensions relevant to SEL, including information on theories and research on the social and emotional development and the knowledge and skills necessary for creating classroom learning contexts that are well-managed and promote student mental health, along with increased attention to identifying strategies and supports for their own social and emotional competence and well-being (see Hon, Suave, Mahfouz, & Schonert-Reichl, Chapter 6, this volume).

Adult SEL is critical for student SEL to occur effectively (Schonert-Reichl, 2017) and we cannot assume that the conditions of school naturally create space and time for teachers to develop and grow so that they can better meet the needs of their students. Society keeps changing, and teachers constantly need to refresh their skills to meet youths' needs. Developing cultural competence has new meaning in the 2020s. Teachers need to better understand where students are socially and psychologically given the influx of electronic devices in youths' lives. As a society, we depend on the people who have devoted their careers to supporting children and youth in classrooms and schools. We owe it to them to create the best possible policies, conditions, and professional development to support them to do their best work.

Conclusion

As we bring this book to a close, our hope is that the exposure to the work shared by the authors in this book has provided fuel for thought for readers' efforts and those educators who share a committed vision to create conditions that bring SEL into action. We recognize that it may feel unsatisfying that we are not providing strong recommendations on the issues we raise in this final chapter; however, this is intentional. Throughout this book, we are rooted in the most contemporary research and practice, yet clear answers are elusive because of the rapid changes in students' school experiences, new directions in SEL research that have not yet been fully realized, and the tremendous variation in schools in the United States. The three issues we raised here—SEL and mindsets, the varieties of diversity, and educators' SEL—are complex matters, and addressing these issues is still a work in progress. So, while we offer some suggestions on future directions, we are hesitant to prematurely put a stake in the ground for any one of them. To do so should require strong evidence, which is not yet available. The future of this work requires the effort of researchers and practitioners, ideally working collaboratively to better understand these complex issues.

What we can confidently say, however, is that we now have very strong evidence on the value of SEL for producing important life outcomes for youth and adults (Durlak et al., 2011; Jones et al., 2015; Taylor et al., 2017). This evidence is only becoming stronger with time, and this means we need a clear vision for how we create state, district, school, community conditions that are conducive to SEL.

Our hope is that the those of you reading this book—SEL advocates and critics alike—will join the effort to further advance our knowledge and practices. Our call to action is that we work together to implement policies and practices that create conditions in schools that promote human flourishing.

REFERENCES

Alvarez, B. (2019). Why social justice in school matters. Retrieved from *www.nea.org/advocating-for-change/new-from-nea/why-social-justice-school-matters.*

Alvarez, H. K. (2007). The impact of teacher preparation on responses to student aggression in the classroom. *Teaching and Teacher Education, 23*(7), 1113–1126.

American Psychological Association. (2022). Civic engagement. Retrieved from *www.apa.org/education-career/undergrad/civic-engagement#:~:text=one%20useful%20definition%20of%20civic,organizational%20involvement%20to%20electoral%20participation.*

Diliberti, M., Schwartz, H. L., & Grant, D. M. (2021). *Stress topped the reasons why public school teachers quit, even before COVID-19.* RAND.

Durlak, J. A., Weissberg, R. P., Dymnicki, A. B., Taylor, R. D., & Schellinger, K. B. (2011). The impact of enhancing students' social and emotional learning: A meta-analysis of school-based universal interventions. *Child Development, 82*(1), 405–432.

Dweck, C. S. (2006). *Mindset: The new psychology of success.* Random House.

Dweck, C. S., & Yeager, D. S. (2019). Mindsets: A view from two eras. Perspectives on *Psychological Science, 14*(3), 481–496.

Fishkin, J. (2016). Bottlenecks, disability, and preference-formation: A reply. *Social Philosophy Today, 32.*

Gallup. (2022). K–12 workers have the highest burnout rate in the U.S. Retrieved from *https://news.gallup.com/poll/393500/workers-highest-burnout-rate.aspx.*

Ioverno, S., Belser, A. B., Baiocco, R., Grossman, A. H., & Russell, S. T. (2016). The protective role of gay–straight alliances for lesbian, gay, bisexual, and questioning students: A prospective analysis. *Psychology of Sexual Orientation and Gender Diversity, 3*(4), 397–406.

Jones, D. E., Greenberg, M., & Crowley, M. (2015). Early social–emotional functioning and public health: The relationship between kindergarten social competence and future wellness. *American Journal of Public Health, 105*(11), 2283–2290.

National Commission on Teaching and America's Future. (2007). *The high cost of teacher turnover* (Policy brief). Author.

Powell, J., Menendian, S., & Ake, W. (2019). *Targeted universalism: Policy and practice.* Haas Institute for a Fair and Inclusive Society, University of California, Berkeley. Retrieved from *www.haasinstitute.berkeley.edu/targeteduniversalism.*

Schonert-Reichl, K. A. (2017). Social and emotional learning and teachers. *Future of Children, 27,* 137–155.

Schonert-Reichl, K. A., Kitil, M. J., & Hanson-Peterson, J. (2017). *To reach the students, teach the teachers: A national scan of teacher preparation and social and emotional learning (a report prepared for the Collaborative for Academic, Social, and Emotional Learning [CASEL]).* University of British Columbia.

Skinner, R. (2004). Character education. Retrieved from *www.edweek.org/leadership/character-education/2004/09.*

Steiner, E. D., & Woo, A. (2021). Job-related stress threatens the teacher supply. Retrieved from *www.rand.org/pubs/research_reports/rra1108-1.html.*

Strambler, M. J. (2021). A universal perspective is key to diversity and equity in schools. The Hill. Retrieved from *https://thehill.com/changing-america/opinion/576345-prioritizing-our-universal-ties-instead-of-identity-is-the-key-to.*

Taylor, R. D., Oberle, E., Durlak, J. A., & Weissberg, R. P. (2017). Promoting positive youth development through school-based social and emotional learning interventions: A meta-analysis of follow-up effects. *Child Development, 88*(4), 1156–1171.

Toomey, R. B., Ryan, C., Diaz, R. M., & Russell, S. T. (2011). High school gay–straight alliances (GSAs) and young adult well-being: An examination of GSA presence, participation, and perceived effectiveness. *Applied Developmental Science, 15*(4), 175–185.

Yeager, D. S., Hanselman, P., Walton, G. M., Murray, J. S., Crosnow, R., Muller, C., . . . Dweck, C. S. (2019). A national experiment reveals where a growth mindset improves achievement. *Nature, 573*, 364–369.

Yeager, D. S., Trzesniewski, K. H., & Dweck, C. S. (2013). An implicit theories of personality intervention reduces adolescent aggression in response to victimization and exclusion. *Child Development, 84*(3), 970–988.

Index

Note. *f* or *t* after a page number indicates a figure or a table.

D

J

K

L

M

O

P

T

U

V

W